AF323692

European Security in NATO's Shadow

NATO has been a successful forum for managing European security policy. Yet European governments have repeatedly tried to build a new security institution in NATO's shadow. In this innovative book, Stephanie C. Hofmann asks why governments attempted to create an additional institution despite no obvious functional necessity, and why some attempts failed while others succeeded. *European Security in NATO's Shadow* considers security cooperation through the lens of party ideologies to shed new light on these questions. She observes that political parties are motivated to propose new institutions by their multidimensional ideologies. Moreover, the success of efforts to create such institutions depends on the degree of ideological congruence among parties in power. In particular, the relationship between the values of multilateralism, sovereignty and Europe informed the impetus and success rate of the attempts made during negotiations for the Maastricht, Amsterdam and Nice treaties to create a European security institution.

STEPHANIE C. HOFMANN is Assistant Professor at the Graduate Institute of International and Development Studies in Geneva, where she also holds the post of Deputy Director of the Center on Conflict, Development and Peacebuilding.

"Using European security initiatives as a test case, Stephanie C. Hofmann shows that the convergence of party ideologies across countries creates opportunities for international cooperation. Sharply argued, carefully researched and well written, this book makes the exciting argument that party ideologies matter in international relations.

Hofmann also shows that it is impossible to understand European security initiatives such as CFSP and ESDP without taking into account the presence of an alternative, namely NATO, which makes the creation of a new European institution costly and perhaps superfluous unless one factors ideological preferences in."

Frédéric Mérand,
Associate Professor of Political Science,
Deputy Director at the Centre for
International Peace and Security Studies,
University of Montreal

"Debates over European security too often stress its *sui generis* nature. In this important new book, Stephanie Hofmann argues that its study should instead be grounded in broader debates and theoretical schools within comparative politics and international relations. Adopting a resolutely eclectic stand, Hofmann argues – and shows in richly documented case studies – that security cooperation in Europe can only be understood if we build systematic linkages between the international and the domestic. Indeed, domestic politics – in the form of political parties and their ideologies – play a central role in explaining why Europeans have persisted in efforts at security cooperation 'in NATO's shadow.' Hofmann's book is thus a must-read for Europeanists as well as the broader community of international relations scholars."

Jeffrey T. Checkel,
Simons Chair in International Law and Human Security,
Simon Fraser University and Research Professor

"This gem of a book bundles what we know from existing theories of international relations and domestic party politics and refracts that knowledge in an analytically subtle and original manner. Beautifully written, this book yields fresh insights into the largely unknown evolution of European security during the past two decades."

Peter J. Katzenstein,
Walter S. Carpenter, Jr. Professor of International Studies,
Cornell University

"By bridging the fields of comparative politics and international relations, this book provides a unique and superb analysis of the way party ideology informs intergovernmental bargaining on matters of international security. It is a must-read for all students of party politics, international security and European politics."

Catherine E. de Vries,
Professor of European Politics,
Department of Politics and International Relations,
University of Oxford

"NATO has cast a long shadow over efforts to carve out an autonomous European defence capability. Why these efforts have persisted and why they have reached fruition in the guise of the European Security and Defence Policy of the EU are matters deftly and expertly dealt with in this volume. Hofmann offers an explanation that focuses less on inter-state negotiation and the institutional rivalries of NATO and the EU, and more on the ideological configurations of domestic politics. Focusing principally on France, Germany and the UK, we are offered an approach that breaks new ground in its view of domestic preferences as an explanation of foreign policy and institutional development. At a time when the shadow of NATO may be waning, this is an important route to understanding just how durable is the EU as the basis of a greater European responsibility in international affairs."

Mark Webber,
Professor of International Politics and
Head of the School of Government and Society,
University of Birmingham

European Security in NATO's Shadow

Party Ideologies and Institution Building

Stephanie C. Hofmann

CAMBRIDGE
UNIVERSITY PRESS

CAMBRIDGE UNIVERSITY PRESS
Cambridge, New York, Melbourne, Madrid, Cape Town,
Singapore, São Paulo, Delhi, Mexico City

Cambridge University Press
The Edinburgh Building, Cambridge CB2 8RU, UK

Published in the United States of America by Cambridge University Press,
New York

www.cambridge.org
Information on this title: www.cambridge.org/9781107029095

First published 2013

Printed and bound in Great Britain by the MPG Books Group

A catalogue record for this publication is available from the British Library

Library of Congress Cataloguing in Publication data
Hofmann, Stephanie C., 1977–
    European security in NATO's shadow : party ideologies and
    institution building / Stephanie C. Hofmann.
        p.   cm.
    Includes bibliographical references and index.
    ISBN 978-1-107-02909-5 (hardback)
    1. National security–Europe.   2. Europe–Politics and
    government–1945–   3. North Atlantic Treaty
    Organization.   I. Title.
    JZ6009.E85H64 2013
    355′.03304–dc23
    2012026435

ISBN 978-1-107-02909-5 Hardback

Contents

Figures

Tables

Acknowledgments

"Think eclectic" is a credo I took away from Peter Katzenstein. This book has become just that, eclectic not only in its theoretical foundations but also in terms of the support I have received from various individuals and organizations throughout the years and the places in which I conducted my research and wrote the book. The subject of the book dates back to my stay at the University of Washington, Seattle, where I had the good fortune to attend a lecture by Jolyon Howorth. Had he not sparked my interest in European security, this book would likely have been written on a very different topic.

The first version of this book appeared in the form of my Ph.D. dissertation at Cornell. Peter Katzenstein was a wonderful *Doktorvater*, teaching me much about research, writing and pedagogy. Matt Evangelista wisely suggested that I not lose sight of the United States when writing about European security. And Chris Anderson did much to sharpen my understanding of party politics.

Throughout the years, discussions with friends sharpened my thinking about International Relations and politics more generally. My fellow colleagues at Cornell helped keep life stimulating, particularly Michelle Renée Smith, Scott Siegel, Jason Lyall, Maria Zaitseva, Eryn MacDonald, Seo-Hyun Park, Ute Tellmann, Irene Mittelberg, Leila Mohsen Ibrahim, Ryan Plumley and Andrew Yeo. In Geneva, Nicolas Berman, Jovi Carapic, Catherine de Vries, Oliver Jütersonke, Celine Poilly, Emily Meierding, Rahul Mukherjee and Melanie Wahl have provided me with a great support system and inspiration.

Helpful comments, sometimes verging on heated discussions, improved this book profoundly. Among others, I want to extend my gratitude to Frédéric Mérand, Chris Reynolds, Brian Rathbun, Catherine de Vries, Gail McElroy, Nick Onuf, Anand Menon, Rob Weiner, François Heisbourg, David Sylvan, Michael Clarke, Paul Cornish, Andrew Bennett, Lee Seymour, Andrea Volkens, Zeljko Branovic, Eva Gross, Kathleen McNamara, Lora Viola and Keith Krause – as well as to my students at the Graduate Institute who have patiently listened to me spinning my arguments to them and, luckily, always enjoyed engaging with them.

I was very impressed by how many officials, both in capitals and at the IO-level in Brussels, were willing to share their expertise with me. Many of the most interesting interviews were with policy-makers who asked to remain anonymous. I am thankful for the access and information they provided. A number of policy-makers I interviewed deserve special mention for opening their doors to me. In New York, Sir Emyr Jones Parry was gracious enough to share his unique insights into European security policy in the 1990s over tea; the same can be said of Hubert Védrine in Paris, though as per French custom, tea was not served. Interviews with Joschka Fischer, Joachim Bitterlich and Klaus Scharioth were most helpful in illuminating German perspectives.

The financial support from the VolkswagenStiftung, Compagnia di San Paolo and Riksbankens Jubileumsfond Grant greatly facilitated the research for this book. Furthermore, within their joint research and training program "European Foreign and Security Policy Studies," an unwieldy title for an excellent network of scholars on European security, I was able to present and discuss my ideas to fellow scholars working on the same policy field. I also benefited from support from the German Academic Exchange (DAAD), a Luigi Einaudi Fellowship from Cornell's Institute for European Studies and a Mellon grant.

The *Stiftung Wissenschaft und Politik* (SWP) in Berlin was kind enough to host me for three years of research and writing. SWP credentials provided excellent access to policy-makers and scholars in Germany and throughout Europe. Particular thanks go to Heinz Kramer, Olga Ott, Volker Heise and Peter Schmidt. Though much shorter, my stay at the Centre d'Etudes de Recherches Internationales (CERI) in Paris was highly beneficial and would not have been possible without help from Bastien Irondelle. The EUI in Fiesole provided me with culinary and intellectual support to find the courage to revise the book (also called Jean Monnet Fellowship). Most recently, my new academic home in Geneva has provided just the right incentive to transform the dissertation into a book.

To write this book, I needed to be able to move around and, at times, be distracted. Cafés in Paris and Vienna of the eighteenth century have the reputation for instigating and nurturing politically controversial thought or, at least, as places where one can share ideas, read, write and talk. While the cafés in which I wrote and thought about this book might not correspond to those of Paris or Vienna in the eighteenth century, they nonetheless provided me with a great environment to write. Allegro, Gimme!, La Cité Sankt Oberholz and Livresse deserve a special thanks – they have become my offices whenever I am in Berlin, Ithaca, Florence Seattle or Geneva.

I am grateful to my research assistant, Jon Strandquist, for helping me with the copyediting. I also want to thank Cambridge University Press, and John Haslam in particular, for their support throughout the publishing process. A disclaimer should be voiced: though research and writing has never been a strictly individual endeavor, all errors are mine.

At times, I wished my parents had found European security issues as exciting as I do; however, with time, I realized that this was a blessing. They provided the calm I needed to realize that I was "just writing a book." Danke Euch Beiden, dass ihr mich nicht das Wichtige aus den Augen habt verlieren lassen.

1 Introduction

Do political party ideologies matter in international relations? Politicians speak of "the national interest," singular, in defending their national security policies, claiming to set aside their ideological differences in matters of "high politics." Yet, arguments between politicians reveal fundamental differences in how political parties conceive of national interests. Indeed, government turnover can result in major alterations in foreign and security policy. Political party ideologies are the root cause for such changes. They consist of interrelated values that signal group membership and suggest appropriate ways of dealing with other actors, both domestically and internationally. Thucydides (1951: 43–4) already argued that preferences are based on the interrelationship between the values of security, wealth and the honor of one's political community. Since politicians belonging to political parties derive specific policies from the core values they uphold, their ideologies constrain their policies. The study of core values and their interrelationships help us understand what "national" interests drive governments' policies at particular points in time.

In the realm of international cooperation, members of political parties in government are faced with three fundamental questions: what policy issues should be institutionalized multilaterally? With whom should one share responsibilities? To what degree should these responsibilities be shared? Governments are left to choose between acting unilaterally or multilaterally in policy fields such as security, attuning their actions to a political community which they perceive themselves to be a part of. Governments also must decide between delegating responsibilities to a supranational organization or retaining control by devising intergovernmental institutions. These value dimensions manifest themselves in the form of three core values in the realm of cooperation: multilateralism, political community and sovereignty. Since the subject of this book is European security, Europe is the political community in question.

Not only do political parties matter for the foreign and security policies of individual states, but the aggregation of political party ideologies at the international level has important consequences in international relations. Insofar as party ideologies drive domestic political competition over the definition of the national interest, international cooperation among democracies cannot be divorced from the preferences of national political parties. Politics does not stop at the water's edge. Instead, the world of politics is one of ideological conflict. When the ideologies of parties in government are congruent across countries, opportunities for international cooperation arise. Parties in power form policy-entrepreneurial coalitions based on ideological congruence. However, when we observe ideological incongruence across governing parties, governments fail to form such coalitions and attempts to initiate international cooperation are likely to fail. In general, party ideologies define and delimit the scope of possible compromises.

European security cooperation

The particular instances of international cooperation with which this book is concerned are the various European security institutions such as the North Atlantic Treaty Organization (NATO), the Western European Union (WEU) and the European Security and Defense Policy (ESDP).[1] Since the 1950s, NATO has provided a comprehensive security guarantee and military policy forum for its member states. Nonetheless, over the years European governments have faced many choices when devising their security and defense policy. They could renationalize security, or they could transform NATO into a security institution geared towards a new set of threats and challenges. They could reform existing institutions such as the WEU or the Conference for Security and Cooperation in Europe (CSCE), or European governments could create an entirely new multilateral institution. While European states have pursued all of these options at various junctures, they have repeatedly returned to attempts to build a new autonomous European institution in NATO's imposing shadow.

This choice is puzzling. Since European multilateral security policy has successfully been addressed in NATO, there would appear to be no need to create an additional, autonomous security institution – understood to be "explicit arrangements, negotiated among

---

[1] Since the Lisbon Treaty came into force (December 2009), ESDP has been renamed Common Security and Defense Policy (CSDP). Because the book's time frame ends at the year 2000, however, I will refrain from using the new acronym.

international actors, that prescribe, proscribe, and/or authorize behavior" (Koremenos *et al.* 2001: 2). Why create an institution that fulfills a mandate very similar to NATO's, that resembles NATO in institutional design, that has largely the same membership as NATO, and that draws on resources already designated for NATO? This is a costly choice. There are costs to national autonomy as states assume yet more international commitments and obligations. The choice also involves the diplomatic costs of negotiating with allies over institutional design and the financial costs associated with founding a new institution. Another important cost for European governments has been the political fallout of managing US attempts to deny European governments an autonomous security institution outside of NATO.

Yet various European governments persisted in their efforts. Over the past six decades, European governments repeatedly turned their attention to new security institutions in NATO's shadow. They did so in 1950–4 with the European Defense Community (EDC), from 1960 to 1963 with the Fouchet Plans, in 1970 with the European Political Cooperation (EPC), in 1975 with the Tindemans Report on the European Union, in 1981 with the Genscher-Colombo initiative, from 1990 to 1992 with the Common Foreign and Security Policy (CFSP), from 1995 to 1997 with the renegotiation of the Maastricht Treaty that cumulated in the Amsterdam Treaty, and again from 1999 to 2000 with the creation of ESDP. Each attempt substantially overlapped with NATO in terms of membership, mandate and resources (Hofmann 2009).

The outcomes of these attempts varied among outright failure (e.g. EDC, Amsterdam Treaty), compromises that led to weak institutionalization (Maastricht Treaty), and success with the ESDP, which also substantially overlaps with NATO. ESDP is the only attempt that resulted in a robust European security institution. To be considered robust, an institution must be autonomous and endowed with the resources and capacities to fulfill its mandate. Since its creation, ESDP has conducted over 20 crisis management operations and has competed with NATO for member states' resources and attention. Thus, it is not surprising that, at each attempt, the US government has voiced concern about European security autonomy (Hoffmann 2003: 1030). In perhaps the most forceful statement about such attempts, then-US ambassador to NATO Nicholas Burns called ESDP "the most serious threat to the future of NATO" (Burns quoted in Koch 2003).

I derive two research questions from these observations. First, why do states try to create additional institutions in a pre-existing institutionalized policy space? And second, why do we observe variation in the outcomes of these attempts? In other words, what explains the different outcomes of attempts to create a European security institution? Why did the proposal to include a European security dimension in the Amsterdam Treaty fail? Why was CFSP created in such a weak form despite the end of the Cold War and the changes that came with it? And why were European states able to build a security institution with ESDP? These questions address the creation of intersecting centers of authority and power on the international level in the form of institutionalized cooperative arrangements that overlap.

The argument: political parties and institutional overlap

I trace the answers to the questions back to the ideologies of political parties. The impetus for proposals to create security institutions lies in individual political party *ideologies* and the ability to institutionalize such proposals depends on the *degree* of ideological *congruence* between political parties in power in key European states. Since party ideologies affect the security policy of states, the creation of an additional security institution in Europe has been a political project that stands and falls with cross-national ideological congruence. The existence and form that the proposed institution has assumed across various attempts has depended on the configuration of party ideologies both within and among national governments on the European level.

The emphasis on ideologies in this explanation suggests that what much of the International Relations (IR) literature understands as national interests are generated through policy debates amongst domestic actors. Parties disagree on security policy, the extent to which international cooperation furthers state interests, with whom cooperation should take place, and the forms it should take. My theoretical approach draws upon insights in two theoretical domains – Comparative Politics (CP) and IR – because neither one alone can adequately explain the puzzle. I account for the variation in relations between states by integrating arguments about parties, belief systems, domestic institutions and international cooperation. As a result, I explain why the same states sometimes cooperate with one another and at other times do not.

Political parties, the central domestic actors in this account, rotate into and out of government bringing with them often divergent ideologies. In examining the substance of political party ideologies, I look for the manifestation of three core values: multilateralism in the use of force, sovereignty and Europe. Multilateralism is shorthand for a continuum that runs from unilateralism to multilateralism-as-an-end-in-itself.

Sovereignty represents the intergovernmentalism through supranationalism continuum. It is less obvious that we can characterize Europe on a continuum but, for consistency's sake, I will represent Europe as capturing the range of understandings of Europe-as-a-geographic-space to Europe-as-a-political-community. Political parties have linked these values in different ways: in general, parties have either defined the relationship between the values independently of one another or they have prioritized one or two values over others, making them the actual core of the ideology from which the meaning of other values is derived. For example, should a party value multilateralism-as-a-means-to-another-end, this is an indication that multilateralism is not a core value of this party but is instead derived from either sovereignty or Europe (both other "possible ends").

Based on the core values, embodied in a party ideology, national governments formulate distinctive security policies and value alternative (potential) multilateral security actors differently. Following from this, parties find different strength and weaknesses in existing institutions, as reflected in core values, which then affects their policies towards the creation of an institution that would overlap with an existing one. Such configurations make it difficult to study individual international institutions in isolation. Thus, NATO factors into the decision whether or not to create an additional institution via political ideologies. NATO becomes politically meaningful through parties' interpretations of it.

Proposals for a European security institution have always taken place in the context of NATO's supreme presence in the European security order. The existence of NATO has provided states with various options in security policy. They could privilege NATO, participate in European proposals while continuing to value NATO, or privilege an autonomous European security institution to the detriment of NATO. Their choices, I argue, reflect the core values of parties in power around multilateralism, sovereignty and Europe. Former British Foreign Secretary Douglas Hurd said of EC security cooperation, "As any builder knows, it is important to get the foundations and the framework of the structure right first" (Hurd 1994: 427). The blueprints that define these structures, in my formulation, are party ideologies.

Under the Conservatives, for example, the United Kingdom's (UK) government vetoed the merger of the WEU and the EU in 1991 and 1996, and instead pushed for a European security pillar *inside* NATO. The Conservatives did so because they continued to privilege NATO as the pillar of British security policy. Staying with the example of the United Kingdom, the Labour Party has a very different understanding of the European Union and NATO than the British Conservatives, despite EU issues being very unpopular with British voters. In October 2000, for example, Prime Minister Tony Blair stressed that he wanted the European Union to become a "superpower but not a superstate" (Black and Watt 2000). The *Guardian* judged this stance to be "positive and engaged and in striking contrast to the Tories' negative policy towards the EU" (Black and Watt 2000). The ideological congruence between Labour and other parties in power in key European states, particularly the Rally for the Republic (RPR) in France and the Social Democrats (SPD) in Germany, created conditions under which proposals for a new security institution could move forward. Proposals for ESDP reflected values shared by Labour, the RPR and the SPD around the role of multilateralism in security policy, the place of their respective states within Europe, and intergovernmental rather than supranational institutions. ESDP thus emerged despite NATO reforms that took it in the same direction as proposals for ESDP.

Alternative explanations

I examine my own argument in relation to three alternative explanations to avoid spuriousness. First, from Comparative Politics, I examine an alternative approach that is close to my own explanation. Despite this superficial similarity, this approach conceptualizes ideology differently, conceiving of it on a single left–right continuum. This one-dimensional explanation challenges my understanding of ideology, which draws on three values: multilateralism in the use of force, sovereignty and Europe. I argue that the content of security policy in individual states and the congruence of ideologies across governments require this more nuanced understanding of ideology.

Two additional alternative explanations, realism (soft balancing) and rational choice institutionalism (institutional choice and adoption), are drawn from International Relations theory. In security studies, realism remains predominant, while the leading theoretical approach in the study of international institutions is rational choice institutionalism. Relying on different variables to explain why institutions are created and maintained, they advance explanations at odds with my focus on political party ideologies. Realism emphasizes power aggregation and security through strategies of balancing and binding as reasons for security cooperation; cooperation lasts only as long as it serves these particular purposes. Rational choice institutionalism stresses cooperation problems which, in the interest of efficiency and mutual gains, are resolved through the creation of an institution. Realist explanations emphasize the role the United States has played in the creation of a European security institution autonomous from NATO. Rational choice institutionalist scholarship focuses on actual events that occurred during the time period under investigation and how these events have changed the calculations for a new security institution. Despite their differences, the two approaches both pay little – if any – attention to domestic politics and share a functional understanding of international institutions.

My own explanation takes seriously inter- and intrastate differences in how governments interpret power distributions and institutional cooperation problems across time. This sets it apart from realism and rational choice institutionalism.[2] I nonetheless draw important insights from these theoretical approaches to explain how political parties operate. Parties' preferences that rest on ideological foundations can resemble the sorts that realism or rational choice institutionalism attribute to states. The behavior of both British Conservatives and French Socialists conform to realist predictions. The policies of the British Labour Party, on the other hand, resemble behavior predicted by rational choice institutionalism. The explanation found in this book diverges from realist and institutionalist explanations in that it shows that efficiency and power concerns exist within a larger universe of values that compose political ideologies based on the three values of multilateralism in the use of force, sovereignty and Europe. Power constellations and cooperation problems are not universally accessible constraints that are interpreted the same way across all governments and political parties. Instead, political parties within and across states have particular understandings of power and cooperation problems.

In order to assess the relative explanatory weight of potential causal factors, I focus on the creation of the weak Common Foreign and Security Policy (1990–1), the Amsterdam Treaty negotiations (1996–7) that failed to create a security institution, and the creation of the robust European Security and Defense Policy (1998–2000). The main actors on which I concentrate are France, Germany, and the United Kingdom. To be more precise, these states are the units-of-analysis for the rational choice institutionalist and realist approaches, while the parties in power are the units-of-analysis for my own approach and the

---

[2] As former Foreign Minister Fischer said, "Europe is not just a rational but also an emotional event (*Veranstaltung*)." Interview with the author in Princeton (February 21, 2007).

partisan values approach. The main reason for my selection of these three states is that they are the three biggest militaries in the EU and an effective autonomous security organization is possible only with their consent.

Claims and contributions

My analytical lens and argument contribute to various debates within political science and policy debates about European security: the role of material power, cost–benefit calculations of multilateral action, as well as institutionalization dynamics and political ideologies in international and European cooperation. First, I demonstrate that major European states created an autonomous European security institution in spite of US concerns. The success of ESDP was dependent on neither the US geopolitical position, nor its policy preferences. Neither was it dependent upon European member states' structural positions. In fact, the US government has voiced concern in all the cases of attempted European security autonomy (Kissinger 1965; Sloan 2000). Instead, I observe an important variance in political parties' attitudes toward the United States and multilateral European security policy. At any given point in time, major European governments understood the relationship toward the United States differently despite their similar structural position as medium-sized powers in the international system. Nonetheless, a few political parties exhibit realist logics of balancing in security policy.

Second, *European Security in NATO's Shadow* shows that the creation of international institutions cannot be studied without their broader institutional context in mind. Observing the proliferation of international organizations is not enough to explain why there are overlapping institutions. One needs to look at the concrete processes through which institutions come to overlap with each other. Until now, regime complexity has been predominantly studied in terms of taxonomy of institutional constellations (Young 2008). This happened at the expense of the analysis of the origins of overlap. In this regard, ESDP – let alone attempts to create an autonomous security institution – has received little attention. ESDP, however, challenges NATO's purpose as Europe's security provider as it overlaps significantly with NATO's membership, mandate and resources. Despite the decision to create an additional institution in an already institutionalized space, the major concern of most governments has not been the creation of an efficient division of labor between the two institutions. Instead, governments have formed this additional institution for their own ideological purposes, showing remarkable tolerance for the costs and inefficiencies this involves. By studying how the already-existing NATO has affected the likelihood of the creation of another institution, I attempt to fill a serious gap in the IR literature.

Third, the book advances our understanding of national preference formation, with special attention to the dimensionality of political ideologies, by pointing to the neglected role of political party ideologies and party positions in security policy. Its argument is derived from scholarship in IR theory and Comparative Politics that provides insight into why and how the political ideologies of parties matter. I suggest that the left–right dimension does not structure party positions on issues of European security. Instead, after I derive the main value dimensions deductively from the major IR paradigms, I investigate the ideological structures underlying political preferences inductively. Put differently, my argument makes no assumptions about the relationships between the values. I then show the different political positions that exist in the conceptual space spanned by dimensions, and systematically link these domestic variables to international outcomes.

Fourth, *European Security in NATO's Shadow* emphasizes the fits and starts of the institutionalization of European security cooperation. Though governments have repeatedly come back to proposals for security cooperation, I find that such proposals have never been substantiated when parties in power disagreed about the need for an autonomous security institution. The creation of a European security institution has not been an incremental process. Unlike other domains in which the European Union has slowly incorporated responsibilities, such as the EU internal market, security cooperation has been an exceptionally political project.

A final claim contributes to debates about who should provide for European security, and how – a policy debate that is decades old. In the extensive debate on "soft balancing," for instance, I illustrate that some political parties exhibit realist logics of balancing in security policy, but ideological differences across European states exercise an important influence and constraint on their ability to do so through multilateral cooperation. By extension, I argue that the debate about whether or not ESDP represents a competitor to NATO depends largely on the core values of parties in power in key European states at a particular point in time. Though I examine European attempts to create a security institution in an already institutionalized policy space, the argument has broader relevance for understanding international cooperation in a world with growing instances of institutional density and overlap

(Shanks *et al.* 1996; Pevehouse *et al.* 2003).[3] Some scholars term this development "treaty congestion" (Brown Weiss 1993: 679). Assuming that existing institutions do not significantly interfere with efforts to create new ones, scholars ignore, both empirically and analytically, much of international relations around institutionalized cooperation (Raustiala and Victor 2004: 278). I show how a focus on institutional overlap changes our understanding of European security cooperation.[4]

Plan of the book

The plan of the book is as follows. Chapter 2 presents and describes key building blocks for a theory of ideological congruence and incongruence. To explain how configurations of European political party ideologies affect the outcome of European attempts to create security institutions, I discuss the various ways political parties conceive of political ideology and how those ideologies motivate parties.

Chapter 3 connects political party ideologies to the outcomes of attempts to create a European security institution. It presents the central mechanism of my theory: ideological congruence or incongruence among international actors at a particular time. To come to this conclusion, I study national governments' preference formation and international ideological configurations. This chapter demonstrates ways to systematically combine International Relations and Comparative Politics literatures so as to be able to explain both the *origins* of government preferences and how these preferences *influence* international policy. This chapter also positions my theory against alternative explanations rooted in realism (soft balancing), rational choice institutionalism (institutional choice and adaptation) and Comparative Politics (party politics).

Chapters 4 through 6 consist of the empirical case studies that provide evidence for the claim that political ideologies structure the evaluation of specific policies and influence international outcomes. In Chapter 4, I look at the creation of CFSP in 1990–1 and show that it was institutionalized in only declaratory form as a result of minimal ideological congruence on issues of European security institutions and European

---

[3] The security field has witnessed the proliferation of crisis management actors (Bellamy and Williams 2005). The EU–NATO overlap is the most significant example of overlap in the field of international security – both in functional and geographic terms.

[4] For example, the creation of the European Political Cooperation (EPC) in 1970 has not been considered in terms of a failed attempt to create a security institution. Instead, it has been portrayed as a compromise to institutionalize foreign policy in a non-binding way, though NATO's existence and concerns about overlap explain why EPC looked the way it did (Nuttall 1992).

security writ large between parties in power in key states. Authors argue that the upheaval caused by the end of the Cold War and German reunification led European governments to grow closer together (Jones 2007). This makes CFSP's weakness, despite proposals for a stronger institution, puzzling. Attention to political ideologies shows that many governments in fact disagreed over the international institutions with which one should face new security threats and the conditions under which force should be used. Whereas French Socialists wanted a strong European institution autonomous of NATO, British Conservatives opposed the creation of a robust institution *outside* NATO. The CDU/CSU–FDP government in Germany split the difference between these positions. The compromise between them was a watered-down institution, in the form of a declaration of policy goals called CFSP – without its own military assets and capabilities. This compromise was seen as temporary for some, for example for the CDU/CSU, and final for others, such as the Conservatives.

In Chapter 5, I examine attempts during the Amsterdam negotiations to integrate the WEU with its military capabilities into the European Union (1996–7). Despite external incentives in the form of the disintegration of Yugoslavia and the EU's confrontation with its powerlessness, and despite Article N in the Maastricht Treaty, which called for reform in areas such as security and defense, the ideologies of major European governments were too incongruent, especially around the core value of Europe, to create anything more than they had already done in Maastricht. These basic differences in core values resulted in major disagreements between national governments that led to the failure of WEU–EU integration. While alternative explanations stress the political tensions between "Europe" and the United States at the time, evidence shows that American opposition did not in fact intimidate several European governments. No collective interest had emerged since Maastricht to underpin the idea for a European security institution.

Chapter 6 focuses on the creation of ESDP in 1998–2000. The key shift that explains the creation of a robust European security institution autonomous of NATO was a change in the parties in power, particularly in the United Kingdom and France. Concerns about NATO were minimal. With ideological congruence, ESDP was created along common interests as a robust institution that reflected shared ideological core values between key national governments. Thus, despite no external security threat calling for such an institution, as NATO was transforming in the same direction, ESDP was created as a robust institution. In fact, ESDP was established despite the material and political costs entailed in replicating NATO and despite US reluctance to allow an autonomous European security institution to form.

In the conclusion, Chapter 7, I discuss my theory's broader relevance for scholarly and policy debates and avenues for future research. The chapter also addresses the current state of EU–NATO relations. I discuss how party ideologies have implications for how states make use of the institutional opportunities and constraints that overlapping institutions have given them – and the implications of this for the transatlantic security community, and security cooperation more generally.

2 Political party ideologies and security cooperation

What are political ideologies in the realm of security cooperation? Who carries them and with what consequences? Are political ideologies stable over time or do they simply reflect the strategic calculations of political leaders who want to stay in office? The content and impact of party ideology has hardly been studied to explain foreign and security policy or institution building, nor have repeated European attempts to create a European security institution received systematic attention in either the IR or EU literatures. Most IR scholars see governments primarily as representatives of national interests. These interests, in turn, are understood as reflecting a country's geopolitical position or economic structure, but not the political leanings of parties. Overall, foreign and security policy is either understood as consensual or idiosyncratic. Party politics and the values that feed it are deemed to be of little relevance.

This neglect is surprising given the centrality of political parties in the government of consolidated democracies. One can observe that many foreign and security policies are not backed by a national consensus but instead divide "the national." The German Social Democrats' concept of *Ostpolitik* represented a major shift from Germany's foreign and security policy orientation under the Christian Democrats. The parties in Taiwan are split on the issue of the island's independence from China with the Democratic Progressive Party historically favoring this goal, whereas the Kuomintang favor a continuation of the current status quo across the Taiwan Strait (mainly *de facto* separation from the mainland without a formal declaration of this status). The issue of going to war in Iraq from 2003 onwards and whether to continue the support also split "the national interest" in countries such as Germany, Spain, Poland and Italy. Manow *et al.* (2008: 20–1) observe "anecdotal evidence highlights the importance of the party-political complexion of national governments … [but] has not yet generated much academic activity in collecting systematic evidence on party-political governments' composition." Such evidence, however, is necessary if we want to theorize and systematically evaluate the role that political parties play in international cooperation.

This chapter lays the foundation for the argument that international politics and policies cannot be explained by international factors alone. Policy options are left to national governments. National governments represent partisan orientations. They play an important role in key foreign and security policy changes. Some political parties are willing to transfer responsibilities and policy issues to the European level whereas others are not. As a result, explanations for the outcomes of different attempts to cooperate in the security field vary, both within and across cases. In making the case that political party ideologies matter, I first define and conceptualize political ideologies. To conceptualize political ideologies, I rely on findings in Comparative Politics and elite/public opinion studies. I then show in the second section how ideologies are formed within parties and are articulated by them.

Political ideologies

Domestic actors disagree on foreign and security policy issues. They often have different assessments of national interests and identity, and different views about the multilateral use of force, international institutions and European integration. So-called "national interests" are shaped by policy debates between domestic actors. These debates have consequences for foreign and security policy. But the key actors in these debates, political parties that aggregate and express diverse political interests, have hardly been theorized in IR, and even less so in security studies.[1] This is the more surprising since even scholars such as Andrew Moravcsik, who emphasize material preferences, have admitted that when it comes to European security policy "national preferences are ... dependent on ideology" (Moravcsik and Nicolaïdis 1999: 61). Indeed, in regard to ideational variables in general and political ideology in particular the field of security studies lags behind others dealing with ideational preference constitution.[2] Based on this

[1]   Three notable exceptions are Brian Rathbun (2004), Mark Haas (2005) and Michael Desch (2007/8), who demonstrate that ideology plays an important role in structuring elite attitudes in foreign policy. Rathbun focuses on humanitarian intervention, Haas on great power threat perceptions and Desch on US foreign and security policy. Studies relying on game theoretic models, on the other hand, such as Kenneth Schultz's (2005), assume that there are ideological party differences and preferences in security policy *despite* little research on it. Schultz (2005: 18, 26) argues that international cooperation under distrust between two states is more likely and more durable depending on which parties (hawkish or dovish) are in power in the respective states.

[2]   Scholars working on issues of International Political Economy have begun to integrate ideational variables and the nature of ideologies (Hall 1989; Oatley 1999; Thérien and Noël 2000; Iversen and Stephens 2007; Mukherjee and Singer 2008; Noël and Thérien 2008), as has research on immigration and European identity (Lahav 1997).

neglect and various conceptualizations of ideology in different fields of political science, the following paragraphs tackle the issue of political ideologies.

Defining and mapping political ideologies

Political ideologies can be understood as different ways of organizing values at abstract as well as relatively concrete levels: they present and order the political, economic and social goals and values of political actors and they are programmatic and action-oriented, recommending domestic and international policy prescriptions and animating political action (Schurmann 1973: 18, 20–1). A relatively coherent and discrete value system forms the basis of each political ideology (Downs 1957; Geertz 1964; Schurmann 1973: 18; Seliger 1976; Simon 1982; Boudon 1989).[3] The value system consists of (core) values and their relationship(s) to one another. *Values* are conceptions of the desirable (Williams 1979). They serve as criteria for selection in political action and competition. *Core* values are "the point or set of points in 'policy space' that cannot be defeated by any other(s)" (Warwick 1992: 355; see also Laver and Schofield 1990: 122–6; Feldman and Zaller 1992: 271–2). As such, ideologies are empirically ascertainable attitudes and preferences toward political issues.

Different ideologies are characterized by how they relate their (core) values to one another. Actors interpret values a certain way and link them together in a non-random and non-contradictory fashion (Gerring 1997: 980; see also Williams 1979: 21–2; Conover and Feldman 1981). These resulting sets of values offer visions of social and political order and explain how resources and power should be allocated and to what ends they should be used – both on the domestic and international level.

Ideologies can be based on one or more core values. Studies on party politics, voting behavior in legislatures, government coalitions and public opinion have tackled the issue of how to conceptualize ideologies or

---

[3] This definition contrasts with a normative definition. In political theory, ideology is understood as ideas, which are in some ways misleading, one-sided and illusory and often serve the interests of powerful groups (Gramsci 1971; Althusser 1984; Thompson 1990; Marx and Engels 2006 [1848]). Ideology carries a negative connotation in these works. Karl Mannheim (1936) tried to change the conceptual interpretation of ideology, accepting the historical and social genesis of thought but also expanding the understanding of the concept to cover multiple social understandings of diverse social groups. Mannheim introduced ideology as a feature of sociopolitical thinking and unmasked Marxism as an ideology. Empirical studies of ideology bypass the question of truth and favor studying the input ideology gives into the political system.

belief systems[4] (Patterson 1963; Stokes 1963; Holsti and Rosenau 1990: 95; Warwick 1992: 340; Aldrich *et al.* 2006: 485). In these studies, political competition and conflict often is portrayed as taking place over a *given* set of value dimensions. Some prominent studies have argued in favor of one dimension only (Downs 1957; Rathbun 2004), others have argued in favor of two (Wittkopf 1990, 1994; Holsti 1998/9; Thérien and Noël 2000) or three dimensions (Chittick *et al.* 1995).

I argue, and show, however, that one, two or three core values are not a priori sufficient to describe the range of (foreign and security) policy attitudes.[5] The concept of political space is neither natural nor obvious (Laver *et al.* 2006: 672; Kam *et al.* 2010; Benoit and Laver 2012; De Vries and Marks 2012; see also Lipset and Rokkan 1967). It is an open question as to how many core values (or value dimensions) adequately explain the cleavages that inform preferences. Some value dimensions are independent of the predominant left–right continuum (Noël and Thérien 2008: 10, 25–6, 28–9); knowing a party's position on the left–right continuum does not mean that we can predict that party's position on other value dimension(s) (Wittkopf 1981, 1990; Laver and Hunt 1992: 15; Chittick *et al.* 1995: 323). Other value dimensions, by extension, can be collapsed onto the left–right continuum. Overall, given the "the splendid complexity of tastes" (Laver and Hunt 1992: 15), the use of a single value dimension to describe the structure underlying a policy space in any real political system is often an oversimplification (Stokes 1963; Conover and Feldman 1981, 1984: 113). For example, if the "right's" core value is considered to be liberty in the realm of foreign policy, we have a hard time explaining how this value translates to either more interventionist or isolationist policy preferences (Budge *et al.* 2001; Clare 2010).[6] Both are conceivable options.[7]

---

[4] Public opinion scholars tend to talk of goal-beliefs and belief systems instead of ideology to distinguish their concepts from the predominant left–right dimension of ideology (Chittick *et al.* 1995: 319–20; Herrmann *et al.* 1999: 554). As belief systems rely on core value dispositions, however, my definition of ideology can accommodate this view.

[5] Humphreys and Laver (2010) have shown that these multidimensional spaces can also have an equilibrium. For an interesting discussion on different possible dimensions (language, religion, race, region, tribe, caste) that inform ethnic preferences and cleavages see Posner (2005).

[6] Murray and Cowden (1999: 470–2) start from a one-dimensional assumption and postulate that liberals act differently from conservatives on the domestic and the international level. However, their statistical tests show that additional dimensions (such as militant or cooperative internationalism) are important as well. Lahav (1997: 388–9, 397–8) cannot capture a large variance falling outside the left–right dimension.

[7] Noël and Thérien (2008) show that left and right are not stable categories but change over time and across space.

This indeterminacy points to the insufficiency of a single core value to explain a party's foreign and security policy ideology. Employing one dimension to organize political conflict can be too broad to account for the variety of ways in which national governments can respond to and understand international challenges and international cooperation. This "complexity of tastes" also explains that ideologies can be *domain specific*. The same values do not have to inform both economic and security policy preferences, for example (Conover and Feldman 1984: 120; Feldman and Zaller 1992: 278; Holsti 1998/9: 30; Noël and Thérien 2008: 10). There is no theoretical reason that ideologies should be informed by a given set of value dimensions.

Existing empirical studies show how a single value dimension can misconstrue ideological leanings and instead point toward the many different dimensions that could exist. In the aggregate, the results of these empirical studies show that one, two or three dimensions cannot be assumed a priori. Instead, one should be able to account for all analytically relevant core values. Indeed, my conceptualization of political ideology builds on a growing literature that is moving beyond the left–right divide, particularly when it comes to the EU or European parties, by looking at more precise divides such as the sovereignty–integration cleavage (Tsebelis 1994; Hix and Lord 1997; Baker and Seawright 1998b: 77; Hix 1999; Moravcsik and Nicolaïdis 1999; Tsebelis and Garrett 2000; Hooghe *et al.* 2002; Marks *et al.* 2002; Benoit 2009), and the libertarian–authoritarian cleavage (Hooghe *et al.* 2002; Mattila 2004; Hix *et al.* 2007; McElroy and Benoit 2007; Hagemann 2008).[8] Hix (1999) and Franklin *et al.* (1996) argue that European integration and left–right contestation are independent of each other. Others again argue that Europe and the left–right dimensions are neither fused together nor independent of each other but are correlated, at least in some policy domains (Hooghe and Marks 1999). Recent research on European integration and party-political complexions has shown that while some political parties assimilate the emerging issue of European integration within existing structures of ideological frames (Hellström 2008), for other parties Europe can cross-cut existing ideological frames (Parsons and Weber 2011; De Vries and Hobolt 2012).[9]

---

[8] When scholars dissect EU integration into particular domains, they ignore security policy and foreign affairs.

[9] Evidence can also be found outside EU studies. The US political spectrum shows how hard it can be to consider one party more on the right or more on the left. "Wilsonianism with boots," as some characterize George W. Bush's foreign policy, has elements of both so-called left and right. Research on parties in France shows that

Support for my argument can be found in political thought as the preceding discussion reflects a long-standing debate in this field. It is very difficult to find a common linking strand in what is considered "right" and "left." The historical source of the spatial analogy is the seating arrangements in the post-revolutionary French Constitutive Assembly of 1789. Overall, the ideological structure of seating arrangements is invariably one-dimensional in parliamentarian systems. However, the choice of which dimension this should be can cause problems. Downs' argument (1957: 116), for example, that the level of government intervention in the economy determines "right" and "left" is problematic. In ideological terms this could categorize fascism as more center-right whereas libertarians could be considered extreme right (Eatwell 1989a: 42).[10] Authors such as Laponce (1981: 8), Brittan (1968: 88–9) or Eysenck (1954: 110) have conceived of the ideological spectrum as based on two dimensions. Shils writes of the "obsolete belief that all political, social and economic philosophies can be classified on the Right-Left continuum" (Shils 1954: 28). Schapiro (1972: 84) argues that "[t]here are probably no two terms in the language of politics which are more imprecise and subjective in the meanings which are attached to them than 'left' and 'right', and which are more misleading in their common usage ... there is no illumination to be derived from the misleading 'Left-Right' classification." Furthering this point, Green (1987: 2) says that it is "helpful to abandon altogether the habit of thinking about political philosophies as if they can be ranged along a straight line from left to right."

Political ideologies and security cooperation

Ideology in the realm of security and foreign affairs is rooted in a set of values upon which actors understand the means and ends of security or,

one dimension taken for granted, cultural liberalism, cannot be perceived as one single ideological dimension but rather as a number of independent dimensions. Issues such as homosexuality, the death penalty and immigration cannot be used to map French parties along a single cultural liberalism scale but instead two fundamental value sets are at play: progressive-traditional and socially egalitarian-hierarchical elements (Grunberg and Schweisguth 1997: 164; Andersen and Evans 2003: 183–4).

[10] The "right" can encompass both libertarianism and (moral) authoritarianism. It stresses collectivism (O'Sullivan 1976) or individualism, both based on the value of (ordered) liberty. The issue of abortion, for example, cannot be boiled down to equality and liberty. Liberty should recommend that one should be free to choose but the right also holds up moral standards and a certain notion of the "collective" – as a result the "right" is often against abortion. The "left" traditionally is understood to emphasize equality. In the case of abortion, it should stress that the unborn and the mother have the same rights but instead the left is often advocating choice. Liberty and equality by themselves are often not enough to derive policy preferences.

more precisely, the security threats as well as the means to tackle them. These domain-specific ideologies package a set of normative and causal claims that define parties' and, consequently, national governments' understandings of their neighbors and how best to address them. As research has shown, liberal democracies agree that political actors with political ideologies far removed from the values of rule of law, human rights and democracy constitute a threat to their security (Russett 1996; Haas 2003, 2005), but disagree on how to deal with such threats and risks.

When conceiving of the domain of security cooperation and the choice of responding to security threats, three fundamental questions structure the political debate: for what reasons should one act multilaterally in using force (*substance and importance of cooperation*); to what degree should responsibilities be shared (*depth of cooperation*); and with whom should one share responsibilities (*is there a community*)? While these questions delineate the fundamental dimensions in which national governments need to find answers, they also resonate with three major IR schools of thought. When looking at security cooperation, realists are mainly interested in the rationale for not acting alone (substance), while rational choice institutionalists are primarily concerned with the depth of cooperation. Constructivists want to know whether states act together because they feel part of a community. Based on these questions, national governments face three choices: (1) whether to address security threats unilaterally or multilaterally, (2) whether to integrate their policies into supranational institutions (i.e. delegating responsibility for confronting threats to a higher locus of authority) or to cooperate on an intergovernmental basis, and (3) whether to engage in world politics as part of a larger political community or, instead, with a group that acts together, whether because of some functional logic or simply by accident.

From actors' answers to these three broad choice scenarios can be derived three values: *multilateralism-in-the-use-of-force, sovereignty* and *Europe*. All three values can take on interpretations that make them core values, but not necessarily so. Unlike left–right distinctions in which certain values cluster together, my theory of preference formation makes no assumptions about the relationships between these different values. Instead, after deductively constraining the set of possible value choices, one needs to investigate the value relationships underlying political preferences. If any one of those values is defined in terms of another, it is subsumed and therefore ceases to exist as a motivational force (or core value) in its own right.

Each of these three values can have various manifestations that, metaphorically speaking, line up along three respective dimensions;

calling them multilateralism, sovereignty and Europe is simply a shortcut. First, I examine the various notions an actor such as a political party can assign to the *importance* of international institutions in national security policy. The value of *multilateralism-in-the-use-of-force* is understood as recurring efforts to coordinate "relations among three or more states on the basis of 'generalized' principles of conduct" (Ruggie 1992: 51) such as indivisibility and expectations of reciprocity (Keohane 1990; Caporaso 1992; Ruggie 1992; Tierney 2011). However, this can be interpreted in many different ways. Does the actor prefer to further its interests through committed multilateral cooperation (Risse-Kappen 1996; Rathbun 2011a, 2011b), selective modes of cooperation (Brooks and Wohlforth 2005), or does it prefer to "go it alone" (Waltz 1979; Mearsheimer 1990)? Does the actor value self-sufficiency and autonomy over (selective) cooperation? Is multilateral action only a tool to promote other values and interests (Keohane 1984; Martin 1992; Fioretos 2011), or is it perceived as an-end-in-itself (Pouliot 2011)? This value defines a dimension that extends from unilateralism through multilateralism-as-a-means-to-another-end to multilateralism-as-an-end-in-itself at the other end of the spectrum. Multilateralism-as-an-end-in-itself is a core value, a value from which actors think "as the 'natural' way to go about" (Pouliot 2011: 9) social interactions and, hence, it cannot be subsumed by any other value. However, it still can relate very differently to various manifestations of other values such as sovereignty and Europe. Just because an actor values multilateralism-as-an-end-in-itself, this does not foreclose valuing sovereignty, for example, in terms of either intergovernmentalism or supranationalism. Multilateralism-as-a-means-to-another-end, on the other hand, rests with an end defined by another value and, consequently, can be subsumed by core values derived from Europe or sovereignty. For example, Europe-as-a-political-community, a core value, in conjunction with multilateralism-as-a-means-to-another-end results in favoring multilateral cooperation within the European framework to any other. Based on the various connotations and interpretations of multilateralism, actors might (1) want to proceed in as many international institutions as possible, (2) not at all, or (3) prefer one multilateral setting over others.

Second, the *depth* of potential cooperation matters. How does a political actor such as a political party value *sovereignty*? Is the actor in favor of isolationism, supranational institution building that concedes national sovereignty, or intergovernmental institution building that retains national sovereignty? That is, do parties perceive cooperative arrangements more according to Moravcsik's (1998) logic of liberal intergovernmentalism, Haas' (1964) almost apolitical role for states in integration, or as an entanglement to be avoided outright (Rabkin 2004)? Are they willing to pool or delegate sovereignty, handing powers to international bureaucracies and/or to qualified majority voting? Are these decisions conditional upon other factors, such as Europe, or do they inform other values? Sovereignty can extend from isolationism through intergovernmentalism to supranationalism. Again, not every actor has to uphold the same understanding of sovereignty. It is very unlikely that a national actor is in favor of supranationalism at large, allocating sovereignty to a new locus of authority. However, it is conceivable that in conjunction with valuing a preferred political community some actors see supranationalism as informing their preferences.

Third, I examine the value of *Europe* in a political security ideology in order to locate the preferred *venue* or *community* of cooperation.[11] Does the actor privilege relations with European partners and institutions over any other countries and institutions; that is, is Europe understood as a political community (Adler and Barnett 1998; Mérand 2008)? Or is Europe understood only as a geographic area with no political claim attached to it (Hitchcock 1998: 170)? This value informs a dimension that reaches from Europe-as-a-geographic-space through Europe-as-a -community-among-others to Europe-as-a-political-community. Some political actors and parties value Europe as such. They prefer interacting with their European neighbors over interacting with any other potential country. This understanding of Europe is rooted in a shared history of wars and friendship, a *Schicksalsgemeinschaft* (a community of shared destiny) (Manners 2002). Nonetheless, not every actor that favors Europe-as-a-political-community has to also be in favor of such values as supranationalism. Instead, these dimensions, derived from different underlying values, have to be distinguished analytically. Yet other actors favor Europe only as a means-to-another-end (geographic space), making it derivative of multilateralism or sovereignty (Parsons 2002, 2003). Europe *can* be specific to a policy domain (Moravcsik and Nicolaïdis 1999: 63; Wüst and Schmitt 2007: 89–90). In cases where actors have a nuanced approach toward Europe based on the policy

---

[11] While the third value is specific to Europe, the other two are not. Issues of international cooperation in security policy have come up with increasing frequency in Africa and Asia. The African Union as well as the Economic Community of West African States and the Southern African Development Community, for example, have included the maintenance of peace and security in their mandate – as have the Association of South East Asian Nations and the Shanghai Cooperation Organization (Bellamy and Williams 2005; Williams 2009). In these cases, Europe needs to be substituted with other political communities.

domain in question, the value of Europe is unlikely to cut across other dimensions of political contestation such as multilateralism–unilateralism. However, actors can also be simply for or against Europe, in which case Europe cross-cuts other value dimensions. For example, the French Socialists and the German CDU/CSU are in favor of deeper European cooperation across all policy domains, while the British Conservatives have tended to be skeptical of Europe since it became more political – and, hence, encroached more on national sovereignty.[12]

These three values and their relationships form the main policy space structuring preferences and specific issue positions about security institutions in a non-randomized and meaningful way. Depending on the particular political ideology, this set of values can either be independent, interdependent, or derivative of one another. Given these different value manifestations, ideologies around European security cooperation cannot necessarily be captured through one dimension, as with a left–right continuum employed by partisan values explanations (Rathbun 2004), especially if the continuum simply measures attitudes for or against cooperation in a certain policy domain. Instead, several dimensions can jointly structure political parties' policy preferences. The reasons and forms to organize multilaterally vary. Most of these options involve some form of international cooperation in security institutions, either in the form of narrow military alliances, or in comprehensive security institutions. A study of ideologies draws attention to the various possible manifestations of security institutions. Based on more or less subtle differences in actors' positioning on various aspects of support for the scope of security cooperation, we can start thinking about why some actors favor one security institution over all others, while other actors want as many security institutions as possible. By not deciding *a priori* how many core values exist, we receive a more nuanced picture of the different motivations for creating international institutions in an already institutionalized policy space.

A key factor shaping party preferences around the creation of an autonomous European security institution has been NATO. I argue that NATO's impact on European attempts to create a security institution has not existed as an objective constraint, but rather has been *filtered* and interpreted through the values of multilateralism-in-the-use-of-force, sovereignty and Europe. Parties that are pro-European and favor the multilateral use of force are likely to be inclined to create a European

---

[12] Evans (2003: 164), for example, shows that when it comes to "Europe" some political parties are close to other parties that are otherwise traditionally not ideologically inclined to side with them.

security institution – regardless of what happens inside NATO. However, political parties that value the multilateral use of force as a means, but are not attached to Europe, are likely to favor NATO or other established and successful security institutions. NATO's existence stresses the fact that looking at multilateralism-in-the-use-of-force and sovereignty is insufficient to explain whether a party is in favor of a European security institution.

If one maintains the metaphor of three dimensions on which these values line up, one can map the values that constitute security ideology in a simplified three-dimensional space (as in Figure 2.1). The first examines the willingness to engage in international cooperation by employing the value of multilateralism-in-the-use-of-force. The second dimension concerns sovereignty; that is, whether the actor is in favor of supra- or intergovernmentalism, or instead prefers isolationism. Finally, the third dimension concerns an actor's ideological affiliation in regard to a political community. As Figure 2.1 illustrates, ideological inclinations are influenced by a set of values that do not necessarily correlate with each other. However, any of these dimensions can be collapsed onto the others, depending on the exact manifestation of each value. This is indicated by the bold lines (one-dimensional policy space), the shaded area (two-dimensional policy space) and the cube (three-dimensional policy space). The multidimensional scheme allows one to measure not just *if* a party favors security cooperation, but also *what kind* of institutionalized cooperation, and with *which* partners.

The basic argument here is that the more party ideologies converge in terms of multilateralism, Europe and sovereignty, the higher the likelihood that a European autonomous security institution will be created. Conversely, a European security institution becomes less likely when key states diverge ideologically; this divergence could take the form of values tending toward unilateralism, of emphasizing the transatlantic relationship over Europe, or could diverge over the inter- versus supragovernmental nature of security cooperation.

Interpreters of values: political parties and party factions

Ideologies construct the interests of purposive actors. Collective actors are attached to different manifestations of (core) values, translate them into ideologies and identify with their meaning. This is a process of interpretation (Weldes 1996). There are many meaningful ways in which values can be related to one another. As a result, not every actor

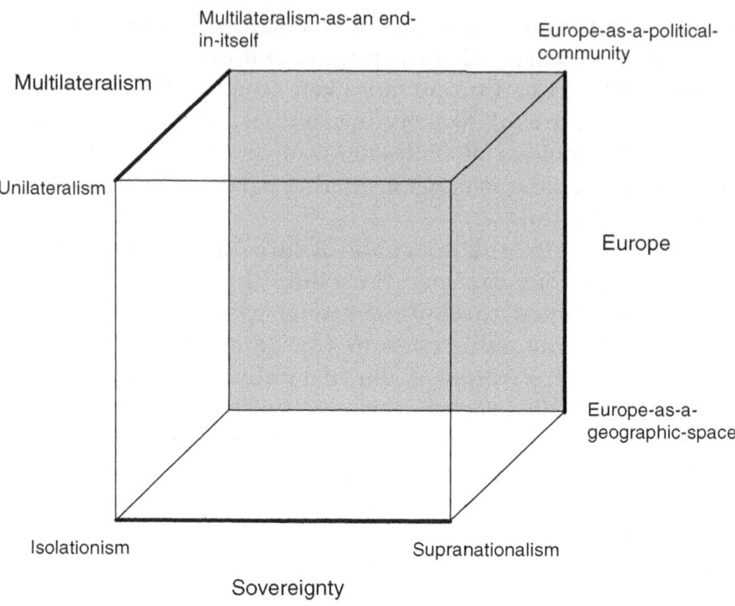

Figure 2.1 Mapping party ideologies in a multidimensional space

views the world in the same terms. These collectively held values – or hierarchy of values – define appropriate conduct and influence actors' interests and political position within the broader environment. The actors of interest here are political parties. Parties aggregate values and are central to political contestation and competition (but not exclusively); they are a specific kind of collective political actor as they are legitimate representatives of a set, and of the salience, of political ideas over time (Budge and Farlie 1983; Cox 1987; Döring 1995). There are many different (domain-specific) policy positions that parties can take (Linhart and Shikano 2009; Pappi and Seher 2009) whose meaning is not necessarily shared by other national or international actors. To account for the ways in which ideology influences parties, one first needs to explain their composition, possibilities for ideological change, and the reasons that certain parties adhere to particular ideologies in the first place.

Political parties, policies and policy change

In this analysis, I focus on advanced representative democracies where political parties are the interpreters of political ideologies and have agenda-setting authority (Beyme 1985: 29).[13] In democracies, parties in power are vested with authority to commit or withhold resources, for example, with regard to making foreign and security policy.[14] The ideologies that parties uphold are long-standing (Van der Brug *et al.* 2007: 179). Political ideologies reflect how and why elites construct their political world (Aldrich 1995; De Vries and Hobolt 2012). Political elites that share a commitment to a particular way of ordering political life – based on economic, social and/or environmental issues or goals, for example – are likely to form groups in the interest of contributing to the organization of political life; often these groups take the form of political parties. Parties in other states can claim allegiance to the same value-set underlying an ideology. Ideology has transnational elements in the sense that it is based in political thought, but is also domestically rooted since it derives important reference points from its national context that can be specific to only one country.

Parties and ideologies   Inter-party competition on the domestic level is often, to a large degree, driven ideologically. Parties offer structured alternatives through distinct ideological profiles (Hinich and Munger 1992, 1997). As a result, national interest and policies are not static and all-enduring but may be altered over a short period of time due to elections and changes of government. Even if politics is at times sold as bipartisan to the electorate, this does not foreclose the possibility that parties and politicians see the world through ideological and partisan spectacles.[15] The so-called "political color" of a government matters. As Jennings (1992: 436) has shown, "even though the political parties are routinely accused of being indistinguishable, the cleavages run long and deep at the elite level." This holds particularly for party systems with firm party discipline (Jäger *et al.* 2009: 425; Mikhaylov *et al.* 2012: 2). As I have shown in the previous section, political ideology in the realm of security policy and foreign affairs can have many different manifestations. Parties differ on what political institution should

[13] "The difficulty that regimes have in suppressing party politics is one indicator of just how central parties are to governing a modern state" (Ware 1996: 1).

[14] The interpreters of political ideologies can be manifold; they can be any kind of social and political grouping of individuals. Next to political parties, ruling families (as is the case in some states in the Persian Gulf) or authoritarian leaders might hold onto political ideologies. However, depending on the particular kind of grouping, we can expect different mechanisms with which ideologies are upheld and reinforced.

[15] Ideological influences on security policy preferences might be masked by other rationales that are electorally more popular. The George W. Bush administration has undertaken several attempts to resell the decision to go to Iraq (Desch 2007/8). However, this does not dampen the ideological nature of this policy.

provide for security, with what means, and in what fashion. These pro-grammatic distinctions among parties serve to organize political debate and preferences among parties (Kiewiet and McCubbins 1991; Cox and McCubbins 1993; Aldrich 1995; Schultz 2005: 8–9).

Political parties offer not only distinct but also relatively stable pol-icies and communicate a coherent set of policy propositions. Ideology matters to political parties in ways that shape a relatively stable set of policies.[16] The realization of particular policies motivates parties (Laver and Hunt 1992; Klingemann *et al.* 1994; Müller and Strøm 1999). Ware (1996: 47) tests the longevity of party ideologies and finds the "ten-dency for party ideologies to persist; values and views that were present at a party's founding seem to have survived for a long time." In the end, party and ideology are inextricably linked and partisanship and ideo-logical orientation exist side by side (Inglehart 1979: 353; Dalton 1988; Huber 1989).

The link between parties and ideology has been contested in the CP lit-erature. A key debate has been whether political parties are policy-seekers with rooted ideologies, or are office-keepers or vote-seekers for whom ideology is merely a way of attracting votes.[17] If ideologies are merely a way to court votes, the argument goes, there is likely to be little rela-tion between party ideologies and government policy (Strøm 1990). However, already Edmund Burke in 1770 defined parties as "a body of men united for promoting by their joint endeavors the national interest upon some particular principle in which they are all agreed" (quoted in Ware 1996: 5). Burke's view of parties as policy-seekers has more contemporary empirical backing based on different studies providing considerable evidence for the policy-seeking view of political parties (Laver and Budge 1992; Klingemann *et al.* 1994; Rathbun 2004; Clare 2010). Other prominent political scientists have called political parties "the agents of collective purpose in a democracy … [T]hey distill the multiple strands of social sentiment into concrete programs backed by a particular moral vision" (Hall 1986: 91; see also Risse-Kappen 1994) or, in the words of Lipset and Rokkan, political parties are "alliances in conflicts over policies and value commitments within the larger body politic" (Lipset and Rokkan 1967: 5).

---

[16] This argument does not discount observations that ideologies allow for a certain dynamism in which values can be reinterpreted and new parties can introduce new values to the political stage (Noël and Thérien 2008; De Vries and Hobolt 2012).

[17] Some also argue that parties are primarily cohesion-seekers who care most about keeping party activists in the fold (Aldrich 1983; Steenbergen and Scott 2004; Parsons and Weber 2011). To do so, they have to rely primarily on ideological commitments and, hence, show incentive structures congruent with the policy-seeking argument.

The policy-seeking versus office-keeping or vote-seeking dimensions of parties should not be understood as dichotomous but instead should be thought of as a matter of *degree* (Aldrich 1995: 22–3; Müller and Strøm 1999; Schumacher *et al.* forthcoming). Parties "reflect both strategic considerations of how to shape policy positions in the current election so as to consolidate or attract votes, and the constraints imposed by long-standing ideology" (Klingemann *et al.* 2007: 108; see also Strøm 1990; Moravcsik 1993: 481–3; Budge 1994; Adams 2001; Adams *et al.* 2004; Hanson 2010: xv). Ideology establishes limits from which parties rarely escape – especially because of leadership *commitments* and electoral *attachments*. None of this excludes parties from occupying an ideological position that they believe will be electorally popular. The argument, however, is that elections do not change the party ideology, especially not in regard to security policy as this is hardly ever a policy field which determines the timing outcome of an election. Instead, elections affect the relative attention and salience that parties give to particular issues. The preferences themselves do not change (Klingemann *et al.* 1994; Rathbun 2004).

Factions, ideological emphasis and policy redirection   Rather than locating changes in party ideologies in elections, I argue and show that they are better explained through change in party leadership and party factions. At times these changes may coincide with general elections. I conceive of ideology construction and value interpretation as a party-driven process that reflects the ideological leanings of the dominant party faction at the time.[18] Though political parties are relatively unitary structures, it is possible that some value interpretations constitutive of a particular ideology are contested within parties. Variance in value emphasis and salience finds expression in party factions – they often form within parties around certain issue domains (Schurmann 1973: 32–3; Budge and Farlie 1983; Rathbun 2008; Jäger *et al.* 2009: 422; Oppermann and Viehrig 2009). Some factions are more invested

---

[18] Most German political parties, though they include their party base in the framing of the party program, write the program in the party headquarters. Interview with Andreas Körner, consultant of the Green Faction in the German Parliament (Fraktionsreferent Sicherheitspolitik) in Berlin (December 21, 2006) and interview with Dr. Markus Engels, Deputy Director Department for International Affairs, Deputy International Secretary, in Berlin (December 19, 2006). In the UK, in the Labour Party, the National Executive Committee drafts the party manifesto. The leadership is more dominant in framing party policy in the Conservative Party (Peele 1980: 186). As a result, Heath had alienated his party on ideological grounds (Peele 1980: 186). When Thatcher won, she re-oriented the party toward its majority view.

in certain policy fields than others and carry a party line more or less passionately. The exact preferences of any particular government depend on the faction that controls the party at a particular point in time (Schultz 2005: 3, 9).[19]

Tensions and value conflicts are more likely in parties with more than one core value. Not only the values' particular manifestations but also their exact alignments can be debated (Tetlock 1984, 1985, 1986; Feldman and Zaller 1992; De Vries and Hobolt 2012). Especially when new values are introduced to a party ideology, they might not sit easily with established values, and intra-party debate is very likely. Evans (2003) and De Vries (2007, 2010) show that some previously cohesive parties had a hard time introducing Europe into their party ideology. The British Labour Party heavily debated the issue in the 1960s and 1970s (Baker and Seawright 1998b: 58; Forster 1999: 23). Europe cannot easily be derived from a single core value.

Party leaders, who came to power through an internal party election, try to reconcile value conflicts across factions. They translate the different value manifestations, as well as their salience, and link them up into an ideology in which the majority of the party can find itself (Cox 1987; Chiou and Rothenberg 2003; Kam 2009; De Vries 2010; Kam *et al.* 2010; see also Rhode 1991). This task is manageable because the differences between the various factions are mostly over emphasis. This emphasis is bound by party standards. Party leaders forge compromises within parties to develop a common platform. These platforms have an integrative and ideological function. They communicate to party members some ideological compromises but at the same time express the factions' and leaders' leanings (Katz and Mair 1994).

Individual leaders might choose to move their party away from some well-established party standards, but if this move is not just one of emphasis, but of real change in core values, their commitments and electoral attachments are called into question and the party and voters are likely to punish this move (Laver *et al.* 2006). More radical divisions can prove disruptive and can lead to party splits, as has been the case in the UK with the split from Labour and the creation of the Social Democratic Party in 1981, for example.

Overall, political parties selectively emphasize or de-emphasize issues in their policy inventory – also around election time (Budge and

---

[19] Even an IR scholar such as Glenn Snyder, who argues that the systemic level can best explain the creation of alliances, admits: "Since the relative influence of parties and factions is subject to change, a state's alliance preferences may also change as groups move up or down the domestic political ladder" (Snyder 1997: 132).

Farlie 1983; Klingemann *et al.* 1994: 24). More often than not it is the emphasis, instead of the actual value orientation, that changes over the course of a single election campaign – a shift that can nonetheless adjust policy preferences. Party election platforms not only represent the ideology of the party, but also the tendencies of the dominant faction at the time. Party leaders do not come to power out of a vacuum and, as a result, they cannot change values at will. Different parties have more or less well established factions, with their own meetings, think tanks and names (Reiter 2004).[20] The Social Democrats (SPD) in Germany, for example, have a socialist-leaning faction known as *Frankfurter Kreis/ Parlamentarische Linke* and a neoliberal *Seeheimer Kreis*. Recently, a group known as the *Netzwerker* has been formed as well, which sees itself in between those two factions. The German Greens are split between *Realos* ("pragmatic") and *Fundis* ("principled"). The British Conservatives are divided into groups such as the *No Turning Back Group*, *European Reform Group*, *Friends of Bruges* and the *Conservative Mainstream*; all are skeptical of European integration, but to different degrees. In France, the *Centre d'Etudes, de Recherche, et d'Education Socialiste* (CERES) in the *Parti Socialiste* (PS) was critical of European integration in the 1970s and 1980s because of the neoliberal thrust of the European Community (EC) (Gordon 1993: 109; Haywood 1993: 270–2). A party's ideological lens structures the interpretation of the external environment and politicians act on behalf of a set of party standards that they often take for granted. Any reinterpretation of value manifestations and configurations needs to be justified in light of the existing ideology.

This book is concerned with the build-up and consequences of group membership rather than the origins of the grouping. Suffice it to say here that when new political regimes are put in place, and new foreign and security policies need to be formulated, such as after World War II, political elites, under the guidance of leaders such as Charles de Gaulle or Konrad Adenauer, impacted the particular configuration of values describing an ideology (Hanson 2010). Multilateralism, sovereignty and Europe are not values that came about with the end of the Cold War but instead existed in the political sphere long before (Krasner 1999; Parsons 2003; Rathbun 2011a). Party leadership, at the party's initial stage, had influenced their institutionalization, which resulted in politicians adhering to these values and referring to their party's tradition in

---

[20] In 1999, when ESDP was debated, it mattered that the *Realo* Joschka Fischer was heading the foreign ministry and not for example the *Fundi* Jürgen Trittin (Hooghe *et al.* 2002: 983).

justifying their policy choices. For example, Adenauer, the first head of the CDU after the war, entrenched the value of Europe-as-a-political-community as a core value for his party, firmly stressing "Germany's" ideological congruence with the "West"; that is, a common political community based on a liberal orientation, its penchant toward a market-oriented economy and institutionalized protection of individual rights, while being "fully aware that such an alignment might well rule out the possibility of reunification for the foreseeable future" (Turner 1987: 68, see also Döring-Manteuffel 1983; Sontheimer 1991). The CDU shared with all German postwar parties the belief in multilateralism-as-an-end-in-itself based on the historical experience with the Nazi regime (Duffield 1998). Sovereignty, by consequence, was understood contextually. Nonetheless, Adenauer faced fierce resistance from Kurt Schumacher and most of the SPD. Schumacher, who headed the SPD in the initial postwar period, understood Europe not as an anchor for Germany but as a community-among-others (Turner 1987; Sontheimer 1991). As a result, from the beginning of the Federal Republic, the CDU and the SPD had different agendas regarding foreign and security policy. The CDU under Adenauer and the SPD under Schumacher valued immediate reunification of Germany and its aligned status differently based on different ideological foundations.

The lack of strong representational linkages

An important question concerns why parties adhere to their particular ideology. The previous sections have argued that ideology affects security policy preferences and that it is of secondary importance whether national governments behave in this fashion because of a sincere commitment to their ideology, or because they fear that compromising those values will be electorally damaging. This section advances the argument for ideologies as the main motivator of preferences a little further by making the case that the common value system of the party socializes politicians and influences their worldviews. Socialized into an ideology, politicians are biased to pursue the preferences of their party – they abide by the ideology as a function of being a party member and out of a desire to keep the party distinct and together. In this sense, ideologies are "principled beliefs" (Goldstein and Keohane 1993).[21] Empirical

---

[21] Even the literature on internal and external strategic settings that explains party cohesion (Krehbiel 1991, 1993; Cox and McCubbins 2005; Dewan and Spirling 2011; Diermeier and Vlaicu 2011; Richman 2011) does not deny the impact of partisan identities and preference alignment, but instead argues that it is a matter of degree.

evidence supports this theoretical argument as it has shown that the general public often does not vote based on security issues (except on issues of war, and then only occasionally) (Aldrich *et al.* 2006).

The emphasis on beliefs within parties contrasts with two mechanisms in the Comparative Politics literature used to explain the ideological consistency of parties in government in line with the office-keeping or vote-seeking arguments: vested interests push parties for a certain policy, or the general public votes for a certain issue and holds the parties accountable for their policies.

Security ideology and vested interests   One argument centers on the relationship between parties and particular constituencies, such as business sectors or classes. Some have studied security cooperation from the perspective of promoting trade, protection of foreign investment, and the generation of income for actors involved in the provision of strategic goods. Such arguments often employ the logic that different interest groups have divergent preferences on these issues which are reflected in parties and, subsequently, in policies (Fordham 1998a, 1998b; Moravcsik and Nicolaïdis 1999; Narizny 2007).

By contrast, I argue that there is no powerful constituency, policy elite, class or sector in favor of a European security institution autonomous from NATO. Though the arms industry could be considered the constituency of parties favoring market-creating policies to promote trade and to generate income for actors involved in the provision of strategic goods, this does not automatically translate into a preference for a European market as opposed to the transatlantic, bilateral or globalized markets. Even in 2007, nine years after the initiation of ESDP, Darnis *et al.* (2007: 13) have observed: "The idea of European defence industrial autonomy is unrealistic for the time being since large parts of the European defence industry remain fragmented, while other parts of the industry are increasingly 'globalising' their supply chains." As the empirical evidence will show later, parties that favor market-creating policies and that have been involved in cooperation in the arms industry, such as the British Conservatives, have not been in favor of a European security institution. Also, defense industries in Europe are at least partly state-owned (Jones 2006). As such, their motivations cannot be thought of independently from the government and the political parties in power.

Second, there are few (re)distributive effects to begin with and the gains that could be made through multilateral security cooperation beneficial to vested interests have already been obtained through NATO membership. Even though policies have both public and private components, the private gains associated with the creation of an autonomous security institution are not major (Wallander 2000). NATO membership has organized its member states' security and arms production. NATO had already established a Military Production and Supply Board in 1949. It became the Defense Production Committee in 1954. It coordinates production, standardization and technical research in the weapons industry and has expanded its reach further ever since, giving rise to such things as air defense weapons systems (Jones 2006: 252).

Third, projects for bilateral and multilateral cooperation on arms procurement have existed independently of a European security institution (Jones 2006; Keohane 2008). The creation of a European security institution does not involve new arms procurements for all member states so much as a sharing of existing national assets between NATO and an autonomous European institution. One example is the creation of the European Airlift Center in Eindhoven which provides air transport to France, Germany, the United Kingdom, Belgium, Italy, the Netherlands, and Spain. The Airlift Center can be used for NATO or EU purposes. Since the end of the Cold War, defense budgets across Europe have been static while the cost of equipment has been rising (Darnis *et al.* 2007; Keohane 2008). National defense industries have never been completely autonomous from those of other states but instead NATO and bilateral security partnerships, such as those existing between France and Germany, have made their militaries more interoperable (SIPRI 2008).[22]

Security ideology and the electorate   A second general argument focuses on the electorate and national elections, as well as referenda, as the key mechanisms enforcing party adherence to their declared ideologies. Through the mechanism of democratic accountability, political parties need to demonstrate responsibility, credibility, and reliability (no matter if the parties are primarily office-, policy- or vote-seeking) while pushing them to deliver on their promises (Downs 1957: 103–5; Castles 1982; Budge and Keman 1990; McDonald and Budge 2005: 3, 13–14). Nevertheless, the general public is more attentive to some policies than to others (Carmines and Stimson 1980). When it comes to the European Union, scholars have observed that

---

[22] Article 296 of the Treaty on the European Union allows member states to exempt defense contracts from EC procurement rules if such a move is necessary for the protection of their essential security interests (Keohane 2008). Only very slowly does the arms industry turn to the European Commission to lobby for an increase in spending on anti-terrorist technology or the removal of arms export barriers (Andersson and Malm 2006; Darnis *et al.* 2007). Both sets of policies exist despite the existence of ESDP.

"Europe's population is not insulated from the consequences of Union policies" (van der Eijk and van der Brug 2007: 5). Since at least the Maastricht Treaty and the end of the Cold War, more domestic attention has been given to European integration (De Vries 2007; van der Brug and van der Eijk 2007), as well as to international crises (Tomz 2007) from the electorate. As long as the electorate is not completely cynical about politics, parties will have to care about their credibility and therefore will need to act cohesively at the national and the international levels.

Elections and referenda give citizens influence over the distribution of legislative power and "to the extent that political parties and their leaders support different policy packages, also indirectly over the policy direction of their national government" (van der Eijk and van der Brug 2007: 6; see also Hooghe and Marks 1999: 72). Scholars have come to different conclusions as to how the public perceives European integration or foreign policy (in uni- or multi-dimensional terms) and whether their attitudinal position toward European integration matters to the general voter's choice of party (and hence implicitly to the formulations of policy). For those who argue that attitudes toward Europe can be captured on a left–right spectrum, parties mobilize voters by fusing Europe with other left–right issues (Gabel and Anderson 2004).[23] As such Europe is one issue among many that motivates voters' choices. Others argue that Europe cross-cuts a left–right dichotomy making it difficult to mobilize voters on this basis (Holsti 1998/9; Van der Brug *et al.* 2007: 183), except for extremist parties (De Vries 2007).[24] This reduces the possible outlet for political public opinion. One therefore needs to dissect the issue on the basis of particular policy domains.

In domains such as political economy, a left–right dichotomy might be sufficient to explain different attitudes and preferences toward domestic and European policies. As some have pointed out, "Left/ Right contestation shapes positioning only on European policies that

---

[23] However, as already mentioned in the context of ideological space, Gabel and Anderson have to admit that "there are subtle and systematic distinctions in the structure of the EU policy space that would be missed by assuming only one dimension to the policy space. These distinctions are meaningful" (2004: 28; see also Scheuer and van der Brug 2007: 105).

[24] By examining *entre autre* election manifestos, the book's case studies will show that election manifestos can be quite explicit in their preferences towards the EU. The British Conservatives, for example, ran on an anti-EU campaign in 1997 based on their ideological inclination, but to no electoral success (Evans and Norris 1999). The CDU/CSU always included European issues in its election campaign, even such unpopular ones as the EMU, and still won elections.

are concerned with redistribution and regulating capitalism" (Hooghe *et al.* 2002: 971; see also Fiorina 1981). Foreign and security policy issues, however, are issues distant from regulatory concerns with concentrated gains (Miller and Stokes 1963; Lowi 1964; Gowa 1998: 321–2; Koenig-Archibugi 2004: 165). While initial research on public opinion regarding questions of foreign and security policy (mostly on intervention and war) in the United States has shown that the public is uninformed and unstructured (the so-called Almond-Lippman consensus), ever since the Vietnam War research on the US public has shown that the public takes cues from international and domestic elites or events (Aldrich *et al.* 2006: 485–6) and has "sophisticated and nuanced views" (Aldrich *et al.* 2006: 483; see also Herrmann *et al.* 1999: 565). However, these attitudes do not regularly translate into votes (Aldrich *et al.* 1989; Oppermann and Viehrig 2009). Isernia *et al.* (2002) and Van der Brug *et al.* (2007) have observed that the European public is less informed and motivated by foreign policy issues than the US public. For the general European public, European security cooperation is not a policy priority, despite a generally positive view of the issue.[25] Issues such as security institutions neither impact the public nor a specific group of the electorate directly. It is unlikely that the issue informs their party choice or provides incentives for parties to mobilize around the issue. Research that dissects European integration into policy domains has shown that both political elites and the public want to shift different policy domains to the EU level: "Elites desire a European Union capable of governing a large, competitive market and projecting political muscle; citizens are more in favor of a caring European Union, which protects them from the vagaries of capitalist markets" (Hooghe 2003: 296; see also Koenig-Archibugi 2004: 165–6).[26] Voters care about European security cooperation, but they care less about it than about policies with redistributive consequences. As a result, overall multilateral security institutions are not very salient to elections, though they might be more important to some political parties than to others based on different ideological commitments. As a consequence, political parties are less tempted to simplify their electoral platform along a one-dimensional message when it comes to security institutions.

---

[25] For data on public opinion around European security, see Eurobarometer 32 (1989: 43–5), Eurobarometer 35 (1991: 27–31), and Eurobarometer 45 (1996: 55–7).

[26] Wüst and Schmitt (2007: 89–90) show that while voters and parties align in regard to general pro- and anti-European stands, they do not in certain policy domains. This indicates that certain domains are interpreted differently from the general attitude toward Europe.

Not all politics is reduced to elections. Political leadership matters. While the political elite is not insulated from the general electorate, "the fate of the European Union still lies in the hands of the political leadership of Europe" (Ray 2003: 991), and this political leadership can give cues to voters (Ray 2003; Aldrich *et al.* 2006; Marsh 2007; Wüst and Schmitt 2007). Research has shown that "the position taken by a political party on the issue of European integration *can* act as a cue for supporters of that party" (Ray 2003: 990, emphasis added; see also Risse-Kappen 1991; Isernia *et al.* 2002: 204, 215). When a party does not attach much importance to an issue, because it either does not rank high on its priority list or the party is not united on the issue, then voters do not necessarily follow party cues (Gabel and Scheve 2007). Overall, the salience of Europe and European integration for political parties, as indicated in their party manifestos for example, has increased – but not in a uniform manner (Hooghe and Marks 2006; Benoit 2009; Oppermann and Viehrig 2009).

In sum, parties primarily adhere to a particular ideology in devising security policy, not as a response to social forces, whether vested interests or the general electorate, but due to the socialization of party members into a set of (hierarchically) ordered values that constitute a party ideology. Indeed, the autonomous view of party ideology here underscores how social forces can follow party ideology.

3 The success and failure of European security cooperation

What accounts for the failure to merge the WEU and the EU during the Maastricht Treaty and Amsterdam Treaty negotiations? Does the British Conservatives' resistance to European integration in security policy explain it? What explains rapprochement between France and NATO in the mid 1990s? Is it only a coincidence that ESDP was created soon after Labour came to power in the UK?

The following chapter provides a framework for tackling such questions. The theory presented here explains why European governments repeatedly attempted to replicate NATO among themselves, and why their attempts met with different degrees of success. I argue that at key junctures in the history of European security, the ideologies of parties in power shaped the preferences of states around questions of institutional overlap and generated opportunities and constraints for institutional cooperation. In international cooperation, what matters is not only party ideology (or ideologies) in a single state, but the extent to which ideologies are shared across national governments. The central mechanism in my theory is ideological congruence or incongruence among international actors at a particular time. The core argument is that this ideological congruence or incongruence among national governments explains outcomes in European security cooperation. Ideological configurations have historically both impeded and facilitated the creation of an international institution similar to NATO, but autonomous from it. If governments in power in key states have ideologies with different core values, efforts to create a new security institution fail, or assume only the weakest institutional form. If governments in power in key states have ideologies with similar core values, efforts to create a security institution can succeed along the basis of these shared values, possibly resulting in a strong security institution. By combining insights from International Relations and Comparative Politics theories, this chapter traces how the effect of partisan orientation can explain policy-making settings and the success, or lack thereof, of interstate cooperation.

This chapter provides the second building block for a theory of how configurations of European political party ideologies affect the outcomes of European attempts to create security institutions. The first section explains the causal processes through which party ideologies affect state policies and the outcomes of international cooperation. I examine the effects of party ideologies on security policy and the specific behavioral prescriptions associated with particular sets of values. In the second section, I situate my argument in the broader International Relations and European Studies literature. The third section contrasts my argument with alternative explanations derived from realism, rational choice institutionalism, and a partisan values argument. In the last two sections, I discuss the research design and case selection for the chapters to come.

The causal logic

To answer the questions motivating this book, it is not enough to point to the kinds of ideologies present on the national level. One also needs to study how a particular ideological orientation is translated into national policy preferences and interstate policy outcomes. Thus, my causal argument incorporates two steps. In the first step, ideologies are translated into government policy within states with different institutional contexts. By focusing on party ideologies and changes in government, we can specify when changes in preferences of EU member states toward specific institutional paths occur; something that historical institutionalists such as Pierson (1996: 140, 263) suggest needs further specification and analytical rigor. In the second step, party ideologies create consequences for multilateral security cooperation across states by constraining or enabling attempts to create security institutions on the basis of congruent ideologies. As Hix and Lord (1997: 4) have pointed out, "key players may rush to form agreements while there is a favourable conjuncture in the domestic politics of member states" to lock "successor governments into EU-level agreements." Ideological congruence among EU member states is one such "favourable conjuncture," I argue.

Ideologically minded coalitions are crucial both on the domestic and international level. I show how parties' ideological orientations argue their way through domestic and international institutional settings. On both levels of analysis, the coalition's main characteristic is the degree of ideological congruence. Should we observe instances of ideological congruence, coalitions are formed internationally and nationally, trying to limit ideological conflict by defining the range of appropriate policies. Policy proposals are not just being discussed but also successfully ratified. However, should we observe ideological incongruence, international coalitions will falter or national coalitions will hesitate to formulate policies; as a result, policy proposals will not see the light of day.[1]

Party ideologies and the national interest

National preference formation is the first step in the causal process through which party ideologies affect security cooperation for governments in power, the so-called ideology-to-policy linkage. Parties across Europe operate in different institutional contexts, involving different constitutional principles, producing either unitary or coalition governments, or situations of *cohabitation*, and act according to different conventional practices. These different structures and practices affect the translation of political ideologies into government policy (McGillivray and Smith 2004: 569). Ideology cannot always be translated directly into policy.[2] As Cheibub and Limongi (2002: 156) point out, "Government action is necessarily limited to the area that contains policy proposals preferred by its supporters over the status quo" (see also Howorth 2010).

The institutional setting has an influence on whether political parties can govern alone or need to look for like-minded supporters to translate their programs into policy. The institutional framework can mediate the impact of ideologies on policy. In general, two variables affect a government's preference formation and decision-making process: first, parties find themselves either in parliamentary, semi-presidential or presidential state institutions; second, they compete in either proportional representation or majoritarian electoral systems depending on the electoral laws in the particular countries.[3] These variables have an

---

[1] While there are many commonalities between the international and national coalitions, this is not to say that coalition dynamics and characteristics are the same for government coalitions and international coalitions. For example, small coalitions might be advantageous on the domestic level while on the international level large coalitions are often favored (Abramson *et al.* 2008). Also, on the international level coalitions do not have to govern for a preset period of time. And the costs of cooperating are different: at the international level, not cooperating at all could be more costly than symbolic cooperation, while on the domestic level, it is likely to be the other way around.

[2] While much work in Comparative Politics addresses the *origins* of party preferences, shows their stability and how they relate to the electorate's attitudes, little work actually shows whether and how these preferences *influence* policy content (Hellström 2008; Manow *et al.* 2008; for exceptions see Erikson *et al.* 2002; Soroka and Wlezien 2010).

[3] Admittedly, the representation of different regimes is prototypical and there exists variance in the way the decision-making process is organized (Cheibub and Limongi 2002).

impact on the number of parties that form the government and hence also the ideological "pureness" through which ideological programs are translated into policy (Laver and Schofield 1990; Tsebelis 1995; Cheibub and Limongi 2002: 162).

Not all government practices can be deduced from institutional settings, however. Extra-constitutional practices, the size of the parliamentary majority and the principle of collective cabinet responsibility, for example, matter as well. In the following section, I will explain the different institutional settings and conventional practices and how they relate to ideological policy preferences.

Straightforward translation of ideology into policy   The few parliamentary democracies with majority voting rules in single member districts (SMD) (almost) invariably produce a majority for a single party for government formation (Duverger 1954; Katz 1980; McDonald and Budge 2005: 9) – though the British national elections in 2010 have shown that it is not impossible for third parties to attain power in coalition with a major party.[4] When political government coalitions are unlikely to form, no compromises need to be forged with other parties. The only compromises that matter are those that keep individual parties together and support the practice of party discipline. When considering party leadership and discipline, what matters is the margin the party has in parliament. Small margins can empower small factions of backbenchers in the party (Puchala 1975: 507; Aspinwall 2000: 416). The Conservative Prime Minister John Major, for example, was constrained in terms of what he could and could not do by the slender nature of his majority – he needed to buy votes in his own party (Baker *et al.* 1994). It is nonetheless possible in these instances that ideology can be translated into policy straightforwardly.

When there is little or no need to rely on other parties, formal cooperation is not encouraged and parties tend to be confrontational. Based upon the fusion of legislative and executive powers, the cabinet has complete control over the legislative agenda (Loewenberg and Patterson 1979). In such a system, we can expect the major parties to represent two different ideological stances on many policy issues as they distinguish themselves from one another. Looking at the data from Laver and Hunt (1992), for example, one observes that the major parties in the UK (Labour and Conservatives) were perceived by party experts to be further apart than parties in Germany and France which were operating in different political and institutional contexts.

---

[4] India is also an exception. I thank one of the anonymous reviewers for this point.

Coalitions and ideological compromises   Coalition government is common practice in a multiparty parliamentary system with proportional representation (PR) voting rules (Katz 1997: 5; Lijphart 1999; McDonald and Budge 2005: 9; Strøm *et al.* 2010: 519).[5] As a result, different political parties have to agree on a common policy stance based on ideological compromises. Often these are written down in coalition treaties or agreements that are either made public before or after elections, and which define the margin of common ideological ground and policies (Müller and Strøm 2000, 2008; Strøm *et al.* 2010: 521, 528–30). They constrain cabinet ministers.

Ideological compromises are not necessarily made in proportion to party share but in proportion to the leverage smaller parties have over larger parties (Kaarbo 2008; Kaarbo and Beasley 2008; Müller and Strøm 2008; Clare 2010). A state characterized by two big parties that stand for different sets of values, plus a few smaller parties, gives considerable leverage to the smaller parties in getting concessions during the formation of coalition governments in which they are included as junior partners. The allocation of ministerial portfolios influences government policies at the national level (Laver and Shepsle 1996; Hallerberg 2003; Pappi and Seher 2009).[6] In Germany this is known as the *Ressortprinzip*.

Furthermore the scope of the coalition is conditional on policy preferences in the sense of Axelrod's (1970) argument that government coalitions are policy-connected in ways that bring together ideologically adjacent parties. In other words ideological configurations explain the range of policies the new government will adopt (Clare 2010). Since a single party will not be able to translate its ideology directly into policy, but instead has to build compromises with its coalition partner(s), it will look for parties that are close to its ideological core; parties are selective when it comes to their governmental partners (de Swaan 1973; Laver and Schofield 1990: 104–42; Warwick 1995; Müller and Strøm 2000, 2008) because political parties are not free to move along the ideological spectrum at will.

On issues where coalition parties are ideologically congruent, it is very likely that they agree on a common policy that will last. As Budge and Keman (1990) showed, concessions made by parties in order to

---

[5] If these states adopt an entry hurdle to parliament (in Germany, e.g. 5 percent, in Turkey 10 percent), party fragmentation can be reduced.

[6] "If elites of one ideology control foreign policy, the state will follow one set of strategic preferences; if no ideology dominates, the state's policy will be incoherent" (Owen 2001/2: 122).

successfully form a coalition government can lead to conflict among parties down the line. Concessions are not always possible either. If the government coalition parties fundamentally disagree on one issue, as has been the case with Turkey's possible membership of the EU in Germany's *Grosse Koalition* 2005–9, the issue is generally left out of the coalition treaty and subsequent policy.[7] Warwick shows that the "ideological diversion within governments" determines the duration of the coalition (1992: 334, see also Sartori 1976 and Clare 2010).[8] Looking at three independent dimensions that define political ideology (Warwick 1992: 340), Warwick presents evidence from his study of 16 different countries showing that if ideological distance prevents the formulation of common policies, governments become very unstable and will terminate (Warwick 1992: 347). Hence, domestic government coalitions are ideologically constrained – as are international coalitions of states.

Power-sharing and possible ideological compromises   Compromises and coalitions are not only seen in parliamentary systems. Semi-presidential systems such as the Fifth Republic of France (since 1958) are based on power-sharing, to a degree, because the president shares power with a prime minister whose support is linked to the national parliament (Sartori 1997: 121–37).[9] If the president and the prime minister are from different parties, the so-called *cohabitation*, compromises have to be forged between the parties for policy to be agreed upon. Overall both gridlock and compromise are possible and party agendas may not be implemented to their fullest (Budge and Hofferbert 1990; Mayhew 1991).

The party landscape in France is highly fractionalized but semi-presidentialism has helped produce dualistic tendencies in

---

[7] Or minority governments emerge (Strøm 1990). "The emergence of minority governments can be explained in terms of the calculus made by party leaders about the costs and benefits of participating in government, given that they are concerned not only with achieving office but also with the policies to be implemented by the government" (Cheibub and Limongi 2002: 154).

[8] See also Döring and Hallerberg (2004) for an overview on different coalition making modes.

[9] In a presidential system, the separation of powers between the legislature and the executive means that the party controlling the government may not have control over the legislature. In such divided governments, the exact pervasiveness of deadlock depends on institutional features such as the share of seats controlled by the president's party in parliament and on the specific provisions regarding the presidential veto (Cheibub and Limongi 2002: 154–5, 171). France tried to alleviate the problem in its reform of 2007. The elections for president and parliament are now held at the same time, reducing the presidency term from seven to five years.

presidential election campaigns, where coalitions are forged within different camps based on *familles spirituelles* – ideologically like-minded groups (Chagnollaud and Quermonne 2000c: 220; Cheibub and Limongi 2002: 166–8; Clift 2003: 45; Hanley 2003).[10] It has not led, however, to a two-party system and parliamentary elections are still dominated by multiple parties (Ware 1996: 195).[11] "The logics of electoral coalitions on the one hand and of demarcation between the different moderate-right parties on the other are obviously mirrored in the definition of ideologies within each organisation" (Sauger 2003: 109). The issue of Europe, for example, has been so divisive in France that Euroskeptics of the moderate right and left have left their respective parties to create new ones (Knapp 2003: 126). The presidential electoral system can create a temporary ideological assimilation or simplification. But once elections are over, this dichotomy relaxes again and compromises must be forged.

The notion that presidents are "above parties" (Bell 2000: 7) is at best contested and, most likely, simply a myth (Chagnollaud and Quermonne 2000c: 138–47). Presidents need party support for their (re)election (Knapp 2003: 123), and the president is involved in the selection of candidates for the next legislative election in his own party. Presidential candidates are members and leaders of political parties. Presidential elections involve parties, not just individuals, and presidents change not only the emphasis of national policies but also their content; they do not mask their political affiliation (Hayward 1993a, 1993b: 41; Machin 1993). Mitterrand is quoted as having said, "I am elected by people of the left, but am the president of all the French people" (quoted in Chagnollaud and Quermonne 2000b: 94), a statement reflecting the ambivalent character of the president's function in representing both state and party. During *cohabitation* it becomes especially clear that the

---

[10] Some have therefore argued in favor of a "de-ideologization" and "drastic reduction in the party's ideological baggage" (Kirchheimer 1990: 58); however, while coalitions exist, ideological orientations are confirmed and reaffirmed (Bartolini and Mair 1984; Bell 2003; Clift 2003: 44–6). Admittedly, the party system in France is more fluid with regard to coalitions than is Germany, for example. Renaming of parties, new party formations, and splits happen regularly (Sauger 2003: 108). In addition, some parties are heavily factionalized which can make the difference between them and a coalition minimal.

[11] For its presidential elections, France has a two-ballot majoritarian system which requires parties to reach a 12.5 percent threshold in the first ballot with only two candidates progressing to the second ballot. This is a hurdle to smaller parties favoring the creation of alliance candidates though the general rule is that each party runs on its own electoral program (Evans 2003: 166). Since 1985, the National Assembly is elected through proportional representation (Chagnollaud and Quermonne 2000c: 201).

French president is partisan and that his party in the National Assembly is on his side (Guilbert 1997; Chagnollaud and Quermonne 2000a: 330–5). Quoting Michel Barnier, former Minister of European Affairs (1995–7) and Foreign Affairs (2004–5), the party expects the president to "determine the common framework [*fixe l'horizon*]" of the "community of destiny" which unites the party with its president (Guilbert 1997). As Hayward puts it (1993b: 75), "France has forged a partisan statesman with a democratic authority." Additionally, as Machin argues, "His partisanship is not only crucial to his election, it is also an indispensable element of his exercise of power as President" (1993: 147).

It is worthwhile examining the French case in more detail because of its extra-constitutional practices in the arena of foreign and security policy. The president claims primacy over the portfolio of foreign and security policies based on the established practice of the *domaine réservé* upon the strength of which he can push for his party's ideological stance. This so-called *domaine réservé* is a "*convention constitutionelle*," a constitutional custom (Chagnollaud and Quermonne 2000b: 89; see also Chevallier *et al.* 2007: 319–22) which is not a written rule in the constitution and is contested at times – especially when the prime minister and the president disagree ideologically over the country's foreign and security policy outlook.[12]

Under *cohabitation*, when the parties controlling the executive and legislative branches are different, the prime minister often tries to impose on foreign and security policy. For example, "Europe ... has remained to date very much within the presidential domain first" (Evans 2003: 167). However, Michel Foucher, formerly head of the policy planning unit in the Quai d'Orsay (the French ministry of foreign affairs) and later Hubert Védrine's political advisor, said there is a "constant power struggle"[13] between Matignon, the Prime Minister's

---

[12] The *domaine réservé* draws on Article 5 and Article 15 of the French Constitution of October 4, 1958. Article 5 reads "the President of the Republic shall see that the Constitution is observed. He shall ensure, by his arbitration, the proper functioning of the public authorities and the continuity of the State." Article 15 states, "The President of the Republic shall be commander-in-chief of the armed forces. He shall preside over the higher national defence councils and committees." Articles 20 and 21 also grant some power to the prime minister saying that he disposes of the armed forces and is responsible for national defense. The president's *domaine réservé* in foreign, security and defense policy has a long history beginning with De Gaulle's insistence that he needs an enhanced role as president to conduct the wars in Algeria (Chagnollaud and Quermonne 2000b: 62, 67). See http://www.assemblee-nationale. fr/english/8ab.asp#TITLE%20II for the entire French constitution.

[13] Interview with Michel Foucher in Paris (May 30, 2008). See Howorth (1993) and Cohen (1989) for a detailed discussion on the tensions between Elysée and Matignon in the formulation of foreign and security policy.

office, and the Elysée, the President's office – after all, the parliament prevails over the national budget and the president needs the signature of the prime minister and the responsible minister for the signing of international treaties (Chagnollaud and Quermonne 2000b: 60–1).[14] What inhibits the full exercise of the *domaine réservé* is also the fact that national foreign and security policy is negotiated and formulated in the Defense Committee (*conseil de défense*) which consists of the president, the prime minister, the minister of foreign affairs, the defense minister, the minister of interior, the finance minister and certain military representatives (Art. 15 of the French Constitution). The president heads the committee and often, but not always, the president decides in the end (Chagnollaud and Quermonne 2000b: 86, 99).[15] Overall, political ideologies define the realm of the politically possible.

Bureaucracy on a leash   In the first step of national preference formation, I question arguments of bureaucratic autonomy in favor of a perspective privileging party politicians and party ideology and their implications for national policy. Regarding preference and policy formulation, my argument bears resemblances to Krasner's critique of Allison's take on bureaucratic politics (Krasner 1972). During the policy formulation process the political elite is crucial, while bureaucrats take over once the policy has to be implemented on an everyday basis.

The "personal filter" (Krasner 1972: 166) that Krasner attributes to variables such as culture and values is, in this case, political ideology. No matter the institutional or electoral context within which parties operate, once they assume power in government the party occupies the top of the national administration of the ministries. Party representatives who are also ministers, or occupy senior staff positions in the ministries, introduce their policy priorities to the senior civil servants of the ministries. Furthermore, it is common practice that they appoint civil servants with their party affiliation to decision-shaping positions. They also tend to privilege divisions of the ministry that are more ideologically aligned with their policy outlook – they keep an entourage of politically like-minded people around them. After all, the head of the ministry is the policy-maker and has to negotiate policy decisions with other cabinet members. Bureaucrats present the ministers with proposals and

---

[14] Article 52 of the constitution says that the president negotiates and ratifies international treaties but Article 19 states that these treaties need to be countersigned by the prime minister and the responsible minister.

[15] Interview with Michel Foucher in Paris (May 30, 2008).

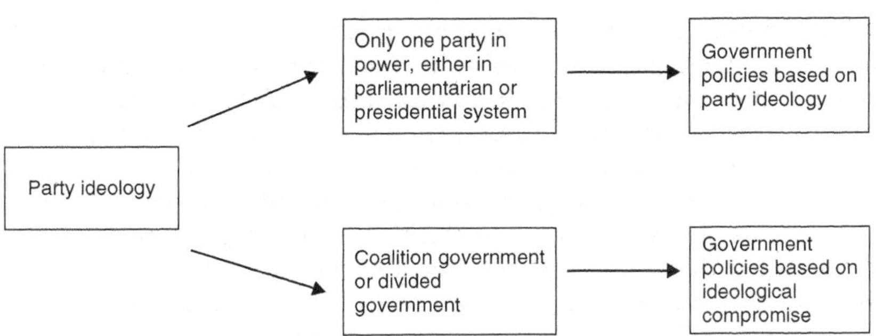

Figure 3.1 Step 1 – government preference formation

have the opportunity to become policy-shapers. Proposals that do not
fit with the ideology of the party are often dismissed. While bureaucrats
in various ministries and in the office of the head of state or government
make policy suggestions, it is up to the political actors, such as the ministers or heads of state or government, to let these ideas materialize or
not. They are the gatekeepers, so to speak, who let those ideas closest to
their political ideology come to the forefront.

Through this process of national preference formation (as in
Figure 3.1) a set of national interests emerge that governments bring
to the international level on the basis of party ideologies. Ideologically
connected, values are translated into preferences and policy differently,
depending on the domestic institutional context and political partners.
Proposals for international institutions will emerge or be denied based
on the ideological content of the government. The negotiations that
lead to either the acceptance or the veto of a new institution, which
would encompass commonly agreed procedures and treaty provisions,
can be based on attempts to persuade and convince national counterparts. They might be successful but only as far as the national red
lines, drawn by ideologies, allow. Bilateral and international negotiations are marked by the margin of maneuver that political ideologies
leave to politicians. A second step involves attempts to cooperate with
other national governments whose own policies reflect the ideologies
of parties in power in other states, drawing attention to the issue of
ideological congruence.

International ideological configurations

The second step in the causal process examines how these national
preferences influence international policy. I argue that their impact is
mediated through the degree of ideological congruence across political

parties in power in the three most powerful states at the European level. The overall ideological divisiveness in international politics can change with changes of governments in power. In one of the major textbooks on the EU, Neill Nugent (1999: 474) observes that "fixed alliances ... between particular governments do not exist. Rather, governments tend to come together in different combinations on different issues." These combinations, I assert, are characterized by ideological congruence. In the setting of multilateral cooperation, the extent to which shared ideologies create overlapping policy preferences – or international coalitions of the willing in the true sense of the term – shapes the outcomes of institutionalized security cooperation.[16] When one observes ideological congruence around the creation of a new institution, the expectation is that this creates opportunities for institutionalizing cooperation. Conversely, ideological incongruence among the member states of a potential international institution is expected to have an inhibiting effect, such that proposals for a new institution will fail or assume only weak forms (as in Figure 3.2).[17]

The Fouchet Plans for a European security and defense institution brought forward by France's De Gaulle government in the beginning of the 1960s, for example, broke down because the Gaullist party advanced a vision of confederal Europe at odds with the federal vision of other European governments, such as the German CDU/CSU government (Bodenheimer 1967; Howorth 1996: 28).[18] Taking note of this, the French Defense White Paper of 1972 noted that a common European defense policy depended on the political will of the various partners and on the reality of their commitments (David 1989: 45–65), stressing that the diversity of ideologies clearly ruled out European military union (Ministère de la Défense 1989: 45–63).

---

[16] See McElroy and Benoit (2010) for a discussion of how ideological congruence among European national parties influences their decision to join European political groups in the European Parliament.

[17] Research has shown that national executives have neither emerged as a single unit nor converged as a result of their EU membership (Kassim 2003, 2005; Bulmer and Lequesne 2005; Zimmer et al. 2005). Though European security policy has received no attention, in recent years, EU studies scholars investigated issues such as party voting behavior in the Council (Mattila 2004; Zimmer et al. 2005), the EP (Kreppel and Tsebelis 1999; Kreppel and Hix 2003), and national party competition over European issues (Marks and Wilson 2000; Pennings 2002). These studies demonstrate that party affiliation turns out to be the significant predictor for the voting patterns in the Council, the European Parliament or IGC (Johansson 1999, 2002; Aspinwall 2002) – often better than regional economic interest or nationality. "Governments seek EU policies that are in line with their electoral commitments" (Hix 2005: 409).

[18] The same can be said about the failure of the EDC (Hitchcock 1998: 171, 176, 193).

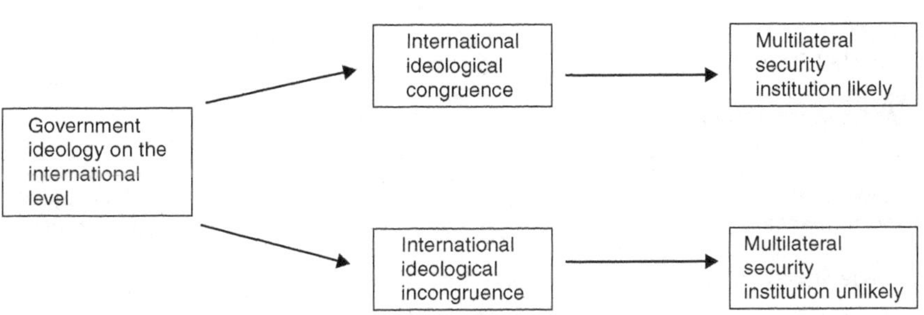

Figure 3.2 Step 2 – international ideological configurations

While political party ideologies significantly constrain political choices, they should not be understood to be deterministic. Ideological congruence on the international level leaves national governments room to pursue various strategies to attain their policy goals. While all governments might agree to create a new security institution based on the fact that they share pro-Europe, pro-multilateral and pro-intergovernmental values, individual political parties might also pursue different specific goals with the creation of an additional institution.

Political parties are more prone to compromise on some values than on others. While Europe (either in its expression as political community or geographic space) leaves parties in an "either-or" situation, multilateralism (understood either as end in itself or as a means to another end), on the other hand, allows compromise. For example, while some governments might see the new institution as increasing their range of action (multilateralism-as-a-means-to-another-end), others might view it as part of a general preference for multilateralism (end-in-itself). Though multilateralism finds different expressions here, the general direction – pro-multilateralism – allows for a degree of congruence. As long as there is overlap among core values, these different visions can be accommodated within a single institution. A perfect overlap is unlikely but, as with national coalitions, as long as the congruence is significant, parties involved will try to reduce the ideological conflict that could emerge. Compromises are possible on the national and the international level – given that ideological congruence exists in the first place.

Ideological incongruence and congruence are the end points of a continuum. At one end, no agreement between national governments on the international level is probable, while at the other a substantive agreement is probable (as in Figure 3.3). I argue that less controversial and often unspecific procedural norms and rules of an institution

Ideological incongruence		Ideological congruence
EDC Fouchet Plans EPC **Amsterdam Treaty**	**CFSP** WEU	**ESDP**

*Case studies in bold

Figure 3.3 Cases along the ideological congruence continuum

need less ideological congruence. Substantive norms, rules and procedures can only be agreed upon once there is ideological congruence. The degree of ideological incongruence or congruence is thus central to explaining outcomes.

Veto players, salience and trade-offs

Three final qualifications in the causal process concern the role of veto players in government, the salience certain governments attribute to particular values in their ideologies, and the possibility of trade-offs in international negotiations. Where veto players are present on the domestic level, there is the potential that an international agreement signed on the basis of values shared internationally, will be vetoed due to ideological disagreements domestically. If veto players are staunchly opposed to e.g. a new institution, it is unlikely that an international agreement favoring a new institution will be ratified (e.g. the French National Assembly during the EDC ratification process; the referendum in Denmark on the Maastricht Treaty; the referenda in France and the Netherlands on the European constitutional treaty; or the Irish referendum on the Lisbon Treaty).[19] However, when so-called veto players are either absent, or in favor of creating a new institution, the plans can proceed.[20]

[19] Voters' motivations in these referenda are not exclusively based on the voter's orientation toward the EU, but also toward domestic politics (Franklin *et al.* 1994).

[20] This point relies on the findings of the veto player's literature. It has mostly found resonance in the field of political economy (see Birchfeld and Crepaz 1998; Hallerberg and Basinger 1998; Tsebelis 2002; and MacIntyre 2003). It has found less application in security studies. Peterson and Wenk (2001) and Spruyt (2005) are notable exceptions.

Second, when an international policy proposal resonates with a national government, but this government does not perceive this policy issue as a policy priority (Budge and Farlie 1983), then bureaucrats can become policy-shapers because the government is most likely to ask them to be more involved in the formulation of the national policy. As I discuss in Chapter 6, German bureaucrats shaped the government's position on ESDP due to the salience of the ruling SPD–Green coalition government attached to the issue, though keeping within the general parameters of the coalition's ideology. In general, though, the heads of state and governments delegate detailed considerations of substantive policy to the relevant ministries, but take the lead in EU (institutional) matters.

Third, in focusing on the domestic and international levels, my argument superficially resembles the heuristic of a two-level game (Putnam 1988) and a liberal intergovernmentalist theoretical outlook (Moravcsik 1998). However, while Putnam and Moravcsik argue that the choices at the international and domestic levels are strategically interdependent, this is not necessarily the case in my theory. International pressure does not force national leaders and parties to commit to anything, in my theory. Domestic accountability is also weak because, as I demonstrated before, the representational linkages between parties and constituencies in security policy are weak; instead, I argue that political parties in government are interested in policy based on a set of values that inform their ideology. Insofar as domestic politics affects international bargaining over security in my theory, it revolves around party factions or coalition partners imposing constraints on political leaders. In negotiations over European security, government officials sometimes recognize the constraints of factions within their government in setting limits to their position. Again, however, these constraints are not strategic but ideological. Furthermore, in contrast to liberal intergovernmentalism, I argue (and show) that international negotiations result in the creation of robust international institutions when party ideologies held across governments in power are highly congruent. Trade-offs, compromise and issue linkages between national governments do not originate from exogenously assessed interdependencies and structural power constellations but, instead, are only made possible once ideological congruence among national governments exists.[21] International

---

[21] Rathbun (2011b) shows that a so-called bipartisan consensus actually consists of ideological compromises where agreement could only be found on the margins – and only for a restricted period of time. Gheciu (2005) argues that ideological congruence is a prerequisite for learning and persuasion among international actors.

negotiations offer a venue in which ideological boundaries can be tested and communicated to international counterparts.

The theoretical lens: domestic and ideational variables and Europe

This argument asserts the primacy of domestic actors in creating institutional outcomes on the international level and uses insights from Comparative Politics to ascertain the origins of state preferences. While the argument can be situated in the constructivist tradition of International Relations since it looks at ideational variables to explain political outcomes, it focuses on an ideational variable – political party ideology – that has received little attention in the literature.

Ideational variables and the domestic–international nexus

My argument finds inspiration from work that has focused on ideational variables when explaining the creation and management of international institutions. However, I focus on a different level of aggregation than preceding studies in order to account for changes in "national" preferences, as well as continuity. Work in the tradition of ideational variables and mechanisms has focused on either less aggregate constructs such as ideas held by individuals (Parsons 2002, 2003), or more aggregate constructs such as national identity, national ideology, transgovernmental field, security community or culture that transcend party divides (Kier 1995;[22] Katzenstein 1996; Duffield 1998; Glarbo 1999; Tonra 2001; Nau 2002; Haas 2005; Meyer 2005; Mérand 2008; Hofmann and Mérand 2012). I claim that including party ideologies in explaining the foreign and security policies of democracies is not only insightful but also meaningful for analysis. Craig Parsons' (2002, 2003) work on ideas, for example, argues that individuals are interpreters of ideas and if these individuals are institutionally empowered, they explain French foreign policies. Parsons writes about the influence of ideas in times of major geopolitical change with no guiding social structure in place but the state (i.e. the end of World War II and of the Cold War). Neither international nor domestic structures can explain how ideas fall across party lines, as "ideas [are] irreducible to other factors" (Parsons 2002: 76). Despite this assertion, he admits that centrist coalitions – even in times of great political uncertainty – played an important role in forging

---

[22] Interestingly, Kier (1995: 72) writes about subcultures that for all intents and purposes are actually party ideologies.

policies (2002: 64). He does so without examining parties systematic-ally where, arguably, ideas "float less freely." Mark Haas (2005), on the other hand, presents international ideological distance as the source of national threat perceptions. While he draws attention to the fact that ideological distances are of consequence, he defines ideology mainly in terms of domestic order and hardly focuses on intra-state ideological differences or ideological content. As a result, democratic governments are portrayed as ideological look-alikes.

In the IR literature, aggregate variables such as national identity or culture are often discussed as a fixed variable deduced from domestic politics (Nau 2002). Where does change in identity or culture come from? Political parties and political coalitions are a possible instiga-tor of such change. Scholars focusing on national culture argue that there are distinctly national norms regarding, for example, the utility of force (Meyer 2005). Using this variable, one would expect consist-ency of government policy over time in each country. However, as long as some national ideological differences can be noted, examining political party ideologies captures more of the dynamic nature and variability in preferences than national culture does (Legro 2005). If, on the other hand, one understands identity as multiple, contingent and fluid (Hopf 2002), then who is the interpreter of these various strands of identity? If it is the state, one gets back to a static concept, and if it is the domestic process (which is underspecified in Hopf's work), I argue that in a democratic system the most likely interpreter of identities are political parties which are the vehicle of particular ideologies.

While scholars working in the tradition of constructivism argue that the distinction between domestic politics and international relations is tenuous, IR scholars have criticized constructivist neglect of domestic structures and variables (Checkel 1998, 2004; Hopf 1998; Finnemore and Sikkink 2001). My argument contributes to a refinement of the domestic–international nexus.[23] I challenge the predominant

---

[23] The introduction of domestic variables into the study of international relations explaining divergent state policies is not new but instead found applicability in the comparative study of foreign policy. Domestic structures have been studied under the rubrics of second image (Waltz 1959) and second image reversed (Gourevitch 1978), making domestic structures either an independent, intervening or dependent variable. Its primary operationalization is in terms of state–society relations and soci-etal actors (Katzenstein 1976; Migdal 1988; Moravcsik 1998), with various degrees of refinement of these variables such as the nature of political institutions (Bueno de Mesquita *et al.* 1999; Weeks 2008), degree of their centralization (Risse-Kappen 1991), and structure of society (Holsti 1992). In theoretical terms, most of these stud-ies showed how to bridge realist and liberal explanations by defining the scope con-ditions under which each approach operates. See Waltz (1959); Katzenstein (1976,

understanding that states can be characterized as unitary actors by analyzing variables such as a state's position in the international system, national interest, national culture and national identity. Even authors such as Glenn Snyder, who insist that the origins of state preferences can be derived from the international system, stress the "domestic politics prism consisting of the perceptions and values of decision makers and the domestic constraints that bear on them." He goes on to say "usually, domestic politics limits decisional choices within narrower bounds than do systemic constraints, but that may not always be true. The *broadest domestic constraints* ... [are] *ideological predilections and repulsions*" (Snyder 1997: 132, emphasis added). Snyder, however, does not examine domestic ideologies systematically. Like many other rational choice scholars, Snyder argues that national interests are exogenous (Waltz 1979, 1993, 2000; Keohane 1984; Martin and Simmons 1998). However, I show that the state is not a single rational actor but a "conglomerate of coalitions and interests, representing individuals and groups" (Doyle 1997: 19), and that this has important consequences for the formulation of national preferences and for the prospect of international cooperation.

In some instances, the study of partisan politics has found its way into IR, but it has done so in the form of material societal interests rather than party ideologies per se. In areas such as the use of force, rearmament policies, or economic foreign policy, scholars have studied executives as representative of their partisan coalitions' economic interest, rejecting the concept of national interest (McKeown 1991; Morrow 1993; Fordham 1998a, 1998b; Trubowitz 1998; Narizny 2003a, 2003b). They focus on military spending and foreign policy-making in conjunction with class or sectoral interests underlying political coalitions. Narizny (2003a), for example, argues that class interests are the primary causal force behind partisan differences over responses to threat and connects budgetary politics to rearmament with a focus on left and right parties. Alesina and Rosenthal (1995), as well as Epstein and O'Halloran (1996), observe domestic policy divergence in the realm of foreign economic policies and stress that party platforms are non-convergent because political parties represent the interests and values of different constituencies. Ideological biases play only a minor role in these accounts, if any. This book goes beyond an analysis that views national governments mainly as representatives

1978); Doyle (1986); Putnam (1988); Mastanduno *et al.* (1989); Levy (1989); Snyder (1991); Schweller (1992); Goldstein (1995); Mansfield and Snyder (1995); Moravcsik (1997, 1998); Evangelista (1999); and Drezner (2003).

of vested (economic) interests, instead seeing them as principled representatives of the political parties that form these governments; ideologies are seen as based on values that define the realm of the appropriate policy.

European security cooperation, institutions and junctures

The degree of ideological congruence of governing parties explains the *timing* and *outcomes* of the different attempts to create a European security institution. At various points in time, national governments have chosen to work within and/or outside NATO. The prospect of European security cooperation was founded at a specific juncture which was made possible through ideological congruence rather than European integration or path dependent dynamics. These junctures are not to be confused with critical junctures that are based on events that were "not expected to take place" (Mahoney 2000: 513; see also Pierson 2000). Instead, national elections and resulting international ideological configurations can be expected to have an impact on institution-building and development. Ideological "junctures" are not contingent but have lasting consequences. By focusing on failed and successful attempts that stretch over a ten-year period, I can show that the moment of institutional creation resulting in ESDP is not a silent revolution of incremental adjustment and integration dynamics. National governments decide *what* to create, *when* and *how*, and whether other institutions will move along or not. This is not to say that institutional constraints do not play a role in the choice selection, rather their constraint is mediated through ideological lenses. Institutional constraints can be understood as "a past that is sticky but interpretable" (Abbott 2001: 227).

The three institutions I study – the EU, NATO and political parties – all have their particular characteristics and qualities. The EU, for instance, has variously been called a "multilevel system" (Marks *et al.* 1996) or a "multi-perspectival polity" (Ruggie 1993: 172). Based on the complexity of the EU in regard to actors, policy spaces, degrees and formality of institutionalization, key theoretical relationships are different between issue areas. No single general theory has been able to capture this to date (Jupille *et al.* 2003; Diez and Wiener 2004).[24]

---

[24] Regarding the question of whether the EU is an example of interstate cooperation (Hoffmann 1966; Moravcsik 1998; Pollack 2005) or an international institution *sui generis* (Hix 1994, 1996; Caporaso 1996), in the end, the answer to these questions is: it depends on the policy space. Most of the European integration literature has been devoted to supranational elements of the EU. See for example Bulmer (1983);

The European Commission and the European Court of Justice have variably been held responsible for the deeper integration of such policy fields as economic and social policy (Burley and Mattli 1993; Alter 1998). I argue that these potential integration dynamics are not the prime drivers of the creation of intergovernmental European security institutions in or outside of the Union's structure since they rely on a different set of actors, institutional structures and policy content (Lowi 1964; Tsebelis and Garrett 2000).[25] ESDP, in the end, has been created within the EU but as a new institution, with a new set of institutional bodies and capabilities. "Junior" ambassador positions were created in all EU member states' Permanent Representations to represent their national interests in the newly appointed decision-making body known as the Political and Security Committee (PSC). Foreign ministers have from that point met on issues related to crisis management, not only in NATO but also in the ESDP format.

Others have made the argument that ESDP was created incrementally (Glarbo 1999; Tonra 2001; M. Smith 2004; Mérand 2008; Reynolds 2010), along a particular path, with a few hiccups on the way (Regelsberger and Wessels 2005). European states have tried to create a security institution since the 1950s, mentioned its possibility in the treaties for the first time in the beginning of the 1990s, and institutionalized it in 2000. Its resemblance with NATO – an institution that persisted and changed after the end of the Cold War – could be called coincidental and a result of unintended consequences rooted in an institution's increasing returns once it has been established (Thelen 1999; Pierson 2000; Wallander 2000; Mérand 2008; Reynolds 2010). According to path dependence arguments, change happens within existing policy bounds (Pierson 2000); preferences are formulated in the institutional context and are not separable from them (Thelen 1999: 375).[26] But what if national governments are members of several institutions at once? Which policy bounds do their preferences reflect? My theoretical lens makes clear that we cannot look at NATO and the EU in isolation. I suggest that regime complexity does not render national governments schizophrenic. Instead, national governments' ideologies are mediating and interpreting the international institutions' policy bounds. Policy

Milward (1984, 1992); Taylor (1991); Hix (1994, 1996); Marks *et al.* (1996); and Menon and Hurrell (1996).

[25] It is telling that in their comprehensive book on European integration theory, Diez and Wiener (2004) do not discuss European security policy in any of their chapters.

[26] Historical institutionalists explain change by focusing on either formal policy changes (Thelen 1999; Pierson 2000), drift (Hacker 2004: 246) or conversion (Thelen 2003). The different mechanisms hinge on policy specific factors – and not actors.

bounds are not objectively given institutional constraints. It is the governments' ideological lens that lets them interpret their institutional environment and not vice versa. As I argue here and will show later, ESDP was not created incrementally, and NATO persisted based on member-states' choices rooted in the party ideologies. The failure to institutionalize an ESDP-like institution during the Amsterdam Treaty negotiations in the mid 1990s was an *event* that can be explained when studying ideological configurations. Scholars working in the tradition of historical institutionalism, on the other hand, argue that such failures qualify as nonevents (Hacker 2004: 245).

Some argue that national identities and preferences are becoming more alike through everyday encounters in the EU. We should therefore observe an assimilation of political party ideologies within and across European countries.[27] This argument suffers from many weaknesses. There are few indications that the EU influences national party systems, especially not in terms of ideological distance among national parties, however (Mair 2000; Pogunkte *et al.* 2007). Party organization and leadership as well as homegrown ideational structures are important variables that should be considered. Even if party ideologies would all be Europeanized, this would not necessarily lead to a cross-national consensus in regard to European integration because – as this book shows – different parties value Europe differently. One observes significant differences among parties on the national and the international level. Furthermore, scholars arguing that EU member states become more uniform over time dismiss the national preference formation that exists independent of the European level. EU member states have responded differently to identical EU input even under similar external conditions (Kohler-Koch 1999; Héritier and Knill 2001). Jachtenfuchs and Kohler-Koch (2004: 110) come to the conclusion that "decades of EU attempts at harmonization and system competition have left a mark on national systems but they have no unifying effect." In my view, cooperation and institutionalization are hampered as long as national governments are overseeing the process and there is ideological incongruence. There is no one particular "EU interest" that all parties have started to share over time. "Even if one accepts the multi-actor complexity of the EU, it is still possible to assert the dominance of the member-state governments and the primacy of intergovernmental decisions" (Rosamond 2000: 159; see also Slapin 2008). By stressing that sovereign statehood is retained in the EU security policy field, one can compare cooperation

---

[27] See for example Jørgensen (1997); Ohrgaard (1997); Glarbo (1999, 2001); Radaelli (2000); Caporaso *et al.* (2001); and Smith (2004).

among EU states in this policy field with other international institutions that institutionalized security, such as NATO.

One role that the EU, and its previous incarnations, definitely plays is that it offers its member states a forum for discussion. Based on this possibility, valuing isolationism and unilateralism is – though possible – rendered unlikely. As such, international institutions do suggest policy bounds to some degree. As unlikely as the success of some policy proposals might be, the EU offers a venue where they can be presented and discussed. This however has no significant impact on the actual outcome of the negotiations since "the European Union (EU) is run by party politicians" (Hix and Lord 1997: 1), who adhere to their ideologies.[28] The composition of the governments of the member states affects the composition of the European Council and the Council of Ministers, which again has a major impact on European Union politics and policies.

My theoretical focus on domestic and ideational variables contrasts with the two leading IR explanations I examine – rational choice institutionalism and realism. In neorealist/realist and rational choice institutionalist accounts, political actors labeled "United Kingdom" etc. are the bearers of national interests (Grieco 1995), or spokespersons of domestic economic coalitions (Moravcsik 1998). Both theoretical approaches are based on a universal – as opposed to context-specific – rationality assumption but distinguish themselves in terms of the substantive specifications of what utility should be maximized. While realists focus on power, rational choice institutionalists focus on prosperity. These values trump all other possible values (Finnemore and Sikkink 2001: 393). Whether the party-political government complexion matters has been ignored. To take national preferences seriously means to take the political positions of parties seriously. When political parties form a government they "do not simply represent but interpret and shape what the national interest is" (Manow et al. 2008: 22). To test whether my theoretical take on ideology has much traction, I also test it against the partisan values explanation in Comparative Politics that is built on the left–right dimension of political contestation.

Alternative explanations

My own argument can be distinguished from established schools of thought both in International Relations and Comparative Politics. The

---

[28] Hix and Lord go on to say, "All three branches of its political leadership – the Commission, the Council of Ministers and the European Council – are predominantly recruited from political parties" (1997: 1).

three alternative explanations considered here are, first, an explanation of partisan values that understands the left–right dimension of political contestation as fundamental to party politics, second, rational choice institutionalism, and third, realism with a focus on soft balancing and binding strategies.

Partisan values: the left–right dimension

One alternative to the argument presented above is a partisan values explanation that conceptualizes ideology in terms of only one dimension, the left–right dimension of political contestation. The argument goes that left–right is the major policy referent for political parties subsuming any other possible value dimensions. This argument has been made in the Comparative Politics' party politics literature as well as in IR under the heading of constructivism.

Many scholars studying political parties have argued that political contestation and competition are organized along one single dimension: the left–right dimension (Downs 1957; Budge *et al.* 1987; McDonald and Budge 2005). They furthermore argue that new possible values (or patterns of conflict) that might cross-cut the left–right divide will instead be absorbed by it, otherwise the new value will have no policy implications, especially in terms of voter mobilization. As a result, the left–right dimension will retain its dominance (Schattschneider 1960; Silverman 1985; Kitschelt 1988; Kitschelt and Hellemans 1999). But what does it mean to be on the "left" or on the "right"? Lipset, for example, brought forth a definition of left and right that is widely accepted: "By 'left' we shall mean advocating social change in the direction of greater equality – political, economic, or social; by 'right' we shall mean supporting a traditional, more or less hierarchical social order, and opposing change towards greater equality" (Lipset *et al.* 1954: 1135; see also Dodd 1976; Browne *et al.* 1984; Castles and Mair 1984). The left is often thought of either in terms of equality or liberty, and the right in terms of liberty or authority. The particular issues over which the left and right have contested have changed over time.[29] The economic sphere, in combination with welfare state provisions, has however always remained at the

---

[29] There is a debate whether the left–right continuum can be divided into an economic and libertarian–authoritarian dimension (Kitschelt 1994) or old versus new politics (Franklin *et al.* 1992). One has to distinguish between the economic policy domain and the sociopolitical one. In the economic domain, liberty and equality conflict and the left chooses equality over liberty, while the right is more libertarian. But the same cannot be said of the right in the sociopolitical sphere. Instead of being libertarian, here the right stresses authority.

heart of the issue (Laver and Garry 2000). But "new left" and "new right" issues such as civil liberties also established themselves bringing to the fore the libertarian–authoritarian dimension (Kitschelt 1995). This points to cross-cutting issues among liberty and equality.

Some of those who study the EU argue that European integration can be subsumed into a left–right dimension of political contestation. Marks and Steenbergen (2004) call this the regulation model. The argument rests most often on the economic policy space (Kreppel and Tsebelis 1999; Moravcsik and Nicolaïdis 1999; Tsebelis and Garrett 2000). European integration is understood in terms of how the EU affects the market: the left pushes for more common economic regulation across Europe and the right favors less regulation.

None of these CP studies mentioned above have tested for the foreign and security policy space. However, some IR scholars have translated this view onto foreign and security policies, most prominently Brian Rathbun (2004), who argues that equality and liberty, on a continuum, explain foreign policies.[30] These two fundamental values, according to him, inform three foreign policy continua: inclusiveness or exclusiveness, appropriateness of using forceful means, and multilateralism or unilateralism (Rathbun 2011b). Equality stands for an inclusive, dovish, multilateral foreign policy that encompasses concern for others, and liberty implies an exclusive, hawkish, unilateral foreign policy based on narrow national interests.[31] Based on this distinction, political parties are either in favor of multilateral security institutions when their ideology is based in equality, or less so when their ideology emphasizes liberty. Hence, the more to the left a party is, the more it favors multilateral security institutions, while the more to the right, the less it wants multilateral security institutions.

This alternative explanation will only be tested for in the first step of my causal chain. In the preference formation phase, we should observe that the values, multilateralism, sovereignty and Europe, align around "left" and "right" – an understanding of political contestation that transcends policy spaces. The left is then pro-Europe, pro-multilateralism and pro-supranationalism, and the right is Euroskeptical, favoring

---

[30] Two other fundamental values that might characterize left from right – liberty (left) and authority (right) – are not considered. In later work on US foreign policy, Rathbun (2007) switched to community and hierarchy as the two core values explaining foreign policy attitudes, arguing that equality and liberty are not necessarily antagonistic.

[31] Rathbun (2004) examines cases of humanitarian intervention in the Balkans, a geographical region close to the EU that arguably is more "equal" than conflict and crisis regions further abroad. However, this selectivity of interventions cannot be captured with only two core values.

unilateralism and insisting on intergovernmental cooperation or isolationism. Though Rathbun (2004) does not address ideological congruence, we then should see parties from one political leaning align when pushing for a European security institution, though in his understanding, "right" parties are not very keen on multilateral cooperation which, in effect, leaves the initiatives to build new multilateral forums to the "left."

While this explanation shares my emphasis on party ideology and a view of parties as policy-seeking, meaning that "parties win elections to formulate policies rather than formulate policies to win elections" (Rathbun 2004: 8), we differ in the conceptualization of ideology. This has major repercussions for policy preferences. My argument is that multilateralism, sovereignty and Europe cannot be fused to the two fundamental values of equality and liberty. I argue that this unidimensional conceptualization of ideology fails to capture more than just subtle differences between parties and instead distorts policy preferences, and hence the possibility of international ideological congruence and institution-building.

Rational choice institutionalism: overcoming the barriers to Pareto efficiency

One important alternative to my argument that originates in IR theory is based on rational choice institutionalism, mainly the rational design school and what I call the institutional choice school (Aggarwal 1998; Koremenos *et al.* 2001; Jupille and Snidal 2005; Alter and Meunier 2009). Rational choice institutionalists work on the presumption "that states use international institutions to further their own goals, and they design institutions accordingly" (Koremenos *et al.* 2001: 762). That is, states act based on a hierarchy of values in which welfare-maximizing or prosperity trump all other incentive structures. In the context of rational choice institutionalism, multilateralism is understood as a means to an end, not as an end in itself. One major research question has been the following: under what conditions do actors choose to alter existing institutions or create new ones – a question with obvious relevance for European states attempting to cooperate in the shadow of NATO. Based on a long-standing tradition of explaining the creation of international institutions, these theories have elaborated a research program to explain variation in international institutions through different types of cooperation problems.[32]

---

[32] The questions of why and how international institutions proliferate and how they overlap have been studied under the rubrics of nested institutions (Aggarwal 1998),

The functional logic that underlies these approaches argues that cooperation problems generate incentives for creating (or attempting to create) additional European security institutions next to NATO, as well as maintaining NATO.[33] Issue-specific interdependence informs the national interest in overcoming dilemmas of strategic interaction. National security is costly to provide unilaterally. By exchanging information with other states and pooling military capabilities, states can reduce this cost – given that they can trust their fellow collaborators. Actors either fear that other states they interact with will defect from cooperative interactions or that the distributional gains will be divided too unevenly (Martin 1992). States show an interest in "making an exchange," if cooperation increases their security and if vulnerability to opportunism can be held at bay.

NATO was created and maintained with two functions in mind: security among its membership (e.g. Greece and Turkey) and external security (Lepgold 1998; Haftendorn *et al.* 1999). Transaction costs are reduced through the creation of institutional arrangements that enforce cooperation and formalize the division of mutual gains and losses,[34] thereby reducing uncertainty about the state of the world and, in our case, uncertainty about the impact of alternative institutional choices (Jupille and Snidal 2005: 8–10; see also Aggarwal 1998; Koremenos *et al.* 2001; Weiss 2011).[35]

As long as existing institutions are apt to overcome particular cooperation problems, there should be no need for a new institution, but "the lower this suitability, the more likely costlier and riskier strategies such as institutional change and creation become" (Jupille and Snidal 2005: 7). Exogenous shocks to the international system – such as the end of the Cold War – and the emergence of new actors that threaten states' security create new cooperation problems.

---

regime density (Young 1996), complex interdependence (Jervis 1997), regime complexity (Raustiala and Victor 2004; Alter and Meunier 2009), institutional interaction (Gehring and Oberthür 2004, 2006) or institutional selection and choice (Jupille and Snidal 2005).

[33] Though basic cooperative structures were already in place in the EU, this does not necessarily reduce the transaction costs in regard to the creation of new institutions inside the EU. Transaction costs are issue specific; their benefits cannot be assumed to be able to be transferred to other domains.

[34] In IR, Robert Keohane's work was ground-breaking when he introduced the micro-economic concept of "transaction costs" into political science. The most important dimension of transaction costs is asset specificity: "durable investments that are undertaken in support of particular transactions, the opportunity cost of which investments is much lower in best alternative uses or by alternative users, should the original transaction be prematurely determined" (Williamson 1985: 55).

[35] See Abbott and Snidal (2000) and Weber (2000) for variants of this argument.

Existing institutions either have to adapt to generate or sustain their institution's efficiency, or states create a new institution. The security environment of the end of the Cold War required not narrow military alliances but security management institutions that could face a diverse set of threats and risks originating not just from states but also non-state actors (Wallander 2000: 715). As Lepgold (1998: 89) points out, NATO's "three traditional functions [nuclear and conventional protection, security community] have not disappeared; they have, however, receded in political and strategic importance as compared to the two types of peace-operations tasks: humanitarian operations and operations designed to affect the political incentives of the actors in the conflict."

A number of claims follow from such a perspective. Creating a new institution in an already institutionalized policy space is said to be costly, hence the stakes surrounding a cooperation problem must be high. Governments will therefore first try other options to alleviate their cooperation problem. When contemplating this new cooperation problem we should first observe states looking for existing alternatives to NATO, such as the WEU or the CSCE/OSCE. If they find these alternatives to be inappropriate, we should observe them trying to reform NATO to address the new cooperation problem. Celeste Wallander (2000) and Jae-Jung Suh (2007), for example, focus on instances of institutional adaptation, explaining why states maintain and adapt international institutions once their initial function has disappeared. "Changed circumstances, such as shifts in the distribution of power ... are likely to alter the original cost/benefit relationship. Yet if the marginal costs of maintaining an existing institution outweigh the considerable costs of creating an entirely new set of norms, rules, and procedures, states will choose to sustain existing arrangements rather than abandon them" (Wallander 2000: 706). Wallander sees increasing returns to scale as sources of institutional persistence. This is what Williamson (1985: 116) and Suh (2007: 13) call "first mover advantage." Along this line, Suh argues that NATO's asset specificity confers on it an enormous cost advantage over its competitors (Suh 2007: 179–87). In support of this argument, Lepgold (1998: 80) points out that NATO's functions since the early 1990s have also included peace operations – together with conventional and nuclear protection and provision of security community to its members.

When the focal institution remains unsatisfactory and institutional change inside does not lead to the desired outcome, then new institutional arrangements will be created. The rational choice institutionalist tradition points to particular cooperation problems and the attempts to solve them as the source of variance in European attempts to create an institution autonomous of NATO. The creation of a new institution will "be done with its relationship to existing IOs firmly in mind" (Jupille and Snidal 2005: 37). European states either create an additional security institution next to NATO because it is collectively more attractive to the participants (Abbott and Snidal 1998; Aggarwal 1998; Aggarwal and Fogarty 2005) or a sub-group of states (Young 1996; Mansfield and Reinhardt 2003). Or an additional institution will be created as a follow-up and add-on to NATO (Young 1996; Abbott and Snidal 2004). That is, the cooperation problem at hand is either one of distributional gains where European member states are dissatisfied with the United States and its distribution of the spoils (Weiss 2011), or one of geographic and functional reach where NATO cannot act everywhere, but the EU can, and where the EU provides NATO with additional capabilities. The "strategic and political problems associated with the production of different security goods" (Lepgold 1998: 87) in crisis management operations are very demanding and need specific forces and skills. The creation of a new European security institution is the result.

Whatever the exact cooperation problem, as European states also want to maintain NATO, we should observe the creation of a new institution with a division of labor in mind which, while not tackling the exact same cooperation problem, operates in the same policy space, emphasizing institutional compatibility, or "institutional reconciliation" (Aggarwal 1998: 2; see also Young 1996) in the interest of efficiency (Weiss 2011). The failure to institutionalize European security at Amsterdam, despite having a proposal on the table, and the weak institutionalization at Maastricht are explained by the absence of cooperation problems in the early 1990s. As the case studies illustrate, however, cooperation problems existed during the early 1990s. A functional logic was rarely paramount in the policies of national governments. Instead, governments create new institutions for reasons unrelated to cooperation problems and prove remarkably tolerant of inefficiencies in the creation of new institutions.

Realism: power aggregation and soft-balancing

A key critique of the rational design school is that power is essentially missing from its account of institutional creation.[36] There have been

---

[36] Grieco (1993). Wallander (2000: 730) admits that power, and the role of the United States, is not theorized much in rational choice institutionalism.

a growing number of realist studies on European security cooperation[37] pointing to the role of the distribution of capabilities and US
power. A key claim here is that military capabilities and assets make
states more secure by being able to project power and increase their
autonomy from other states. Hence, states pursue the accumulation
of power as their main policy goal. Power or security is the main
value driving actors to create or not create international institutions.
Krasner, for example, argues that one can ignore the domestic level
of analysis in the security domain because "it could be assumed that
all groups in society would support the preservation of territorial and
political integrity" (Krasner 1978: 70). Institutionalized cooperation
in the security policy field is a tool in a state's arsenal for augmenting
its power through external balancing.

Realists share an understanding of structural factors as the most
powerful influences on state behavior. However, structure can be
mediated through unit-level factors (Rose 1998). Realist studies on
European security cooperation all have in common the argument that
states cooperate in the security policy space for the purpose of power
aggregation in the interest of security maximization (Posen 2004,
2006; Pape 2005; Paul 2005; Walt 2005). With the end of the Cold
War, the threat environment has changed. "As the threat (or any component of dependence) declines, alliance cohesion will also decline"
(Snyder 1997: 172). It is at these junctures that alternatives to the existing alliance come to the forefront. Alternatives are used as a source of
leverage in negotiations within existing alliances (Snyder 1997: 149).
Realists observe that European states have created a new security institution next to NATO "through external alignment" (Art 2005/6: 178).
What exactly these security concerns are based on is contested in the
general theoretical orientation of realism. Some argue that European
states perceive the United States as a potential security threat, which
leads Europeans to hard balancing (Posen 2004, 2006; Art 2005/6).
According to this view, Europe is engaged in forming countervailing
alliances and investing in arms build-up which could escalate to hard

---

[37] Alternatively to European security cooperation one could define the European
attempts as alliance-building. "Alliances are formal associations of states for the
use (or nonuse) of military force, in specified circumstances, against states outside
their own membership" (Snyder 1997: 4). States engage in such behavior "to ease the
general insecurity of anarchy, not because they fear attack by any particular state"
(Snyder 1997: 24). The value and meaning of an alliance to a state is to have a greater
deterrent from external attacks, greater capability to defend itself, to balance against
the preponderance of another power or to further (militarily) the national security of
the signatory states. In this sense, both NATO and the European efforts to create a
European security institution can be considered alliances.

balancing.[38] Others again argue that the Europeans are "simply" dissatisfied with the unipolar position of the United States which results in soft balancing (Pape 2005; Paul 2005; Jones 2007). Soft balancing is defined as the efforts of "second-tier great power states" to pursue "limited, tacit, or indirect balancing strategies largely through coalition building and diplomatic bargaining within international institutions" in order "to constrain US power" (Paul 2005: 58). In this scenario, Europeans do not fear losing their sovereignty to the United States (Jones 2007: 24; see also Pape 2005; Paul 2005). Instead, European states soft balance when they are dissatisfied with the United States for reasons such as NATO transformation according to US wishes (Posen 2004: 9).[39] Hard and soft balancing distinguish themselves through the assets used to offset the advantage of the predominant power (robust armament or rearmament policy vs. tacit non-offensive coalition building) and the purpose for the creation of the international security institution.

Despite these disagreements, realists agree that the EU is institutionalizing power capabilities and potentialities (Lieber and Alexander 2005: 124) to generate military power in response to the United States and by extension in response to American hegemony inside NATO.[40]

[38] If one argues that European states do not balance against US power alone but because it forms a threat, one also needs to look at the intentions of the United States. Threats are understood as "an inherently perceptual concept. While capabilities play an important role in determining what is deemed threatening, the other essential ingredient is intention" (Weitsman 2004: 33; see also Walt 1987: 22ff.). Furthermore, geographic proximity and offensive power matter (Walt 1987: 23–5). While Walt (2005) and Jones (2007) argue that balancing is based on intentions, Art (2005/6) argues that an increase in US power suffices. As the alternative explanation presented here rests on Jones mostly, I will look for intentions.

[39] Surprisingly, none of the (soft) balancing arguments take account of NATO and the continued existence of this transatlantic alliance of which European states are a part. With the end of the Cold War, realists first argued that NATO would cease to exist (Mearsheimer 1990; Waltz 1993); later on, they adopted a more complex explanation (Snyder 1997; Schweller 2001). NATO's persistence is not incompatible with the realist research program as long as it is understood as a tool of US power politics. However, the existence of both NATO and ESDP is troubling for realists as they cannot account for why European states continue to be members of NATO.

[40] Brooks and Wohlforth (2005, 2008) and Wohlforth (1999) do not observe a systemic balancing imperative based on Waltz's structural realism. They argue that unipolarity renders balancing inoperative. They present an alternative explanation for ESDP's existence: the "demand for regional policy coordination" (Brooks and Wohlforth 2005: 79). However, if this is so, one wonders where this demand is coming from and why the region has been redefined as Europe instead of the transatlantic region. Also, Wohlforth (1999: 31) initially argued "many Americans support an EU 'security identity.' If all goes well, Europe will become a more useful and outward-looking partner while posing virtually no chance of becoming a geopolitical competitor." *If all goes well* remains underspecified, however.

"There is considerable evidence that EU foreign policy, led by Paris and Berlin, will actively seek to balance ... US power" (Cimbalo 2004: 115). Posen (2006) sees the UK and France as the driving forces.

Jones (2007) presents the most systematic approach about repeated attempts to create a European security institution. He argues that depending on the international and regional structure, European attempts to create a security institution failed at times and succeeded at others. As long as the world was dominated by a bipolar security structure, European states could rely on US forces to take care of their external and internal security since the United States saved Europe from both the Soviet Union and German militarism. These structural factors discouraged European security cooperation. However, with the end of the Cold War and the manifestation of a global unipolar system, the United States became preoccupied with other security issues and regions. European states felt abandoned and needed to find other means to project power globally. "Aggregating power allows smaller states to project greater power in the international system ... a failure to project power abroad decreases states' ability to provide for their own security" (Jones 2007: 24–5). In addition "weaker states may also aggregate power in a unipolar system to decrease the likelihood that the dominant power will impose its will on them in areas of strategic importance" (Jones 2007: 29).[41] This second notion corresponds to soft balancing. In addition, Jones argues that, with the end of the Cold War, European states felt threatened anew with Germany's reunification. As Germany is a status quo power and learned from its past experiences, it was willing to pursue a "'binding' strategy to ensure long-term peace on the continent" (Jones 2007: 5). The unipolarity of the system explains the timing and motivation for aggregating power in the form of ESDP (Jones 2007: 24). If the dissatisfaction with the United States and Germany is not shared, proposals for additional cooperation fail.

In the following empirical chapters, I look for evidence of soft balancing or balancing efforts. A key argument of mine, however, is that the outcomes of European security cooperation are shaped less by the uniform desire to balance, and more on how political parties in power in key European states perceive their relationship to the United States.

---

[41] However, when states may or may not do so is underdetermined in Jones' theory as well as in realist thought in general. In addition, Jones (as do for example Posen 2004; Pape 2005; and Paul 2005) simply assumes that the international system is unipolar without referring to the debates that existed especially in the mid 1990s over whether the international system was multi- or unipolar.

Research method and operationalization of key variables

The empirical expectations based on the four different theoretical approaches – my own argument and the three alternatives – vary along several dimensions. The focus on ideologies in my explanation assumes that policy preferences in security vary across parties. There should be cross-temporal variation in the formulation of national preferences in regard to security policy based on different parties in power. Furthermore, a focus on parties as the main actors should leave open whether we can observe cross-national variation in policy preferences at the same point in time. A partisan values argument based on a left–right continuum shares this assumption and can be measured in a relatively similar fashion.

Conversely, rational choice institutionalism and realism both disregard domestic differences. Instead they argue that structural incentives will ensure that national preferences remain constant and consistent over time as long as cooperation problems or the international structure do not change. While the rational design school leaves open whether cross-national differences exist at the same point in time, according to realist logic we should be able to observe the same national preferences among structurally similarly situated states such as the UK, France and Germany.

Degree of ideological congruence

The independent variable of my argument is the *ideological distance* across parties in power in major European states, and over time. I focus on the parties that have been in and out of government in the time period of 1990–2000. The parties in question are the Labour Party and the Conservative Party in the case of the UK. When it comes to France, I focus mostly on the Socialists (PS) and the Rally for the Republic (RPR), with occasional mention of the Union for French Democracy (UDF), the Communist Party and the Greens. In Germany, I concentrate on the Christian Democratic Union/Christian Social Union (CDU/CSU), the Social Democrats (SPD), the Greens and the Free Democrats (FDP).

Many have pointed out that the dimensionality of ideologies and ideological diversity across countries is hard to measure (Warwick 1992: 352; Laver and Benoit 2006; Debus 2009; Benoit and Laver 2012). So far dimensionality has mainly been studied quantitatively and within countries, holding the institutional context constant to account for equivalence (Laver and Benoit 2005; Laver *et al.* 2006; Benoit 2009;

Debus 2009). Scholars have selected a set of party, public opinion or voter categories and located them on pre-selected scales (Pappi and Seher 2009: 406). This "choice must be defended on methodological and substantive grounds" (Lowe *et al.* 2011: 126; see also Benoit *et al.* 2009: 443) but "choosing between dimensional representations of a given space is to a large extent a substantive modeling decision taken by the analyst" (Laver and Benoit 2006: 51). Whether scholars rely on a manifesto dataset, political documents, public opinion polls, voting returns, or expert surveys and then apply factor analysis, logit scale, content analysis computerized word scoring, or the relative proportional difference approach (Mikhaylov *et al.* 2012: 23),[42] they identify the most salient political dimensions defining the policy space and look at whether they are correlated *overall* (Laver *et al.* 2006: 678–81; see also Thomson 2009: 765–6; Benoit and Laver 2012; De Vries and Marks 2012). When solely working deductively, assumptions can misconstrue the policy space (Laver *et al.* 2006: 690–1). By assuming the relevant ideological dimensions that inform a policy space, the potential to foreclose possible ideological alignments is high. However, when scholars work inductively, for example with factor analysis, factors might be omitted because they are not plausible theoretically (Chittick *et al.* 1995: 316). "This is a generic problem for spatial models and reflects the limits of any method used to estimate a common policy space when some party policy priorities do not fit into the dimensional structure used to describe the system as a whole" (Laver *et al.* 2006: 691; see also Holsti and Rosenau 1990: 121). Quantitative work still looks at "how different techniques handle positioning in higher dimensional spaces" (Benoit *et al.* 2009: 445; see also Gabel and Hix 2004: 93).

In order to get to the fine-grained configuration of individual parties' ideology and the choices parties make with regard to the three values, qualitative research in the form of interviews and archival research is better suited to this task than most quantitative methods. As I have shown in Chapter 2, there is no *a priori* reason for (core) values to relate to one another in a particular way. The literature on parties and public opinion shows that there is no agreement on whether one, two or three dimensions structure an ideological space.[43] To overcome theoretical

---

[42] For a discussion on the weaknesses and strengths of each method see Debus (2009: 286–94) as well as Linhart and Shikano (2009). A problem with public opinion surveys, for example, has been that questions can be interpreted one way or the other (Chittick *et al.* 1995: 319). Expert surveys use different and non-comparable scales.

[43] As Gabel and Hix (2004: 93) have pointed out: "Scholars of EU policy-making have adopted conflicting assumptions about the dimensionality and character of the EU policy space. Since the shape of the political space – the number of dimensions, the

and methodological preconceptions outlined above, I first provide three major value dimensions that are derived deductively from three different, and major, IR theoretical traditions before I measure actual ideological party positions inductively. This does not require an *a priori* determination of an ideological space (Eatwell 1989b: 60; Pappi and Seher 2009: 411). I treat the number of core values as an empirical question – especially as I am not only interested in policy positions but also in how those positions affect national and international policy outcomes. After all, nuances that can best be captured qualitatively are important to show whether ideologies are congruent or not.

I measure ideology based on over 60 interviews in France, Germany and the UK (conducted between 2006 and 2008), archival and primary data such as parliamentary debates, government statements, coalition treaties where appropriate, party platforms/resolutions, mission statements (Pelizzo 2003: 87; Klingemann *et al.* 2007), writings and speeches by party leaders as well as secondary sources with a focus on *histoires engagées* written by participants. Major national newspapers were also used to understand and lay out domestic debates.[44] Operationalizing ideology involves a two-step process. In the first step I dissect the core values of national governments and major opposition parties along the three dimensions of unilateralism–multilateralism-as-an-end-in-itself, supranationalism–intergovernmentalism, and Europe-as-a-geographic-space–Europe-as-a-political-community. As ideology can be mistaken for a strategy to get into office (the so-called office-seeking argument in the Comparative Politics literature), I point to occasions when political parties' value interpretations were unpopular with the general public, but still informed the party's major policy goal (e.g. Labour's insistence on building ESDP) to control for this explanation.

Different interview and text sources reveal information about their authors' political preferences and whether actors explain and justify their actions in similar ways in different settings. Interview information "can be the kiss of death to objectivity" (Seldon quoted in Forster 1998: 4) – the quality of evidence varied with interviewee and some made the interview conditional on anonymity in the text. Care was therefore taken to interview as wide a range of national and European

policy content of these dimensions, and the location of actors in this space – is a central determinant of political competition and outcomes, their conflicting assumptions often lead to different conclusions about and interpretations of EU policy-making. This is a serious impediment to advancing our theoretical understanding of EU politics. A resolution of this theoretical conflict depends on assessing the relative value of the conflicting assumptions."

[44] Most public records, departmental and government papers remain officially classified. In addition, intergovernmental negotiations were conducted in private.

officials as possible, focusing especially on bureaucrats who experienced changes in government. To identify the relevant personnel to interview, I scanned the organizational chart of government ministries and political parties in France, Germany, the UK, the United States as well as in the EU and NATO institutions. Wherever possible, information was verified against evidence presented in the secondary literature, written witness accounts, and in other interviews.

I look at different types of political text such as party programs, coalition treaties, government declarations, party documents, legislative debates, and party convention speeches. Party programs and coalition treaties deserve special mention. They are policy agreements and the "most reliable and unbiased source of preferences of political actors" (Benoit *et al.* 2009: 443). Party manifestos are often written a few months before the election. "Parties use these documents to announce their policy positions to voters, as well as to mark their starting positions for the process of government formation following an election" (Benoit *et al.* 2009: 450). Next to signaling the general contours of the party's governmental program and to informing possible coalition partners about policy priorities, party manifestos also "serve as an intra-party platform offering diverse factions an opportunity to push their policy goals for specific problem areas" (Pappi and Seher 2009: 403).

In the second step, I make comparisons across states at different points in time in order to ascertain the degree of ideological congruence. To avoid tautology, I measure the degree of ideological congruence among parties independently of behavior. The measure is qualitative, based on party manifestos, interviews and expert judgments. I make reference to the different sets of value interpretations of each party in government. As Van der Brug *et al.* have pointed out, "differences between parties is qualitative in nature" (2007: 170), a nominal level variable and therefore not to be captured with regression methods.[45] I pay particular attention to whether parties across countries use similar language and speak of congruent values when legitimizing their policy decisions. Do parties and governments refer to common values across national borders with counterparts at a particular moment in time? Do other parties and governments condemn or criticize these values? Measuring the precise distance between parties or governments across countries is

---

[45] To simplify, scholars have used the left–right dimension, dichotomous variables which arguably are comparable across countries, but "the drawback of such procedures is that the redefined dependent variable only captures a single aspect of party choice" (2007: 170).

difficult but it is possible to point to whether the ideological congruence between national governments is greater or lesser over time as a result of domestic shifts in government.

Partisan values

An alternative explanation based on a left–right continuum relies on the same method of measurement as my own argument. But rather than locating particular values around multilateralism, sovereignty and Europe at the center of my theory, I focus on where parties are located on the political spectrum in terms of left and right, using the benchmark values of equality and liberty respectively (Rathbun 2004). I thereby test whether the various interpretations of multilateralism, sovereignty and Europe can be collapsed onto this single value dimension of political conflict.

Nature of the cooperation problem

According to the logic underlying rational choice institutionalism, the nature of the cooperation problem determines whether and what kind of international institutions can be created. Jupille and Snidal (2005: 6–10) conceptualize cooperation problems based on the following dimensions: issue characteristics, overall efficiency, uncertainty about the state of the world coupled with uncertainty about the impact of alternative institutional choices, and transaction costs. An issue characteristic is "defined as nature of the problem with respect to which institutionalized cooperation is being contemplated" (Jupille and Snidal 2005: 7). Is the issue a political or a technical one? If all actors gain from additional cooperative arrangements, then creating a new institution is very likely. Uncertainty, in the rationalist logic, exists because in an anarchic system there is always a lack of information regarding the power, interests and intentions of other actors in the system; it "concerns the actual costs or benefits and the likelihood that an anticipated event will actually occur" (Woll 2008: 26). As such, uncertainty will never vanish but can be reduced. The information is understood as objective in the sense that similarly situated actors will perceive and interpret it similarly (Lake and Powell 1999: 31); it is not filtered through ideational lenses. As actors want to maximize their utility within these structural constraints within which cheating can be reduced through credible institutional cooperative structures, they engage in cooperation where information about potential cooperation partners is credible. Transaction costs can be defined as "equipment, process, human asset and location specificity" (Suh 2007: 16; see also Weber 2000: 20–5).[46] Asset specificity in military institutions is defined as "consultation mechanisms, military planning and command structures, common infrastructure, joint exercises, inter-operable weapons systems, and integrated forces" (Suh 2007: 13). In tracing cooperation problems, I rely primarily on existing studies, including Lepgold (1998), Weber (2000), Wallander (2000) and Suh (2007), as well as interview material, government statements and parliamentary debates.

Power

The power variable has been thoroughly studied by Jones (2007) whose insights will serve as a template but are supplemented by interview data, parliamentary debates, government statements, as well as defense production and force posture data from the IISS's Military Balance. Concerns about relative power, be it in the sense of balancing or soft balancing, can be measured through a steady investment in military capabilities, or at least in the rhetoric thereof. If these investments on the part of Europeans are made to become more independent of the United States – that is, if military hardware is built in Europe instead of being bought in the United States and Europeans invest in European military headquarters structures to the exclusion of participating in NATO – balancing can be said to take place. If rhetoric and institution-building rather than hardware production take place, then we observe soft balancing. Either way, one should expect a coordinated move among European governments based on shared power-induced incentives.

Institutional robustness

In essence, the variable that I set out to explain – institutional robustness – is about whether institutional performance (Gutner and Thompson 2010) is fundamentally guaranteed. Robustness is a question of institutional design (Koremenos *et al.* 2001). It varies according to: (1) degree of autonomy from other international institutions; (2) level of precision, formality of rights and authority in the legal

---

[46] Transaction costs have been variably operationalized. Weber (2000: 114) adds to the above definition two more components, namely technological development and heterogeneity. She admits, however, that the two have minor effects on preferences. Wallander defines assets as norms, rules and procedures (Wallander 2000: 706). This definition, as Suh (2007: 67) points out, "muddles the differences between the national and NATO assets." This is why I rely mostly on Suh's conceptualization.

framework (treaties, strategic concepts, etc.) as well as legal transformative capacities (Abbott and Snidal 2000; Koremenos *et al.* 2001); and (3) human/material resources (March and Olsen 1995: 92–5).

The degree of autonomy denotes whether the newly created institution is hierarchically subordinate to another international institution, as was for example the case of the WEU with NATO. The level of precision and formality probes whether the international institution receives any mention, and if so a precise one (Abbott and Snidal 2000), in the legal framework and whether the text commits the member states credibly to the multilateral performance in a given issue area (Moravcsik 1998). Of course, commitments can only be fulfilled if the institution is also manned with the appropriate permanent staff, administrative structures and material resources. In the case of security institutions, military (or civil-military) capabilities and assets are of interest. I will refrain from establishing absolute measures of appropriate staffing and resourcing. Instead, I will make ample note of the relative capacities of each institution (or proposed) under investigation. With the help of these dimensions we can look beyond the agreed-upon legal framework to see whether signatory states have implemented their promises and compromises.

A relatively strong institution thereby is an institution which is autonomous from other institutions with which it might overlap (Hofmann 2009), is based on precise language in the legal framework, and has material and human resources and capacities at hand that, at least in the abstract, give it the capacity to achieve the agreed-upon objectives. A weak institution receives hardly any (or very vague) mention in the legal framework and has scarcely any resources and capacities at its disposal.[47]

Research design and case selection

This book adopts a comparative qualitative approach. I test the different hypotheses through cross-case comparison and within-case analysis through process tracing.[48] The tracing of the independent variables across cases and the causal process observations within the cases allow for explaining the particular outcome. As Thérien and Noël (2000: 160) point out, the process through which partisan orientation

---

[47] Whether an institution is weak or not does not automatically correlate with institutional independence (Barnett and Finnemore 1999; Haftel and Thompson 2006; Bradley and Kelly 2008) or the depth of cooperation (Mansfield *et al.* 2008).

[48] The many advantages of such an approach have been discussed elsewhere. See George (1979: 113–14); George and McKeown (1985: 34–41); Collier *et al.* (2004); and George and Bennett (2005).

becomes effective "can only be assessed with case studies." Through process tracing, I examine the national governments' decision-making processes on the international level in order to determine whether they acted for the reasons hypothesized and whether the factors postulated by various theories actually shaped the outcomes.

To examine the impact of domestic forces on international policy-making and institution building systematically, I focus on three cases. The three cases that form the empirical chapters of this book are the creation of the Common Foreign and Security Policy (1990–1), the Amsterdam Treaty negotiations (1996–7) and the creation of the European Security and Defense Policy (1998–2000). Each is chosen on the basis of several criteria. First, they encompass the full-range of variance on the dependent variable. The Amsterdam case is an example of a failed attempt to create a European security institution. The CFSP case captures the creation of a weak institution. And ESDP illustrates the creation of a robust institution. Hence these cases allow for rigorous hypothesis testing in which different causal logics are assessed and compared.[49] Second, the number of cases allows for contextual knowledge and facilitates operationalization of the underdeveloped causal impact of (1) political ideologies and (2) a pre-existing institution on institutional creation – in this case NATO.[50] The cases permit observation and explanation of the causal mechanism of ideological congruence as explained above. And third, despite a large literature on ESDP, little theoretical attention has been given to ESDP in relation to NATO and to the cases that preceded it. Looking at instances of failure of institutionalizing European security (Amsterdam) and weak institutionalization (Maastricht), as well as NATO transformation, helps us in our understanding of why ESDP succeeded.

One could argue that the empirical cases are not temporally independent of each other (King *et al.* 1994: 222), but that one observes path-dependent institution building instead (Steinmo and Thelen 1992; Pierson 2004). However, through within-case analysis, it is possible "to identify and analyze the temporal sequences through which hypothesized explanatory variables affect outcomes" (Munck 2004: 111). CFSP and ESDP might not be completely independent of each other. However, the fact that ESDP came into existence eight years after CFSP, despite prior attempts to create such an institution with

---

[49] See King *et al.* (1994) and Brady and Collier (2004) on hypotheses testing. The typology of institutional overlap allows for determining cases that can be productively compared. See Stinchcombe (1968: 43–7); George and McKeown (1985: 28–9, 45); Ragin (1987: 20, 149); and Munck (2004: 111).

[50] See Brady *et al.* (2004: 10) for the treatment of underdeveloped concepts.

the Amsterdam Treaty in the mid 1990s, demonstrates that one cannot speak of an "automatic" transfer of responsibilities or linear institutional evolution. In this regard, ESDP can be considered independent of CFSP, allowing valid and rigorous inferences (Ragin 2004: 125). In addition, the temporal proximity of the three cases allows me to control for international structure, a factor stressed by realists, which remains relatively constant across the three cases.

The units-of-analysis in the three empirical cases are France, Germany and the United Kingdom. Or to be more precise, states are the units-of-analysis for the rational choice institutionalist and realist approaches, while political parties are the units-of-analysis for my own approach and the partisan values approach. The intergovernmental decision-making structures of ESDP and NATO predispose larger states to exercise more influence. Furthermore, without the biggest three militaries in Europe, an effective autonomous security organization would be impossible; hence I focus on those three.[51] They also have what Naurin (2007) and Naurin and Lindahl (2008) call the most network capital within the European Union and are representative of many different attitudes towards European security cooperation (Giegerich 2006). Germany, France and the UK provide for adequate cross-national ideological and institutional variation to test my argument. Parties with different ideologies went in and out of office during the time period of investigation: in the UK, the Conservatives were in power during the Maastricht Treaty negotiations until 1997, when Labour came to power during the final stages of the Amsterdam Treaty negotiations; in France, a Socialist government was in power during Maastricht, followed by cohabitation prior to Amsterdam, which was negotiated by an RPR government, and cohabitation for ESDP; in Germany, finally, a CDU/CSU and FDP coalition was in government until 1998, when a SPD–Green coalition took over. This change of governing parties within and across cases allows for the evaluation of cross-temporal and intra- and cross-national change.

Finally, a brief consideration of the theory's scope conditions and assumptions is in order. One scope condition is the nature of the political regime. The scope of the argument is limited to advanced democracies. I do not simply argue that partisan positions matter across regime types. Instead, I focus on the mechanisms of how these positions translate into government preferences and then into international

---

[51] However, this does not mean that the other member states are not important. When they oppose the proposed institution, they can opt out (see Denmark) *but* without much material effect to the institution.

outcomes. The domestic mechanism is based on a democratic institutional set-up. That is, once a particular party or party coalition comes to power, it constrains the articulation of national preferences. Elections bear the potential for a fair and accepted party turnover, which allows different (and stable) preferences to come to the fore.[52] The causal mechanism on the international level assumes that the norms of consultation and bounded competition are the main organizing principle of international negotiations (Dixon 1994; Moravcsik 1997). My argument is thus confined to stable democratic regimes with well-established parties and democratic institutions.

A second scope condition concerns the actors. My argument has the most purchase in stable party systems that are not based on clientelistic relations. Clientelistic parties might also represent a particular set of values; however, the longevity and consistency of political ideologies might depend on many factors outside of the causal mechanisms presented here. The theory I present throughout this book is based on the assumption that politicians have access to long-term collectively held values due to their party membership. And parties present a distinct and relatively stable value-system that is not reducible to mere clientelistic and volatile pressures. I assume that in parliamentarian systems especially, the head of government acts according to the will of her faction and, by extension, her party. Betrayal of fundamental party values would cause members to leave the party and/or diminish its support in parliament. Though the cases presented here are all European and cover the security policy domain, my argument can travel across issues and regions as long as the two (interrelated) conditions – institutionalized democracy and stable party systems – are fulfilled.

Based on this research design, I am able to provide a systematic explanation to abundant anecdotal evidence. Government turnovers are often cited as a source of alterations in national policy. David Allen and William Wallace, for example, say that in the mid 1970s Europeans were inclined to create a European security institution: "the decisive event, without doubt, was the death of President Pompidou on 2 April 1974 ... The changed tone of French policy was rapid enough to throw its diplomatic representative into some confusion" (Allen and Wallace 1982: 30). The relationship to the United States improved as well; this

---

[52] Acharya observes that "regional organizations offer an avenue for states to pursue distinctive foreign policy goals which may reflect their political and ideological orientation" (Acharya 2004). However, we should expect different causal mechanisms at play in organizations such as ASEAN, ASEAN Security Community (ASC), ASEAN Regional Forum (ARF) and APEC that explain how and whose ideological orientations matter.

was "primarily the result of fortuitous changes of leadership in the UK, France and West Germany" (Allen 1982: 72). CFSP was a "response to the collective challenges facing Europe at the end of the 1980s – or, at least, to the challenges as they were perceived by European leaders at that time" (de Schoutheete de Tervarent 1997: 41). Just before the creation of ESDP, "Britain was not at the center of this Europeanization process, but before the Kosovo war Prime Minister Tony Blair reset the agenda for European security cooperation. In a substantial change in policy, the British government initiated a joint plan with France" (Katzenstein 2005: 130). Even realists like Schweller argue: "The incentive structure of elites, even foreign policy ones, is primarily a function of domestic, not international, politics" (Schweller 2001: 174). Posen (2006: 172) refers to differences between the SPD and CDU in Germany to account for different German foreign policies toward the United States. And neoliberal institutionalists broadly state that "the pressures from domestic interests, and those generated by the competitiveness of the state system, exert much stronger effect on state policy than do international institutions, even broadly defined" (Keohane 1989: 7). As the next chapters will show, party ideologies inform national preferences influencing cooperation in multilateral security policy.

4   The end of the Cold War and the Maastricht Treaty: the weak Common Foreign and Security Policy

With the Cold War drawing to a close in 1989, a redefinition of the Western alliance's security strategy was to be expected. As French president François Mitterrand observed at the time: "There is no longer an imposed order. Europe is now master of its choices, or it can be" (quoted in Cogan 2001: 26).[1] What Mitterrand and others perceived as a new window of political opportunity for restructuring European security confronted European governments with several choices: (1) they could renationalize security, relying less on their transatlantic allies, (2) they could transform NATO into a security institution geared towards a new set of threats and challenges, (3) they could reform existing institutions such as the WEU or the CSCE that had played a negligible security role during the Cold War (Gordon 1997) to build a sustainable pan-European security system (Flynn and Farrell 1999) or (4) European governments could create a new multilateral institution outside the existing institutional framework.

So why, among these choices, did European governments choose to create the Common Foreign and Security Policy (CFSP) as a second pillar of the newly created EU outside the framework of the existing NATO alliance? Why was CFSP institutionalized only as a weak and declaratory institution? And why was NATO transformed?

Existing explanations attribute CFSP to a number of factors, including the dissolution of the Soviet Union, the violent disintegration of Yugoslavia and fear of similar violence in Eastern Europe, and the desire to avoid the uncoordinated involvement of EU governments in conflicts like the Gulf War (Attina and Repucci 2004: 59, 68). For realists, the structural changes created a regional security dilemma that prompted the creation of CFSP in order to bind a reunited Germany

---

[1] Longtime Reagan advisor Jeane Kirkpatrick observed at the time, "Everyone who thinks about such things knows that familiar patterns of international relations are changing in fundamental ways, and it is still not clear how governments will relate to one another in the post-Cold War era" (Kirkpatrick 1990: A11).

while "soft balancing" against the United States. Institutionalist arguments explain the persistence of NATO in the absence of the Soviet threat by the sunk costs states invested in the institution and the adaptability of its assets toward meeting new security threats. However, these explanations are problematic. For realists, not all European governments pursued strategies of binding Germany and soft balancing against the United States. Why did different governments pursue different strategies in spite of their similar structural positions in the distribution of capabilities? The institutionalist argument stumbles on the fact that CFSP was created outside of NATO, increasing the potential for conflict between the two institutions rather than establishing an efficient division of labor between them. If European governments were in need of a multilateral venue for organizing security, why was NATO suddenly insufficient? After all, significant reforms were taking place within NATO to meet exactly the sorts of security threats seen as motivating CFSP.

In this chapter, I make the argument that national parties in power understood the changing security environment differently, leading European governments to favor different policy priorities. Based on their ideological positions, the French and German governments at the time advanced proposals for a European security institution outside of NATO to take advantage of the opportunity presented by the end of the Cold War, while the British government opposed such a proposal. The fact that national governments in similarly situated states drew different conclusions around fundamental security issues points to the salience of non-systemic variables. As early as 1990, there was no consensus among European governments regarding the post-Cold War security order, nor did it seem likely that one would emerge. Governments within Europe and across the Atlantic disagreed over the international institutions with which one should face new security threats and the conditions under which force should be used. Whereas French Socialists wanted a strong European institution autonomous of NATO, British Conservatives opposed the creation of a robust institution *outside* NATO. The CDU/CSU–FDP government in Germany split the difference between these positions. These differences are grounded in different ideologies. The compromise between them was therefore a weak institution, mostly in the form of a declaration of policy goals called CFSP.[2] Its legal foundation in the Maastricht

---

[2] CFSP is not the first time that turning points or potential breakthroughs have been identifiable in the field of European security policy autonomous from NATO; however, it is the first time after the end of the bipolar world order.

Treaty[3] was left intentionally vague, often not offering any definitions of the new tools created (Ginsberg 1997: 23), and – most importantly – CFSP did not receive its own military hardware. Instead, loose ties were initiated between the EU and the WEU[4] at the same time as the WEU was being considered a bridge between the EU and NATO, leaving open the question of how exactly the security institutions would be connected to one another.

This chapter is organized in four parts. First, I examine the changes in the international environment and the options governments perceived in responding to new security challenges. The second section develops my own argument around party ideologies, focusing on party attitudes towards European security within the UK, France and Germany. The section demonstrates the absence of strong ideological congruence based on the core values of multilateralism in the use of force, sovereignty and Europe across the parties in government. Third, I examine the ways that party ideologies shaped the creation of CFSP as a weak security institution against the backdrop of reforms within NATO. The final section lays out alternative explanations based on partisan values, realism and rational institutionalism.

Confronting uncertainty after the fall of the Berlin Wall

The rapid and unforeseen disintegration of the Soviet Union, the retreat of the Soviet armies, German reunification and the disintegration of Yugoslavia changed the international security environment, especially in Europe. The sort of systemic change that the end of the Cold War brought about increased strategic uncertainty (Bueno de Mesquita 1978; Glaser 1993; Press-Barnathan 2006: 272). Uncertainty about how to tackle the new challenges led to strong disagreements, even among actors that had been bound together in the NATO alliance for decades. While the

[3] This treaty is officially called Treaty on European Union (TEU). However, to distinguish between the Maastricht, Amsterdam and Nice negotiations and their outcomes, I will refer to it as the Maastricht Treaty.

[4] In the Brussels Treaty of 1948, France, the United Kingdom, Belgium, Luxembourg and the Netherlands pledged mutual armed assistance against aggression. But the North Atlantic Treaty overtook this treaty a year later. While NATO was institutionalized in the early 1950s, the Brussels Treaty was institutionalized only in 1954 as the WEU – after the failure of creating the EDC (Duke 1996: 168). From the outset, NATO marginalized the WEU. The Modified Brussels Treaty of 1954 stipulated that the WEU would rely on the appropriate military authorities of NATO for information and advice on military matters. "[A]dditional functions could have reached widely; but ... NATO was the key defense structure, so that it would make no sense for WEU to duplicate its military planning" (Quinlan 2001: 3).

European continent would "no longer live under the shadow of a threat to its very survival" (Hurd 1994: 423), security and stability threats were already apparent in the break up of Yugoslavia. Furthermore, as NATO Secretary General at the time, Manfred Wörner, observed: "The risk is in uncertainty – about the future political structure of the Soviet Union, the bad economic situation, and all its consequences, in a country which still has more than three million people under arms and tens of thousands of nuclear weapons" (Wörner quoted in Whitney 1991: 1).

While the full implications of the eclipse of bipolar competition between rival ideological camps might not have been realized at the turn of the decade, governments agreed that security threats had changed in the emerging post-Cold War era. A sole reliance on military capabilities for the purpose of deterring threats was ill-suited to solving the myriad new security problems faced by states.

To some, at the end of the 1980s, NATO's posture of deterrence seemed poorly adapted to tackling new security challenges, while its military structure rendered it poorly adapted to crisis management tasks, particularly around ethnic conflicts that were increasingly on the agenda. Some governments, therefore, pushed for reforms that would add a political dimension to NATO's long-standing military mandate. These reforms were premised on the notion that NATO had to transform not just its military structure but also its political outlook – especially in order to manage relations with Eastern European states. In the new international system, approaching states as a purely military alliance would send the wrong signals.[5] Instead, so the argument goes, NATO had to develop political forums for discussion and consultation.

Other governments drew the conclusion that changes in the post-Cold War world made it possible to present proposals for a new security institution outside of NATO. These two postures did not necessarily create a zero-sum game because governments could be in favor of NATO reform, while concurrently supporting the creation of a new security institution. Thus, at the same time that NATO members began to discuss the reform of their organization to demonstrate and ensure its future relevance, the French Socialist government, together with the German Christian Democrat–Liberal coalition government, presented several proposals to the other ten EC members to create an autonomous European security institution and a multinational military force managed through the EC. This was to be accomplished by moving the WEU under EC control (Smith 1991a: A27).

---

[5] Phone interview with Brigadier General Helmut Ganser, military representative of Germany to NATO, Brussels (January 17, 2008).

Political parties in Europe

To understand how European governments responded to this changing security landscape, I argue that it is necessary to examine party ideologies around the issue of security cooperation. At the end of the Cold War, the Conservative government in the UK, the Socialist government in France, and the coalition government of the CDU/CSU and FDP in Germany had different views of the world. Even among different political parties within these countries, there was no consensus regarding either NATO's purpose or its relationship to other organizations. Electoral results could therefore shift international ideological configurations. In any case, the ideologies of political parties in power shaped government views on NATO and the EC. As a consequence, governments adopted different policies despite confronting a similar set of systemic changes and structural constraints. A key result of ideological disagreements was different approaches toward the sorts of power and efficiency concerns that realists and rational choice institutionalists see as motivating state policy.

In what follows, I discuss the different interpretations of core values and their relationships to other values. These underlie the security ideologies of European parties in power at the end of the 1980s. In focusing on the values of the parties in power, and those in opposition, I demonstrate variance both within and across European states, and underscore how these differences shape preferences toward both NATO and an autonomous alternative to it.

The United Kingdom: Euroskeptics in power

Consecutive British governments' policies toward the EU have been described in terms of the UK's "enduring awkwardness" vis-à-vis Europe. It is a common argument that the UK's unique history, its geography and its culture have all combined to engender Euroskepticism and strong Atlanticism (Wallace 1991; George 1998).[6] Yet national culture arguments cannot explain the variance in UK's preferences with respect to the European project, NATO and security institutions in general. While certain similarities between parties are difficult to deny, the idea that there are culturally entrenched attitudes that program the behavior of the British governments in EU negotiations does not hold. As Kassim argues, this cultural perspective fails to "provide a

---

[6] Additionally, Aspinwall (2000) shows that the UK is not unique in its skepticism.

satisfactory explanation for the development or content of UK prefer-ences" (Kassim 2004: 263).

It is necessary to empirically investigate British party ideologies in the domain of European security. The Conservative and Labour parties have different ideologies around security. As one observer put it, the differences between the parties are the "values which the par-ties have attempted to advance in the international sphere" (Peele 1980: 191). "Much of the controversy over Europe and its persist-ence as an issue in British politics is due to different perceptions and definitions of the national interest" between parties (Gamble 1998: 27). These different conceptions of "national interest" in regard to a potential European security institution are based on different understandings of core values. One major point of contention since the Cold War has been the issue of strengthening NATO, especially by additional defense expenditure (Peele 1980: 193). The fact that the Conservatives were in power during Maastricht negotiations had important consequences for CFSP, making party ideology more revealing of government interests than arguments around national culture. A new *initiative* for an autonomous European security insti-tution would have been unlikely from the UK government no mat-ter which party was in power. Labour prioritized a European social policy and the Conservatives remained firmly grounded in NATO. Nevertheless, when the UK's European allies tabled such proposals, the parties reacted differently to them.

The Conservative Party: European realists   In the 1987 UK elections, the Conservative government won power with a clear majority – their third mandate in a row. Throughout the Cold War, the Conservative Party was a staunch supporter of NATO in the field of security, while supporting economic liberalization within the European Community after the UK joined in 1973 (Thatcher 1993: 742–6; Gamble 1998: 22; Forster 1999: 5, 30; Major 1999: 265). These policy preferences have deep roots in Conservative Party values. Values of sovereignty, and multilateralism in the use of force, that underlie security policy cannot be discussed independently of each other in the case of the Conservatives. This is because the party has traditionally set these values in a clear hierarchy whereby British sovereignty is the primary core value from which multilateralism-as-a-means-to-another-end is derived. Europe-as-a-geographic-space can be understood as another core value. While many European integra-tion issues were framed as taking away sovereignty, the Conservative Party has been Euroskeptic even when a European policy field has been organized intergovernmentally and, consequently, did not impact national sovereignty.

The Conservatives have given "absolute priority to national sovereignty over any move to supranational institutions" (Gamble 1998: 22). Any participation in international venues has to be organized intergovernmentally so as to ensure the party the option to reto or opt out. The Conservative Party has long argued that the overriding priority of the country's foreign and security policy process should be the maintenance of sovereignty. "Britain is once again giving a lead in world affairs ... We stand up vigorously for Britain's interests abroad" (Conservative Party Manifesto 1987: 308). Hence, "Europe should be no more than an association of nation states" (Gamble 1998: 22), and it should not involve a long-term commitment (Ludlam 1998: 35).

Interlinked with sovereignty is multilateralism-as-a-means-to-another-end. Multilateralism-as-an-end-in-itself finds no traction in the party. Rather, multilateralism has only been accepted as a way of retaining British sovereignty. Because national sovereignty is so prominent in Conservative political thinking, security threats are conceived primarily, if not exclusively, in military terms. The focus on stability alongside national defense, which began to dominate the security understanding in Europe with the end of the Cold War, was perceived as naïve and idealistic from the Conservative perspective because a world where liberal democracy is the exception, not the norm, is dangerous to the goal of assuring peace. As a result, military defense has been seen as a national goal and central interest. "Strong defence is still the surest foundation for building peace" (Conservative Party Manifesto 1987: 309). Hence, the Conservative Party was a vehement critic of Labour Party proposals for nuclear disarmament – which Labour was pushing for, if necessary unilaterally. The Conservatives saw the necessity of holding on to these established military means as a way of granting security in times of strategic uncertainty. "Labour's policy is to give up Britain's independent nuclear deterrent without asking anything in return" (Conservative Party Manifesto 1987: 308). The United Kingdom cannot deter all threats alone, however. Not for the sake of multilateral action per se, but to "the end" of being safe and at the same time heard and understood in international security politics (informed by multilateralism-as-a-means-to-another-end), the Conservatives have supported NATO. NATO is the most powerful alliance of the world and the US a close partner of the UK with which it consults on a regular basis (Fair and Hutcheson 1987; Chuter 1997: 115). Through NATO, the Conservatives argue, national security and sovereignty are hence guaranteed. One does not need to risk additional membership in a sovereignty-infringing security institution. An additional security institution, establishing yet another international authority, might even weaken UK national security. "Such an approach – which one might dub 'realism' – made the pronouncement of Conservatives very different from either Labour or Liberal attitudes" (Peele 1980: 191).

These two values by themselves cannot explain why the Conservatives would not vote for an intergovernmental security institution that would incorporate military capabilities (such as a merger of the EC and the WEU would suggest) in Europe. After all, sovereignty can also be pursued through different international institutions by playing each institution against the other through a strategy of forum shopping (Alter and Meunier 2006). It is therefore crucial to understand how the Conservative Party valued Europe, a value that is not derivative of sovereignty and multilateralism. When it comes to Europe, the Conservatives have not perceived Europe as anything more than a geographic region and an economic opportunity. In the economic sphere, the Conservative Party has regarded the EC as an opportune venue for pushing for free trade. This emphasis on an economic Europe has been shaped by the Conservative Party's commitment to free markets and trade. As a result, the party had been in favor of European economic integration in the 1970s and 1980s, not in the interest of an ever-closer Europe, but in the interest of free trade and deregulation in a geographic space with strong economies that happened to be in Europe; they were in favor of market making but not market regulating policies.[7] Prime minister John Major summarized the Conservatives' interest in Europe as follows: "essentially we mean two things: a Europe that is open for trade, a free market and a tolerant Europe" (Major quoted in Wall 2008: 111). Europe is about economic competitiveness and flexible cooperation: "Europe should allow for some countries to further integrate and leave others who do not want to participate out ... Never should one try to force an agreement."[8] In the security sphere, the party as a whole was even more skeptical of Europe.

---

[7] A senior German official has pointed out that in the mid 1990s "the whole notion of Brussels changed for the Brits." Whereas before it was all about nonsense aspects of economic integration (e.g. straight bananas), it is now about elections in Congo and peace in the Balkans. They see the EU as serving a different purpose. Interview # 1 in Berlin (November 16, 2006).

[8] Interview # 7 with Conservative advisor in London (December 6, 2006), with Chris Newton, Special Advisor on defense questions in the Conservative Research Department and with Liam Fox, in London (December 5, 2006). The British membership in the EC works as long as it is in Britain's interest, which according to Conservative ideology is based on free trade. "This government has taken Britain from the sidelines into the mainstream of Europe ... genuine common market ... freer trade" (Conservative Party Manifesto 1987: 309). Nowhere can one find a remark of a Conservative politician of the time that the EU could or should become more.

It is worthwhile pointing out that the Conservative Party is not completely unified on the issue of European integration, though the overall party stance is Euroskeptic (Ludlam 1998: 38, 44; Bulmer and Burch 2005: 867, 876; Wall 2008: 108). Party leadership has managed to keep the various factions together (Forster 1999: 28; Parsons and Weber 2011). What binds the party together is that its members are absolutists when it comes to national sovereignty. Party leaders have to stress this value over all others.[9]

This interpretation of a set of values has undergirded specific policy preferences of Conservative governments. Based on this understanding of Europe and multilateralism, as well as a strong desire to maintain British sovereignty, the Conservative Party has historically been against European security initiatives outside of NATO. The Conservatives support NATO, regardless of which party is in power in the United States, and as long as NATO puts emphasis on its military might. The issue of NATO primacy has been undisputed in the Conservative Party (Forster 1999: 108); "European security is NATO."[10] Conservative values around the issues of sovereignty and skepticism of multilateralism have been at the root of the strong support in the party for NATO. Its understanding of Europe-as-a-geographic-space has informed its fear of integration dynamics that would take away sovereign rights. As one British official argued, NATO is the "cornerstone of our security and the most important international security organization. It has been established over several decades, has been tested, and combines European and US capabilities. It is a broad and united expression of shared values. Europe is primarily and fundamentally based on a market and hence should look differently than it currently does."[11] As the Conservative Party manifesto observed, "We still stand fully by our obligations to our European and American allies in NATO" (Conservative Party Manifesto 1987: 308). This relationship had created an understanding in the Conservative Party that "European security would only be discussed in the presence of the United States" (Chuter 1997: 115), that is, in forums where the United States and its partner, the UK, have the dominant voice. This has informed Conservative

---

[9] One example illustrates this point. When the party leadership went from Thatcher to Major in November 1990, Major did not change the Conservatives' EU policy. Though there was no change of substance, the tone changed as Major used less aggressive language (Wall 2008: 109–11). Divisions within the party only became prominent with Black Wednesday and the beef crises, when party backbenchers debated what exactly the internal market should encompass. No such disagreement existed in regard to security policy issues. These debates never led to a party split. While, those who did not accept Major's leadership defected to other parties (Ludlam 1998: 32–3).

[10] Interview # 7 with Conservative advisor in London (December 6, 2006).

[11] Interview with Chris Newton in London (December 5, 2006).

reluctance about political integration in the EC. As long as military security needs to be organized multilaterally, Conservatives will value NATO over any other institution. NATO's persistence and transformation, therefore, makes the creation of an overlapping institution not only superfluous but also dangerous to the British influential position in the formulation of multilateral security policy. The preference for NATO has ruled out a strategy of forum shopping for the Conservatives.

As a result, the British government under the Conservatives was hostile to any downgrading of NATO and concerned with the risk of American abandonment of Britain and Europe. In addition, it favored only intergovernmental cooperation in the security policy domain, based on the understanding that institutions work best on the basis of sovereign states (Wall 2008: 100). To this end, Prime Minister Margaret Thatcher sought "to strike the balance between preserving the present military character of the alliance and giving it a new political dimension ... NATO, the European Community and the 35-nation Conference on Security and Co-operation in Europe should all have distinct but complementary roles in the new architecture of Europe" (Stephens and Mauthner 1990: 1).

The Labour Party: peace and stability   The Conservative government's Labour counterpart, in opposition during the negotiations leading to CFSP, has largely shared the concern for preserving British sovereignty, but differed with the Conservatives on issues of Europe and multilateralism in the use of force. For both parties, the insistence on national sovereignty forms a core value in their party ideologies. As Thomas Risse pointed out, "The distinctive nationalist English identity is incompatible with federalist or supranationalist visions of European political order. It explains why British governments, whether Conservative or Labour, have consistently been reluctant to support a deepening of European integration" (Risse 2001: 199). However, deepening refers not only to supranationalism, but also to the inclusion of new policy fields into the realm of EU authority. It is here where the Conservative and Labour parties differ. European policies are "one of the dominant and most divisive issues of modern British politics" (Baker and Seawright 1998a: 1; see also Gamble 1998). As a result, the Labour Party stressed different policies for British security policy in times of international change.

When it comes to sovereignty, Labour has traditionally agreed with the Conservative Party that supranational institutions in the security policy domain are out of the question. However, the Labour Party has not linked sovereignty to multilateralism in the same way as the

Conservatives. In its party manifesto of 1987, Labour committed the party to the UN and multilateral action in general, arguing against institutional cherry-picking (Labour Party Manifesto 1987: 320); this is based on interpreting multilateralism-as-an-end-in-itself as a core value. As a party that values inclusive multilateral action, Labour was critical of US action and condemned US foreign policies that favored cherry-picking over consultation with allies (Labour Party Manifesto 1987: 320). Based on its fundamental multilateral approach, Labour has understood different international organizations as venues for pursuing security and stability policy (Peele 1980: 191). International institutions are not primarily understood as instruments for pursuing power and sovereignty, but as arenas for consultation and information exchange where disagreements are not uncommon but where consensus is sought when possible. It is therefore not surprising that Labour, while in favor of the UK's membership in NATO (Labour Party Manifesto 1987: 321), was at times a vehement critic of NATO policy and nuclear deterrence.

In regard to Europe, Labour does not define it as a core value but instead as derivative of multilateralism and sovereignty. Europe is interpreted as one community among others, where multilateral policy can be conducted. Critical of economic neoliberal European integration at first, the inclusion of more political elements into the EU was more in line with Labour's other ideological learnings. As a consequence, under the leadership of Neil Kinnock, Labour had become critical of the Conservative Euroskeptic policy (Baker and Seawright 1998b: 58–9). In its manifesto, it stressed that "Labour's aim is to work constructively with our EEC partners to promote economic expansion and combat unemployment" (Labour Party Manifesto 1987: 321). Labour supported European efforts to multilateralize policy spaces, including security policy, though it traditionally had been skeptical of economic cooperation toward market liberalization.[12] Hence, it was conceivable that Labour would have committed more strongly than the Conservatives to a European institution outside of NATO.

---

[12] During the period when the Conservatives agreed to cooperation with European counterparts under the condition that cooperation would be constrained to the realm of trade policy, the Labour Party had criticized the EC for its economic liberalization. This culminated in Labour asking for a British withdrawal from the EC in its 1983 party manifesto, criticizing the EC's exclusive emphasis on markets and liberalization and undermining a social policy dimension (Gamble 1998: 28).

France: the Socialist reign

French foreign and security policy has often been ascribed to "Gaullism," implying a national consensus across parties. However, such a Gaullist consensus is a myth. "Differing opinions, usually masked by the protective cover of a few simplistic 'catch-phrases' concerning France's autonomy and its *rang,* reveal the largely illusory nature of 'consensus'" (Menon 1996: 158). Hubert Védrine[13] speaks of "false ideas of consensus ... it's a lazy consensus that exists only because of laziness and ignorance. It's very hollow – a pseudo consensus."[14] As with the notion of British awkwardness in Europe, it neglects empirical investigation of party preferences.

Looking inside France, important differences can be observed between parties that shape government policy. The range of interpretations as to what constitutes Gaullism is extensive, allowing parties to variously emphasize the French *force de frappe,* national independence in decision-making (understood either as attachment to liberty of action or as unilateralism), refusal to accept subordination to the United States, the search for *grandeur* and *rang,* the primacy of the nation-state, the importance of national defense, and the insistence on a European security order (understood either as means or end) (Newhouse 1970; Paolini 1989; Gordon 1993: 3–21; Howorth 1996).[15]

The various interpretations of sovereignty and Europe lead parties such as the RPR to argue that both values are complementary, while others like the PS say that Europe will eventually lead to a reduction of national sovereignty.[16] Rejoining NATO has not been a consensus issue, while creating a European security institution has been consensual – though the understanding of, and reason for, European integration and cooperation vary. While the RPR pursues multilateral (European) policies in the interest of widening France's range of action, the Socialists

[13] At the beginning of the 1990s, Védrine was first advisor and then secretary general of the Elysée. In 1997, he became foreign minister.

[14] He goes on to say that the same goes for *Europe puissance* as nobody defines it the same way or even knows what it means. While the RPR sees it as a toolbox for its conception of security policy, the PS insists on *Europe* rather than *puissance.* "European defense remains undefined." Interview with Hubert Védrine in Paris (May 29, 2008).

[15] De Gaulle himself said in 1966: "What is independence? Certainly not isolationism or narrow nationalism. A country can be a member of an alliance, such as the Atlantic Alliance, and remain independent ... to be independent means that one is not at the mercy of any foreign power" (quoted in Howorth 1996: 22).

[16] There are at least two visions of how best to promote the cause of a stronger Europe and more balanced alliance: integration or confederation. These visions had already manifested themselves during the debates on EDC in the 1950s (Hitchcock 1998: 170–93; Parsons 2002).

have been in favor of Europe per se, without a functional need. Based on different methods of arriving at the objective of a European security institution, parties have disagreed on what such an institution should look like; their level of commitment to such an institution has also differed.

Socialists: Europe first   The PS has interpreted Europe as an important value, as did De Gaulle. But while De Gaulle saw Europe as a means to an end such as French *grandeur*, the PS understands Europe as an end in itself and disconnected in this sense from issues of sovereignty and multilateralism. Europe-as-a-political-community forms a core value in the French Socialist party ideology. Europe has been more than an instrumental institution for Socialists. It is an idea that needed constant affirmation and evolution. Mitterrand made Europe a principal focus of his 1988 election campaign.[17] In his *Lettre à tous les Français* Mitterrand argued, "Europe will develop by itself [*L'Europe se fera par elle même*]," and Europe is "an idea that follows its own path." There was an "expectation of a steady, meaningful progress" (Grant 1996: 60). Moreover, Europe provides France with the political community to feel secure in its environment. Seeing "an international environment in disorder" (Parti Socialiste Manifesto 1988: 8), the Socialists complained about "the slow construction of Europe" (Parti Socialiste Manifesto 1988: 8) and argued that international crises "marginalize Europe" (Parti Socialiste Manifesto 1988: 8). The party understands France as a possible engine of European integration.[18] "In the international context, France occupies a special place. Its role will be increasingly important as it pushes for a stronger Europe" (Parti Socialiste Manifesto 1988: 10). Mitterrand once said, "We are at home in Europe" (Mitterrand quoted in Kirkpatrick 1990: A11). All of this has led Socialists to pursue projects that deepen European integration without necessarily attaching a functional need to them, except that it is European. "To fix Europe, it is insufficient to evoke symbolic dates and passively wait for them ... As Europe is insufficiently present

[17] During the *cohabitation* from 1986 to 1988, there was constant tension between *Matignon* and *Elysée* as to who makes European politics (Lequesne 1998: 130–1). Mitterrand tried to keep the policy domain to himself. Chirac challenged the president's exclusive control. The different manifestations of the value "Europe" were exemplified in the election campaign of 1988, where Mitterrand made Europe a principal theme (Mazzucelli 1997: 47; Lequesne 1998: 128).

[18] The party even conceived of extending its deterrence capabilities to encompass all of Europe. "[France's] global deterrence, in due course, will be effectively exercised to the benefit of western Europe, if Europe so desires" (Parti Socialiste Manifesto 1988: 10).

and absent from certain policy domains ... we need a European project" (Parti Socialiste Manifesto 1988: 11). Throughout the year 1990, Mitterrand mentioned on several occasions that "the Europeans would take charge of their own security; NATO would be continued but remain confined to its traditional geographic zone of Western Europe and North America" (Cogan 2001: 23).

Multilateralism in the use of force has traditionally been valued as-a-means-to-another-end; multilateralism is derivative of Europe-as-a-political-community. Mitterrand lamented the dominance of the United States inside NATO wherever possible. In this sense, the French Socialist Party presented itself as a soft-balancing realist in traditional IR terms – but instead of material grounds it reasoned on ideological grounds.[19] The PS has had strong reservations about France's membership in NATO, which ties its members to American economic and military imperialism (Gordon 1993: 107).[20] The PS has drawn on a strain of Gaullism that has sought to prevent French and European "vassalization" by the United States.[21] Of the PS, Védrine says that it dislikes American hegemony not because of the sheer concentration of power in the United States, but primarily because it is the *United States* that is the hegemon.[22] He contrasts his party to "Occidentalists" that see France and the United States as coming from the same occidental family and hence sharing the same ideas and values. The PS "emphasized the limits of the Atlantic link and demonstrated Western Europe's continued dependence on the United States. Indeed, Mitterrand was well aware ... 'it would be just as dangerous for Europe to abandon itself to the protection of a country outside of our own continent'" (Gordon 1993: 124).

[19] The Conservatives, while also sounding realist, value NATO for its continued security provision. The French Socialists saw the changing international environment as a chance to voice their dislike of US security policies. This is one major difference between the two parties.

[20] The PS was against an alignment with "imperialist positions" in the world (Parti Socialiste 1980: 340).

[21] Interview with Admiral Jean Dufourcq in Paris (May 27, 2008).

[22] Interview with Hubert Védrine in Paris (May 29, 2008). He turns around Ruggie's argument that multilateralism is favored because it happens under US hegemony (Ruggie 1992). The Socialists have a notion of anti-Americanism based on disagreement on social, economic and political dimensions that translated into pronounced skepticism in NATO (Védrine 1997). On the other hand, Gaullist parties traditionally disagree with the United States on political questions, more so than economic and social ones. Their opposition to NATO originates from their insistence on France's sovereignty and independence.

Sovereignty, while important to the Socialist Party, also has been valued contextually. Where European affairs are concerned, the PS has been willing to give up sovereign rights for the end goal of a federal Europe (Party Socialist Manifesto 1988:10). However, in other multilateral institutions, such as NATO for example, intergovernmentalism has been the valued form of interaction.

As a result, whereas De Gaulle felt that by concentrating on foreign and security policy he could strengthen and expand intergovernmentalism, and thereby arrive at his confederal solution, the PS and Mitterrand felt that by prioritizing technical aspects of economic and monetary union they could progressively foster federalism, thereby generating a common foreign and security policy (Mazzucelli 1997: 139). The PS's ideological position predisposed its leadership to not only support a proposal to create a European security institution, but also to table it.

RPR: national sovereignty first   The ideology of the PS's main competitor, the RPR Party centered on Jacques Chirac, differed on the values of multilateralism, sovereignty and Europe.[23] The RPR and PS disagreed over the nature of France's role in the world and in Europe, and how best to achieve it – especially in the realm of security policy. The parties held a "genuinely different view about France's proper military role in Europe" (Gordon 1993: 157). Both were in favor of more European engagement with security issues,[24] but disagreed over what this means and how it could be achieved.[25]

The RPR has traditionally adhered to the core value of French sovereignty. In conjunction with sovereignty, Europe has been seen as a means to achieve other policy goals, rather than a value in itself. The RPR has seen Europe as a tool to exercise influence, stressing the nationalist *étatist* element of Gaullism. The party has not refrained from using the term patriotism in its manifesto to stress France's exclusiveness and interprets Europe in more functionalist terms as a community-among-others: it is

[23] See Howorth (1993: 154–63) for a discussion on all the different foreign and security policy issues where the RPR differed from the PS and the tension that resulted from these differences during *cohabitation*.

[24] However, there is a consensus in France that defense issues have to be taken seriously and threats and risks are similarly assessed across parties. Interview with Francois Heisbourg in Paris (May 27, 2008).

[25] UDF and RPR are apart in visions of France in the EU even if their economic and cultural attitudes are close (Andersen and Evans 2003: 185). In the context of European institution building, Simon Nuttall once observed, "The motives of successive French governments in promoting a European identity, whether along inter-governmental or integrationist lines, are complex and shifting" (Nuttall 1992: 3).

not about what France can do for Europe, but what Europe can do for France. Chirac has said, "One has to be ambitious for France" (Chirac 1988: 15), and "turn France into the first nation of Europe" (Chirac 1988: 37). He goes on to say, "I invite all the French people with courage and with heart to distinguish between the essential and the incidental land to join my struggle – a struggle against socialism, a struggle for the individual, and a fight for France" (Chirac 1988: 38). Room for maneuver on the international stage has been very important for the RPR (Parsons 2003).[26]

Multilateralism in the use of force has been valued contextually. The RPR has insisted on sovereignty and, as long as sovereignty is guaranteed, has been in favor of multilateral security cooperation. As a result, the RPR has been much less critical of the United States.[27] This is so because the RPR's "Americanskepticism" has originated as a response to American power and not American political ideology. Before the end of the Cold War and with the diminishing role of nuclear weapons, Chirac, as prime minister in the first cohabitation (1986–8), pushed for France's rapprochement with NATO, but Mitterrand blocked it (Cogan 2001: 77).

While the tendency of the French military was to harmonize its relationship with NATO, President Mitterrand was wary of encouraging a rapprochement. In a restricted Defense Committee meeting on January 16, 1990, Mitterrand stated that previously in his presidency, during the first "cohabitation" government (1986–1988), headed by his political rival, Jacques Chirac, France was "within the snap of a finger of returning to integration with NATO. It was my refusal that prevented this." (Cogan 2001: 13; see also Gordon 1993: 151–5)

On a more symbolic level, when Prime Minister Chirac decided to break a precedent in 1988 and attended the March NATO summit, Mitterrand joined him in order not to leave the playing field to his political rival (Gordon 1993: 146).[28]

As a result of these value interpretations, the RPR and Chirac were much more in favor of a French security policy pursued in a variety

[26] Interview with Francois Heisbourg in Paris (May 27, 2008).

[27] Interview with Admiral Jean Dufourcq in Paris (May 27, 2008). During the Cold War, much more emphasis was put on nuclear deterrence than on conventional forces and the RPR was opposed to cooperation in nuclear policy in NATO. Once the importance of nuclear weapons in guaranteeing France's sovereignty diminished, the party opened up to cooperation in NATO.

[28] Another situation in which Chirac and the RPR sided with NATO, and the Socialists with Mitterrand against, is in regard to nuclear posture: Chirac was in favor of flexible response whereas Mitterrand stressed the deterrence component (Gordon 1993: 146–51, 156). Their division thereby reflected a major transformation in NATO that took place in the 1960s which granted European governments (except France) more say in nuclear policy through the creation of the Nuclear Planning Group in 1966. A shift in nuclear strategy from massive retaliation to flexible response in 1967 was a compromise between conflicting US and European perspectives on the requirement of deterrence (Sloan 2003: 55).

of international multilateral security institutions of which NATO and CFSP are possible expressions. The EC and NATO were both seen as options to pursue multilateral security policy as long as France's sovereignty was guaranteed. The RPR sought to give France a greater margin of latitude to act (Chirac 2000). Overall, the RPR was open to different multilateral forums while not being committed to them per se.

Germany: in favor of multilateralism

With German reunification, Joseph Joffe asked, "What does a nation do with its liberated power in the post-bipolar age when the 40-year-old strategic threat has disappeared that previously posed all major questions and delivered most of the major answers?" (1994: 83). The answer came with the traditional view of Germany as a civilian power embracing multilateralism and willing to pool national sovereignty as a result of its historical experiences with militarism and nationalism during the Third Reich. German parties have thus cherished multilateralism and tight restrictions on the use of force (Maull 1990/1, 2000; Berger 1996; Duffield 1998). Multilateralism-as-an-end-in-itself has been much more pronounced in most German parties than in France and the United Kingdom due to the country's historical experience.

Unlike the UK where Conservatives and Labour have had divergent views on the value of Europe and multilateralism, or in France, where the Socialists and RPR have disagreed about France's relationship to NATO based on their different understanding of multilateralism, sovereignty and Europe, in Germany policy debates relevant to European security cooperation were more nuanced, often hinging on values such as Europe's inclusiveness and supranational versus intergovernmental cooperation. In which multilateral forum force can be used, to what ends (only defense or also security crisis management) and where have been debated. These nuances were nonetheless consequential. The CDU/CSU and SPD have diverged over many foreign and security policies as, for example, the CDU's policy of *Westintegration* that was heavily attacked by the SPD, or the SPD's *Ostpolitik* which resulted in the CDU calling Willy Brandt a traitor [*Vaterlandsverräter*]. As with the previous cases, German parties have diverged on value interpretations and consequently policy preferences. As a result, they think of the "national interest" differently.[29] Differences between the government

---

[29] Asked about the meaning of national interest, Joschka Fischer said, "when one mentions national interest, one automatically makes others think about national idiocy that is sold with this term, this is like sweet wine. The actions of politicians are often juxtaposed to national interest, they often act irrational." Interview in Princeton

and opposition parties were pronounced at the end of the Cold War, as the SPD and the Greens were both dominated by their more radical factions, the *Frankfurter Kreis/Parlamentarische Linke* and the *Fundis*, respectively.[30]

CDU/CSU: Europe first The Christian Democrats' ideology in terms of security institutions has been characterized by no clear hierarchy of values – as the French Socialists, the CDU/CSU values Europe independently of sovereignty and multilateralism. Europe-as-a-political-community and multilateralism-as-an-end-in-itself have been core values for the party.

The CDU/CSU ideology has informed the principle of *Westintegration*, where policies are premised on integration in multilateral institutions based on "Western" principles such as democracy and the free market (Thränhardt 1996). While Europe was seen as part of *Westintegration*, the CDU/CSU has regarded it as more than a multilateral framework. Europe has been a cultural and political community coinciding with the institutional expression of the EEC/EC/EU. European partnership and the EC have therefore been stressed prominently in the party manifesto of 1990 (CDU Party Manifesto 1990: 28–9), and especially the Franco-German engine therein (CDU Party Manifesto 1990: 29). As with the French Socialists, the value of Europe has cross-cut multilateralism in the use of force and sovereignty.

In regard to multilateralism in the use of force, the CDU/CSU has valued it as an-end-in-itself. It forms another core value in the party's ideology. The policy field of European foreign and security policy found an explicit mention in the CDU/CSU manifesto – before the Maastricht negotiations had even started. "Only with a common foreign and security policy can Europe represent its common interests effectively and meet its responsibilities to solve global problems" (CDU Party Manifesto 1990: 29). However, as much as Europe has been valued, the CDU/CSU also

(February 21, 2007). The Green position papers and manifestos all avoid the usage of the term "national interest." Constanze Stelzenmüller, journalist for *Die Zeit*, referred to national interest as the *"Ausschwitzkeule."*

[30] The US government was aware of the ideological differences between German parties. For example, Hutchings said that the US government observed the German elections in 1990 very closely: "Election cycles matter and the party in power matters for the US to assess European efforts." The US government was very much in favor of the CDU/CSU–FDP government winning the election rather than the SPD under Lafontaine, as Kohl and Bush shared a similar understanding of the transatlantic relationship, whereas Lafontaine and Bush did not. Hence, "in the US, some tried to help Kohl in subtle ways such as to invite him over often, etc., to win over Lafontaine." Interview in Princeton (Februrary 21, 2007).

valued its existing membership in NATO. "NATO and the Bundeswehr remain indispensable ... The stability of an overarching security structure in Europe demands transatlantic cooperation with North America" (CDU Party Manifesto 1990: 33). Based on its core values, the CDU/CSU did not the EC or NATO over one another, nor did it perceive that one institution's mandate was restricted by the existence of the other, but instead valued the concept of interlocking institutions.[31] The party wanted to be an initiator in creating a new security institution network. "Germany will fulfill its responsibility in Europe. It will energetically participate in building a new European security structure in which the European Community, the WEU, NATO and CSCE complement one another" (CDU Party Manifesto 1990: 33).

The value of sovereignty has to be understood in context. Based on the understanding of Europe-as-a-political-community, the CDU/CSU has been in favor of a federal European Union in which subsidiarity and parliamentary control are guaranteed. As a result, the CDU/CSU has favored supranationalism in regard to European integration. But sovereign rights would only be ceded to the EC; no other multilateral institution has been conceived in such supranational terms. Instead, intergovernmentalism has been the preferred mode of interaction in other multilateral forums.

Based on this interpretation of values, the CDU/CSU ideology has influenced its leadership's worldviews. The CDU/CSU party leadership pushed for further integration in the EC, including security policy, while at the same time seeking to coordinate these efforts with NATO. While the CDU was in favor of a broad mandate for NATO, it did not see tensions between this and the possibility of the EC developing also into a crisis management institution. The party made clear to its counterparts – mainly France and the United States – that it was not willing or able to choose between the two international organizations when it came to multilateral security policy.

FDP: Europe and multilateralism The FDP shared many values with its CDU/CSU coalition partner, especially in regard to multilateralism-in-the-use-of-force as an-end-in-itself, and had a very similar understanding of the transforming international context. The FDP has been very much in favor of NATO's persistence and transformation. "The FDP pledges itself to the active membership of a unified Germany in the transatlantic alliance (NATO). A neutralized, unified Germany is unimaginable for the FDP" (FDP

---

[31] Interview with Joachim Bitterlich in Berlin (October 23, 2006).

Party Manifesto 1990: 25). NATO transformation was a policy priority for the party.

> The political character of NATO needs to be strengthened ... strong bonds exist in security policy between the North American democracies and the European continent ... Multinational forces are a model of the future structures that build trust. As a first step, the FDP supports all initiatives towards the formation of multinational associations in the Alliance. (FDP Party Manifesto 1990: 26)

In addition, the FDP has stressed the importance of the UN and the OSCE in building and strengthening security and stability (FDP Party Manifesto 1990: 22, 29–30).

The FDP also valued Europe-as-a-political-community but has not made sovereignty a derivative of it. Multilateralism, sovereignty and Europe are, therefore, core values. As a result, the FDP has been more hesitant in the supranationalization of policy fields in the EC than the CDU/CSU. "Our constitution tells us to preserve our national and state unity, to serve peace in the world as an equal partner in a unified Europe and to bring about in free self-determination the unified liberty of our country" (FDP Party Manifesto 1990: 11). Nonetheless, it has shared with the CDU/CSU the drive to initiate changes in the EC and broaden its policy scope. The FDP has underlined its strong European vocation and has explicitly favored a common foreign and security policy.

> In the future, the EC needs to exercise political influence even more strongly through a common front [*geschlossenes Auftreten*] in a way that corresponds to its importance and economic power. The European Political Coordination (EPC) of the national governments needs to be brought together with the foreign relations of the community in the interest of a unified European foreign policy. This policy needs to extend to all aspects of security. (FDP Party Manifesto 1990: 24)

Overall, European security policy cannot go against NATO. Instead, both NATO and a European security institution have to be "embedded with each other."[32] The relationship between the European security institution and NATO should not be one of a division of labor but, instead, needs to function on the basis of close cooperation and consultation.

---

[32] Interview with Friedel Eggelmeyer, Advisor in Security Affairs to the FDP, in Berlin (October 31, 2006).

The CDU/CSU and FDP coalition government   In the CDU/ CSU and FDP coalition, in power at the time of Maastricht, values overlapped almost completely when it came to informing a European security policy. While Europe did not factor prominently in the coalition treaty of 1991, with the implications of German reunification taking up most of the text, the treaty nonetheless stressed finding new policy responsibilities for the EC (Koalitionsvereinbarungen 1991: 35, 59). Foreign Minister Genscher (FDP) was quoted as saying, "the more European our foreign policy, the more national it is" (quoted in Ash 1993: 23).[33] Before the general elections in 1990, Kohl, in front of a French audience, said that it is time to push for future integration in the sphere of foreign and security policy (Kohl 1989: 758).[34]

SPD: multilateralism, above all   At the end of the Cold War, the SPD was influenced by its chancellor candidate and vice chairman Oskar Lafontaine, who belonged to the *Frankfurter Kreis/Parlamentarische Linke faction.*[35] The SPD, as did the CDU/CSU at the time, understood Europe in connection with sovereignty arguing for a federally organized United States of Europe based on the principle of solidarity (SPD Party Manifesto 1990: 23); despite this, its overall core value has been multilateralism-as-an-end-in-itself. As such, Europe has not solely been understood in its institutional expression of the EEC/EC/EU. Instead, the SPD has been in favor of an inclusive understanding of Europe, one that would leave "no state behind." The party has stressed the necessity to engage in a dialogue with Germany's neighboring states to the East in order to foster pan-European institutions. The EC had no priority in this.

In regard to multilateralism in the use of force, the SPD – in the tradition of multilateralism-as-an-end-in-itself, which was foundational to its *Ostpolitik* – was critical of NATO and the use of force. The party

---

[33] When the CDU/CSU–FDP coalition first formed in 1982, FDP politicians such as Rudolf Baum were not in favor of it and refused to take a minister's post (Kohl 2005: 27). This can be seen as an indicator that coalitions are created with those factions that are most inclined to agree ideologically with the coalition partner.

[34] In his autobiography, former Chancellor Kohl observes two camps regarding foreign and security policy: CDU/CSU and FDP on one side and SPD and the Greens on the other (Kohl 2005: 294).

[35] In September 1990, the East German SPD merged with the West German SPD at the Berlin convention. The SPD's new basic program was not even a year old at the time. For a detailed analysis of the process of the Berlin basic program of 1989 see Braunthal (1993).

argued: "the end of a divided Germany is not the end of all crises in the world, as the Gulf crisis shows, but has nonetheless made Germany and Europe more secure. Now it is time to reevalute [Germany's] position in light of this détente" (SPD Party Manifesto 1990: 21). Its ultimate aim has been to end military alliances: "Military blocs have lost their function. We want to replace them. Our goal remains a treaty for the creation of a European security system in the framework of the CSCE in which the former military alliances can be dissolved" (SPD Party Manifesto 1990: 22). The SPD perceived a need for the persistence of security institutions, favoring the pan-European CSCE in attempting to overcome the East–West divide. NATO, which the party regarded as a Cold War relic, was deemed impossible to reform and transform (SPD Party Manifesto 1990: 22). The SPD's *Frankfurter Kreis* understood NATO as an exclusive West European club with a Cold War focus on security, i.e. deterrence.

As a result, with regard to multilateral security policy initiatives with military implications, the SPD was more hesitant than the CDU/CSU. In addition, the SPD conducted a more differentiated and nuanced policy toward the United States, which at times resembled euro-Gaullist tendencies. The *Frankfurter Kreis* faction of the SPD, in particular, sought to strengthen Europe and was critical of US policy, regarding it as focused too narrowly on the military and of cherry-picking foreign policy goals and allies to conduct security policy with.[36]

The Greens: peaceful cooperation   The radical *Fundis* faction dominated the Green Party at the beginning of the 1990s (Betz 1995: 205–6; Klein and Falter 2003).[37] Similar to the SPD at the time, the Green party valued multilateralism-as-an-end-in-itself. Europe and sovereignty had

[36] Interview with Karsten Voigt, at the time foreign policy spokesperson for the SPD, in Berlin (October 23, 2007).

[37] At the end of the 1970s, the Greens formed out of two very heterogeneous movements: a left wing anti-militarist radical movement, and a "save the environment" movement that could be described as ecologically-minded middle class. As a result, the Greens had a very broad range of political goals and splitting was a possibility. But the German political system with its 5 percent hurdle to enter Parliament pressured them to stay together and push for the common denominator, environment, as primary political goal (Klein and Falter 2003: 53). The biggest division has been between *Fundis* and *Realos*; the division is also understood as *Ökosozialisten* versus *Ökoliberale*. While the first group sees ecological problems as a consequence of capitalism and does not want to be part of the government, the latter does not criticize the economic system of Germany but wants to live according to an ecological humanism. These controversies dominated the first decade of the party's existence with *Fundis* being the majority (Klein and Falter 2003: 56–9). The division peaked with unification and then many *Ökosozialisten* left the party to join the PDS (Betz 1995: 206).

to be understood contextually. It was critical of the use of force as it had been exercised thus far, namely in the form of NATO. "The goal must be the abolishment of military alliances and the complete demilitarization of Europe" (Grünen Party Manifesto 1990: 7). Like the SPD, the Greens perceived NATO in Cold War terms, regarding it as a mere instrument of weapons proliferation (Grünen Party Manifesto 1990: 18). They doubted that NATO could be reformed, seeking instead "a world without military blocs and a society without weapons and armies" (Grünen Party Manifesto 1990: 18) as a long-term goal. However, the party manifesto of the time also mirrors the tensions that existed in the party. The *Realos* had a more moderate understanding of NATO and did not seek an immediate and unconditional exit from NATO, as did the *Fundis*. Hence, within the party, a compromise was formulated that *if* NATO was unwilling to commence unilateral disarmament *then* Germany should exit the institution (Grünen Party Manifesto 1990: 18–19).[38]

The party has been in favor of multilateralism in the interests of peace and security. In general, the party sought to create a new institutional network that would induce peaceful coexistence with all European states. As with the SPD, the Greens favored CSCE transformation, regarding it as the most inclusive institution in the post-Cold War order. "The CSCE can be the appropriate venue for the construction of a new and peaceful European order and the elaboration of the idea of a 'common European home'" (Grünen Party Manifesto 1990: 21).[39] The Greens at the time regarded multilateral institutions as an-end-in-itself (instead of a "national" policy) (Grünen Party Manifesto 1990: 21).

The insistence on multilateralism has informed their stance on Europe. Europe is valued not as a special political community but as a community-among-others that happens to be in Germany's immediate neighborhood which, again, is a natural environment within which to create multilateral frameworks to foster peace. The Greens have no direct stance on sovereignty. They seem agnostic as to whether or not Germany should give up sovereign powers to an international institution; however, they insist that whatever happens will happen "with the

---

[38] "When discussions regarding the implementation of unilateral disarmament lead to questioning German NATO membership or dismantling NATO, then we are willing to leave NATO. We have to leave NATO because there can be no peace with NATO and the weakening, disintegration and finally dissolution of the military pact is inevitable to create peace. A policy of peace cannot be based on military blocs" (Grünen Party Manifesto 1990: 18–19).

[39] "In order to prevent war, a new pan-European collective structure linking all nation-states needs to replace the confrontational bipolar structure in which the Federal Republic of Germany and other states were embedded" (Grünen Party Manifesto 1990: 21).

people," i.e. in close cooperation with the parliaments (be they national or European).

As a result, the Green's policy preference is to create an inclusive framework in Europe that would foster peaceful relations. As long as a European security institution would present itself this way, while at the same time not insisting on military means to create security, the Greens under the leadership of the *Fundis* would favor such an institution.

As the preceding discussion has shown, ideological differences within and across the UK, France and Germany characterized the period during which the Cold War unraveled. Table 4.1 summarizes the different value interpretations that translate into the ideological positions of each party in government.

NATO transformation and the creation of CFSP

Between 1989 and 1991 governments of Western European states experienced policy overload. Initially, managing German reunification and Central and Eastern European states' demands for economic and political assistance occupied European governments. Soon after, in the beginning of 1991, European governments were also confronted with the Soviet aggression in the Baltic states, the launch of Operation Desert Storm, and the Soviet August putsch. In the second half of 1991, the disintegration of Yugoslavia accelerated – a further demand on European attention.

Despite these fundamental changes, the external events neither marked a *moment fondateur* for a robust European security institution, nor did this trigger France's re-entry to NATO. Instead, in the midst of these historical events, two major directions for European security cooperation were pursued. First, some NATO members began a process of NATO transformation from a collective defense alliance to a more political organization that included crisis management in its mandate. Second, several governments pushed for a new European security institution independent of NATO. In neither the EC nor NATO was there a consensus concerning either the politicization of NATO or the militarization of the EC (Kissinger 1990: D7; Glaser 1993). Zbigniew Brzezinski, former National Security advisor to US President Jimmy Carter, for example, observed that "there is unanimity that the North Atlantic Treaty Organization should be continued. But there are contentious issues, too: how NATO should relate to Europe's emerging political unity" (Brzezinski 1993: A23).

The three governments all had their own concepts for organizing European security, each rooted in the ideological position of

Table 4.1 *Domestic and international party configuration, 1990*

Country	Party/ies	Multilateralism	Europe	Sovereignty
United Kingdom	Conservatives†	Means-to-another-end	**Europe-as-a-geographic-space**	**Intergovernmental**
	Labour	**End-in-itself**	Europe-as-a-community-among-others	Intergovernmental
France	Socialists (PS)†	Means-to-another-end	**Europe-as-a-political-community**	Supranational/ intergovernmental
	RPR	Means-to-another-end	Europe-as-a-community-among-others	**Intergovernmental**
Germany	CDU/CSU†	**End-in-itself**	**Europe-as-a-political-community**	Supranational/ intergovernmental
	FDP†	**End-in-itself**	**Europe-as-a-political community**	**Intergovernmental/ supranational**
	SPD	**End-in-itself**	Europe-as-a-community-among-others	Supranational/ intergovernmental
	Greens	**End-in-itself**	Europe-as-a-community-among-others	Supranational/ intergovernmental

Notes
Core values in bold; † party/ies in government.

ruling parties. As a result, they made different ideologically structured demands and proposals. The British sought to reform NATO to become more political and to manage new security threats. In direct competition with this push for reforming NATO was the French government, which sought to endow the EC with a more political security policy, limiting NATO's mandate to collective defense. Bridging these antagonistic positions was the German proposal for "interlocking institutions." In the end, NATO was transformed and CFSP was created, but in a very vague fashion, which accommodated the competing visions of interlocking or autonomous institutions, allowing the direction of European security to be decided at a later date.

NATO's transformation at the end of the Cold War

In 1990, former NATO Secretary General Lord Carrington observed: "The structures of NATO are flexible enough to accommodate almost anything. Whether the countries of NATO are flexible enough to adjust themselves to what is happening is another matter" (quoted in Frankel 1990: A1). Indeed, strategic debates inside NATO regarding its functional and geographic scope were intensified with the end of the Cold War.[40] While every member state wanted to maintain the multilateral security structure, they disagreed about the purpose of the institution.

First steps toward collective security and France's opposition   With the Cold War coming to an end and the security climate changing, governments in Europe and North America started focusing on complex new risks to their peace and stability including ethnic and civil conflict, economic distress, the collapse of political order, and the proliferation of weapons of mass destruction. With broader security concerns gaining prominence, some NATO members sought to transform the Alliance so as to include complex crisis management, peace-building, comprehensive security and human security (Yost 1998: 1, 199–200; SIPRI 2005).[41] To negotiate the future of NATO, the first important summit after the end of the Cold War took place in London in July 1990. In

---

[40] NATO has stressed political aspects of security from its inception. These were subject also during the Cold War: for example, the Alliance renegotiated its mandate with the Harmel Report in 1967. Two functions were stressed: collective defense and détente in East–West relations. The report accommodated different ideological leanings of political parties in power at the time (Sloan 2003: 49).

[41] Large-scale reductions in US nuclear forces in Europe, based on the concept of extended deterrence, began in the late 1970s and increased from 1987 onward based on the Intermediate-range Nuclear Forces (INF) Treaty.

preparation for this meeting, some NATO member states had started work in different NATO committees to discuss a new nuclear strategy, a more politically oriented Alliance, and initiatives aimed at deepening the relationship with Eastern Europe (Cogan 2001: 32). In the 1990 London Declaration ("Declaration on a Transformed North Atlantic Alliance") member states agreed to "enhance the political component" of the Alliance. Article 2 of the North Atlantic Treaty from 1949 provided one such basis for transformation. "The Alliance declared itself, in effect, as much a political institution as an instrument for the collective defense of Western Europe" (Cogan 2001: 32). NATO confirmed that it no longer considered the Soviet Union and the Warsaw Pact as a threat and announced its interest in friendly diplomatic relations with them.[42] Furthermore, NATO stated that it can, as "an agent of change ... help build the structures of a more united continent, supporting security and stability with the strength of our shared faith in democracy, the rights of the individual, and the peaceful resolution of disputes" (London Declaration, par. 2).

The declaration precipitated a sharp disagreement between the US and French governments (Bozo 1991: 186–7; Lellouche 1991). The Mitterrand government sought to block NATO efforts to become more political, reflecting the PS understanding of NATO as an institution that should remain focused on collective defense (Gordon 1993: 169). For the French, a political role for NATO would enhance American control over European affairs and inhibit the extension of Europe-as-a-political-community. In the end, Mitterrand did not sign up to the July 1990 NATO summit decision despite the fact that the declaration also acknowledged developments toward European security efforts in the EC (Boniface 1997).[43]

Circumventing the French Socialists' ideological opposition As France sought to hinder or at least delay NATO transformation, other NATO members in favor of NATO's transformation, especially the British government, decided to act. Reformulated, NATO's purpose meant not only to change the strategic vision, but also adapting NATO's resources and military structures. In May 1991, the Major government secured the creation of a Alliance Rapid Reaction Corps (ARRC) with

[42] In November 1990, NATO and the Warsaw Pact signed the Treaty on Conventional Forces in Europe and a joint declaration on commitment to nonaggression.
[43] "The move within the European Community towards political union, including the development of a European identity in the domain of security, will also contribute to Atlantic solidarity and to the establishment of a just and lasting order of peace throughout the whole of Europe" (London Declaration 1990: par. 5).

the support of the American and German governments. This was part of NATO's shift in military strategy from positional defense based upon the Main Defense Forces to the other two already existing categories of NATO forces, Immediate and Rapid Reaction Forces and Augmentation Forces. The ARRC became a highly mobile fighting force under permanent British command and German command over the air component.[44] The British and German governments both valued NATO – though for different reasons – as a highly capable security institution. The German coalition government was in favor of NATO transformation to strengthen multilateral cooperation in general, while the British government wanted to make sure that its range of actions would not be constrained in the new security environment.

The French government, operating with a different notion of NATO's importance and purpose, opposed these reforms. From a PS perspective, by creating the ARRC, NATO was trying to appropriate new roles and missions by first creating the forces that would deal with them – bringing European forces under the aegis of NATO and US security policy instead of the EC – and thereby attempting to preempt the creation of a more autonomous European security institution (Fitchett 1991). The French government also rejected the more political turn of NATO and was against new consultative councils of NATO with former Warsaw Pact members (Riding 1992a, 1992b; Boniface 1996).

To circumvent French opposition, the British and the Americans conspired to switch decision-making bodies, moving discussions from the North Atlantic Council, where France had a veto, to the Defense Planning Committee (DPC), from which France had withdrawn under De Gaulle (Robin 1995; Cogan 2001: 54).[45] Second, they moved the date of the DPC meeting up to occur well in advance of the Maastricht Treaty Conclusions (Forster 1999: 113).[46] NATO's status quo had been changed with the initiation of the ARRC without France being able to halt the transformation.

---

[44] Also, NATO started to restructure its integrated command structure, reducing the number of major NATO commands. These changes were reinforced through institutional changes, as new political bodies were created (such as the Partnership for Peace and the Euro-Atlantic Partnership Council).

[45] The DPC was created in 1963 as co-equal to the NAC. The DPC was charged with NATO's core security business, including questions relating to Article V. In 1966, when France withdrew from NATO's integrated military structure, the DPC assumed responsibility. This allowed the Alliance to continue to function effectively, avoiding a French veto over matters related to NATO's core security mission (Robin 1995: 173).

[46] Some argue that the DPC meeting had been moved forward to reduce the European security initiative to a European pillar in NATO under American control (Dumoulin 1991: 69).

A year later, the call for transformation and a more political NATO was embraced in Rome in November 1991, where NATO's military strategy was under review. The meeting resulted in the *New Strategic Concept* on November 7. In the 1991 Rome Declaration, the Allies announced the construction of a new "security architecture" based on "interlocking institutions" that would "complement each other" (New Strategic Concept 1991: par. 3). It was also in Rome that President George H.W. Bush gave a hesitant green light to a European security initiative under the condition that it would not divide NATO (Mazzucelli 1997: 153). Cautious observers pointed out that these arrangements would be "inter-blocking" or "inter-knocking" rather than "interlocking" (Yost 2007).

Based on a liberal interpretation of Article 4 of the North Atlantic Treaty as "a catchall for other missions" (Cogan 2001: 51), the Strategic Concept defined new military roles and a more political identity for NATO, effectively putting the Alliance in the crisis management business. Based on the recognition that "the risks to Allied security that remain are multi-faceted in nature and multi-directional, which makes them hard to predict and assess" (New Strategic Concept 1991: par. 8), NATO developed new roles outside the range of actions that it originally acted upon and expanded on in the North Atlantic Treaty of 1949. These roles include peacekeeping, peace enforcement, crisis management and outright military intervention (non-Article V operations) for reasons not related to the common defense but to humanitarian or collective security ends. Based on this change in mandate, in June 1992 NATO foreign ministers formally declared that NATO was willing to support peacekeeping operations under the auspices of the CSCE and then later that year agreed to make troops and equipment available to the CSCE and the UN in their efforts to bring peace in former Yugoslavia. The guiding principle of NATO has remained "security is indivisible" (Rotfeld and Stützle 1991: 217–18), but its means to achieve these goals have changed.

To the British government, the NATO Rome Summit on November 7–8, 1991 was key to the preparation for the final phase of the EC's Maastricht negotiations. NATO's primacy was recognized by its members. It was a Conservative understanding of the situation that "responsibility should continue to belong to the Atlantic Alliance with its central British role and proven efficacy. The key element of the British strategy was, however, to secure the restructuring of the Alliance before the question of expanded EC defence competence could be considered" (Forster 1999: 111). It was the British understanding that by keeping the transformation of NATO ahead of the EC and CFSP, NATO would set the parameters for European efforts, ensuring that European efforts would remain subordinate to NATO.[47]

The creation of CFSP

Debates inside NATO resonated within the EC regarding the need and shape of a new European security institution. Member states in favor of Europe-as-a-political-community took the end of the Cold War as an opportunity to advance integration into a different domain, that of security, by using the events to demonstrate the benefits of an autonomous European security institution. International events such as the disintegration of the USSR

> shaped the immediate context and parallel nature of the IGCs [Intergovernmental Conference] on EMU [Economic and Monetary Union] and political union. But these events did not directly affect the content of the IGCs, which were concerned with an existing West European agenda and took little account of the implications of changes in Central and Eastern Europe. In this sense Maastricht was a backward-looking treaty. (Forster 1999: 2)

Nonetheless, or, indeed, because European security cooperation did not originate from a functional need-based standpoint, these proposals met opposition from governments whose security ideologies were at odds with this European vision.

French President Mitterrand and German Chancellor Kohl, who had been in favor of greater foreign and security cooperation in Europe even before German reunification (Riding 1991b; Mazzucelli 1997: 47), took the initiative.[48] Indicative of this political will is that, at Kohl's and Mitterrand's first bilateral meeting, they committed to implement the long-dormant defense clause of the 1963 Elysée Treaty. In July 1987, Kohl suggested a French–German brigade (4,200 troops), which came into being in January 1988 under the newly created French–German Defense and Security Council. Sophie-Caroline de Margerie, Mitterrand's advisor on European questions at the time, says a European security institution signified "a will to give Europe a political dimension in which defense is a component."[49] These views were rooted in the PS's

[47] As an observer at the time said, "By announcing radical changes in NATO's military structure in response to a sharply reduced Soviet threat, the Western alliance has simultaneously sought to forestall moves by the European Community to develop an independent defense capability" (Riding 1991a: A3). Or at least some of the NATO members had this intention.

[48] Sophie de Margerie organized meetings between the *Elysée*, *Matignon* and *Quai D'Orsay*. Politicians facilitating this coordination task from the same party led to very little domestic constraint in the formulation of French foreign and security policy. Interview with Sophie-Caroline de Margerie in Paris (May 29, 2008).

[49] Interview with Sophie-Caroline de Margerie in Paris (May 29, 2008).

political ideology. To Mitterrand, both capabilities and the symbolism of autonomy from NATO mattered.[50] However, he also had another pet European project that had been in preparation for a longer time period: the EMU, Mitterrand's "primordial objective" (Bozo 2005: 304; see also Mazzucelli 1997: 36ff.).[51] Just after the Berlin Wall fell, the EC member states met at the European Council in Strasbourg in December 1989, where they decided to have an IGC on EMU in late 1990, prioritizing monetary cooperation before turning to security.[52]

Bilateral Franco-German initiatives and British ideological opposition   With an IGC on EMU secured, Kohl and Mitterrand turned their attention to foreign and security policy. Based on a Franco-German initiative – two letters addressed to the EC presidencies dated April 19, 1990 and December 6, 1990[53] – the EC members began negotiations on whether to have an IGC on political union, including a common foreign and security policy (Cornish 1996: 756).[54]

The Franco-German letters advanced the notion of a federal Europe based on the values of Europe-as-a-political-community and supranationalism, which Kohl's Christian Democratic party as well as the French Socialists valued, signaling that European integration and community-building go hand-in-hand and should be indivisible (Mazzucelli 1997: 17; Bitterlich 2005; Bozo 2005: 304–5). On November 28, 1989, Kohl addressed the Bundestag proclaiming, "the future architecture of Germany must be fitted into the future architecture of Europe" (quoted in Dinan 1999: 131). At the first party congress

[50] Mitterrand presented his rather exclusive idea of Europe on December 31, 1989 and then officially in Prague in June 1991. His European confederation idea proposed an association agreement with Central and Eastern European states but not full EC membership (Cogan 2001: 7). This proposal failed (Bozo 2005: 303).

[51] Chirac argued in favor of a common currency, but against a single currency, because a single currency would lead to transfers of sovereignty to the EC level.

[52] In general, in preparation for an IGC, the national representatives to the EC/EU meet once a week, the ministers once a month, and the heads of state twice a semester. Because of the negotiations surrounding German reunification, Germany asked to postpone the date of the IGC until after the German general elections in November 1990. As a result, they started in December, though Mitterrand had hoped that they would start at the beginning of 1990 (Mazzucelli 1997: 45).

[53] The letters are reproduced in Laursen and Vanhoonacker (1992).

[54] It was not the first time that a German and French government tried to push for an European security institution. In 1987, they had wanted to reactivate the WEU (Gordon 1993: 146). Until then, the WEU was cast in the form of a dependent relationship to NATO; some called the WEU a "shadow alliance" (Schell 1991). The WEU "Platform for European Security Interests" issued in The Hague in 1987 considered two options for the WEU: either as the European pillar inside NATO or the nucleus for an EU security and defense institution. It was then that NATO and WEU moved into "latent competition" (Schmidt 1992: 215). However, the British government disagreed with the proposal and the reactivation failed.

of the reunited CDU/CSU in 1991, he noted that "German unity and European unity are two sides of the same coin" (quoted in Markovits and Reich 1997: 45). At the same time, Kohl insisted that the initiative was not against NATO in any way (Kohl 1992: 77; Mazzucelli 1997: 197; Sarotte 2010: 113).[55] The CDU/CSU and FDP both regarded NATO and European integration as complementary processes. Mitterrand and his PS supported the federal view of Europe and stayed silent in regard to NATO. France's Europe Minister Elisabeth Guigou saw the letters as a sign to "march towards a federal Europe" (Wall 2008: 123). However, "although Mitterrand advocated a federal Europe in his joint letter with Kohl, he was no doubt aware of the danger in pushing the idea too fast and too far" (Mazzucelli 1997: 160). In the end, on June 26, 1990, the other EC member states officially endorsed the proposal agreeing to negotiate a second IGC with the aim of a political union (IGC-PU) at the European Council in Dublin in June 1990; the conference started in parallel with the EMU conference in Rome in December 1990 (Lequesne 1998: 141).

In Britain, the Conservatives did not welcome this Franco-German proposal, a reflection of their skepticism of Brussels and the European community idea (Wall 2008: 96). Prime Minister Thatcher asked the Foreign Office to come up with British counterproposals making sure that nothing would weaken the role of NATO (Gamble 1998: 22; Wall 2008: 97). "I had at least put down a marker against the sort of proposals" (Thatcher quoted in Wall 2008: 98). The British government argued that the European agenda was already full enough (Forster 1999: 6). Trying to get the British government on his side, Mitterrand argued that European integration would be one way of embedding a unified Germany though Thatcher remained unconvinced. Her party's understanding of the EU was informed by a realist understanding of international institutions. While the French Socialist government perceived Germany as an integral part of Europe, Thatcher argued that further deepening of the EU would instead provide Germany with more tools to dominate Europe (Wall 2008: 96). Furthermore, Thatcher's reaction is indicative that not every international institution of which the UK is member is valued in the same way; they all are means to various ends and security policy has already been effectively addressed in NATO.

The beginning of the IGC and the unraveling of ideological disagreements   The negotiations that culminated in the Maastricht Treaty

---

[55] Interview with Sophie-Caroline de Margerie in Paris (May 29, 2008).

took place over the course of one year, between December 1990 and December 1991. They were composed of two distinct elements: an Intergovernmental Conference on Economic and Monetary Union (IGC-EMU) and an Intergovernmental Conference on Political Union (IGC-PU) both of which led to the Maastricht European Council in December 1991.[56] The IGC on political union, which opened in December 1990, began acrimoniously. The Presidency Conclusion (under the Italian presidency) that launched the IGC-PU ended "for the first and only time in the history of the EC ... with one member state, the UK, dissenting via a separate footnote" (Wall 2008: 106). Thatcher announced, "What is being proposed ... is the back door to a federal Europe, which we totally and utterly reject" (quoted in Wall 2008: 106). Since an IGC can be convened with a simple majority, the IGC was nonetheless launched on December 15, 1990.

Around the same time, Thatcher failed to pass the first leadership ballot at the Conservative Party convention and resigned.[57] John Major was then elected leader and became prime minister. While Major might have changed the British style of negotiating with his European partners, he remained skeptical of Europe and sought to preserve British sovereignty, reflecting his party's majority ideological position (Major 1993; Ludlam 1998: 52; Wall 2008: 115). The change in political style between Thatcher and Major was not sufficient to obscure the fundamental difference between the British government and its partners on the substance of policy under discussion at the IGCs. As Major said:

I shared many of her concerns. I recoiled at the prospect of a "federal" Europe. I was deeply suspicious of political union. I did not wish to ditch sterling. I believed the conditions the Social Chapter sought to impose would add to employers' costs and push up unemployment. I did not wish to see a more powerful Commission. I did believe that it was right to enlarge the Community and bring in the nation states of Central Europe. (Major 1999: 266)

The Conservatives therefore continued to negotiate "without any commitment to closer European integration" (Forster 1999: 180).

Major was hardly in power when Mitterrand approached him in January 1991 regarding an autonomous European security institution. Mitterrand tried to convince the new prime minister that the UK should join France and Germany in the endeavor of creating a European security

---

[56] Political union encompasses a wide array of issues such as enlarging the scope of the EC's competencies, in social or security policy, as well as institutional questions regarding the role of different EC and national actors.

[57] Her autocratic style figured prominently in her downfall (Forster 1999: 26). For the differences in style between Thatcher and Major see comments made by Sir Charles Powell quoted in Junor (1993: 209–10).

institution within the EC, recalls Major's Private Secretary for Foreign Affairs, Stephen Wall (Wall 2008: 115). Mitterrand wanted to bring the WEU – and especially the WEU's military assets and capabilities – within the EC treaties, but Major could not accept this. Instead, he insisted on an arrangement whereby the WEU would remain an appendix to NATO. "Britain wanted to build up a European capability through WEU but under the NATO umbrella. Mitterrand said WEU should be alongside NATO with bridges between the two organisations" (Wall 2008: 116). In the end, as Stephen Wall recalls, the ideological differences between the French and British governments of the time were too large (Wall 2008: 116). Instead, in February 1991 a letter by Foreign Ministers Dumas (France) and Genscher (Germany) called for close association between the WEU and the Union (Mazzucelli 1997: 138, 153).

At the same time, US Secretary of State James Baker drew attention to US concerns about the relations between the European Community and NATO. He asked that discussions should begin regarding a common foreign and security policy between the Community and those NATO countries that were not members of the Community (de Schoutheete de Tervarent 1997). US concerns resonated with British and Italian initiatives. After NATO had agreed to the ARRC, and after a British–Italian proposal suggested that a non-permanent European rapid reaction force subordinate to NATO could be created to act where NATO could not (Mazzucelli 1997: 152; Forster 1999: 117).

In October 1991 the French and German governments reacted in detailed proposals in a third letter. This letter pushed for the creation of CFSP and the creation of military assets within the EC. The proposed Eurocorps would lay the foundations for a WEU structure outside NATO and move the WEU's capabilities beyond its common defense commitment. As the letter described it, the WEU would become "an integral component of the European unification process" and, over time, the "defence component of the Union" (Wall 2008: 127). Furthermore, its declared objective was to "strengthen the Atlantic alliance overall by reinforcing the role and responsibility of the Europeans and by creating a European pillar in their midst" (Wall 2008: 127; see also Forster 1999). Especially, this last position reflects the German Christian-Democratic government's leaning toward supporting as many multilateral endeavors as possible.

The US government approached France with its concerns on the issue of military control of the proposed European rapid-deployment force at a visit of Secretary of Defense Richard B. Cheney with Mitterrand. Cheney presented the US view that such a force should be designed to strengthen, not weaken, the role of NATO as the pre-eminent regional military entity. Separable, but not separate, was the US attitude. However, Mitterrand and his senior cabinet ministers stated that they preferred placing a new European crisis-reaction force under control of the EC (Smith 1991b: A15). France consented to paying lip service to the Alliance, while the Germans sought reassurance of NATO's and Eurocorps' compatibility.[58] In the end, the commitment to the Atlantic Alliance remained vague, reflecting disagreements between the French and German governments over the importance of NATO.

Observing these disagreements, and reading between the lines, the British government was alarmed by the third Franco-German letter. The Conservatives saw these proposals as deliberate double-speak: endorsing NATO while setting up something new inside the yet-to-be-created EU that, in practice, would undermine NATO. Major wrote to Mitterrand expressing his concerns, particularly regarding the extent to which the proposed CFSP would undermine NATO as the primary security institution in Europe. The letter reflected the Conservatives' ideology informed by the core values of sovereignty in combination with multilateralism-as-a-means-to-another-end. Major addressed his primary concerns and dislike of European policy-making, especially that (1) the proposal suggested that CFSP would cover all questions of security and defense of the EU, (2) the WEU should be the executive arm of the EU exclusively, excluding institutional links to NATO and that the WEU would not be autonomous from the Council of Ministers and (3) that NATO obligations were hardly mentioned (Wall 2008: 127–8).

The discussion on a specific policy domain was paralleled by a much larger discussion about the general institutional structure of the yet-to-be-created European Union that exposed differences between the three major governments regarding the values of sovereignty and Europe. The Luxembourg presidency of the first half of 1991 proposed to create a "temple": a three-pillar structure, where different actors influence and different rules would apply to the three policy areas of the

---

[58] Eurocorps was not created under the aegis of the EC or WEU but was nonetheless officially launched at the French-German summit at La Rochelle, May 21–22, 1992, as a bilateral institution that was joined later by Belgium, Spain and Luxembourg. German Defense Minister Volker Rühe said in a speech to German officers in Leipzig that "the fact that no German soldiers will be withdrawn from their NATO assignment shows that the buildup of European security structures is taking place with, and not against, NATO" (quoted in Drozdiak 1992: A31). At the insistence of the German government, the French government agreed in January 1993 that the Eurocorps would be placed under NATO command should a military crisis arise in Europe. This is known as the Lanxade-Naumann-Shalikashvili agreement. Interview with Joachim Bitterlich in Berlin (October 23, 2006).

EU including: (1) EC, (2) foreign and security policy and (3) justice and home affairs. Opposed to this largely intergovernmental proposal was a vision of a more supranational EU as a "tree": an organic inter-connectedness of all policy areas, which also meant that the EP, the Commission and ECJ would have a say in all policy domains. All policies would be dealt with under the Community structures in which the Commission had the (sole) right of initiative, and in which the EP would play its full part with the arbiter of the law being the ECJ. Kohl was in favor of this supranational "tree" vision (Mazzucelli 1997: 137; Forster 1999: 13; Bitterlich 2005).[59] However, it was anathema to the British government.

Douglas Hurd stressed that

Some of our partners tried to argue that an effective common foreign policy could only be achieved by the adoption of more qualified majority voting, a decisive role for the Commission, possible recourse to the European Court of Justice, and greater power to the European Parliament ... A text incorporating proposals for a CFSP along these lines was put forward by the presidency in September 1991, close to the final stages of the negotiation. The UK argued successfully ... against this approach. (Hurd 1994: 422)

The Conservatives insisted that if there was a mention of foreign and security policy, it would be outside the Treaty of Rome, which estab-lished the EC and supranational structures, repeating that CFSP could not be in competition with NATO (Gordon 1997/8). "Defence was to become a key British preoccupation as the Maastricht dead-line approached" (Wall 2008: 124). "One cannot understand the shape of the Treaty without understanding the role of Britain in the negoti-ations" (Forster 1999: 1) and the British government at the time was committed to preventing the merger between the WEU and EU from happening. Major held a Commons debate on November 20, 1991 to gain approval for his negotiation stance. "The debate worked well" (Major 1999: 274) and the Cabinet approved the position on December 5. As a result, the British:

political method of doing business, of refusing to accept linkages between dif-ferent policy sectors and accepting concessions from others, by refusing to give anything in return, the style was clearly awkward. A key problem was that there were few positive goals that the government wanted to achieve and there

---

[59] During the entire negotiation period, the German Chancellor's office kept close con-tact with the Auswärtiges Amt (Foreign Ministry). "The Chancellor's office provided Genscher's personal representative, Ambassador Jürgen Trumpf, with general guide-lines on German administrative positions as he negotiated in Brussels" (Mazzucelli 1997: 79).

was virtually nothing on either IGC agenda to attract the government. (Forster 1999: 179)

The French, having a more evolutionary view of the EU, adopted a position somewhere in between. It favored the mentioning of "federal vocation" in the treaty and had supported Germany's call for more rights to EU institutions. With France in a pivotal position it "could tilt the balance of the negotiations either way" (Mazzucelli 1997: 144; see also Mazzucelli 1997: 80, 151; Lequesne 1998: 147). Mitterrand therefore struck a compromise with the British government whereby the more intergovernmental model was adopted that in Mitterrand's view could later be integrated further. Kohl, though he aspired for more, agreed to the condition that the decision be reviewed in five years, codified in Article N, which called for a stocktaking of existing procedures and policies (Lequesne 1998: 146; Forster 1999: 15).

The Maastricht Treaty: no robust CFSP   The negotiations ended in December 1991. The treaty was signed on February 7, 1992, and the final ratification took place in Germany on October 12, 1993. The ratification in France, for example, was indicative of the different ideological stances of the major parties toward Europe. It was problematic because the treaty needed constitutional revision due to its infringement on national sovereignty. The RPR was against many clauses of the Treaty. Alain Juppé, the party's secretary general, argued along sovereignist lines (Davidson 1992; see also Chevallier *et al.* 2007: 386–8). However, the treaty passed in the National Assembly and Senate with Gaullist abstentions (Mazzucelli 1997: 208–16), and in the national referendum (Mazzucelli 1997: 221).

In the end, the Maastricht Treaty created an institutional framework for three different policy complexes: first, the EC, second, CFSP, and third, Justice and Home Affairs (JHA). CFSP represented the lowest common ideologically-bound denominator amongst the divergent ideologies of governments in power in the three major European states.[60] Each government was forced to compromise; each was pushed as far as their party ideologies would allow – but no farther. The main actors at the time could not agree on which institutions should be responsible for

---

[60] The already existing EPC was being institutionalized as the "F" dimension in CFSP, with F standing for foreign policy (M. Smith 2004), but the "S" dimension covering security and defense remained underdeveloped (Delors 1997: vii). European foreign policy goes beyond the declaratory diplomacy of the weakly institutionalized European Political Cooperation (EPC) toward action by institutionalizing a new policy instrument, i.e. joint actions and common positions (Holland 1997: 1; Müller and van Dassen 1997; Forster and Wallace 2000).

multilateral use of force or on the extent to which a European security institution would impinge on their sovereignty. As a result, European security policy in the form of CFSP received declaratory mention in the treaty. The security dimension of CFSP remained little more than a symbolic institution, modest in scope. In the coming years, CFSP would be responsible for such issues as the EU's non-proliferation policy supporting the renewal of the NPT, arms control, joint action on limits of exports of dual-use goods, the administration of Mostar and the training of Palestinian police forces.[61]

In terms of the predictions of my theory, the security dimension of CFSP is far from robust. "It lacks a clearly defined objective, measurement criteria to achieve it, a timetable for institutional change, sanctions for defectors, and a central bureaucracy with a firm mandate for its operations" (Smith 1998: 150; see also Ginsberg 1997: 12–14). On the one hand, the EC member states were pushed beyond European *foreign* policy-making, granting the EU inclusion of *security* policy in its mandate. The security dimension of CFSP found its first ratified juridical foundation in Title V of the Treaty. "The common foreign and security policy shall include all questions related to the security of the European Union, including the framing of a common defence policy, which might in time lead to a common defence" (Maastricht Treaty 1992: Title V, Article J4). The language suggests that neither overall objectives and principles for the conduct of the EU's external relations, nor the competencies of the different institutions, have been precisely stated.

As Douglas Hurd, British Secretary of State for Foreign and Commonwealth Affairs at the time of Maastricht, put it:

it is obvious that on defence matters CFSP was at Maastricht only able to come up with a compromise. The key sentence (in Article J4) refers to the inclusion in CFSP of "the eventual framing of a common defence policy which might in time lead to a common defence". These words were the result of much debate and argument. Some member states wanted to go much further and faster in the development of a defence element in the European Union, while others argued against any mention of defence. The Treaty leaves the question open. It refers to a common defence policy but makes clear that it is a long way off, *and the prospects of a common defence may only follow if all member states agree to it in the*

---

[61] In the five years after the treaty's ratification, the EU established over 25 common positions, joint declarations and about 40 joint actions such as supervising elections in South Africa and Russia, delivering aid to the Palestinian authority, organizing humanitarian aid in Bosnia, and negotiating and implementing the Stability Pact to ensure stability in Eastern Europe (European Commission 1997: 18–20; Ginsberg 1997: 18–22).

future. In the meantime, the treaty also makes clear that any European Union policy on security issues should be compatible with NATO policy. NATO remains vital to ensuring European security and stability. (Hurd 1994: 425–6, emphasis added)[62]

The treaty mentions the newly created Union's interest in pursuing common defense (Maastricht Treaty 1992: Title V, Article J4.1) but did not provide the EU with its own military capabilities to act since the Franco-German proposal to merge the WEU with the EU failed.[63] The British Conservative government vetoed the merger, deeming the endeavor dangerous "inasmuch as it could put trans-Atlantic solidarity and the functioning of NATO at risk" (de Schoutheete de Tervarent 1997: 50; see also Major 1999: 264). As a result, the Dutch presidency redrafted clauses pertaining to CFSP's relationship with NATO indicating the compatibility of the two and that the eventual framing of a common defense would be subject to an evaluation (Mazzucelli 1997: 187). The British concession about "eventual framing" was sufficiently nuanced to guarantee a national veto. The Franco-German proposal regarding an autonomous security institution was completely watered down.

In terms of human and institutional resources, CFSP inherited the foreign policy structures of the EPC secretariat (Nuttall 2000: 251) and witnessed the establishment of the Commission's Directorate-General IA (later DG RELEX) with a nucleus of approximately 200 staff (Nuttall 2000: 255), as well as an immediate staffing freeze (Duke 2006: 9). The CFSP Secretariat in the Council started out with 27 staff members (one staff member from each member state plus permanent Council staff) (M. Smith 2004: 188). Directorate

---

[62] Other observers agree with Hurd: the result at Maastricht "was the best offer available at the moment and for the near future" (Wessels 1994: 446). The "ambiguities of the overall text ... a product of a diplomatic and political bargaining process" (Wessels 1994: 448). In regard to CFSP, one observes "European defense identity was made explicit, albeit in a conditional fashion, at the Maastricht Summit on December 9–10, 1991" (Cogan 2001: 55). Others call it an "unsatisfactory compromise" (Holland 1997: 1). Hurd himself calls it a "nebulous concept" (Hurd 1994: 421).

[63] From the EU perspective, the WEU was described as "an integral part of the development of the Union" and can be requested "to elaborate and implement decisions and actions of the Union which have defence implications." It is also said that the EU "shall respect the obligations of certain Member States under the North Atlantic Treaty and be compatible with the common security and defence policy established within that framework." The WEU foreign ministers were meeting at the margins of the European Council under the presidency of Genscher. They welcomed the EU initiative but announced that they would act "in conformity with the positions adopted in the Atlantic Alliance" (WEU Secretariat General 1991) indicating that the WEU was seen as both the defense component of the European Union and as the means to strengthen the European pillar of the Atlantic Alliance (WEU 1991).

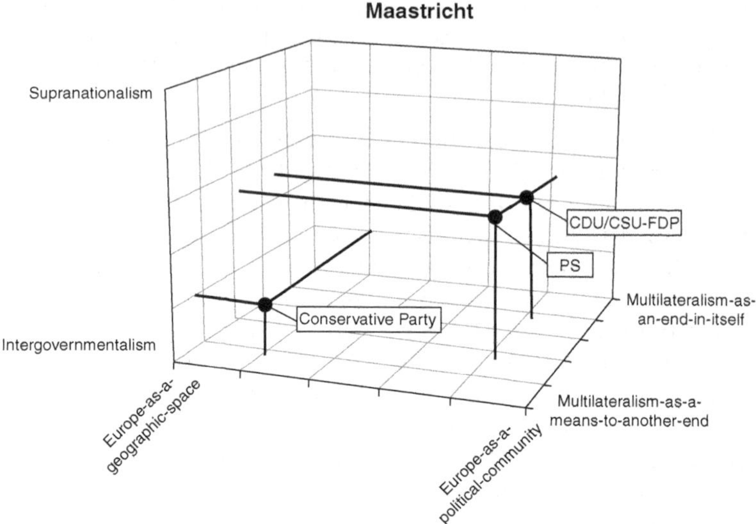

Figure 4.1 Degree of ideological congruence, 1990

General E (External Relations) was placed under a Director General. Two branches were under his control: external economic relations and CFSP (Nuttall 2000: 251). This number would not grow significantly (except for accommodating seconded staff from the new member states 1995) until the Cologne decisions at the end of the decade (Smith 1998: 158).

This weak institutionalization can be explained by the minimal ideological congruence among the major actors across core security values (see Figure 4.1). As Hurd says, only an "intergovernmental process based on consensus" is possible (Hurd 1994: 421).[64] The Major government stayed true to the sovereignist and NATO tendencies of the Conservative Party, resisting the formal subordination of the WEU to NATO. "Cooperation in these areas, yes; compulsion, no" (Major 1999: 274). And Major went on to say, "It [the Maastricht Treaty]

[64] In addition, as a reflection of its skeptical view toward Europe and insistence upon national sovereignty, the British government also opted out of EMU and the Social Chapter. "Conservative governments had spent years ending restrictive practices, promoting supply-side policies and forcing businesses to take decisions to promote their profitability. I did not wish to see all this wrecked by the job-destroying legislation that coalition governments across the Community had inflicted on their electorates" (Major 1999: 273).

kept foreign and security policy where it belonged, in NATO and with individual nation states" (Major 1999: 363).

Joachim Bitterlich, Kohl's Europe and security advisor, recalled that the German government was disappointed, given how short CFSP fell of German aims.[65] It was disappointed about the negotiation results as it thought that it had proven its transatlantic credentials enough to be trusted by the British on issues of European integration. Showing how the participants themselves recognized the importance of parties, Kohl hoped that with new governments in power, particularly since Neil Kinnock's Labour Party showed greater interest in Europe,[66] a more communitarian EU could be negotiated.[67] Kohl also believed that the integration momentum would lead to a more robust CFSP at the next round of IGC negotiations, a prediction that would prove incorrect (Kohl 2007: 387). Arguing along the same line, German political scientist Wolfgang Wessels suggested that things might change with new political leaders in office (Wessels 1994: 447, 454). But it was not just the British Conservatives that stymied a more supranational EU. Based on different priorities regarding multilateralism, the German Christian-Democratic and French Socialist governments also could not agree amongst themselves about what role NATO should play in European security (Mazzucelli 1997: 140). Yet serious European security efforts could not move forward until there was agreement on what to do with the Alliance.[68] The Franco-German disagreement was overshadowed by British opposition and the fact that Kohl and Mitterrand were committed to a very similar idea of Europe. Kohl was reassured by the Socialist intention to further European integration which also favored giving up sovereignty to the European level.

For the French, as for the German government, CFSP was a disappointment. Mitterrand argued that while the creation of an autonomous

[65] Interview with Joachim Bitterlich in Berlin (October 23, 2006).

[66] Labour had voted against the Maastricht Treaty in the House of Commons especially because of the British opt-out of the Social Chapter (Forster 1999: 170; Wall 2008: 164). Neil Kinnock (Labour), in the House of Commons, criticized the UK government's role in signing the Maastricht Treaty arguing that the conservatives were "a double opt-out government … has isolated Britain on most vital issues of economic and monetary union and the social charter" (quoted in Wall 2008: 137). This reflects Labour's ideological stance that values not only sovereignty but also multilateralism-as-an-end-in-itself.

[67] Interview with Joachim Bitterlich in Berlin (October 23, 2006). The 1992 general elections in the UK were on the horizon and Labour seemed to have had a good chance at the time of Maastricht to win the elections.

[68] Interview with Hubert Védrine in Paris (May 29, 2008). Védrine describes *l'état d'esprit* of Mitterrand and the Socialist Party as wanting to advance European integration, but as being blocked by the UK and a hesitant Germany when it comes to security and defense.

European security institution was "inevitable" in the long run, it did not seem "imminent" (quoted in Gordon 1993: 178). Mitterrand's "long run" would last until 1998, when the British and French governments initiated, in Saint Malo, the creation of an ESDP autonomous from NATO.

Alternative explanations

Existing theories provide different explanations for CFSP. Below, I focus first on the partisan values explanation before I look at the realist and institutionalist readings of the end of the Cold War and its implications for European security, arguing that all theories fail to explain the outcome adequately and leave important aspects of the case unaddressed.

The importance of conceptualizing ideology based on the various interpretations and relationships of multilateralism, sovereignty and Europe can be underscored by looking at the weaknesses of an approach resting on a single dimension of policy contestation. By narrowing the focus to a single dimension of equality versus liberty, Rathbun (2004) cannot capture the choices parties have made between different multilateral forums. There are few political parties in Europe that favor unilateral security policy, a policy position that is informed by the value liberty. The differences concern the forums – whether NATO, the EC/EU, or both, as well as the kind of cooperation (intergovernmental or supranational). Multilateralism, sovereignty and Europe are variably core values for different parties and in different configurations.

As the preceding discussion has shown, both "left" and "right" can support European cooperation. Both the Conservatives and the CDU/CSU are parties considered to be on the right (Marks and Steenbergen 2004); however, the German CDU/CSU was much closer aligned to the French PS than to the British Conservatives when it came to European security. This policy stance cannot be understood without dissecting the ideology into several dimensions. Also, while the PS favors multilateral cooperation, it does not do so in all political forums. Again, this policy preference cannot simply be captured by looking at equality or liberty. In both cases, the value of Europe-as-a-political-community is a core value apart from the left–right dimension (Andersen and Evans 2003: 171; Sauger 2003: 109–10; van der Brug and van der Eijk 2007; Parsons and Weber 2011). And the Conservatives' antipathy to Europe also is independent from their willingness to cooperate multilaterally in security institutions outside of Europe.

The one-dimensional emphasis on liberty equality and the neglect of the wider international institutional environment in which political parties act is particularly problematic in light of NATO because European

efforts take place in the shadow of this already-existing security institution. Liberty motivates exclusive, sovereignist and often unilateral
security policies. In a world with several international institutions, this
value's policy recommendation is indeterminate. The research program
around regime complexity has shown that governments that favor liberty could use additional international institutions in the same policy
domain to increase their range of action through forum shopping (Alter
and Meunier 2006, 2009). Additional international institutions can be
seen not as constraining governments, but instead as giving them more
liberty. At the same time, liberty might recommend avoiding participation in international institutions. As we have seen, parties known to
be on the right, such as the British Conservatives, are neither in favor
of overlapping European and transatlantic security institutions, nor do
they favor unilateralism in the sphere of security policy. In the realm of
European security policy, their policy position can only be captured by
analyzing several core values.

Realist arguments draw attention to the distribution of capabilities
and US power, in particular. They hinge on two explanations for CFSP.
The first is that it represented an initial attempt to "soft-balance" against
the United States in a unipolar international system in order to provide
Europeans greater autonomy (Art 2005/6; Pape 2005; Paul 2005; Jones
2007: 33, 55).[69] There are three problems with this argument. First,
realists themselves are unable to agree on whether the international
system was indeed unipolar, especially in 1991 before the USSR collapsed (Krauthammer 1990/1; Mearsheimer 1990; Mastanduno 1997;
Wohlforth 1999). Second, as I have shown, only the French proposed
policies that could be perceived as "soft balancing," and even here
the Mitterrand government wanted the United States to maintain its
presence in Europe for collective defense. Moreover, the French push
for autonomy from the US-dominated NATO alliance was rooted in
Socialist ideologies rather than changes in the balance of capabilities
at the international level. The British and the Germans, on the other
hand, worked to frustrate French ambitions to curb both NATO's transformation into the more political domain of crisis management, and
an autonomous European security institution that would compromise NATO's role in European security. As a weak institution, CFSP
lacked the substance to (soft-)balance against the United States. A third
problem is that, far from aggregating power, European states under-
took troop reductions that totaled half a million personnel (Wallander

---

[69] At the turn of the decade, Mearsheimer (1990) presented yet another hypothesis
arguing that Europeans would renationalize to balance against each other.

2000: 718; Waltz 2000: 27), in the process increasing their dependence on US forces in crisis management; Europe's inability to handle the Bosnian civil war reinforces this point.

A related realist argument is that US disengagement increased the security dilemma in Europe. A reunified Germany, no longer kept down by the Americans, engendered fears in other European states. European states could no longer depend on American forces to maintain the peace and keep Germany "enmeshed in a security institution" (Jones 2007: 84). "There was an important cost to relying on NATO: it was unclear how long the United States would remain in Europe" (Jones 2007: 83; see also US Defense Department 1993).[70] Germany needed to be "tied in" (Gordon 1997/8: 85), according to this binding argument, and the solution was CFSP. These authors also note that Germany itself wanted to assure its European (though apparently not American) allies of its good intentions.

This argument fails to account for the Bush administration's strong rhetoric as well as policy proposals submitted to NATO to start transformation. President Bush was critical of an autonomous European security institution. His administration perceived NATO as the primary foundation of European security and as an institution that would allow the United States to remain pre-eminent in European security – as expressed in the Bartholomew memorandum (Schweller 2001: 181; Sarotte 2010: 112–13). When the US government got ready for the NATO Rome Summit in 1991, Reginald Bartholomew and James Dobbins sent a memorandum in February 1991 to the European allies warning them against duplication and the development of an independent force, and presenting the Europeans with a list of "dos and don'ts" regarding the development of a European security institution (Lambert 1991; Usborne 1991; Duke 1994: 172). Madeleine Albright would echo this letter after the Franco-British Saint Malo meeting that launched ESDP in the beginning of 1999. Later in 1991, Bush said, "If your ultimate aim is to provide independently for your own defense, then the time to tell us is today" (quoted in Buchan 1993: 155). The United States was worried about the potential for a more action-oriented European voice outside of NATO that would undermine the transatlantic coherence in security matters.[71] Early on, the Bush administration had a clear

---

[70] The US congressional elections of 1994 reinforced European fears of American neo-isolationism in that they ushered in a Republican majority and Senator Jesse Helms appointed as chair of the Senate Foreign Relations committee.

[71] Interview with Robert Hutchings, former Director for European Affairs in the National Security Council, in Princeton (February 21, 2007). There were nuances in expressing skepticism: Secretary of State James Baker was more in favor of a pro-EC

conception of the European security architecture and the continued political and military role of the United States therein.[72] The realist argument also ignores the fact that US force reductions were a commonly agreed-upon policy. Moreover, as mentioned, the Europeans also reduced their forces, including those governments that should have had the most to fear from a potentially revanchist German power. Most fundamentally, this argument disregards the institutional outcome of a weak CFSP. If European governments truly sought to bind Germany, why did they not create a more binding institution? The British government was more than hesitant in creating CFSP and instead pushed hard for NATO transformation, thereby mirroring the US government's policy position within the EC. As a result, CFSP did not become robust, binding, or equipped with any meaningful military hardware – and it had not become a robust institution even though strategic uncertainty was at its peak.

A second explanation rooted in IR comes from rational choice institutionalists. As the preceding pages have laid out, the international environment in which the United States and European states found themselves was greatly changed during the course of two years. New security threats and related cooperation problems arose. However, national governments did not act in the most cost-efficient way, either adapting one already existing institution or creating a new one to face the challenge. Instead, both paths were pursued half-heartedly.

In terms of NATO, the rational choice institutionalist argument begins with the premise that NATO members perceived the need for the continued existence of a transatlantic security organization. NATO had the general institutional assets to adapt to the changing international environment, transforming from a collective defense institution into a crisis management institution – something ignored by realist analysis. Though CFSP does not factor into the most prominent application of

line while Secretary of Defense Richard Cheney was more pro-NATO and wanted to make sure that any European attempt to create another security institution would be placed under NATO authority (Mastanduno 1997: 68; Forster 1999: 112). Secretary of Defense Cheney said about CFSP that it could come into existence "with the caveat that we are not interested in ... anything that's going to undermine NATO" (quoted in Smith 1991a: A27). The Pentagon pushed harder for this line than the Presidency and the State Department, though the latter two shared similar concerns. What exactly would undermine NATO was not defined. Interview with Karsten Voigt in Berlin (October 23, 2007). Over the next decade the United States would remain hostile, or at best ambivalent, regarding European security cooperation outside NATO.

[72] Reagan was much more attentive to keeping good relations with the USSR. Bush gave more attention to allies (and is therefore called the strongest Atlanticist since Truman, or maybe Kennedy).

this rational choice institutionalist approach to European security, a set of logical implications can be derived from Celeste Wallander's (2000) account of NATO's transformation.

Wallander (2000) and Suh (2007: 175, 183) argue that NATO has been the most attractive security institution after the end of the Cold War because of its sunk costs and adaptability.[73] For a new institution to be created, it would have had to offer lower costs than NATO or tackle new cooperation problems. Suh argues that NATO persisted "because the rationalistic, economistic criterion … values the efficiency gains resulting from asset specificities over the costs of maintaining the alliance" (2007: 185). The Bush administration had encouraged the development of a European security identity within the transatlantic Alliance. In a speech in East Berlin on December 12, 1989, Secretary of State James Baker spoke of a new European political architecture and a new Atlanticism, with a NATO that was to be more political. Baker assured the Europeans that the United States had no interest in NATO either going away or simply concentrating on a collective defense mandate that looked less relevant as the Soviet threat was reduced (Bozo 1999: 593; Cogan 2001: 27). Instead, he made clear that the US government continued to perceive NATO as the pre-eminent security institution in Europe, arguing at the same time that NATO should transform from a mainly military alliance to a more political one (Friedman 1989). For these reasons, and writing as late as 2000 and 2007, Wallander and Suh argue that no alternative to NATO has emerged – ignoring CFSP and ESDP.

CFSP, however, was created. It reflects the fact that some European governments, particularly the French and German, sought to create a new institution despite no functional need. Rather than reintegrating into NATO in the interests of efficiency, or building a new institution inside NATO to increase coordination, the French and German governments sought to construct a new institution and were willing to incur the political and financial costs of creating it for reasons rooted in political ideology. Far from concerns with efficiency (after all, NATO's assets proved to be adaptable), the French and German policy reflected French Socialist and German Christian-Democratic party notions of Europe-as-a-political-community. It is problematic for rational choice institutionalist accounts that the attempt to create an *autonomous* European security institution occurred *in parallel* with the transformation process of NATO, but not in coordination with it.

---

[73] See also Keohane (1984: 247) for a discussion on sunk costs.

As the realist and rational choice institutionalist theories argue in favor of structural constraints in which *all* states should *either* act according to realist *or* institutionalist thinking, both alternative theories fail to explain the full range of variance in government positions. In trying to explain the CFSP initiative and its shape, they have overlooked important variables that find expression in the little ideological congruence among the major European governments.

Conclusion

As German Chancellor Angela Merkel would later remark, "Rarely do we have the experience of witnessing firsthand the end of one epoch and the beginning of another" (Merkel 2003: A39). Despite strategic uncertainties and interdependencies, no ideological consensus around a European post-Cold War security order emerged between the governments in power in Europe's three most important states at the beginning of the 1990s. Differences in party positions persisted.[74] And despite the sense of urgency created by the outbreak of war in Yugoslavia three months before the final negotiations, the European governments could not agree on the extent to which security and military policy should be brought into the EU.

Based on their various ideologies, national parties read the history of 1989 in different ways. British, French and German governments of the time remained divided on the importance of NATO and the desirability of an autonomous European alternative.[75] As a result, the European NATO member states set out to create a new but symbolic security institution that moved the newly created EU into a policy space previously reserved for NATO. The institution remained modest because the British Conservative government did not want to create something European that could challenge NATO, an interpretation of the situation that was far removed from that of the German government, for example, which saw the process of NATO transformation and the new CFSP as complementary and, as a result, wanted to strengthen both.

Different political parties in power reflected logics of action that resonated either with realist or rational choice institutionalist arguments: based on valuing Europe above other multilateral venues,

[74] This happened despite strong public support for CFSP – even in the UK (*Agence Europe* 1995; Forster 1999: 109).
[75] In 1990 when the institutional security set up in Europe was in flux, one observer summarized it as such: "France wants a strong Europe. Britain wants a strong Atlantic Alliance" (Kirkpatrick 1990: A11).

particularly NATO, the French government saw CFSP as a way of counteracting US influence in Europe – impersonating actions that resonate with the soft-balancing argument in realism (Posen 2006; Jones 2007) – though material balancing was not the main motivation driving the PS government's policies toward Europe. On the other hand, the RPR's preferences toward institutions reflected rational institutionalist logics. The British Conservative government opposed further European deepening, thus also resonating realist insights – but instead of reflecting realist thought *à la* Posen (2006) and Jones (2007), the Conservatives acted more along the sovereignist lines predicted by the work of John Mearsheimer (1990). Labour's ideology resembled the logic of rational institutionalism. Also the German government's actions resonate best with rational institutionalist insights, with a major caveat being that the German government was ignorant of the costs of institution-building and adaptation. The CDU/CSU–FDP government wanted to create multiple complementary security institutions that would foster peace and stability. Based on its understanding of Europe and NATO, the German government was pushing for a position that could be summarized as "show the US and Europe we care," while the French government took the position "show the US we can," while the British government wanted to "show the US we care." While all three governments' actions *partially resemble* different IR theories' predictions, their motivations cannot be deduced from international structure or functional needs. Instead, ideologies inform their preferences.

Hypothetically speaking, the period between the collapse of the Berlin Wall (November 1989) and the end of the Persian Gulf War (February 1991) offered a window of opportunity during which France might have greatly reduced its opposition to NATO integration and sought better military relations with the United States, and the UK could have improved its relations to the EC.

French leaders could plausibly have argued that the European security situation had greatly changed since the 1960s, that Gaullist reticence toward a hegemonic United States was no longer necessary in the wake of the announced US troop reductions, and that a new French attitude toward NATO had become both possible and necessary. With the dominant American role in Europe greatly reduced and as a means to balance the new German power, France could have cast its lot with the proponents of a "New Atlanticism" and sought to join its allies in a new transatlantic consensus. (Gordon 1993: 165–6)

However, this did not occur, as the Mitterrand government decided not to take part in a number of aspects of NATO reform. It also marked an opportunity for the British to argue that security issues should not be handled by NATO alone anymore. This opportunity was not taken either. "An approach which emphasized the separateness of Europe would seriously weaken our real security ... The common foreign and security policy should include some broad security issues ... but it should not compete with the military tasks in NATO" (Hurd 1991: 13).

In addition, the close examination of party ideologies has shown that particular values transcend a left–right dichotomy, such as Europe-as-a-political-community for the French Socialist and the German Christian Democratic Party. Some have argued that the PS's core value is equality – informing its political preferences and behavior – and that it is therefore in favor of multilateralism, which again explains its preference for a European security institution (Rathbun 2004). However, this would misrepresent the PS's attitudes toward many other international institutions, especially NATO. These different attitudes cannot simply be dismissed as nuances, since they inform policy proposals, especially in the realm of international security. In reducing the PS attitude to equality, it is difficult to explain why the PS opposes France's full membership in NATO and the Alliance's increasing political scope (Favier and Martin 1996: 251).[76] CFSP was not "against the US."[77] Rather than push for a debate about reforming NATO, the PS's policy was to question NATO's organization, content and scope and continue to refuse participation in NATO's integrated military commands, to oppose the deployment of foreign forces on French territory and automatic access of allied air forces to French airspace, as well as the automatic engagement of French troops in case of conflict. The PS also refused to participate in NATO's Nuclear Planning Group and its Defense Planning Committee. Its ideology informs the preference for creating a European security institution, not as a European pillar of the Alliance, but autonomous of it.

European cooperation in the realm of security policy is not a linear process. It is made by national governments that have an important degree of national autonomy in managing international and European (institutional) pressures. And there are no irresistible pressures toward integration, precisely because there is an existing alternative: NATO. As one German government official observed, "if Britain overcame its problems with the Atlantic link and its reluctance to give up sovereignty

[76] Interview with Sophie-Caroline de Margerie in Paris (May 29, 2008).
[77] Interview with Sophie-Caroline de Margerie in Paris (May 29, 2008).

could we have a triple alliance?" (quoted in *The Economist* 1991). As British Foreign Secretary, Douglas Hurd announced:

A review of the CFSP provisions will be on the agenda for the 1996 intergovernmental conference. It is too early to speculate with any confidence what the results of that debate will be. One area on which attention is bound to focus is the relationship between CFSP and the WEU. The challenge will be to marry the Europeans' wish and need to play a greater role in contributing to common defence and security with the maintenance of NATO as the essential framework underpinning European security ... by consent, not by coercion. (Hurd 1994: 428)

5   Renegotiating Maastricht at Amsterdam: the failure to go beyond CFSP

Before the Maastricht Treaty could be reviewed during the 1996–7 IGC negotiations ending in the Amsterdam Treaty, the disintegration of Yugoslavia created an opportunity for EC members to finally give CFSP some boots, i.e. military hardware. After all, it was during this time that the European NATO member states experienced what it means to be fighting on the ground without the Americans. For some governments, the glaring limitations of European capabilities in Yugoslavia raised the issue of a robust EU institution independent of NATO and the unreliability of US leadership.

Nonetheless, as I show in this chapter, despite these external incentives and cooperation problems, and despite Article N in the Maastricht Treaty, which called for reform in areas such as security and defense, the ideologies of major European governments were too incongruent to create anything more robust than they had already done in Maastricht. Hence, the proposal to merge the WEU and the EU, which would have provided real capabilities to CFSP and increased the range of action significantly, failed. Evidence shows that the British government's strong ideological reservations, along with ideological differences between the French and German governments, led to the failure to develop a robust security institution on the foundations of CFSP. Things only started changing in the last 30 days of the Amsterdam negotiations, which lasted more than one and a half years, when the Labour Party came to power in the UK. The new Labour government signed the treaty, making a few significant adjustments to the British position, and promised to do more in the future once the government had consolidated its position domestically. Until then, no collective interest had emerged since Maastricht to underpin the idea for a European security institution. The Amsterdam negotiations – while the Conservatives were in power in the UK – demonstrated that national governments can be, and remain, a brake; there exists no integration automatism.[1]

---

[1] Much EU studies literature and many official EU texts on the Amsterdam IGC are normatively biased toward European unity and improvements in integration (M.E.

Yet again, examining the attempt to create an autonomous European security institution is only half of the picture. NATO is, for some governments, intimately linked to the issue of European security. One of the reasons for which the British Conservative government dismissed proposals to integrate the WEU into the EU was that it wanted to make sure that NATO's primacy was not undermined (Moravcsik and Nicolaïdis 1999: 64; Wall 2008: 158). The French RPR presidency was not as insistent as the Socialist government in creating a European security institution. Instead, Chirac initiated France's rapprochement with NATO, motivated by increasing France's range of action in multilateral security policy. In addition, around the same time, Chirac, who also introduced a proposal to merge the WEU with the EU along with the German government, had misgivings about the federal notion that the German government sought to introduce to the merger. In the end, Chirac dismissed the proposal.

This chapter first examines the external environment in which European states conceived of NATO and the EU around the time of the Amsterdam negotiations. The experience of fighting in Yugoslavia deeply impacted European governments, yet the ways that each understood the implications of Yugoslavia for European security differed markedly. In the second part, I focus on the domestic ideological configurations that existed at the time and the policy preferences that resulted. There was little consensus on security issues between European parties during the Amsterdam negotiations; this lack of ideological congruence led to the failures of Amsterdam – at least until Labour came to power in the UK. The third part traces the processes with regard to NATO transformation and the attempt to create a European security institution independent of NATO, before turning to alternative explanations. I show that the key to understanding the inability to develop a European security institution autonomous from NATO at Amsterdam is to be found in party ideologies. Amsterdam shows that the development of a robust security institution during the period from CFSP to ESDP was neither path dependent nor inevitable (either in terms of balancing or in terms of solving immanent cooperation problems), but rather a highly politicized process in which outcomes hinged on European governments sharing fundamental values around European security.

Smith 1998, 2004: 81; Schake *et al.* 1999; Andréani 2000; Cornish and Edwards 2001; M. Smith 2004). However, this chapter will show that in the case of a European security institution autonomous of NATO, European integration did not "just" happen nor was it deemed "good" by everyone.

The disintegration of Yugoslavia

Thinking around European security at the time of the Amsterdam negotiations was overwhelmingly shaped by the experiences in Yugoslavia in the early 1990s. But other international developments such as the disintegration of the Soviet Union and the question of how to approach the new states in Central and Eastern Europe (CEE) also impacted the Europeans' understanding of security. Despite the major cooperation problems that arose, not every European government drew the same conclusions about how to alleviate the situation. Some EU member states saw the emerging crisis as an opportunity to confirm the EU's status as a credible international actor (Eyal 1993). Other governments were less inclined to see the EU act on the stage of international security.

The EC's initial reactions to the wars in Bosnia and Herzegovina were of a diplomatic nature and introduced sanctions against Serbia and Montenegro. These sanctions were first carried out by all EC states and, after the EU lobbied for UN sanctions as well, the UN Security Council adopted resolution 713 in 1991. NATO and the WEU were tasked to monitor the Montenegrin coast – most ships involved in these operations were European. Soon after the Maastricht Treaty was ratified, the Bush, and then Clinton, administrations decided to leave crisis management to the Europeans, however (Hutchings 1997; Starr 1997: 19; Vanhoonacker 2001). The US government unilaterally withdrew from enforcing the arms embargo on the former Yugoslavia in 1994. This led European states to question James Baker's earlier commitment to the United States sharing Europe's neighborhood (Nuttall 2000: 62). As the crisis escalated into warfare in Bosnia, some European governments felt compelled to intervene militarily. This intention only had half-hearted political support from the United States, which refused to send ground troops.

In response to the crisis in Bosnia and the US reluctance to intervene, acting through NATO as a lead institution was not an option. Instead, the EC member states relied on a variety of international institutions. The German government, in particular, and its FDP Foreign Minister Genscher (and later Kinkel), informed by the core value of multilateralism-as-an-end-in-itself, tried to tackle the conflict in a variety of international forums such as the CSCE, the EU, the WEU and the UN by activating crisis mechanism tools and peace conferences (Genscher 1995; Hilz 2005: 255–6). Regarding military involvement, the UN was the only multilateral organization (aside from NATO) that, at the time, had the necessary capabilities for conducting a complex peace operation. In June 1992, the UN sent a protection force (UNPROFOR) attempting to protect civilians and to ensure humanitarian relief. The largest contingents to the UNPROFOR mission came from the UK and France (Cameron 1999: 30; Major 1999: 549). The mandate of UNPROFOR was demilitarization, establishment of a no-fly zone and protection of safe areas. The UN Security Council established a no-fly zone over Bosnia and Herzegovina and authorized member states to enforce the decision based on Resolution 816 (1993). The United States participated in establishing the no-fly zone under NATO auspices and in coordination with the UN. However, when the United States started air bombardments based on the concept "lift and strike" (lifting the arms embargo and starting air strikes) against Serbian positions, it did so initially without consulting the Europeans (Giersch 1998: 158; Major 1999: 539). This put European ground troops in danger and aggravated cooperation problems (Lepgold 1998: 91).

Over the next couple of years, the United States became more involved politically, though tensions between European governments with troops on the ground, and the Americans who remained unwilling to commit, remained (Giersch 1998: 155–6; Cogan 2001: 69).[2] After EU and UN mediation attempts failed, and after some NATO air raids, Clinton brought together a Contact Group consisting of the United States, Russia, and EU representatives to negotiate an armistice and eventually foster a truce between the warring parties. These informal negotiations were eventually formalized in the Dayton accords of November 1995 and formally signed in Paris in December 1995 (Giersch 1998: 177, 199, 206–11). To implement the Dayton accord, the United States agreed to lead a NATO implementation force (IFOR) to provide military enforcement of the accord. The force was deployed in December, taking over from UNPROFOR.[3] UNPROFOR had largely been European in composition, but also included considerable numbers of soldiers from developing countries. In the wake of the transition from UN to NATO control of the peace operation, troops from most developing countries left. Meanwhile, US soldiers arrived, making up one-third of the 60,000-strong IFOR, a ratio that steadily fell afterwards.

---

[2] NATO started getting involved in Bosnia around July and August 1995, when it initiated a sustained air campaign to undermine the military capabilities of the Bosnian Serb Army (Operation Deliberate Force).

[3] It was NATO's first out-of-area crisis management operation. Germany contributed logistical, medical and engineering units to IFOR, approved by the parliament in June 1995 (Bundesregierung 2000: 39), and in December 1996 the German parliament approved the government's plan to send 3,000 ground combat forces to Bosnia as part of SFOR (Schöllgen 2000: 11). This was the first deployment of German combat-ready ground forces outside NATO territory since World War II. Of the parliamentarians, 499 were for, 93 against, the deployment.

The Bosnian experience highlighted the mismatch between the EU's declared foreign and security policy objectives and the means available to implement such policies. European initiatives had been ridiculed as "symbolic miscarriages" (Hilz 2005: 332). The Europeans had to wait for the United States in order to act forcefully. Richard Holbrooke observed: "By the spring of 1995 it had become commonplace to say that Washington's relations with European allies were worse than at any time since the 1956 Suez crisis ... Bosnia ... had defined the first phase of the post-Cold War relationship between Europe and the United States and seriously damaged the Atlantic relationship" (Holbrooke 1998: 361; see also Giersch 1998: 158; Lepgold 1998: 91). However, different European actors on the ground in Bosnia drew different conclusions from this. While some argued that Europe should carry more weight and influence on the world stage, others simply saw themselves confirmed in their belief that without NATO and the United States nothing could be done.

Political parties' landscape across Europe

The international developments were interpreted by political parties in Europe through the lens of their distinctive security ideologies. Examining these ideologies reveals both domestic variance, as parties interpreted and understood lessons from the Yugoslav experience differently, and variance across Europe, as parties in similarly situated states drew contrasting conclusions. Remarkably, party ideologies remained constant over the years, making governmental reaction toward a European security institution predictable.

United Kingdom: from the Conservatives to Labour

From the end of the Maastricht negotiations to the end of the Amsterdam negotiations, the UK experienced two general elections. The 1992 elections kept the Conservatives in power while the 1997 election introduced Labour to government – 17 months into the Amsterdam negotiations and only one month before their conclusion. After 18 years of consecutive Conservative governments in the UK, "New" Labour[4] won the general election with a 179-seat majority on May 2.

---

[4] The adjective "new" to the Labour Party stood for a value adjustment. Leadership changes led the party to move away from democratic socialism and instead embrace the mixed economy (rewriting the clause of its constitution that committed it to the public ownership of industry), declaring its support for the political European Union. This also led to the party becoming less critical of the United States in socioeconomic

Though not the primary issue, Europe figured in the 1992 and 1997 campaigns of both parties. The two major parties took opposing views on the issue[5] – except in regard to a *federal* Europe, which both opposed based on their insistence on sovereignty. With the Maastricht Treaty negotiations of 1991 the nature of the EU had changed, and with it the attitudes of Labour and the Conservatives. A more political EU with a social agenda found support with Labour. Conversely, after Maastricht, the Conservatives became critical of the EU's emerging social and political agenda as it moved from the realm of market liberalization into a more ambitious political project.

In its 1997 party manifesto, the Conservative Party stated on the first page: "The European social model is failing." The party was instead interested in returning to a "flexible Europe" (Conservative Party Manifesto 1997: 47) stressing the party's continued economic interests in Europe-as-a-geographic-space.[6] Reflecting the party's core values of Europe-as-a-geographic-space and sovereignty which informs interpretations of multilateralism-as-a-means-to-another-end, the Conservatives spell out what they want Europe to be. "Our priorities for Europe's development will be enlargement of the Community, completion of the single market, reform of the European Court of Justice, and further strengthening of the role of national parliaments" (Conservative Party Manifesto 1997: 47). Regarding Europe and multilateralism in the use of force, Michael Howard, the Home Secretary, called CFSP a threat to the role of NATO, thus underlining the Conservatives' selective understanding of multilateralism (Woodward 1997: 17). The WEU–EU merger was even explicitly mentioned in the election manifesto: "NATO

terms (Labour Party Manifesto 1987, 1997; Coates and Lawler 2000; Hindmoor 2004). Hindmoor (2004: 7, 36) demonstrates nicely that "new" Labour did not move to some objectively given political center in a given political space but that the party leadership during the Kinnock and Blair era had to construct this so-called center.

[5] Prior to the 1997 election campaign, studies by Baker and Seawright (1998a, 1998b) and Ludlam (1998) support this point. Based on surveys of Labour (Baker and Seawright 1998b) and Conservative (Ludlam 1998) MPs and MEPs, both present data showing that in 1996 Labour was supportive of European integration and the pursuit of a range of policies by means of Europe, including security policy. This contrasts strongly with the Conservatives who are much more Euroskeptic on all key policy issues. In addition, the data on Labour suggests that its pro-European stance is much more pronounced in the generation that entered parliament in 1987 than in those cohorts that entered parliament earlier. These preferences also correlate with the change of nature of the EU from an economic to a more political institution.

[6] See Major (1999: 701–3) for how the party's election platform came about and see Major (1999: 583–7) for how he managed the party. In the run-up to the elections, Major "warned voters – on 2 April – that it is vital to send a prime minister prepared to defend the national interest at the EU's June summit in the Dutch capital" (White 1997a: 11).

will remain the cornerstone of our security. We will resist attempts to bring the Western European Union under the control of the European Union, and ensure that defence policy remains a matter for sovereign nations" (Conservative Party Manifesto 1997: 49).[7] The Conservatives lamented any form of duplication in European security institutions and equated the inclusion of security issues into the EU with supranationalization of the policy domain.[8]

Labour, on the other hand, ran an election campaign in which it pronounced itself a reliable leader in Europe thus committing to work with European partners in many policy realms, including security and defense policy, while at the same time also confirming NATO's continued role in security matters (Labour Party Manifesto 1997; Woodward 1997: 17; Baker and Seawright 1998b: 66).[9] Blair had inherited a pro-European policy platform from Neil Kinnock (Hindmoor 2004: 149–50). Blair, on April 21, 1997 during the election campaign in Manchester, presented five key points of his party's negotiation position in Amsterdam, should they win the election. "Making reality of foreign policy cooperation" (Blair quoted in Wall 2008: 162) was one such priority. The manifesto also promised a strategic defense and security review "to reassess our essential security interests and defence needs" (Labour Party Manifesto 1997: 36). The Conservatives had opposed such a review, judging the UK military forces to be capable and well-served in NATO.[10] Blair even went so far as to consider giving up some sovereignty in the implementation of intergovernmentally taken foreign policy decisions, further stressing his European credentials: "We will

---

[7] Also the Conservatives held on to their anti-EMU stance despite a survey of the Confederation of British Industry (CBI) showing that three out of four firms favor the single currency (Perkins and Elliott 1997: 3). The Conservatives and the CBI both issued statements that this disagreement does not cause any deep rift between them. Observers called the Conservative stance toward EMU a "purpose-free piece of ideological posturing" (Brown 1997a: 17). EMU, however, caused the party some rift. A minority of members were more "pro-European" (read: did not want to decide right away whether a single currency is in the interest of the UK) but the majority did not approve of the European policy out of principle, ruling out participation in the single currency. Major placed his party's policy in between. Critical of Europe, he did not want to take a definite position on EMU at the time (Major 1999: 604). Major even resigned from the party leadership on June 22, 1995 only to get re-elected again – he did so to strengthen his position in the party (Major 1999: 614–45).

[8] Interview # 4 with a senior British official in London (December 5, 2007).

[9] Leaving out the explicit mention of European security institutions in the manifesto should not be attributed to Labour's disbelief in the issue, but instead as an election strategy. At the time, the Conservative Party constructed a fear of the "European army" and hence Labour decided not to mention the issue for electoral reasons. Interview # 5 with a British official in London (December 5, 2007).

[10] Interview # 6 with a senior British official in London (December 5, 2007).

consider the extension of Qualified Majority Voting to areas where it is in Britain's interest to do so whilst retaining the veto in areas where it is essential" (Blair quoted in Wall 2008: 162). He also stressed that Britain's role in Europe is one of a shaper, claiming that this is Britain's "traditional role," and implicitly accusing the Conservatives of having hurt Britain's interests:

Labour will be strong in Europe ... strong too in setting the agenda, with the right ideas. That is Britain's traditional role in Europe. That's what our allies are waiting for. For too long they've seen British ministers sent to Brussels to find out what the community is doing and to tell it to stop. They want us to help to decide what the community should do, and how it can do it better. They want us to be on the inside, arguing constructively for new directions and new reform. (Blair speech of April 5, 1995 quoted in Hindmoor 2004: 151)

Already in its 1995 conference report, *The Future of the European Union: Report on Labour's Position in Preparation for the Intergovernmental Conference*, Labour indicated that it would push for a different position than the Conservatives during the negotiations. "Labour in government ... will act to defend and advance our national interests in Europe. We will seek to reform the institutions of Europe where we consider that to be necessary. But unlike the Tories we will act in accordance with our positive vision of Europe" (Labour Party 1995). Labour also indicated in the election campaign that the party would sign up to the EU's Social Chapter (White 1997b: 12). This reflects Labour's multilateralism in the use of force as an-end-in-itself and its pro-European stance based on the value Europe-as-community-among-others.

France: cohabitation, RPR reign and cohabitation again

In France, legislative elections in 1993 brought another situation of *cohabitation* in which a Socialist presidency under François Mitterrand shared power with the Edouard Balladur government (UDF–RPR). The 1995 presidential elections brought Jacques Chirac (RPR) to power and thus ended *cohabitation*. The 1997 legislative elections then led to another period of *cohabitation* with the PS under Lionel Jospin forming the government – only two weeks before the end of the Amsterdam negotiations. During these three episodes, the French government's preferences toward NATO and European security cooperation changed according to which parties were in power, and in what function.

The RPR and the UDF were holding onto French sovereignty as a core value of their ideology and an understanding of multilateralism-as-a-means-to-an other-end, which led them to the conclusion that closer cooperation with NATO was in France's interest. The

PS remained suspicious of NATO, which it saw as damaging to European community building. Instead, the PS pursued a policy in line with its understanding of Europe-as-a-political-community in conjunction with multilateralism-as-a-means-to-an other-end. As a result, during *cohabitation* between 1993 and 1995, France's policy toward NATO could be characterized as a *measured, eclectic rapprochement* between France and NATO. Before *cohabitation*, Mitterrand had opposed any rapprochement to NATO, but once the UDF and RPR held the majority in the National Assembly, Prime Minister Balladur (UDF), Defense Minister Pierre Léotard (UDF) and Foreign Minister Alain Juppé (RPR) pressured him to commit at least to small adjustments. However, they nonetheless had to defer to the presidential prerogative, the *domaine réservé*, despite the fact that Mitterrand had defined the relationship between presidency and prime minister in regard to foreign and security policy as a "*domaine partagé* [shared domain]" (Chagnollaud and Quermonne 2000b: 69). Mitterrand refused to grant the defense minister and the chief of staff permission to attend their respective NATO committees on a regular basis, but allowed periodic – but irregular – contacts. Balladur's reaction was to complain that Mitterrand was way too skeptical of NATO (Lemaitre 1994; Balladur 1995: 81; Menon 1996: 162–5).

The presidential elections of May 1995 ended *cohabitation* and allowed for RPR values to have full effect. Chirac became president of France with an UDF–RPR majority in the National Assembly, allowing him to pursue the same policy that Balladur and Juppé had pursued under *cohabitation* to little avail. With the RPR assuming power from Mitterrand's Socialists, there was an opening for a rapprochement between France and NATO with important consequences for European security efforts. Recall that British skepticism of French ambitions was a major factor in Conservative opposition to a more powerful CFSP because the Conservatives feared that NATO's primacy was seriously challenged and supranationalism was on the rise. In one of his major foreign policy speeches during the election campaign Chirac declared, "our country must participate in all Alliance bodies that are based upon a respect for national sovereignty" (quoted in Grant 1996: 65) and repeated this formulation many times afterwards. Charles Cogan, a former CIA chief in Paris, noted that "Mitterrand restrained Jacques Chirac during the first 'cohabitation' government (1986–1988) from drawing close to NATO. When Chirac returned to the scene as president in May 1995, he wasted little time in initiating a rapprochement with NATO" (2001: 77; see also Gordon 1993: 154). With Chirac reconciled to NATO, many observers saw an opportunity for a new consensus between the two states.

In the 1997 legislative election, the ideological configurations changed again. The RPR–UDF coalition ran on its usual "France first" slogan (RPR–UDF Party Manifesto 1997: 4). NATO rapprochement was made part of the election campaign, with the party promising to continue Chirac's policy of integrating into NATO command structures, a process as yet incomplete.[11] Voters opted for the Socialists, however. Jospin, in a statement to *Agence France Presse* on February 4, 1996, aligned himself with the positions previously taken by former President Mitterrand. Jospin said he was "not favorable" to the rapprochement of France with NATO and hoped that France's "autonomy of decision" would be oriented toward the construction of a European security system (quoted in Cogan 2001: 90). Védrine and Guigou became part of the government, and as they had already been important figures in Mitterrand's government, some speak of the "*continuité maastrichtienne* [continuity from Maastricht]" (Delattre 1997). The PS held on to integrationist ideas and the United States as imperial model (Noblecourt 1997).

There are two conceptions of Europe that go against each other … The one that we always defended, is the one of an independent Europe … the affirmation of a social model, the loyalty to a civilization. Today, the real Europeans are those who refuse to let Europe glide into ultralibertarianism, which would lead into the dissolution of Europe … staying loyal to the history of the European project is to build a political Europe. (Parti Socialiste Manifesto 1997: 1)

The PS only won 15 days before the Amsterdam negotiations ended and hence had hardly any time to impact the outcome of the negotiations. Its election into government, however, impacted Chirac's rapprochement to NATO.

Germany: same government, more moderate wings in opposition

The 1994 elections kept the CDU/CSU[12] and FDP coalition in power. True to their core values of Europe-as-a-political-community and multilateralism-as-an-end-in-itself, the CDU/CSU and FDP election programs of 1994 underscored the idea of a federal Europe and a broad multilateralism, defining multilateralism as a policy goal in itself (Solms 1997: 10; Kohl 2007: 662). The parties reiterated that they perceived

---

[11] Interview with François Heisbourg in Paris (May 27, 2008).

[12] For a detailed discussion of the CDU party program of 1994 see Kohl (2007: 658–64). Different factions and working groups inside the CDU/CSU debated over different policy priorities and the program reflects a compromise that was negotiated under Kohl's leadership. Kohl furthermore admits that, in general, he sees the party programs as the basis and guide for his government's politics.

the mandates of the EU, NATO and OSCE in terms of a division of labor (Solms 1997: 10), and that they were in favor of the interlocking concept. Their ideological leanings were reflected in the coalition treaty and the Defense White Book of 1994 as well. In their coalition treaty, the German government committed to a common security policy at the 1996 IGC (Koalitionsvereinbarung 1994: 4).[13] The coalition continued to see the Franco-German cooperation as a core element of European integration, not questioning its implications for other member states (Koalitionsvereinbarung 1994: 86). The Maastricht Treaty, the coalition argued, required specification, and the EU needed to become "capable and able to react quickly" (Koalitionsvereinbarung 1994: 87). This should be done through the "development of an autonomous European security and defense identity" (Koalitionsvereinbarung 1994: 88). Several other documents insist on the same policy positions. A 1994 position paper authored by the CDU's prominent foreign policy experts, Wolfgang Schäuble and Karl Lamers, asked for more CFSP capabilities and notes explicitly security capabilities which are seen as an indispensable factor in endowing the EU with an identity of its own (Schäuble and Lamers 1997: 255–60). Just before the elections the government had published a Defense White Book in 1994, outlining central security objectives, and making the argument that there was a direct link between German security and European integration (White Book 1994: 42); however, the White Book also reconfirmed that an increasing investment in CFSP did not mean a reduction of the importance of the transatlantic partnership (White Book 1994: vi–ix). Instead, the German government continued to push for both institutions to transform in similar fashions.[14]

While the SPD and Greens were also committed to a broad and inclusive multilateralism based on their core value of multilateralism-as-an-end-in-itself, their understanding of Europe remained derivative of broad multilateralism, making them more critical of certain aspects in the EU and NATO. In both the SPD and the Green parties, moderate factions that were in the minority in the party at the end of the Cold War, the *Seeheimer Kreis* and *Realos*, respectively, became more powerful throughout the 1990s. As a result, while holding a relatively critical view of NATO and the United States, the SPD and Greens

---

[13] Europe in combination with security policy has its own chapter in the 1994 coalition treaty.
[14] According to the German White Book of 1994 (1994: 23, 30), there is no existential threat to Germany's territorial integrity in the foreseeable future, but peaceful coexistence in Europe is neither given nor irreversible.

nonetheless moved away from a strong critique of NATO – especially in light of the Alliance transforming in ways that are ideologically more compatible with the factions' ideological position. Pushing for an inclusive multilateralism, the SPD wanted the EU to be able to act globally along with other international institutions (Scharping 1999b, 1999c). However, Rudolf Scharping, party chair and the SPD chancellor candidate in the 1994 election, stressed that, in the interests of being inclusive, Germany should not be the initiator of foreign and defense policy initiatives. This contrasted with the CDU's vision of Germany as a motor of integration and multilateralism more generally. Furthermore, the SPD stressed that military means alone did not grant security and that international organizations should act preventively with diplomatic means. A federal Europe was mentioned as a long-term goal without recommending specific supranational policies. In the Alliance 90/Green Party, Joschka Fischer had moved the *Realo* wing into control of the party (Conradt 1995: 13; Silva 1995: 157–65). His understanding of international politics aligned with the shift the SPD experienced with their change in leadership. Hence, especially when talking about the use of force, Fischer announced that his party accepted it as a means of last resort.

Overall, domestic and international ideological differences persisted from the end of the 1980s to the mid 1990s. As a result, the international ideological configuration of 1996 demonstrates ideological incongruence (as in Table 5.1). However, the international ideological configuration of 1996 changed dramatically in 1997 – not only around the value of Europe but also around the notion of multilateralism (as in Table 5.2). As the remainder of this chapter will show, this change had major consequences on security policy in general, and the creation of a European security institution, in particular.

NATO transformation and the Amsterdam negotiations: two alternatives?

Initially, essentially two options emerged from the international configuration of party values. While the US and British governments continued to push for NATO transformation and the creation of a European pillar inside NATO, the French government repeated proposals already made during the previous round of negotiations at Maastricht to merge the WEU with the EU, thus giving the EU capabilities for autonomous crisis management operations. Whereas these governments tended to see these options as exclusive, the German government, later joined by the new Chirac government in France in 1995, pushed for a third option

Table 5.1 *Domestic and international party configuration, 1996*

Country	Party/ies	Multilateralism	Europe	Sovereignty
United Kingdom	Conservatives†	Means-to-another-end	**Europe-as-a-geographic-space**	**Intergovernmental**
	Labour	**End-in-itself**	Europe-as-a-community-among-others	Intergovernmental
France	Socialists (PS)	Means-to-another-end	**Europe-as-a-political-community**	Supranational/intergovernmental
	RPR†	Means-to-another-end	Europe-as-a-community-among-others	**Intergovernmental**
Germany	CDU/CSU†	**End-in-itself**	**Europe-as-a-political-community**	Supranational/intergovernmental
	FDP†	**End-in-itself**	**Europe-as-a-political-community**	**Intergovernmental/supranational**
	SPD	**End-in-itself**	Europe-as-a-community-among-others	Supranational/intergovernmental
	Greens	**End-in-itself**	Europe-as-a-community-among-others	Supranational/intergovernmental

Notes
Core values in bold; † party/ies in government.

Table 5.2 *Domestic and international party configuration, 1997*

Country	Party/ies	Multilateralism	Europe	Sovereignty
United Kingdom	Conservatives	Means-to-another-end	**Europe-as-a-geographic-space**	**Intergovernmental**
	Labour†	**End-in-itself**	Europe-as-a-community-among-others	Intergovernmental
France	Socialists (PS)†	Means-to-another-end	**Europe-as-a-political-community**	Supranational/ intergovernmental
	RPR†	Means-to-another-end	Europe-as-a-community-among-others	**Intergovernmental**
Germany	CDU/CSU†	**End-in-itself**	**Europe-as-a-political-community**	Supranational/ intergovernmental
	FDP†	**End-in-itself**	**Europe-as-a-political-community**	**Intergovernmental/ supranational**
	SPD	**End-in-itself**	Europe-as-a-community-among-others	Supranational/ intergovernmental
	Greens	**End-in-itself**	Europe-as-a-community-among-others	Supranational/ intergovernmental

Notes
Core values in bold; † party/ies in government.

that combined a transformed NATO with an autonomous EU security institution. In 1997, the German and French governments were joined by a Labour government that also viewed NATO transformation and an autonomous EU institution as mutually compatible, rather than mutually exclusive options. Though the Labour government came to power too late to save the proposals for an EU institution at Amsterdam, the alignment of party ideologies it created would have important effects later with ESDP in 1998–9, as I demonstrate in the next chapter. In 1997, however, the conflict these proposals created would end in favor of a European pillar inside NATO, as efforts to develop an autonomous EU capability by merging the WEU and EU failed. This did not put an end to discussion of an autonomous European security institution, however, because a new government in the UK had signaled a change of policy.

Negotiating a European pillar inside NATO

In the mid 1990s, European governments dealt with the fundamental issue of how to provide for their security, particularly whether to cooperate with NATO, the EU, or both, and what to do with the WEU. The British, German and US governments were all interested in NATO's persistence and *adaptation* to the new security environment.[15] Part of NATO's adaptation, from their point of view, had to include more European burden-sharing inside the Alliance. For the United States and British Conservatives, *nesting* a European pillar within NATO was a way of controlling European attempts to build an alternative institution. The German Christian Democrat-led coalition government saw NATO transformation as a way of keeping NATO engaged *without precluding* a European institution outside the Alliance. Out of this relative congruence of interest, the European Security and Defense Identity (ESDI)[16] and the Combined Joint Task Forces (CJTF) initiatives came

---

[15] This also includes the creation of new forums of coordination and cooperation to engage the Central and Eastern European states – most of these initiatives are based on German-American proposals (Hellmann 1997: 39). Hence, the North Atlantic Cooperation Council (NACC), established in 1991 and replaced by the Euro-Atlantic Partnership Council (EAPC) in 1997, the Partnership for Peace (PfP) founded in 1994, the NATO–Russia Permanent Joint Council (PJC) and the NATO–Ukraine Commission, both established in 1997, bring former enemies together. For a thorough discussion on the implications of the cooperation with former enemies see Yost (1998: 91–187). NATO started regarding itself more and more as an instrument to spread democracy (Gheciu 2005) and invited Poland, Hungary and the Czech Republic to join the Alliance in 1997.

[16] In the scholarly and policy literature, ESDI and CFSP/ESDP are often used synonymously though they represent two different institutions. Authors use both acronyms

to life. France's Socialist government was opposed to these developments as it was suspicious of US and British motives and did not want NATO to occupy a policy domain that the PS saw reserved for the EU. But when the RPR came to power in 1995, it paved the way for the French government's endorsement of the ESDI and CJTF initiatives.

NATO transformation toward more flexible institutional structures   The initial shift from the Cold War posture discussed in Chapter 4 led to possibilities for further transforming NATO's command structure and forces.[17] As the Clinton administration's first NATO initiative, the US government initiated reform of NATO's integrated structure, proposing to create a CJTF headquarters at an informal defense minister meeting in late 1993 – a meeting in which France did not participate (Grant 1996: 62).[18] The intention was to provide flexible command arrangements within which allied forces could be organized on a task-specific basis (Yost 1998: 2, 206). The CJTF can be used for collective defense purposes, humanitarian or crisis management tasks by all allies and partners and facilitates operations with non-NATO members (non-Article 5 missions). This would facilitate the dual use of NATO forces and command structures for NATO-led *and* WEU-led operations. Through the link that the CJTF provides with the WEU, the WEU's Petersberg Declaration, which encompasses nearly all military operations that do not result from a collective defense commitment, became part of NATO's activities.[19] At the NATO summit in Brussels in January 1994,[20] the heads of state and governments of NATO member states informally endorsed this initiative (Barry 1996: 83).[21] The US proposal enabled European states to draw on the CJTF for WEU-led operations. CJTF was thus created

to depict only one institution (a European security initiative) to present transatlantic coherence. ESDI was anticipated inside NATO, however, while CFSP/ESDP always was conceived as outside NATO. Different rationales governed the creation of these European security institutions.

[17] The number of command headquarters was reduced from 65 to 20 (Barry 1996: 81).

[18] In NATO parlance, "combined" has to be understood as multinational, and "joint" as multi-service.

[19] At their June 19, 1992 meeting, the WEU member states agreed to strengthen the WEU's operational role, in accordance with the decisions taken in Maastricht and at the NATO Rome Summit. The Petersberg Declaration lists possible operations, participation in which is voluntary. It indicated the WEU's move beyond its common defense commitment. Also, the WEU headquarters moved from London to Brussels to be closer to NATO and the EU (Gordon 1997/8: 91).

[20] On this occasion, NATO member states also made reference to the Maastricht Treaty for the first time.

[21] "In fact, deploying CJTFs will, for the first time, become the primary *modus operandi* of a standing alliance in peacetime" (Barry 1996: 82).

partly to strengthen the European pillar of the Alliance through the Western European Union. The relationship between NATO and WEU was defined as "separable but not separate" forces, which the WEU could use "in pursuit of the CFSP." This eased *some* superficial transatlantic tensions. However, this also put CFSP in a dependent relationship with NATO. NATO members confirmed "the enduring validity and indispensability of our Alliance."[22]

Though the major emphasis of CJTF was on reform of NATO's military structure, it also created the European Security and Defense Identity (ESDI) – that is, a European pillar inside NATO. The US supported a European security identity as a means of strengthening the European pillar *within* NATO, since succeeding US governments were wary of European efforts outside NATO that would divide the alliance politically and divert military resources away from NATO.[23] The British Conservative government supported the CJTF initiative, as it achieved the dual Conservative aim of not only tying the WEU to NATO, but also of subordinating CFSP to the WEU and hence to NATO. The effect of this was to Atlanticize European efforts, so to speak, instead of being confronted with the wish of other European governments to (also) incorporate the WEU into the EU. The German CDU/CSU–FDP government was also in favor of CJTF in order to increase the European voice inside NATO while bridging the divergent views between the British and the French governments that erupted in the Maastricht negotiations, a position based on the German government's understanding of multilateralism-as-an-end-in-itself and strong commitment to both institutions (Hilz 2005).

However, the French Socialist presidency disagreed with this Atlanticization of European efforts (Barry 1996: 67; Gordon 1996: 50). For instance, Hubert Védrine, then Secretary General of the Elysée, saw ESDI as an attempt "to impede something European from developing."[24] This policy stance succeeded a tough bargaining process between the Elysée and Matignon where the Socialist president used the *domaine réservé* to the utmost against his prime minister, Balladur. The 1994 French Defense White Paper, for example, mentioned the possibility of closer cooperation with NATO and specified that the president and the prime minister would decide on a case-by-case basis upon the participation of the defense minister and chief of staff in NATO

---

[22] NATO Press Communique M-1 (94) 3.
[23] At the same time, it was the US government that disappointed European governments when on the ground in Bosnia and Herzegovina.
[24] Interview with Hubert Védrine in Paris (May 29, 2008).

meetings (Ministère de la Défense 1994: 37). In April 1994, however, Mitterrand blocked his chief of staff, Admiral Jacques Lanxade, from attending a Military Committee meeting, reflecting his opposition to the regular participation of France's defense minister and military chief of staff at NATO meetings (Lemaitre 1994; Boniface 1995: 11–12). In late September 1994, Léotard's participation (the first since 1966) in an informal meeting of the Alliance's defense ministers in Seville, Spain, was justified by an agenda centered on peacekeeping in the former Yugoslavia and France's implications in it. Mitterrand insisted that the meeting had to be informal and no decisions be taken (Grant 1996: 62, 64). During this *cohabitation*, a full return to NATO committees and institutionalized cooperation with NATO was impossible, despite the changing nature of NATO.

Due to French and British-American differences, the CJTF proposal could not be implemented in 1994 (Delafon and Sancton 1999: 182; Sloan 2003: 169). The political disagreement of the US, UK and French governments over the future role of NATO left the concept unresolved pending consensus on the political level.[25] The initiative remained informal. While governments debated CJTF, only NATO military committees that France was not a member of started working on the concept. Both ESDI and CJTF would have to wait for Chirac to come to power in 1995 in order to be implemented.

French rapprochement with NATO and a European pillar   Based on the RPR's strong insistence on its core value, national sovereignty, and its derivative understanding of multilateralism-as-a-means-to-an other-end (such as increasing France's range of action), Chirac initiated rapprochement with NATO's military structure and, as a consequence, brought the discussion about potential full membership back to the table (Cogan 2001: 72). Chirac had long signaled his intention to revise the standoffish French position toward NATO that Mitterrand had maintained. In 1993 Chirac concluded:

if France wants to play a determining role in the creation of a European defence entity, it must take into account this state of mind of its partners, and reconsider to a larger degree the form of its relations with NATO. It is clear, in effect, that the necessary rebalancing of relations within the Atlantic Alliance, relying on existing European institutions such as the WEU, can only take place from the inside, not against the United States, but in agreement with it. (Quoted in Grant 1996: 63)

---

[25] Because it is an issue over the non-Article 5 mandate, the French government has a veto.

Michel Foucher, who used to be the head of the policy planning unit in the Quai d'Orsay and later Hubert Védrine's political advisor, says that there was *"une rupture"* between Mitterrand and Chirac especially in regard to NATO.[26] Chirac had started to engage with two security institutions in parallel: NATO and the EU. This policy remained his priority and would only be hindered with *cohabitation*. Socialist foreign policy grandee Hubert Védrine perceived Chirac's rapprochement with NATO as a deviation from the "traditional" Gaullist consensus on security and defense.[27] However, as outlined in Chapter 4, this consensus has been shallow, where different political parties cherry-picked elements of the so-called Gaullism that resonated with their party ideologies in the domain of security policy. As Christian Quesnot, chief of the military staff under Mitterrand who stayed on with Jacques Chirac for several months, recalls, "There was a real break with the Gaullist-Mitterandian heritage with regard to NATO. I am not making a judgment on it; it was a political act" (quoted in Cogan 2001: 72). Waiting for the occasion of a NATO summit, on December 5, 1995, Foreign Minister Hervé de Charette announced the return of France to NATO's Military Committee and that France would also start attending all sessions of NATO Ministers of Defense meetings then in the North Atlantic Council (NAC).[28] From now on, so stated the announcement, the defense minister and the chief of staff of the armed forces could participate normally in NATO meetings, rather than on a case-by-case basis decided by the president and the prime minister (as Mitterrand had established in 1994). As a result of the French policy change, NATO's North Atlantic Council had become again the primary venue within the Alliance for decisions to be taken on Alliance operations. This altered a common practice since for most of NATO's existence the NAC was not the pre-eminent decision-making body. Instead, the Defense Planning Committee was very active from

---

[26] Interview with Michel Foucher in Paris (May 30, 2008).

[27] Interview with Hubert Védrine in Paris (May 29, 2008).

[28] Interview with Francois Heisbourg in Paris (May 27, 2008) and Admiral Jean Dufourcq in Paris (May 27, 2008). Dufourcq was on the policy planning staff at the Quai d'Orsay and then advisor to the joint chief of staff. Before this decision, France had only been an observer in the sessions of NATO Ministers of Defense in the NAC since 1966. The RPR had pushed to rejoin during the *cohabitation*, but to no avail. The chief of staff attended the first MC meeting since 1966 in October 1995. After the de Charette speech, the French government clarified that it would participate at most formal defense minister meetings, but will not automatically attend every regular biannual meeting. The DPC's primary role is to manage the International Military Staff and by extension is involved in the annual review of national defense planning. However, this, Chirac argued, is an infringement on national sovereignty (Grant 1996: 65).

its creation in 1963 until 1995 as a means to overcome France's potential veto as France was not a member. Chirac's NATO policy has effectively shifted NATO decision-making into the NAC and other bodies in which they have a voice and a vote.

The British Conservative government, in the second half of 1995, reading Chirac's signals, wanted to facilitate France's return to the integrated command structures thinking that this might end the French push for an autonomous European security institution. In early 1996, the British and French governments jointly advanced the "Deputies proposal" (Delafon and Sancton 1999: 185; Sloan 2003: 169). Under this proposal for multiple-hatting, the Deputy Supreme Allied Commander Europe (DSACEUR), traditionally a European, would wear a WEU hat, in addition to national and NATO hats. Hence without duplicating resources and personnel, the WEU would have access to NATO command structures for organizing and commanding military operations. This would give ESDI a real operational capability, rather than the merely rhetorical ambitions announced in Brussels in 1994.

At the time of NATO's 1996 Berlin Summit on June 3–4, IGC negotiations at Amsterdam had been under way for a couple of months. The Berlin Summit accepted the Deputies proposal and "as a consequence, the 1994 summit goals were transformed at Berlin into a plan to build a European defense pillar inside the NATO alliance" (Sloan 2003: 170). That is, NATO foreign ministers agreed to move ahead with CJTF and formalized ESDI – the latter being able to create a CJTF based on consensus and on a case-by-case basis (Schake *et al.* 1999: 22; Howorth 2000b). This signals a further "transformation from defense to security management [... and] is a clear break with NATO's military stance as an alliance" (Keohane and Wallander 1998: B7). NATO was moving toward non-Article 5 operations. The EU and CFSP found hardly any mention in this context. Instead, ESDI became the attempt to manage potential functional overlap by defining the relationships that CFSP, ESDI, WEU and NATO should play in regard to European and international security. Some member states, especially the British government, tried to fence in WEU so that it could not be used as a competitor to NATO. The French PS, in the opposition, reacted quite forcefully to the Berlin agreements. Paul Quils, the PS's spokesman for defense questions, asked at the time, "What is the interest for France to align itself with American positions without anything in return, and to neglect the dialogue with Europe." At the National Assembly, he criticized the RPR. "Do you really believe that the United States is prepared to allow Europe to develop a strategic autonomy that will lead it to make its own military decisions? Can one believe that we are going to mobilize our European partners by aligning ourselves with the American view?" (both quoted in Boniface 1997).

Chirac proved that he was willing to negotiate within NATO and NATO, especially the United States, gave in to his demands to give posts to Europeans as possible nodes around which CJTF could be organized (Atkinson 1996: A14). Multiple-hatting had been an important condition for the French government to fully return to NATO.[29] However, then Defense Minister Charles Millon made claims on NATO's regional command in the south (AFSOUTH) in Naples after US Secretary of Defense William Perry gave Millon the impression that it would be negotiable (Delafon and Sancton 1999: 203–4).[30] The French government, being interested in visible military positions in the integrated command structure after its long absence, started to negotiate with the US government. This negotiation has often been misrepresented in the press as France asking for the command over the US 6th fleet. What the French government initially proposed was that AFSOUTH – excluding the 6th fleet – be headed by a European instead of an American, beginning with a French military officer.[31] The negotiations first took place in an exchange of letters between Clinton and Chirac from July to November 1996. When this exchange of letters was leaked to the press, the negotiations were momentarily halted pressure from the domestic oppositions became unmanageable (Delafon and Sancton 1999: 206–7).[32] By December, however, Clinton and Chirac started secret negotiations again (Delafon and Sancton 1999: 251, 266).[33] Both sides were working on a compromise solution that would divide AFSOUTH into two commands, one American the other European, to be presented at the Madrid NATO Summit in July 1997. This compromise was focused on satisfying the French government's demands regarding the Southern Command by creating a regional CJTF at Naples that would

[29] Interview with Admiral Jean Dufourcq in Paris (May 27, 2008).

[30] Interview with François Heisbourg in Paris (May 27, 2008). At the time, the United States held both strategic commands in NATO, SACLANT (which does not exist anymore) and SACEUR.

[31] The French government was very aware of the controversy such a demand would cause and hence mentioned explicitly that its demands had nothing to do with the 6th fleet (Delafon and Sancton 1999: 199–208, 213–18). Chirac did not want to cause a fight with the United States because of it (Delafon and Sancton 1999: 234).

[32] Interview with Admiral Jean Dufourcq in Paris (May 27, 2008).

[33] The new American Secretary of Defense, Cohen, thought that the French government was overreaching and publicly criticized the idea (Cogan 2001: 87). However, the secret negotiations continued. At the time, the German government tried to help mediate the negotiations.

be commanded by a European for operations in the Mediterranean region. By April, the US and French governments were very close to an agreement (Delafon and Sancton 1999: 282).

Around the same time as the negotiations were held, Chirac decided on an "ill-judged snap dissolution of the National Assembly" (Knapp 2003: 127), which resulted in the RPR losing the majority in the National Assembly.[34] The arrival of the new Socialist coalition government, led by Prime Minister Lionel Jospin and Foreign Minister Hubert Védrine, both of whom (especially Védrine) had systematically criticized Chirac's rapprochement with NATO, meant that no further movement in the direction of NATO was possible.[35] "It is a political spectacle that killed the negotiations" (Delafon and Sancton 1999: 283).[36] Chirac tried "de rattraper la betise [to make up for the foolishness]"[37] but the damage was done. In an attempt to demonstrate that foreign and security policy was not the exclusive domain of the president, and to constrain presidential power, the Socialists blocked the initiative by refusing to countersign any such decision. As a Foreign Affairs ministry spokesperson observed, "without prejudging presidential powers, it seems that the conditions for the continued rapprochement are no longer present" (quoted in Delafon and Sancton 1999: 301). Soon after, the Elysée and Matignon presented a joint communiqué declaring that "the conditions for reexamining relations with NATO military structures no longer exist" (quoted in Lamy 1997: 56). The PS was unwilling to restart the negotiations based on its understanding that NATO should concentrate on its old core task and not interfere in European community building. Says Védrine, "this new world is marked by the predominace of the US which is sometimes referred to as hegemony. The key change is that there is not yet a counterweight" (quoted in Lamy 1997: 56). Foucher says of this episode that "Jospin buried the idea of a rapprochement with NATO."[38]

---

[34] "Learning of Chirac's defeat, President Clinton 'rolled his eyes' according to an advisor. 'He knew that this would complicate the relations with France and could bury the accord over AFSOUTH'" (Delafon and Sancton 1999: 288).

[35] The first thing that happened when Védrine came to office under the *cohabitation* was to make "*un bilan d'échec* [survey of the damage]" of the previous government. Védrine argued that being reintegrated completely in NATO would give France not more influence in it, but would make it lose its originality. Interview with Hubert Védrine in Paris (May 29, 2008).

[36] "According to Pentagon officials, a compromise was being worked out in the spring of 1997 that might have been acceptable to Chirac, had his party coalition been returned to power in the elections" (Cogan 2001: 89).

[37] Interview with Admiral Jean Dufourcq in Paris (May 27, 2008).

[38] Interview with Michel Foucher in Paris (May 30, 2008).

After the first round of negotiations had ended, Jospin blocked the idea of trying to renew it. At the NATO Madrid Summit, Clinton offered Chirac a chance to complete the negotiations but Chirac replied that his domestic situation made this impossible (Delafon and Sancton 1999: 305–6; Cogan 2001: 89).[39] In September 1997, in front of the Institut des hautes etudes de défense nationale, Jospin, who was very much in favor of a European security and defense institution, said that his government had the political will to push in the European direction (Isnard 1997). NATO, on the other hand, continued to implement ESDI based on the Berlin Summit decision, making room in its structures, but handing over a regional command to a European was an *"occasion ratée [missed opportunity]"*[40] – and with it the opportunity to create a meaningful European institution within NATO.

Negotiating Amsterdam: trying to merge the WEU with the EU

Spurred on by European failures in the Balkans as well as Article N of the Maastricht Treaty, some EU governments raised the issue of security policy at the IGC negotiations that began in March 1996 (Gordon 1997/8; Kohl 2007: 647). For some, particularly the French RPR and German CDU/CSU–FDP governments, "The construction of a European pillar *within* NATO does not make the construction of a European pillar *outside* NATO superfluous, especially when it comes to … the structures necessary for political control and military command" (Gnesotto 1996: 26–7; see also Mouton and Charpentier 1996).

With the mandate to start the revisions on the Maastricht Treaty, the Italian presidency started the IGC on March 29, 1996 at the European Council of Turin.[41] It would take 18 months to conclude negotiations

---

[39] Heisbourg says that it is very likely that the negotiations would have been successful if Jospin had not come to power. NATO was an issue in the election campaign at the time, but not a major one. Interview with François Heisbourg in Paris (May 27, 2008). And Cogan (2001: 89) observes: "According to one State Department official intimately connected with the NATO process, Chirac's government held out the possibility that France might rejoin the NATO military structure at the time of the Madrid Summit in July 1997. Pentagon officials claim to this day that what halted the French move back toward NATO more than anything else was the imprudent decision of Chirac to schedule the snap legislative election of May 1997, which upset this final attempt at a rapprochement between France and NATO."

[40] Interview with Admiral Jean Dufourcq in Paris (May 27, 2008).

[41] Turin was preceded by six months of preparation by a working group during the Spanish presidency. It was decided then that the primary issues on the IGC agenda would be institutional reform to prepare for enlargement, budgetary reform, and the completion of the single market.

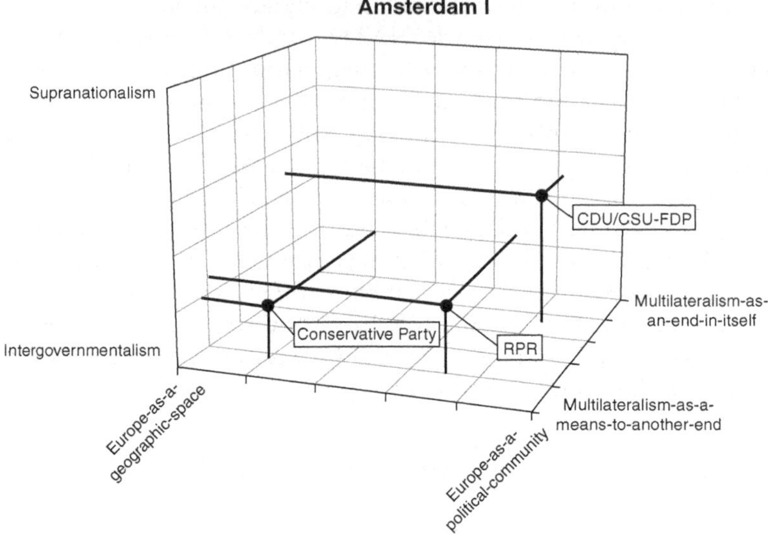

Figure 5.1 Degree of ideological congruence, 1996

at Amsterdam in June 1997. The final version of the treaty was signed on October 2, 1997. The main reason for the length of the IGC was the British government's opposition to further integration on issues such as security policy. Indeed, European governments feared that negotiations would continue into the Luxembourg presidency if the Conservatives won the British election on May 1, 1997. As it happened, however, Labour ousted the Conservatives, paving the way for the treaty to be signed.

Stalled negotiations: the Conservative government refuses WEU–EU integration   The lack of ideological congruence between the French,[42] German and British governments became all too obvious during the Italian and Irish presidencies in 1996 (see Figure 5.1). While the Conservative Party had agreed to review the Maastricht Treaty under Article N, when the treaty was reopened in 1996 the Conservative government still opposed any further integration, insisting on the need to maintain sovereignty against any further devolution of power to Brussels.[43]

[42] See Manin (1996) for a thorough discussion of the French position during the Amsterdam negotiations.
[43] "We were her [US] closest ally in NATO. We shared a language. Our instincts and outlook were more often in tune with North America than with Western Europe. It was no wonder that many Conservatives hankered for an Anglo-Saxon alliance across

Nonetheless, and in light of the improved Franco-NATO relationship under Chirac, the French RPR and German CDU/CSU–FDP governments joined forces in an initiative on December 9, 1996 to create an autonomous European security institution. Reminiscent of the proposal submitted during the previous IGC negotiations in 1990–1, they wrote a letter to the Irish presidency, presenting the *Common Security and Defense Concept* (Vernet 1999; van Ham 2000: 65). The concept proposed a stronger commitment to CFSP, including creation of a general secretary position for CFSP and a three-phased timetable for the integration of the WEU into the EU to be completed by 2010 (Bundesregierung 2000: 43). The first stage would come into force with the Amsterdam Treaty. In this phase the EU would be able to request that the WEU implement agreed-upon security operations using NATO forces. In stage two, EU decisions would be binding on the WEU. Finally, in stage three, the two bodies would be integrated when the EU adopted the WEU mutual defense treaty clause – but would also allow member states to opt out of these commitments (Hilz 2005: 163–78). While Mitterrand and Kohl proposed agreements on CFSP based on their common understanding of Europe-as-a-political-community, Chirac and Kohl had more in common in their appreciation of NATO than Europe. Thus, the Franco-German proposal also explicitly stated that American involvement in Europe is vital. "More than ever, Paris and Bonn link their defense to the Atlantic Alliance" (Delafon and Sancton 1999: 269; see also Mouton and Charpentier 1996: 119).

This results from the RPR's core value of sovereignty tied to multilateralism and Europe leading to preferences for increasing France's possible range of action without giving in to potential supranational pressures as well as the CDU/CSU–FDP's appreciation of multilateralism-as-an-end-in-itself and Europe-as-a-political-community. However, while these party ideologies led to relatively similar policy preferences, their ideological foundations and congruence was modest. Their policy preferences were interpreted through different values (especially regarding sovereignty); this would later result in the abolishment of the proposal. The RPR's insistence on intergovernmentalism goes against the CDU/CSU's valuing of supranationalism in the case of Europe. Chirac was actually very skeptical of the complete transfer of the WEU into the EU as he

the Atlantic, rather than a Continental alliance across the Channel ... We had won many arguments with our European partners. The growth of free trade in the single market had been a British success ... All this moved in a British direction ... And yet our partners wanted a single currency. We did not. They wanted a Social Chapter. We did not. They wanted more harmonisation of policy. We did not. They wanted more Community control of defence. We did not" (Major 1999: 578–9).

liked to have as many multilateral forums as possible at his disposal to conduct French security policy. In addition, like the British government, Chirac was suspicious of a German proposal (supported by Belgium and Greece) to abolish the three-pillar structure of the EU – allowing the Commission, the EP and the ECJ to have more input in all EU policy fields (Gnesotto 1996: 21; Mouton and Charpentier 1996: 114).

While the British government was receptive to the French turn toward NATO, this did not translate into support for the Franco-German proposal. Taking the initiative, the Irish presidency tried to synthesize the various positions presented at the IGC and presented a draft text of treaty changes and a number of options for CFSP reform (Cameron 1999: 63), but the British government refused to sign. Britain's Conservative government stayed consistent with its previous attitude, blocking the merger and resisting any possible pressures and incentives toward integration – despite international changes (Palmer 1997b: 19). Major had already insisted at Maastricht and reiterated on many occasions that "I want to see the Community become a wide union, embracing the whole of democratic Europe, in a single market and with common security arrangements firmly linked to NATO" (Major 1999: 586). To this end, the British government had also sent out a memorandum to its European counterparts on March 1, 1995 in which it objected to a merger of the EU and WEU (Mouton and Charpentier 1996: 120).

Even as other EU member states attempted, in vain, to convince the Conservative government, its own civil service drafted proposals for a European security institution that they thought would be agreeable to the Major government. The experiences of being left fighting alongside the French in Bosnia and Herzegovina from 1992 to 1995, without the Americans, led the defense ministry bureaucrats to propose the creation of a European security institution (with emphasis on capabilities) that would prevent the sorts of problems that came to light in Bosnia. The Conservatives prevented the plan from gaining political momentum, however, arguing that the primacy of NATO should not be questioned.[44] This is indicative of the "bureaucracy on the leash" argument presented in Chapter 3; proposals originating from the bureaucratic level might have a long shelf life but they only come to the light of international politics if the politicians heading the bureaucracies either care about them, attach absolutely no importance to their content or do not pay attention.

A European security institution could not move forward in terms of institutional autonomy, formal and precise legal framework or human and material resources. The Conservative government refused all

---

[44] Interview # 9 with British official in London (December 8, 2006).

political subordination of the WEU to the EU and any move that would place European security and defense in the framework of common EU policies (Gnesotto 1996: 21).[45] Stephen Wall, the British chief negotiator and UK representative to the EU at the time, recalls:

After a months-long preparatory phase led, for Britain, by the European Minister David Davies, the negotiating conference itself was conducted mainly at official level. As the UK representative on the negotiating group, I was on a very tight rein. Every week, before each negotiation session, I would receive pages of minute instructions from the Foreign Office, personally authorised by David Davies. The Foreign Office could have saved themselves a lot of trouble by sending a one-line instruction: "Just say no." There was virtually nothing on the agenda that was palatable to the government. (Wall 2008: 157)

As the Conservative government insisted that security and defense issues stay with national governments and NATO, the Dutch presidency reflected this position in the draft treaty, which it presented to the other EU member states at the beginning of April. The UK's veto on the link between the WEU and the EU could therefore not delay the entire IGC, as what mattered to the Dutch presidency and the other European governments most were issues of greater qualified majority voting and a flexibility clause, which would allow a hard core of member states to pool powers at faster speeds than others – these issues would prepare the EU for further enlargement. By the time of the British election, some observers suggested that about 80 percent of the treaty had been agreed, but based on its ideological position, the British government continued to oppose qualified majority voting and enhanced cooperation (Palmer 1997b: 19).

A quick end to the negotiations: Labour comes to power When Labour came to power in May 1997, the ideological distance among the major governments in Europe shifted (see Figure 5.2). While the Conservatives were blocking the UK's acceptance of Amsterdam, after Blair came to power and met with the Dutch premier, Wim Kok was quoted as stating, "I now believe that it will be possible for us to reach an agreement" (Black and Macaskill 1997: 5). However, the new British government had to familiarize itself with the situation first as it took over the negotiations at a very advanced stage.[46] "The first thing the government had to do was signal its new approach to its partners" (Wall

---

[45] The Conservative government was one of the primary proponents of expanding links between the WEU and NATO. Interview with Paul Cornish in London (December 6, 2006).

[46] Blair needed to know, first, how the negotiations went so far, and where the debates were. He spent his first weeks in office receiving many Foreign Office briefings on every aspect of EU affairs.

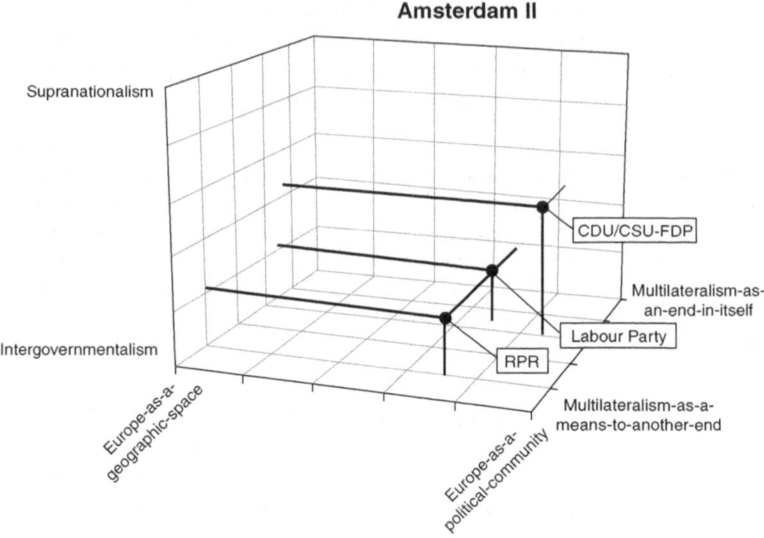

Figure 5.2 Degree of ideological congruence, 1997

2008: 163). In Labour's first weeks in government, it participated in various EU ministerial meetings and two head of state and government meetings when Amsterdam was ready to be signed.

Less than one week into office, Doug Henderson, the Labour Europe minister tasked with setting out the government's policy at a meeting of member state representatives in Brussels, said, "We want to work with you as colleagues in a shared enterprise. Not using the language of opponents. Europe, for the new British government, is an opportunity not a threat" (quoted in Helm 1997b: 6), and confirmed that reaching a deal by the Amsterdam Summit in June would be a top priority "to the relief of his European counterparts after 18 months of stalled talks with his predecessors" (Helm 1997b: 6).[47] Wall, who remained the chief negotiator for the UK during the entire IGC negotiations, also confirmed that the ideological shift in government led to a reorientation of the civil servants working alongside him. With a new government in power, the civil service adapted to the new party's ideological stance:

[47] In the same meeting Doug Henderson said, "I come to this meeting as the representative of a new government with an overwhelming mandate. One of the most important priorities we have identified is to make a fresh start to Britain's relations with the rest of the EU and draw a line under the recent past" (quoted in Wall 2008: 163).

I recall Robin Cook's surprise that officials had prepared for him a draft minute to the Prime Minister about the negotiations that so accurately reflected the positions previously announced by the Labour Party in Opposition. Labour had been out of office for eighteen years. Cook himself had never been in government before. I think he expected to find a Civil Service that would try to persuade him to take Conservative positions, whereas what he in fact found was a Civil Service nervously anxious to satisfy its new boss. (Wall 2008: 163)

Blair met his European counterparts for the first time on May 23 in Noordwijk at a special EU leaders' summit after being in government for about two weeks. To demonstrate its European credentials, one of the new government's first moves was to end the British opt-out from the Social Chapter and support an employment chapter in the treaty.[48] And while John Major and his government were blocking the increase in majority voting in the realm of foreign policy, the Blair government accepted a reduction of the British veto over joint foreign policy *implementation*, as had been promised in the election manifesto, and also agreed to the creation of a position of general secretary representing the EU in foreign policy.[49] But as Sir Emyr Jones Parry, who was Deputy Political Director in the Foreign Office at the time and was soon to become FCO's Director European Union, pointed out, besides the commitments he made in his election program and which were already presented to the EU counterparts by Henderson a week earlier, Blair had had no time to set out his agenda and could only make "small adjustments."[50]

These small adjustments also touched on a common European security institution. First, legal language was added to the treaty. The British government agreed that the goal of common security and defense would be written in the treaty (Amsterdam Treaty 1997a: Article J3 [1]). It also allowed for the wording: "the Union shall accordingly foster closer institutional relations with the WEU with a view to the possibility of the integration of the WEU into the Union"; however, only "should the European Council so decide" (Amsterdam Treaty 1997a: Article J7[1]) leaving every EU member state with a veto over

---

[48] Labour said that joining the first round of EMU would be very unlikely but reasoned with economic arguments which differed greatly from Conservative sovereignist arguments. Also, Labour was the first British government to accept EU money for an information campaign (Perkins and Elliott 1997: 3). On a different note, Labour signed onto the Social Chapter but asked for a two-year transition period on implementing the Chapter. This indicates that Labour had to consolidate its power and ideas in government first before it could really act accordingly.

[49] The latter point had not been negotiated yet with the hope that the Conservatives could be convinced. Interview # 13 with German military official in Berlin (January 24, 2008).

[50] Interview with Emyr Jones Parry in New York (February 22, 2007).

the merger (Palmer and White 1997b: 1).[51] The treaty also established that EU members that are not members of the WEU could participate in some WEU activities. Most importantly, Blair was willing to see the Petersberg tasks of the WEU included among the issues covered by the EU[52] – with the WEU implementing decisions with security implications but NATO remaining the primary framework for mutual defense (Wall 2008: 163–4) – foreshadowing what would come later with ESDP. Thus, under the agreement, the merger of the EU and the WEU would be postponed even as the two bodies would begin to work more closely with one another. Furthermore, in terms of human and institutional resources, the Amsterdam Treaty established the post of High Representative of CFSP, which would also be the Secretary General of the Council of Ministers (hence a bureaucrat) in Article J8 to give more continuity and visibility to the policy field. At his or her side would be the Policy Planning and Early Warning Unit (later known as Policy Unit), an administrative structure that was initially very small in size. On paper, the role of High Representative is modest; mainly he or she would assist the presidency and the Council in preparing and implementing policy decisions (Duke 2006: 12). The decision as to who would fill the post was postponed and, hence, the institutional structure remained an empty shell. The decision at the Cologne Summit in 1999 to give the post to Javier Solana would not only fill this vacant position but also appoint an expert on security. In any case, Labour agreed to issues that had been opposed by the previous British Conservative government. Amsterdam thus represented a "compromise deal over the future of European defence, ending a dispute that had proved a serious obstacle to a final treaty agreement" (Palmer 1997a: 10; Lemaitre 1997).[53]

On issues of security and defense, the Blair government remained reserved at Amsterdam for several reasons. First, the three-phased

[51] In the "Declaration of the Western European Union on the Role of the Western European Union and its Relations with the European Union and with the Atlantic Alliance" attached to the treaty, the WEU declares that "WEU is an integral part of the development of the European Union (EU) providing the Union access to an operational capability, notably in the context of the Petersberg tasks and is an essential element of the development of the ESDI within the Atlantic Alliance in accordance with the Paris Declaration and with the decisions taken by NATO ministers in Berlin" (Amsterdam Treaty 1997b: par. 1).

[52] Interview # 11 with senior German official in Berlin (March 16, 2007).

[53] In another newspaper report it says, "Mr Blair claimed that the final treaty text on a common defence had satisfied his demands that Europe's new defence powers be limited to carrying out humanitarian and peace-keeping tasks" (Helm 1997a: 16). This indicates Blair's willingness to pursue a security institution within the EU while at the same time assuring the British public that the institution will not be completely identical with NATO.

Franco-German proposition included a mutual defense clause – a move that was hard for any British government to accept, let alone the EU's neutral member states.[54] Not much time was left to negotiate a different kind of merger than initially intended by Chirac and Kohl. Second, Labour "proceeded with caution because they did not want to stir up a media hornet's nest. They did not need to worry about the state of opinion in the Parliamentary Labour Party," where MPs strongly backed Blair's European policies (Wall 2008: 166). Major had made his refusal to merge the WEU and the EU very public during the national elections and stirred talk of the creation of a European army. Labour did not want to take on such a controversial issue just after taking over government (Oppermann 2008: 161).[55] Third, foreign and security issues had already been more or less set aside as the Conservatives were very clear on vetoing any reform in this issue area and, at the time Labour came to power, its EU counterparts were mostly preoccupied with voting rights and Commission streamlining to prepare the EU for enlargement.[56] Fourth, Labour had to make sure that the British government structures were well equipped organizationally to conduct a more pro-European policy (Bulmer and Burch 2005: 877). Also, "Labour was out of power for 18 years, European security was not a top priority of the party just after it got to power, but Blair was much more relaxed on European issues."[57] Blair "was pro-European but as he had just entered as prime minister did not want to start on such a note. He was never convinced of what he was doing in Amsterdam."[58] As compensation to European partners, Blair signaled that he intended to go further over time by agreeing to incorporate the Petersberg tasks.[59] "In due course, European defence was to become the area where Tony Blair moved British policy further than any of his predecessors" (Wall 2008: 169).

[54] Article V of the WEU treaty is more far-reaching and automatic than NATO's in its obligations of mutual defense. Hence, not only the UK but also the neutral EU members were against the complete merger of the WEU and EU.

[55] A former senior British official said that in Amsterdam "Blair vetoed because he did not want the press. He was pro-European but as he had just entered as prime minister, he did not want to start on such a revolutionary note." Interview # 3 with former senior British official in London (December 4, 2006).

[56] Two senior officials in the MoD both confirmed that Blair had no real choices in Amsterdam as the negotiations were in an advanced stage and Labour did not run on a detailed EU agenda. Interview # 5 and # 8 in London (December 5 and 7, 2006). "Labour only did not change the British track in Amsterdam because of institutional inertia." Interview # 4 with senior British official in London (December 5, 2006).

[57] Interview # 9 with British official in London (December 8, 2006).

[58] Interview # 3 with former senior British official in London (December 4, 2006).

[59] Interview with Emyr Jones Parry in New York (February 22, 2008) and interview # 9 with British official in London (December 8, 2006).

With the Labour government in power, Chirac signaled at the beginning of May 1997 that he would "abandon Franco-German plans for a *complete* and *timetabled* integration of the EU and the Western European Union (WEU) ... Mr Chirac is not ready to settle for bringing the two organisations closer together effectively deferring plans for a future European defence union" (Palmer and White 1997a: 1, emphasis added; see also Mouton and Charpentier 1996). The compromise solution between Chirac and Kohl, that had held together loosely and through an ideological adversary in the form of a British Conservative government, crumbled with a new potential ideological partner in town that was more closely aligned to the RPR than the German CDU/CSU–FDP coalition. Kohl followed Chirac in abandoning their proposal in order to pave the way for the IGC conclusion. However, Chirac and Kohl asked that the issue of common European security and defense be reviewed at the next IGC (Palmer 1997a: 10; Bitterlich 2005: 44–6). This put less pressure on Blair, who on the other hand, indicated that he would see what he could do once his government had more time to review European security and consolidate its position.

While Labour had an impact on finalizing the IGC negotiations,[60] the PS, which joined Chirac in government only two weeks before the negotiations ended, was basically left out of the process. Jospin accompanied Chirac to Amsterdam, made demands in regard to EMU, and criticized Amsterdam for lacking European spirit; in spite of this, and given the surprise elections, in actuality Jospin had no time to prepare for the IGC (Delafon and Sancton 1999: 295; Chevallier *et al.* 2007: 438–9). Jack Lang, a Socialist Party member and chairman of the Foreign Affairs Commission in the National Assembly in France, resonates this sentiment. He criticized the Amsterdam Treaty which his party had not negotiated but had to sign hardly having been in government. He said that, in regard to foreign and security policy, the treaty did not provide more institutional innovations and that the PS had wanted "the creation of a European federation" (Lang 1997: 1).

Alternative explanations

Despite the impact of party ideologies on bargaining over European security, existing realist and rational choice institutionalist explanations

---

[60] The Conservative Party voted against the European Communities (Amendment) Bill, ratifying the Amsterdam Treaty (White 1997b: 12). Michael Howard, the Conservative shadow foreign secretary, called Amsterdam "an unacceptable step towards an integrated federal superstate" (Howard quoted in Bevins 1997: 7).

ignore the role of government values in formulating security policy. Even a partisan values argument that relies on a left–right continuum misses the specific values that misaligned between governments. Despite all parties coming from "the right" of the political spectrum for the majority of the negotiations, they failed to negotiate an intergovernmental European security institution at Amsterdam. Indeed, as a "failed case" in European security, outcomes at Amsterdam have received relatively little attention in any arguments.

Only one governing party was replaced between Maastricht and Amsterdam, when the ruling party in France changed from the PS to the RPR. The result was a significant revision of France's policy preferences toward NATO and an autonomous European security institution. While the major European states were now all governed by parties from the right, they disagreed on the kind of institution, whether supranational or intergovernmental, and on the forum for institutional cooperation, whether NATO and/or the EU. In fact, despite all parties emphasizing the value of liberty, they could not agree on the creation of a new European security institution. The RPR preference for European security cooperation reflected its multilateralism-as-a-means-to-another-end, insistence on intergovernmentalism and a pro-European orientation; these three values cannot be derived from a putative right-wing preference for liberty. While the British Conservatives define sovereignty and multilateralism the same as the RPR, they differ in their understanding of Europe. The Conservatives are opposed to any community-building policy within Europe, while the RPR values Europe as just another community that could serve France's interest. And the CDU/CSU and FDP coalition differed on all three values with the Conservatives and the RPR, though the German government's interpretation of Europe was more aligned with the one of the RPR than with the Conservatives. As shown, this has resulted in major differences in policy preferences. When set against a partisan values argument, the Amsterdam case demonstrates the importance of looking beyond left–right distinctions emphasizing liberty or equality to the concrete values that motivate security policy, as well as the degree of congruence across European governments.

Among realist explanations, Seth Jones (2007) has argued that the Amsterdam episode was yet another step toward soft-balancing the United States and binding Germany. This argument has three fundamental weaknesses. First, and most importantly, it rests on a misunderstanding of the institutional outcome. Amsterdam did not strengthen the security dimension of CFSP. It introduced neither more balancing nor binding elements to the institution. Second, Jones' binding and balancing arguments completely ignore the parallel developments of CJTF and ESDI inside NATO. The United States wanted to bind European states to NATO through the CJTF mechanism and ESDI. Some European governments agreed with this policy, others did not. As I have shown above, NATO was fundamental to debates about how to develop CFSP and create an autonomous European security institution. Third, arguments about soft balancing against NATO through CFSP ignore the fact that, once the RPR came to power in France, European governments were in favor of a US presence in Europe through NATO. Arguably, CJTF and ESDI substantially strengthened NATO, with European encouragement. This behavior goes counter to soft balancing in the US and, though Jones does not make the argument, could be accounted for through a binding argument – both of the United States and Germany.

From a rational choice institutionalist perspective, it remains puzzling why European governments tolerated inefficiencies in their military operations at the same time that they were engaged in Bosnia and Herzegovina, arguably the most important crisis facing Europe in decades. For years during the Bosnian wars, NATO could not overcome internal disagreements that impeded the ability of allies to act. Celeste Wallander (2000), Joseph Lepgold (1998: 99–101) and Stanley Sloan (1995) argue that ESDI and CJTF were NATO's answer to these problems. However, as the evidence above shows, the success of ESDI and CJTF had less to do with the "adaptability" of NATO assets to new tasks than with two other factors that relate to party ideologies: first, changes of government in France, namely the shift from Socialists skeptical of NATO to an RPR government keen to return France to NATO and, second, the US and British attempt to keep European security cooperation in NATO. "Cooperation problems" are not a given but are understood through ideological lenses. Furthermore, developments in European security in the mid 1990s also go against the rational choice institutionalist argument that when faced with a cooperation problem – that is, disagreements between the United States and European allies over how to act in Bosnia, for example – states will create a new (European) institution to solve the problem. After the launch of ESDI and CJTF, as Wallander (2000) points out, European operations still depended on the consent of all NATO members, including the United States, before a CJTF under WEU command (i.e. an ESDI operation) could be launched. In other words, transformation of NATO did not solve the cooperation problem that rational institutionalists argue motivated ESDI's creation. The Amsterdam episode could have plausibly been the attempt where European governments realized that they needed an *autonomous* security institution to be efficient in the formulation and conduct of multilateral security. However, based on ideologies' incongruence, this did not happen. As I demonstrate, both reforms within NATO and the failures to strengthen CFSP at Amsterdam are rooted in the extent to which fundamental values amongst governments in power overlapped.

Conclusion

The case of the Amsterdam Treaty negotiated between 1996 and 1997 shows that the aspiration to create a security institution, as voiced in the Maastricht Treaty, does not translate into a robust institution *peu à peu*. Despite the claim that Europe is the most highly and deeply institutionalized region in the world, no institution develops automatically and in a linear fashion. Rules, practices and trust do not automatically substitute for political will and preferences. The creation or substantiation of an institution depends on other factors.

After the transatlantic tensions over former Yugoslavia from 1991 to 1995, the European response as to how to overcome these obstacles was not uniform. Some governments wanted to ensure that European security remained in the hands of NATO as a whole, while others desired an autonomous institution. The Amsterdam Treaty did not alter the character of CFSP because of the disagreements among the leading member states' governments whose distinct ideological boundaries prevented them from coming to an agreement. Therefore, "the treaty is a more readable revision of the controversial European Union treaty negotiated in Maastricht" (Whitney 1997: A14). As Cornish says, "Even the most professionally prepared and aesthetically pleasing blueprint failed to eliminate the competition" (Cornish 1996: 752). The treaty negotiations are considered a failure because the EU did not receive any autonomous assets or capabilities. Until Labour came to power in the UK, no serious re-evaluation of CFSP could take place. Several actors were unwilling to create an institution that could potentially compete with NATO. The military hardware stayed with the WEU and NATO instead; NATO provides operational capability to the WEU through the CJTF mechanism. The EU had not become more autonomous in security matters, but arguably more intertwined with NATO.

Some changes to CFSP only happened because of the late change of government in the UK. The Labour government under Blair started a fundamental shift toward the EU but it did not want to be perceived as too hasty. However, Blair did not wait for a next IGC to take the opportunity to change the European security landscape. He did not even wait until the Amsterdam Treaty was ratified. Instead, soon after he consolidated his government and established new EU policy units in the ministries (Bulmer and Burch 2005), he initiated ESDP, a topic to which I turn in the next chapter.

6 Saint Malo, Cologne and Nice: the creation of the robust ESDP

In 1998, NATO scholar David Yost wrote: "NATO has persisted as the central and single most effective multinational security organization in Europe" (Yost 1998: 27). Yet the same year, two European governments met at a bilateral summit to lay the foundations for a robust and autonomous European security institution – despite their membership in NATO. The Franco-British Summit in Saint Malo in December 1998 laid the groundwork for European Councils in Cologne (June 1999) and Helsinki (December 1999) and the IGC in Nice (December 2000) that created ESDP, an independent European crisis management and conflict prevention institution outside NATO-run and NATO-supported institutional structures. Key documents refer to the EU's "autonomous capacity to take decisions" and to "launch and conduct EU-led military operations" (Cologne Presidency Conclusions 1999: II, 7; European Council Nice 2000: Annex VI). New and growing power centers were introduced into the equation of European crisis management: the European Council, the ESDP institutions and EU-led multinational military and civil-military forces.

The formation of ESDP represented the culmination of a European ambition to create a security institution autonomous from NATO – an ambition that waxed and waned in individual European states depending on the party in power. The creation of an autonomous and equipped European security institution was not possible as late as 1996 which, as I have shown in examining the Amsterdam Treaty in Chapter 5, failed due to the inability of major European governments to find common ground. Yet by 1998, the topic of a European security institution was again on the political agenda. By 1999, ESDP had been established – prior to the Nice IGC in 2000, which confirmed ESDP's creation as part of the TEU.

What made the difference? This chapter shows that the key was a change in the parties in power, particularly in the UK and France, and, as a consequence, a change in the international configuration of ideologies of parties in government. ESDP was made possible through congruence of ideologies between Labour in the UK, the RPR in France, and the SPD–Green coalition in Germany. The institution was based on shared ideologies around the intergovernmental nature of security institutions, a common view of Europe, and, to a lesser degree, multilateralism in the use of force. This congruence explains why ESDP was not only created but became robust. Put simply, without attention to the ideological configuration of parties across Europe, one cannot explain the creation of ESDP, its timing, its institutional design, its institutional capacities or its degree of autonomy from NATO.

In this chapter, I first briefly examine the international environment around the time of ESDP's initiation, focusing on the Kosovo War, an event often cited as the motivation for ESDP creation. Second, I examine the ideological spectrum across parties in the UK, France and Germany, showing that important ideological differences remained in the parties on the domestic level, a situation that had important ideological implications for their foreign and security policy. The third section explains the mechanics of the ideological congruence of European political parties around ESDP. The absence of this congruence had earlier been a critical impediment to the creation of a well-equipped European security institution. I discuss ESDP's emergence as a political project in the shadow of NATO and how negotiations between the British, French and German governments were shaped by the values of parties in power are also discussed. The SPD–Green coalition government in Germany, while far from a bystander in ESDP's creation, had a less active role in initiating ESDP than the British or French governments. The German government did, however, leave its mark on ESDP by influencing its design and mandate in ways that reflected SPD–Green values. In the fourth section, I compare my party ideology explanation to rational choice institutionalist, realist and partisan values alternative explanations.

Balkan Wars continued

In the late 1990s, the Balkans still dominated European security. Whereas the early 1990s saw deep differences emerge between European governments and the United States over the handling of Yugoslavia's breakup, the Kosovo War initially saw only minor differences between allies across the Atlantic. Nonetheless, for some authors European reliance on US power exercised through NATO underscored the need for an autonomous European security institution (Cameron 1999; Cohen 1999; Howorth 2007). Yet, as I show below, developments in Kosovo had relatively little to do with ESDP, the origins of which date back to late December 1998.

During 1998, the Serb government responded to a rapidly escalating insurgency in Kosovo with a series of offensives. Unlike in Bosnia, the US government was involved from the beginning. Both sides of the Atlantic were united in condemning both Albanian guerrillas and the Serb government. On March 7, 1998, Madeleine Albright – who had been in favor of an earlier US intervention in Bosnia – declared, "we are not going to stand by and watch the Serbian authorities do in Kosovo what they can no longer get away with doing in Bosnia" (US State Department 1999). The Contact Group began to meet on the issue of Kosovo. Parallel to diplomatic efforts, military intervention was also contemplated relatively soon after the situation in Kosovo escalated, with relatively little disagreement between the United States and major European powers. This was significantly different from Bosnia where such disagreements led to a low point in transatlantic relations. In June 1998, at the NATO ministerial meeting, US Secretary of Defense William Cohen urged his NATO counterparts to begin conceptual planning for a potential intervention in Kosovo. After failing to compel Serb forces to ratchet down violence that was producing large numbers of displaced persons inside Kosovo, NATO issued an activation warning in September 1998 – the first real step toward air strikes.

But in October 1998, US diplomat Richard Holbrooke was able to negotiate the October Agreement introducing OSCE monitors, and in late October Serbia withdrew its forces from Kosovo. This was only a temporary ceasefire, however, and the fighting picked up again at the start of 1999. The Contact Group issued an ultimatum in late January 1999, setting up peace talks in Rambouillet at the beginning of February. It is only at this point that transatlantic differences came to the fore (Woodward 2004: 25). The Rambouillet talks, chaired by France and the UK, failed for many reasons. Michel Foucher, who prepared the talks on the French side, says that the United States was in favor of immediate Kosovo independence, while the British and French governments were more hesitant.[1] On March 24, NATO's air war began. It was then that transatlantic tensions intensified. Europeans complained that the United States did not share important intelligence information with them. There were also debates over the targets of the bombing campaign (Peters *et al.* 2001: 25–6; Woodward 2004: 25). In addition, the technological gap between the United States and Europe made itself felt as "around 80 percent of all strike sorties flown in Allied Force were

---

[1] Interview with Michel Foucher in Paris (May 30, 2008).

carried out by US aircraft" (Lambeth 2001: 168; see also Cohen 1999: A1; Cordesman 2001: 64). Of the members participating in Operation Allied Force, only the United States, the UK and France deployed aircraft that could deliver precision-guided munitions. Because they lacked all-weather or night capabilities, some allies were restricted to day or good weather missions (Nardulli *et al.* 2002: 120). However, it is worth noticing, as Lambeth does, that "two decades of multinational training at Red Flag and elsewhere paid off handsomely in [operation] Allied Force. There were no midair collisions or other near-catastrophic aerial incidents resulting from allies operating from their own private playbooks" (Lambeth 2001: 170). This suggests that, at the operational level, NATO had developed assets that improved cooperation.

The air strikes formally ended on June 20 when Milošević agreed to retreat from Kosovo. Just prior to this, the UN had adopted resolution 1244 and the NATO-led KFOR was launched with around 16,000 troops. Partly to atone for their thin contribution to the bombing campaign, but also to provide the necessary resources to police the Kosovo ceasefire agreement, European forces took on the bulk of the crisis management task that followed the air war. Most observers of transatlantic relations observed that European attitudes toward the United States deteriorated *after* the Kosovo War (Woodward 2004). However, ESDP was already under development at this point, with institutional creation reflecting a new congruence in ideological values across ruling parties in Europe.

Domestic ideological configurations across parties in Europe

Before the Kosovo War unfolded, important steps were being taken that would eventually culminate in ESDP. At the end of the 1990s, the parties in government in the United Kingdom, Germany and France agreed on key policy issues in the realm of security. The political parties in government advocated the same policies toward their countries' relationship to NATO and conceived the possibility of a European security alternative to NATO. However, on the domestic level, each government party continued to face ideological differences with opposition parties – indicating that national interest is ideologically motivated.

The Labour government: changing the relationship with Europe

The Labour Party missed the chance to commit to a full European agenda at Amsterdam because it had just entered government. However, the Labour Party came to power with an agenda that included a commitment to changing the UK's relationship to Europe. The transition from a Conservative to Labour government underscored the sharp changes in policy that can result from new parties coming to power.

The change Labour brought about in the UK's foreign and security policy vis-à-vis both Europe and NATO had a history in the two parties' divergent ideologies. Labour came into government with the aspiration of being at the "heart of Europe" and was looking for an expression of it.[2] This stance was not simply developed during its days in government,[3] but it was part of Labour's conceptualization the UK's place in the world, stressing its European vocation, based on the core value of multilateralism-as-an-end-in-itself in combination with Europe-as-a-community-among-others. The party highlighted the ineffectiveness of the UK's previous position as a reactive "awkward partner" amongst the EU-15 and wanted to demonstrate to its European partners that the new government was determined to play a central role in Europe. As one senior British official put it, "there was the desire of the Labour Party to show European credentials, and there were only limited ways to do this as the UK was a fringe country. Labour wanted to confirm the UK's European identity."[4] Sir Emyr Jones Parry, FCO's political director at the time, said that "the Blair government was much more European [than the Conservatives]. Labour was willing to give European security a go."[5] Labour sought to place the UK in a position of influence as a bridge between the United States and Europe. The focus on Europe was not understood as being at the expense of NATO. Based on its understanding of multilateralism-as-an-end-in-itself, the Labour government saw NATO and ESDP both as expressions of multilateral security policy that would bring peace and stability both within the institutions and internationally.

The Conservatives, on the other hand, reinforced their Euroskepticism after William Hague took over the party leadership. Hague said that he was against the UK joining EMU out of sovereignist principle – even if the UK economy would benefit from it. Hague did not accept any challenge to his leadership and asked those who did not support

[2] Blair was not the first to use the phrase "at the heart of Europe." In a speech in Bonn at the beginning of 1991 Major used the same phrase by which he meant that the British government, not being satisfied with the proposals on the table during the Maastricht negotiations, should introduce its own. However, members of his party who were critical of him on many accounts used this occasion to criticize him as too Euro-friendly – something he claims to be "Copper-bottomed nonsense" (Major 1999: 269).
[3] Interview # 6 with a British senior official in London (December 5, 2006).
[4] Interview # 8 in London (December 7, 2006).
[5] Interview # 10 in New York (February 22, 2007).

his position to leave the front bench. This alienated individual members of the party, which eventually led to Peter Temple-Morris becoming independent (because of his pro-European views) and sitting with Labour (Brown 1997b: 10), and David Churry resigning from the shadow cabinet (White 1997b: 12).[6] The few "Tory Europeans … are an ageing minority" (Gray 1997: 21).

With Labour's election victory in 1997, there was an opportunity for bringing about the changes it desired in the UK's relationship with the EU and multilateral security policy. A robust European security institution was seen as a way to do just this. As Labour was formulating its policy preferences, it looked across the English Channel where French politics had created an opening for Anglo-French cooperation in security that would have broader implications for the rest of Europe.

The RPR presidency cohabitating with the Socialists: NATO has a role in security

While the transition from Conservative to Labour government in the UK brought about a sharp change in policy, developments in France in the late 1990s were more complex as the government moved into consolidated *cohabitation*. Examining the ideological spectrum of French political parties allows us to understand how the congruence between France and the UK occurred, creating an opening for a robust European security institution.

The late 1990s were marked by *cohabitation* between Chirac's RPR presidency and Lionel Jospin's Socialists and their Communist allies. Chirac had to consolidate his position as president. In the very beginning of *cohabitation*, Jospin and Chirac fought over who would represent France on European and foreign policy issues, said RPR president Philippe Séguin in an interview with *Le Monde* (Jarreau *et al.* 1997). While Jospin understood his position as one of two executive positions, Chirac understood Jospin's position as being the prime minister *to* the president (Clift 2001). For Séguin, the beginning of this *cohabitation* was "the national disunion" (Jarreau *et al.* 1997), but eventually Chirac defended his presidential prerogatives, the so-called *domaine réservé an* not without having to make compromises with the Socialist government. After all, the prime minister has to countersign international treaties. As Chapter 5 has outlined, this constitutional power

---

[6] Churry is quoted to have said that there is "no eternal or immutable concept of the nation state" (quoted in White 1997b: 12) that should drive the Conservative Party to treat the European question like a religion instead of politics.

enabled Jospin and the PS to block further French rapprochement to NATO.[7]

The pro-NATO stance of the RPR, based on its core value of sovereignty in conjunction with multilateralism-as-a-means-to-another-end and valuing Europe as one-community-among-others, had changed France's signals regarding its willingness to accommodate British concerns about undermining NATO – a concern both the Conservative and Labour parties shared. And now, with Labour in power, the RPR and Labour also shared a common understanding of European security efforts. The Chirac policy in general sent signals to the British that France was not "out to get the US" and instead could be a potential partner.[8] This assuaged Labour's concerns about developing a European security institution to the detriment of NATO, rather than alongside it. With this ideological congruence around an intergovernmental European security institution autonomous from NATO, but not opposed to it, the two most powerful European states in terms of military capability were one step closer to the creation of what would eventually become ESDP. In Germany, the country's role in an emerging European congruence around what would become ESDP involved both a change from one party to another, but also the predominance of certain factions within the SPD and Green parties. With a transition from the CDU/CSU and FDP coalition government to one consisting of the SPD and Greens, the three major European states could find a consensus that had eluded them at Amsterdam.

The Social Democratic–Green coalition: mediating Political Europe

After 16 years of a CDU/CSU led government in coalition with the FDP, the election result of October 1998 led, for the first time, to a ruling national coalition between the SPD and the Greens. In the 1998 federal elections, all major parties running for the federal parliament

[7] According to Védrine's political advisor, Michel Foucher, NATO exists for the defense of Europe and ESDP for the projection of force outside of Europe. Interview with Michel Foucher in Paris (May 30, 2008).

[8] Chirac also adjusted France's military in response to the changing security environment. Starting in 1996, President Chirac announced a reform program for the French armed forces which were gradually professionalized and transformed so as to be able to perform four different missions: dissuasion, prevention, projection and protection (Irondelle 2011). None of these functions was entirely new, but their order of priorities had changed: the accent of the 1996 reforms is clearly on prevention, and especially, on projection.

were in favor of the European Union.[9] However, while both SPD and CDU/CSU encouraged European policy-making, the two major parties had different inclinations as to the degree of supranationalization and the kind of community the EU should be.

The SPD and the Greens value the EU as one community among others, and insist more on their core value of multilateralism-as-an-end-in-itself. "Europe is no core question."[10] As a result, they are in favor of multilateral cooperation while at the same time are unwilling to prioritize European partners over other multilateral endeavors. Both parties' skepticism toward exclusive partnerships rendered them critical of the CDU/CSU, of American[11] and French power politics and the exclusivity with which the Franco-German engine had been promoted by the CDU/CSU and the PS.[12] Instead, the SPD and Greens have been much more willing to accept the leadership of others in European affairs. This is also reflected in their coalition treaty, where the SPD and the Greens state that they are much more open to a multitude of political forums and critical of Germany taking up leadership in international organizations (Scharping 1997; Koalitionsvereinbarung 1998: par. XI, 1). This policy stance has also translated to issues in NATO. "We are striving for an equal partnership between Europe and the US inside NATO … NATO enlargement should not lead to an exclusion of Russia, should not lead to another division of Europe in regard to

---

[9] Even the PDS was in favor of common European policies, though it disagreed with the ideological outlook of the EU as being too neoliberal in economic terms and too libertarian in social terms.

[10] Interview with Andreas Körner, special advisor for security for the Greens in parliament, in Berlin (December 21, 2006).

[11] The SPD and the Greens have a much more differentiated approach toward the United States than the CDU/CSU and FDP. The CDU/CSU favor the "West" over any other political forums. Goehs said that for the CDU "Europe and the US are two sides of the same coin," implying that the CDU favors both the EU and NATO over any other multilateral forum (Interview with Olav Goehs, the CDU's Special Advisor for Foreign Policy, International Security, and European Affairs at the CDU Headquarters in Berlin [October 18, 2006]). Both the CDU/CSU and FDP are generally in favor of US policies no matter who is in power. As a result, the CDU is more willing to admit and embrace the US role as a superpower. "We want to strengthen and broaden the partnership with the US" (CDU/CSU Party Manifesto 1998: 33). For example, in 2003 Angela Merkel supported the US in its war against Iraq, while the SPD's Chancellor Schröder opposed it.

[12] The SPD and Greens are willing to criticize hegemonic and exclusive (multilateral) policy-making. This differentiates them from the French PS as the French Socialists criticize the United States based on their exclusive understanding of Europe-as-a-political-community. Interview with Winfried Nachtwei, security spokesperson for the Greens in Berlin (November 24, 2006), interview with Uwe Stehr, special advisor for security at the SPD parliament faction says that the SPD wants to be independent of the United States. Interview in Berlin (November 14, 2006), and interview with Joschka Fischer in Princeton (February 21, 2007).

security policy, it should not be linked to proliferation and has to lead to a stronger role for the OSCE" (SPD Party Manifesto 1998: 77).

Relatedly, when it comes to multilateralism in the use of force, the SPD and Greens in particular and their *Seeheimer Kreis* and *Realos* wings have emphasized the use of force as a last resort. Both parties emphasized a comprehensive security approach that includes civilian crisis management and conflict prevention capabilities (Koalitionsvereinbarung 1998: par. XI, 3).[13]

In contrast, the CDU/CSU and FDP were very committed to the general cause of the EU and perceived the EU as a value and political community per se. Valuing Europe in and of itself as a Christian values community with the EU as its expression, the CDU/CSU never moved from its westward strategy. Based on this understanding of community, the CDU/CSU was willing to pursue its policies in a European setting whenever possible. Hence, it has been much more interested in introducing a wide array of policies into the institution's mandate than the Greens or the SPD. It was the CDU/CSU and FDP "who pushed for all the EU initiatives" (CDU/CSU Party Manifesto 1998: 33; see also FDP Party Manifesto 1998), though they did not do so to the exclusion of NATO. Regarding European security, the FDP has stressed that "ESDP has to be understood as [a] European force. But a European force that is there to strengthen NATO."[14] And the CDU/CSU stated, "Germany has to remain a reliant and loyal Partner to the Alliance when taking over responsibility for freedom and liberty ... NATO is a value community and defense alliance and we will continue developing it to an alliance for stability and crisis management ... The West European Union is a European pillar of NATO and the defense arm of the EU" (CDU/CSU Party Manifesto 1998: 32).

While domestic ideological manifestations persisted to the end of the 1990s, the ideological congruence across the British, French and German political parties in government increased significantly (see Table 6.1). This had major consequences on European governments' policy stance toward NATO and a European security institution. Before the British government approached the French government and asked for its support in creating a European security institution,

---

[13] In March 1998, at the Greens' party assembly in Magdeburg, where the party discussed its election manifesto, the first draft included the demand to exit NATO and to reduce the manpower of the *Bundeswehr* by half. However, the dominant *Realo* wing insisted that this be taken out (Klein and Falter 2003: 50).

[14] Interview with Friedel Eggelmeyer, Advisor in Security Affairs to the FDP, in Berlin (October 31, 2006).

Table 6.1 *Domestic and international party configuration, 1999*

Country	Party/ies	Multilateralism	Europe	Sovereignty
United Kingdom	Conservatives	Means-to-another-end	**Europe-as-a-geographic-space**	**Intergovernmental**
	Labour†	**End-in-itself**	Community-among-others	Intergovernmental
France	Socialists (PS)†	Means-to-another-end	**Europe-as-a-political-community**	Supranational/ intergovernmental
	RPR†	Means-to-another-end	Community-among-others	**Intergovernmental**
Germany	CDU/CSU	**End-in-itself**	**Europe-as-a-political-community**	Supranational/ intergovernmental
	FDP	**End-in-itself**	**Europe-as-a-political-community**	**Intergovernmental/ supranational**
	SPD†	**End-in-itself**	Europe-as-a-community-among-others	Supranational/ intergovernmental
	Greens†	**End-in-itself**	Europe-as-a-community-among-others	Supranational/ intergovernmental

the ideological configurations on the international level between the British, French and German governments pointed to the possibility of success in the endeavor.

The mechanics of ideological congruence in European political parties: NATO, ESDI, WEU and ESDP

The late 1990s witnessed not only a stark EU transformation based on ideological congruence between its key member states but also a reconfirmation of the role NATO had found over the last decade. These parallel developments were possible because European governments were in favor of them – and despite the United States wanting to keep multilateral security policy in NATO. The US insisted that ESDI accommodated all European needs, but European governments set out to create a European security institution outside NATO while at the same time confirming their commitment to NATO.

With the Labour government in power in the UK and the RPR in France, there was a congruence of values around the utility of both NATO and a potential European security institution. This marked a departure from the French Socialist policy of promoting a European security institution to the exclusion of NATO, rather than alongside it, a position that had divided France from the UK previously. With the Socialists in parliament, but not in control of the presidency, there was common ideological ground between Labour and the RPR. This ideological configuration between the UK and French governments would drive ESDP.

The CDU/CSU has historically seen its role as an initiator of wider and deeper European integration, including in security. It would thus appear that Germany would be a missing element in the Anglo-French proposal regarding European security cooperation. The SPD and Greens have traditionally been critical of the CDU/CSU's insistence on German leadership in European affairs and instead have been committed to cooperation in general – on the condition that civilian crisis management elements be part of multilateral security policy. As a result, the SPD Green government was responsive to the active Labour and RPR policy. This allowed the UK and France to initiate an EU policy at Saint Malo, making it easier for the British government to sell a European project to its domestic constituency.

Following the Franco-British Saint Malo Summit was the Vienna European Council, December 11–12, 1998, which "welcome[d] the new impetus given to the debate on a common European policy on security and defence" and confirmed that the "CFSP must be backed by credible operational capabilities" (Vienna Council Conclusions

1998: par. 76) inviting the incoming German presidency to continue the debate. Germany also held the WEU presidency at the same time, and used this as an asset to coordinate work in both institutions. At the same time, NATO was preparing for its fiftieth anniversary summit, which would welcome new member states and reinforce American and European commitments to a common security policy and ESDI.

Labour's initial moves in government to be "at the heart of Europe"

Soon after coming to power, Labour started to instigate conversations with its European counterparts on a multitude of issues concerning the European Union. At first, the focus was not on a European security institution per se, as Labour was discussing different policy issues where it could push for a new impetus that started with Amsterdam. Over the years, Blair would repeatedly say that he wanted the United Kingdom to be "at the heart of Europe."[15] For this purpose, Blair increased his advisory team at Downing Street.[16]

To bring about a change in the UK's relationship with its EU partners (Bulmer and Burch 2005: 862; see also Bulmer 2000), Blair had requested the Foreign and Commonwealth Office (FCO) to write a policy review of the 1998 UK EU presidency; the result was the Step Change Programme in September 1998 (FCO 1999). Step change meant to "get away from a passive and reactive approach to the EU" (Bulmer and Burch 2005: 876). During the British EU presidency, the British government felt that it could not introduce its own EU policy. The fact that the government had to preside over the launch of the monetary union, while not itself participating in the eurozone, brought home the idea that its aspirations to play a leading role in the EU needed further consideration. Furthermore, as the preceding Luxembourg presidency officially launched the enlargement process and had named states with which membership negotiations should start, the UK presidency's schedule was filled with issues surrounding this agenda as well (Walker 1998: 10). All in all, there was not much room to conduct a British European policy during the presidency. "The review therefore considered both the substance of UK positions on various policies and the general approach to Europe and how these might be improved. It concentrated on isolating

---

[15] In an interview with French Admiral Jean Dufourcq, who was at the time the advisor of the French joint chiefs of staff, he characterized Blair as a "man of conviction" and *"un homme inspiré* [a man inspired by ideas]." Interview with Admiral Jean Dufourcq in Paris (May 27, 2008).

[16] Interview # 5 with a British official in London (December 5, 2006).

the issues on which the UK could take the lead" (Bulmer and Burch 2005: 877; see also Henderson 1998; Ludlow 1998).

It became clear that the Labour government was not able to push its European policies in the fields of finance[17] or agriculture and, hence, security "came naturally."[18] Most importantly in this regard, "Blair persuaded the Ministry of Defense (MoD), and not the other way around. Until then, the MoD was more inclined to call NATO its multinational organization of choice and see a European security institution as a sideshow. The momentum came from Number 10."[19] Stephen Wall, who had become Blair's Europe advisor, recalls, "It was a combination of conviction and opportunity. He needed to demonstrate to Britain's partners that he meant what he said about Britain being a leader in Europe. Defence was an area where, from conviction, he believed Europe could and should do more" (Wall 2008: 172).

Once the decision was made, Downing Street asked the ministries to formulate the details.[20] Initial information exchange was made with the FCO and the MoD. Facilitating this exchange was the fact that there had been plans for a European security institution already formulated in the FCO and MoD. According to several senior British officials in both the MoD and the FCO, these plans originated from the days of the Major government during the Amsterdam negotiations, but had then been disregarded by the government at the time. The civil service had presented these proposals to the Cabinet but the Conservative government had refused to adopt them because they went against its ideological convictions. The Conservatives acted upon an understanding of multilateralism-as-a-means-to-another-end and Europe-as-a-geographic-space privileging the UK's relationship with the United States and with NATO. ESDP would have brought the Conservative government down as most of the party did not identify with such policy goals.[21] Labour instead tried to balance between Europe and NATO, attempting to pursue collective security through both transatlantic and European efforts based on an understanding of multilateralism-as-an-end-in-itself and Europe-as-a-community-among-others. Now the proposals could return to the fore.

---

[17] A survey showed that Labour MPs were in favor of EMU (Baker and Seawright 1998b: 62), but not the Conservatives (Ludlam 1998). Joining EMU was unlikely because both parties had vowed that they would call a national referendum should the cabinet ever decide to push for entry.

[18] Interview # 5 with a British official in London (December 5, 2006).

[19] Interview # 5 with a British official in London (December 5, 2006) and # 10 with a senior British official in New York (February 22, 2007).

[20] Phone interview with Anthony Forster in London (December 7, 2006).

[21] Interview # 9 with a senior British official in London (December 8, 2006) and # 5 with a British official in London (December 5, 2006).

By mid 1998, the Labour government made it known that it conceived of a WEU–EU merger. British Secretary of State for Defense Robertson said in front of the WEU Assembly, "Some of our Partners have argued for some time for the wholesale merger of the Western European Union into the European Union. The United Kingdom resisted this proposal at Amsterdam ... we do not rule it out today" (Robertson 1998).

Bilateral ideological congruence at Saint Malo: toward ESDP

Based on its government preferences and with the help of the already existing policy proposals in the MoD and the FCO, in fall 1998, British Prime Minister Tony Blair, by now in government for just over a year, launched a new European initiative. This initiative was announced hesitantly during the Amsterdam negotiations, then more forcefully in the British Strategic Defense Review of July 1998, which had been opposed by the Conservative Party,[22] and in a speech at the informal EU summit in Pörtschach on October 24–25, 1998. The British government thereby "worked particularly closely with France and Germany" (Robertson 1999b). In Pörtschach, Blair said that the current situation regarding European foreign and security policy was "unacceptable" and marked by "weakness and confusion" while alluding to the possible integration of the WEU into the EU (*Agence Europe* 1998a). The British government convinced the Austrian EU presidency to call a meeting of EU defense ministers at the beginning of November, though informally and outside the EU framework, in Vienna, Austria.[23] At this meeting, the British government took the lead and Secretary of State for Defense Robertson proposed three alternatives for an enhanced European role in security matters: an enhanced role for the WEU, the merger of the WEU into the EU, or the further development of the "European Dimension" within NATO. The British government, thereby, presented options that the Conservative government previously clearly dismissed as being against "the national interest." The defense ministers came to the conclusion that the military role of the EU should be developed for the solution of

---

[22] Asked whether one could feel a change in the MoD after Labour took over the government from the Conservatives, a senior British official said that suddenly the Strategic Defense Review was welcomed. The Conservatives had opposed it because such a review would have meant cuts but in fact it was a rebalancing of policy, resources, and capabilities. Interview # 4 in London (December 5, 2006). Also see the Conservative Party Manifesto (1997: 48).

[23] This was the first time that the defense ministers of the EU member states met.

crisis in Europe. Based on the informality of the meeting, no concrete decisions could be made but information was exchanged and preferences were heard (*Agence Europe* 1998b).

This exchange of information brought about the subject for the upcoming Franco-British Summit in December 1998, a summit that has been held between the two states on an annual basis since 1979. Hubert Védrine, France's foreign minister at the time, recalls Chirac's interest in a European security institution but "it was not an urgent matter. It was politically ambitious as there was no real threat to which such an institution could respond. We asked ourselves 'What could we do to advance the issue?'"[24] When Gérard Errera, the political director at the Quai d'Orsay, indicated to Védrine and Chirac that there was "a convergence of ideas"[25] between the UK and France and "a British availability and the only possible policy domain was security and defense," Védrine and Chirac answered Errera "that one has to react profoundly [*à fond*]."[26] The ambitious idea now had two ambitious proponents. Labour under Blair thought that cooperation with France on matters of security "was a good thing."[27]

The UK's chief negotiator at the time, Emyr Jones Parry, recalls that Blair and Chirac were determined to start building a European security institution. For that purpose, they let their political directors negotiate the components.

The two days before the Summit, Errera and I exchanged letters but could not agree as to how to cooperate further. Then we met in Saint Malo in a sort of "prisoner's room" and had to start the negotiation with nothing. I insisted to have the Political Director of Defense, Richard Hatfield, with me to cover my back as I was the EU guy. John Holmes [at the time the Head of Blair's office] was in the room too. We finished the negotiations at 3am. I left a copy of the text under the doors of the Chief of Defense Staff, the Secretaries of Defense and Foreign Affairs and Blair later adopted the text with just one minor change: he wanted NATO to be mentioned a little earlier in the text.[28]

The key points of the Saint Malo meeting were that "the Union must have the capacity for autonomous action, backed up by credible military forces, the means to decide to use them and a readiness to do so, in order to respond to international crises" (Franco-British Summit

---

[24] Interview with Hubert Védrine in Paris (May 29, 2008).
[25] Interview with Hubert Védrine in Paris (May 29, 2008).
[26] Interview with Hubert Védrine in Paris (May 29, 2008).
[27] Interview with Emyr Jones Parry in New York (February 22, 2007).
[28] Interview with Emyr Jones Parry in New York (February 22, 2007).

1998: par. 2). Previously, this position was not only very controversial during the Maastricht and Amsterdam negotiations, but also untenable. It was also agreed that the Council be able to take decisions on an intergovernmental basis, that the EU be given appropriate structures and capacities "without unnecessary duplication" (Franco-British Summit 1998: par. 3) but establish its own "appropriate structures and a capacity for analysis of situations, sources of intelligence and a capability for relevant strategic planning" (Franco-British Summit 1998: par. 3). Finally, the EU should have the capacity to "take decisions and approve military action where the Alliance as a whole is not engaged" (Franco-British Summit 1998: par. 3).

Despite the ideological congruence between Labour and the RPR in regard to sovereignty and Europe, the congruence was not a perfect match. Europe and multilateralism was derivative of sovereignty for the RPR, while Labour saw multilateralism-as-an-end-in-itself informing Europe. While these different interpretations did not make European security cooperation impossible as they both favor cooperation, they put different emphasis on the purpose of the institution. Both parties agreed that a European security institution would be one among several, but the RPR understands this as a means to increase France's range of action, while it is yet another expression of Labour's willingness to cooperate with international partners. As a result, the writing of the Saint Malo declaration was contentious, at times resulting in some ambiguity in the text. Britain and France disagreed on specifics and left some components of the declaration vague to work themselves out over time. This luxury of being able to leave language vague signals that enough ideological congruence existed to start the process of creating a European security institution. In other words, the French and British governments agreed to constructive ambiguity thus permitting a range of interpretations.[29]

The declaration remained silent on the *extent* of a capability build-up[30] as well as to what *degree* both governments envisaged a merger of the WEU when referring to "taking account of the existing assets of the WEU and the evolution of its relations with the EU" (Franco-British Summit 1998: par. 3). The RPR, reflecting multilateralism-as-a-means-to-another-end, in conjunction with a core value of sovereignty and valuing Europe-as-a-community-among-others, was much more hesitant than the PS had been a few years before and "made clear that France

---

[29] Constructive ambiguity is made possible rather through disagreements on procedural values, such as multilateralism, than on substantive values, such as sovereignty and Europe.

[30] Interview # 8 with senior British official in London (December 7, 2006).

had no interest in a quick absorption of WEU by the EU, that WEU still played a useful role as a bridge between the EU and NATO" (Jopp 1999: 5). Furthermore, the French government had an interest in maintaining the WEU Article V commitment among its members but was at the same time aware that the British government did not want to bring such a guarantee into the EU.

With regard to the *relative* emphasis of NATO and the EU in security, and ESDP's relationship to NATO, Labour and the RPR did not completely see eye-to-eye but, in the end, managed to negotiate their differences. The French government insisted on the word "autonomous" in the declaration and the British government went along with it.[31] The Conservative Party would never have done so.[32] In return, Blair gave the issue a new spin and managed to convince France to include a clause that said that they would work in support of the Alliance. With this agreement, both parties indicated their recognition of NATO's value as a security institution.[33] "In strengthening the solidarity between the member states of the European Union, in order that Europe can make its voice heard in world affairs while acting in conformity with our respective obligations in NATO, we are contributing to the vitality of a modernised Atlantic Alliance which is the foundation of the collective defence of its members" (Franco-British Summit 1998: par. 2). While the declaration indicates a turn away from "separable but not separate," the agreement stayed silent on the question of whether NATO would have the right of first refusal when deciding on military operations. Chirac announced after the summit that "it is in the interest of the French and the Europeans to be able to weigh in on their destiny and to have the capacity to act together, without depending necessarily on decisions taken elsewhere" (Chirac 1999). In the same speech, however, Chirac also mentioned that "this does not mean that it [ESDP] will replace the Atlantic alliance, which remains a legitimate framework for collective defence and its role in crisis management" (Chirac 1999). Blair announced in reflection on the summit: "We decided that we should go beyond the Berlin arrangements agreed by NATO in 1996 to give Europe a genuine capacity to act" (Blair 1999), and "Europe needs genuine military operational capability, not least forces able to react quickly and work together effectively, and genuine political will. Without these, we will always be talking about an empty shell" (quoted in *European Voice* 1999).

[31] Interview with Emyr Jones Parry in New York (February 22, 2007).
[32] Interview # 7 with Conservative advisor in London (December 6, 2006).
[33] Interview # 3 with former senior British official in London (December 4, 2006).

"Blair went further in Saint Malo than Whitehall wanted."[34] When approached by a senior official who told him about worries in regard to the United States, Blair supposedly answered, "the US owes me one."[35] The British official went on to say that Blair did not listen to the FCO but only to his own party machinery. By doing what he did, Blair allowed ESDP to happen, though "he risked its relationship with the US."[36] US Secretary of State Madeleine Albright voiced her dislike of the Saint Malo initiative right after the summit. She warned the Europeans not to create something that would duplicate NATO, decouple Europe from NATO and discriminate against non-EU NATO members (Albright 1998). Another senior MoD British official said, "The Tory government would not have done so. Saint Malo and ESDP were distinctive Labour responses. The wish to be at the heart of Europe is a remarkable difference between the two parties." The Conservatives attacked the Labour government for its support of ESDP and brandished its own credentials as the party of transatlantic solidarity (Giegerich 2006: 45).

With Saint Malo, the EU "started off on the path towards becoming a military power" (Andréani et al. 2001: 7; see also Mérand 2008: 2). Saint Malo signaled to the other European states that the leading military states of Europe were willing to cooperate in the policy field of European security; and other European states were willing to follow this signal instead of opposing or criticizing it. One interesting feature of the Saint Malo initiative was that it was a Franco-British proposal, as opposed to a Franco-German one, that pushed for a new institution inside the EU. The PS and the CDU/CSU had been the driving forces behind previous initiatives.[37] Foreign Minister Joschka Fischer said that the CDU/CSU at the time complained vehemently that Saint Malo would not have happened without Germany if the CDU/CSU had been in power.[38] Arguably, the CDU/CSU would have delayed this opportunity by insisting on taking a leading role. Instead, Fischer says,

---

[34] Interview # 3 with former senior British official in London (December 4, 2006).

[35] Interview # 3 in London (December 4, 2006).

[36] Interview # 5 with British official in London (December 5, 2006).

[37] Only Germany and France and the UK and France have institutionalized bilateral meetings. Such a mode has not been formally established among Germany and the UK. However, it is common practice that before the communiqué of the bilateral meeting is presented to the broader public, the respective third country will get to know it "out of politeness." It is sent to the political director of the foreign ministry who then distributes it to the relevant departments of his ministry and other ministries. This also happened with the Saint Malo communiqué, which was sent to Klaus Scharioth who sent it over to the defense ministry. Phone interview with Klaus Scharioth (April 12, 2007).

[38] Interview in Princeton (February 21, 2007).

the SPD–Green coalition was relieved that the impasse between France and the UK had finally been resolved.[39] This particular German government did not mind that the other two countries were taking the lead so long as Germany was kept on board. In addition, the SPD–Green coalition was less invested in a European security institution than the CDU/CSU – FDP government before it. It was also much less insistent on supranationalization of a European security institution, as had been its predecessor, despite the opposition of the UK and French governments in Amsterdam. Former special advisor to Kohl, Joachim Bitterlich, pointed out that the Kohl government had been eager and more aggressive to supranationalize the policy field, though both Chirac and Blair disliked this action.[40] This value dimension – supranationalism versus intergovernmentalism – had caused tensions between the three states during negotiations over the Amsterdam Treaty, as Chapter 5 has shown. Bitterlich went on to insist that Kohl would never have let the European Council meeting in Cologne happen the way it did. A CDU/CSU-led government would not have made a decision that should have been taken at an IGC – if only to make sure that ESDP would be created in coordination with a strengthening of other EU institutions such as Justice and Home Affairs. Thus, while it is likely that ESDP would have been created with a CDU or SPD-led government in power, the SPD–Green coalition government made the Franco-British initiative a more promising endeavor.

NATO and ESDI: only one multilateral security option among others

After the Saint Malo summit, and while the German government and its administration were tasked to conceptualized a European security institution, NATO and the WEU held summits and ministerial meetings declaring further institutional changes. The NATO summit in April 1999 confirmed that NATO was moving toward crisis management through further changes to its institutional mandate. "To stand ready, case-by-case and by consensus, in conformity with Article 7 of the Washington Treaty, to contribute to effective conflict prevention

[39] Karsten Voigt agreed with Fischer. He said that at the time of ESDP the party differences in Germany were more rhetorical than of substance as both major parties agreed on the creation of a European security institution, but the SPD leadership was happy that the British and the French government took over the leadership role. That, Voigt insists, would not have happened with a CDU-led German government, which insisted that full European integration can only happen when it is involved as well. Interview with Karsten Voigt, Berlin, October 23, 2007.

[40] Interview with Joachim Bitterlich in Berlin (October 23, 2006).

and to engage actively in crisis management, including crisis response operations" (NATO Strategic Concept 1999: par. 10). Article 7 of the Washington Treaty contains a reference to "the maintenance of international peace and security." The summit bears witness to developments throughout the 1990s, when NATO's priorities shifted dramatically from nuclear and conventional defense to crisis management (Lepgold 1998).

NATO's Washington Summit communiqué and its new Strategic Concept, both issued on April 24, 1999, straddled the issue of where a European security policy would be situated. The communiqué acknowledged "the resolve of the European Union to have the capacity for autonomous action so that it can take decisions and approve military action where the Alliance as a whole is not engaged"[41] (Washington Summit Communiqué 1999: par. 9a). The Strategic Concept, on the other hand, stressed the European pillar *inside* NATO: "On the basis of decisions taken by the Alliance, in Berlin in 1996 and subsequently, the European Security and Defense Identity will continue to be developed within NATO"[42] (NATO Strategic Concept 1999: par. 30). These two statements are the result of a debate where European governments wanted an acknowledgment of their endeavor but the US and Turkish governments were not willing to grant it to them unambiguously.

Before and during the NATO summit, the US government voiced strong reservations about the Saint Malo initiative. US Deputy Secretary of State Strobe Talbott said just before the summit that the United States strongly supported ESDI and NATO transformation in the direction of crisis management (Buhl 1999). Talbott also stressed, "we would not want to see an ESDI that comes into being first within NATO but then grows out of NATO and finally grows away from NATO, since that would lead to an ESDI that initially duplicates NATO but that could eventually compete with NATO" (quoted in Howorth 2007: 42). The US government feared an institution that could eventually compete with NATO for resources, purpose and prestige.

The European governments disagreed – if only subtly. At the NATO summit, British Defense Secretary Robertson spent most of his time on the EU instead of talking about NATO's future (Robertson 1999a).

---

[41] "NATO as a whole" would not be engaged, for example, if France were to veto a proposal.

[42] The NATO Strategic Concept furthermore emphasized the involvement of non-EU NATO members, at Turkey's insistence. NATO "attached the utmost importance to ensuring the fullest possible involvement of non-EU European allies in EU-led crisis response operations building on existing arrangements within the EU." Turkey's position in the WEU as an associate member allowed it to be present in all meetings. However, should the WEU be integrated into the EU, this status would end.

Necessary duplication of institutional assets and functions had become a viable option for the British government based on their core value of multilateralism-as-an-end-in-itself and Europe-as-a-community-among-others. As Robertson pointed out, EU "bodies need to be the right size and shape to support sensible defence decision making. But they must not unnecessarily duplicate the resources and functions that are available from NATO" (Robertson 1999a; see also British-Italian Summit Declaration 1999 and Franco-British Summit 1998). NATO only has *a* role in new security tasks and was not to be the cornerstone for this policy area (Robertson 1999a). German Defense Minister Scharping reiterated the importance of NATO in Europe but at the same time declared the need for Europe to speak with one voice (Scharping 1999a).

The WEU: all European perspectives at the table

The WEU Ministerial in Bremen on May 10–11, 1999 offered a stage for voicing various opinions before the EU summit. The neutral EU member states with observer status in the WEU reiterated their skepticism about a WEU–EU merger. The Swedish government, for example, did not want the transfer of the WEU's mutual defense guarantee to the EU, instead wishing for only certain functions of the WEU to be transferred. In addition, the neutrals appealed in favor of a UN or OSCE mandate. They thereby reminded their fellow EU members that they were about to create an institution which would not act in an isolated policy domain, but instead had to envisage a multitude of other actors in the same policy field – and that NATO should not be the only template. The German Defense Minister, Rudolf Scharping, holding the WEU (and EU) presidency, stressed the German preference for building a European security institution within the EU and reiterated the German position that the WEU should be abandoned and its structures integrated into the EU:

The European capabilities need further development where we Europeans are still dependent on others for support. The first results of our audits showed that we are capable of conducting a limited number of operations with our European capabilities. One of the difficulties at the moment are the decision-making structures for European action as we have to consult, plan and decide in at least three organizations, namely the EU, WEU, and NATO. Personally, I see the solution of this problem in integrating the WEU into the EU and close cooperation between the EU and NATO. (Scharping 1999a)

The EU would need decision-making capabilities and would assume political responsibility for operations where NATO is not engaged. At the same meeting, Fischer stated that "now the time is ripe and the political momentum exists to reach substantive results" (Fischer 1999b). He recalled that the Amsterdam Treaty had only been valid for some weeks and that it could be the task of the Cologne Summit to give the Amsterdam provisions – to which Labour agreed in the last days of the negotiations – substance so that the EU could actually act upon the Petersberg tasks. Fischer stated that while the task of collective defense would continue to be in NATO's hands, a robust European security institution would be a vital complement to NATO. This reflected the Greens' core value of multilateralism-as-an-end-in-itself. As observers in the WEU have no full voting rights, the ministerial did not lead to decisions invoking all EU member states. Instead, member states were waiting for the EU Council meeting in Cologne.

ESDP: multilateralizing a bilateral effort

With the Schröder government's willingness to put the issue of European security on the agenda of its EU and WEU presidencies, ESDP became a realistic possibility – especially when compared with such initiatives as CFSP during Maastricht and the Amsterdam Treaty negotiations. As Klaus Scharioth, the political director of the German foreign ministry at the time, pointed out, Germany made use of this "historical coincidence."[43] Emphasis had still to be negotiated. While the British and French governments focused on a military security institution in their Saint Malo declaration, the Cologne Council under the German presidency introduced a more comprehensive understanding of security. As a result, the language in the Cologne documents resembles that of the Saint Malo declaration, but introduced the idea of civilian crisis management.[44]

Not an ideological priority   The creation of a European security institution was not the first priority of the EU presidency in the form of the SPD–Green coalition government; instead, the German government was preoccupied with a proposal for a European employment pact (which was later agreed). Also, as Saint Malo had taken the German government somewhat by surprise, and it had only been in government for a few months, the SPD–Green coalition needed to consolidate control over policy preferences.[45] Valuing multilateralism-as-an-end-in-itself

---

[43] Phone interview with Klaus Scharioth (April 12, 2007).
[44] Interview # 2 with senior German official in Berlin (November 17, 2006).
[45] Interview with Hubert Védrine in Paris (May 29, 2008).

and Europe-as-a-community worthwhile pursuing if it does not happen to the exclusion of others, the German government was in favor of the Franco-British initiative. Soon into its EU presidency, Fischer outlined NATO's importance for the European security environment and then continued to state that NATO would be strengthened by a stronger and more assertive ESDP. He saw the Franco-British Summit at Saint Malo as the first step toward the congruence of political wills and, as the foreign minister of the country with the double presidency, he promised to translate this opportunity into substance. To this end, he proposed to give the position of "Mr/Mrs CFSP" and the secretary general of the WEU to the same person (Fischer 1999a).

The German government's ideological inclinations and policy priorities opened up the opportunity for its bureaucracy to shape debates under broad guidelines with the ministries and the Chancellery.[46] The ideological frame set out by the German government, however, conditioned the bureaucrats' work. Within this frame, the political director of the German foreign ministry, Klaus Scharioth, became the "*spiritus rector*,"[47] or the tactical promoter of German drafts.[48] He had received "almost *plein pouvoir*"[49] from Fischer. The German Foreign Ministry began work on the basis of its previous attempts in 1991 and 1996, which was to support the merger of the WEU into the EU in three phases and, hence, the militarization of the EU. Fischer, once in a while, would get involved when countersigning proposals. During the drafting period, for example, Fischer intervened by telling Scharioth that he was against a complete militarization and would like civilian elements included as well.[50] He also insisted that the mutual defense clause of the WEU could not be included into the new European security institution – something that Scharioth had contemplated but that went against the Greens' and SPD's understanding of multilateralism in the use of force (and was supported by the EU neutral states).

In the six months after Saint Malo, the German EU and WEU presidencies worked out various plans to institutionalize the Saint Malo initiative into the EU broader framework. The German presidency papers were drafted with little immediate input from other member states – not even from the UK or France, who were content to let the Germans do the

---

[46] Blair and his party, on the other hand, were invested in the issue and stayed in very close contact with their civil servants.

[47] Interview # 12 with former senior German official in Berlin (October 5, 2007).

[48] Interview # 12 with former senior German official in Berlin (October 5, 2007).

[49] Phone interview with Klaus Scharioth (April 12, 2007).

[50] Fischer's politically appointed *Staatssekretär* Pleuger oversaw these draft sessions and meetings.

negotiating with all EU partners after they had initiated the process.[51] While the German government was ideologically aligned with the French and British governments, it presented itself as an arbiter between all EU member states.[52] The basic ideas underlying a European security institution were discussed at formal and informal foreign minister meetings. Various papers were distributed to all member states, comments collected and the papers revised. Scharioth thereby insisted on keeping the WEU in the discussion.[53] At the end of February, before the Kosovo air campaign had started and before NATO's fiftieth anniversary summit, the EU member states received the German presidency's first reflections, a document called "Informal Reflection at WEU on Europe's Security and Defence" (Rutten 2001: 14). In mid-March, at an informal EU foreign minister meeting in Reinhartshausen, a first draft was circulated called "Strengthening the Common Policy on Security and Defence," or simply the "Reinhartshausen Paper" (Jopp 1999). The Reinhartshausen Paper "became the blueprint for the Cologne Presidency Report"[54] focusing EU efforts on the Petersberg tasks and hence the use of force aspect of a European security institution. It raised the questions that defined the succeeding debates concerning the fundamental aims of ESDP.

In regard to the EU–NATO relationship, the paper outlined what is required for a successful ESDP from a German point of view committed to multilateralism-as-an-end-in-itself: non-NATO EU states can participate in operations requiring NATO assets, non-EU NATO members can be associated with Petersberg operations, and transparency and consultation with NATO. Furthermore, the document states that the EU needs to prepare for operations which are EU-led, but with recourse to NATO assets and capabilities, and EU-led with no recourse to NATO assets and capabilities. In pursuit of the latter, the EU needed to ensure "political control and strategic direction of EU-led operations" and that "the EU will need the capacity for analysis of situations, sources of intelligence, and a capacity for relevant strategic planning" (Jopp 1999: 8). This was another way of saying that ESDP would be independent of NATO and, at the same time, that the

---

[51] Interview # 1 with senior German official in Berlin (November 16, 2006).

[52] Other EU states were also content that Germany took over the drafting because they perceived the German government as more neutral in the field of European security. German and British officials pointed out in interviews that they believed that ESDP would not have worked out had it been in French or British hands. Interview # 1 with senior German official in Berlin (November 16, 2006) and interview # 2 with senior German official in Berlin (November 17, 2006).

[53] Interview # 12 with former senior German official in Berlin (October 5, 2007).

[54] Interview # 12 with former senior German official in Berlin (October 5, 2007).

German government and administration perceived ESDP's relationship to NATO to be unproblematic.[55]

The paper also made reference to formal institutionalization and required institutional arrangements: regular General Affairs Council (GAC) meetings, possibly including defense ministers, permanent political and military bodies, an EU military committee consisting of military representatives and a military staff including a situation center, satellite center and the Security Studies Institute lifted from the WEU. The paper was careful to point out that the WEU's Article V would "continue to apply only to those who are NATO allies."

Based on their same interpretation and operationalization of multilateralism-as-an-end-in-itself and Europe-as-a-community-among-others which recommend bridging, EU–NATO relations by trying to include non-EU NATO members as much as possible, the British government agreed very much with the German proposal. Other countries voiced concern. The Dutch government and some neutral countries, especially Ireland, were concerned about establishing a Military Committee in the EU, though for different reasons. The Dutch government saw this as a duplication of NATO, while the neutrals were inclined to see such an institutional body as an unprompted militarization of a European security institution. And, as already mentioned, the French government expressed concern over a rapid merger of the WEU and the EU. It was in favor of "preserving the WEU acquis, whatever the fate of the organisation itself might be" (Jopp 1999: 9). The WEU was yet another tool with which the French RPR government intended to pursue its security policies and was not willing to let it vanish completely. The RPR thought the WEU "could be used in accordance to a given situation either as an alternative or as a complement to the activities of other institutions like the EU, NATO, OSCE or the UN" (Jopp 1999: 14). British chief negotiator Jones Parry pointed out that he negotiated the follow-up issues of the Saint Malo meeting in Brussels on the basis of many bilateral and multilateral meetings. Overall, "80 per cent of the time the French and the British agreed, other times not. When France and the UK agreed everybody just tagged along, if they were not agreeing everybody was watching them argue."[56]

---

[55] The German presidency wanted the terms of reference for the EU–NATO relationship be the Berlin Plus agreements signed between the WEU and NATO. See Reichard (2006) for the *problematique* of transferring an agreement that was made between the WEU and NATO to the EU and NATO.

[56] In the interest of creating a European security institution, Jones Parry initiated that Errera, he and Scharioth would call each other once a week to discuss issues of European interest. Interview with Emyr Jones Parry in New York (22 February 2007).

As a result of the reflections made known to the German presidency, an updated Reinhartshausen Paper also taking into account NATO's Washington Summit conclusions was discussed at the General Affairs Council (GAC) on May 17, 1999. The paper mentioned the possibility of an EU Defense Ministers Council and defined the new suggested permanent body to be established in Brussels as a committee for political and strategic questions composed of permanent representatives which could meet with political and military experts, international military staff with a situation center, and a military committee made of military representatives responsible for the formulation of recommendations to the Permanent Committee. However, the paper deferred decision on a WEU–EU merger to the Cologne Council meeting and, therefore, to the heads of state and government.[57] On May 30–31, 1999 the political directors and foreign ministers met in Brussels one last time before the Cologne Summit. This meeting proved important in finding a compromise for the neutral and non-aligned countries. It was just before the Council meeting that the member states agreed that they would avoid the terms "merger" or "integration" of WEU into the EU, but all agreed that they wanted "to put the WEU to sleep [*Dornröschenschlaf*]" and transfer most of the WEU to the EU.[58]

When the European governments met in Cologne to create a European security institution, all major governments valued the creation of a European security institution independent of NATO (see Figure 6.1). All were in favor of a European force, insisted or agreed on an intergovernmental institution, and perceived both NATO and the EU as providers of their countries' security. NATO was no longer seen as the only multilateral security actor in Europe.

The summit: leaving the final decision to the heads of state and government After all parties in government voiced their ideological preferences regarding the creation and form of a European security institution for almost half a year, two issues found their way into the debates at the EU summit: the institutional set-up and ESDP's relationship to NATO. The German government played the role of mediator on both issues.[59]

---

[57] Pre-empting any EU decisions, on May 29, 1999, at the Franco-German Defense and Security Council Meeting in Toulouse, the French and German governments stated that Eurocorps could be adapted to constitute a European rapid reaction force.

[58] Interview # 12 with former senior German official in Berlin (October 5, 2007).

[59] Interview # 2 with senior German official in Berlin (November 17, 2006).

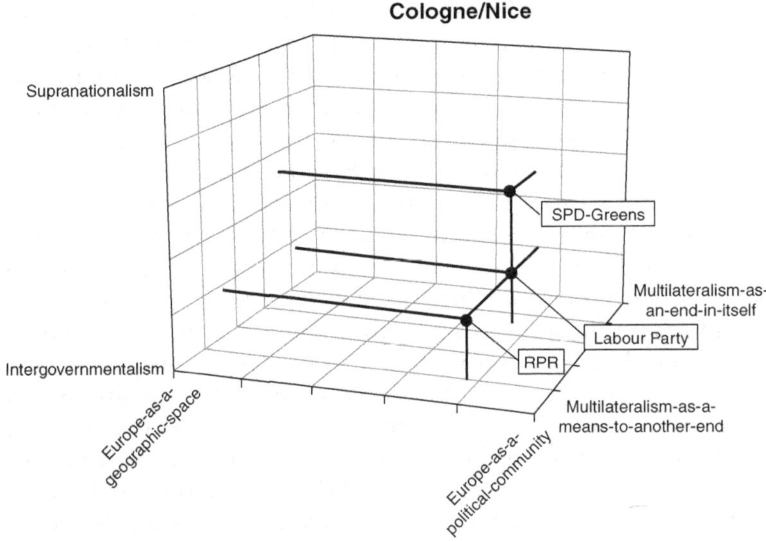

Figure 6.1 Degree of ideological congruence, 1999

The institutional debate turned out to be rather straightforward, even though the relationship between the main political body of the Council of Ministers, the COREPER, and the yet to be created political body called the Political and Security Committee (PSC), which would be responsible for ESDP, posed some problems.[60] Governments disagreed over the seniority of PSC ambassadors in relation to COREPER ambassadors. In the end, the issue of seniority was left to the individual member states to decide and did not prevent the basic ESDP structures from being agreed on as all parties involved were in favor of an intergovernmental and effective institution – in accordance with Art 23 TEU, i.e. unanimously, with abstentions not counting as a veto. The institutional design of the political and military bodies resembled NATO. As two

[60] It was initially intended that the PSC ambassadors should only be in Brussels half-time and the other half close to the minister. Germany did this at first (the political director was also the PSC ambassador). Today the committee is more junior (Head of Division level). Once the interim PSC was set up, COREPER ambassadors, none-theless, insisted at times on holding emergency meetings so that what had been discussed in the PSC could be approved by the COREPER before it went to the Council of Ministers. After the formalization of the PSC, the meetings quickly became more intense (they meet twice and sometimes even three times a week). The PSC can go directly to the Council in cases of urgency, otherwise issues still go through COREPER (Juncos and Reynolds 2007).

German and a British official pointed out, the institutional set-up as such – that is, a political and a military body – was never on the agenda, as NATO's design had already proven itself and, besides, no one came up with an alternative.[61] A German senior official said that the German presidency "wasn't looking to invent the wheel a second time" when it could take proven structures from the WEU and NATO.[62]

The relationship with NATO caused some continued debate. The aspect that caused the most problems was the phrase "where NATO as a whole is not engaged." While the French government had agreed to this wording at the Saint Malo Summit, it wanted to tease out how far it could go in the multilateral setting to give ESDP maximum autonomy from NATO and thereby increase France's range of action.[63] The issue of when and where ESDP could deploy thus dominated the discussion and was rooted in the different interpretations of multilateralism that the RPR, Labour and the SPD–Green coalition upheld. At the end, the heads of state and government decided that they agreed to disagree on the exact definition of the term – which again was possible based on their congruence on the values of Europe and sovereignty. The French government understands the phrase in geographical terms, wanting as much leeway as possible for ESDP. Multilateralism is understood as-a-means-to-another-end – and this "end" was France's range of action. The German and British governments, in the interest of trying to avoid competition between NATO and the EU based on their understanding of multilateralism-as-an-end-in-itself, understand it in more principled terms, meaning that NATO had to decide first whether it was to engage before ESDP should decide on a potential operation. The phrase was included in the conclusions but without any clarification.

The Council conclusions and its Annex III all emphasize that ESDP will be used for the Petersberg tasks and that the EU will receive decision-making bodies and capacity for "autonomous action" (using

---

[61] Interview # 1 with senior German official in Berlin (November 16, 2006) and interview # 2 with senior German official in Berlin (November 17, 2006). "It is not an accident that the EU structures were set up as a mirror of NATO. The key European players did not know anything else … but a strategic view needs all tools at one's disposal and these tools need to be much more closely aligned, one needs to identify all the possible links between the tools … ESDP separates much too much the military and the civilian aspects because its planners and builders were too much NATO inspired." Interview # 5 with British official in London (December 5, 2006).

[62] When asked if there was anything that member states wanted to avoid from what they had seen in NATO, a senior German official said that all EU member states agreed that they did not want as many committees as in NATO [there are over 40 committees in NATO]. Interview # 1 in Berlin (November 16, 2006).

[63] Interviews # 1 and # 2 with senior German officials in Berlin (November 16 and 17, 2006).

Saint Malo language). They also stress the importance of developing more effective military capabilities, the need to strengthen the industrial and technological base, and the importance of non-EU NATO members being able to participate "to the fullest possible extent" (Cologne Presidency Conclusions 1999: Annex III, par. 3). To fulfill the Petersberg tasks "the Union must have the capacity for autonomous action, backed by credible military forces, the means to decide to use them, and a readiness to do so, in order to respond to international crisis without prejudice to actions by NATO" (Cologne Presidency Conclusions 1999: Annex III, par. 1). To that end, the conclusions asked the Finnish presidency to work on the creation of the military arm.

Regarding the WEU, the Presidency Conclusions indicated, "we are now determined to launch a new step in the construction of the European Union" (Cologne Presidency Conclusions: Annex III, par. 5). Therefore, the GAC was tasked with

The definition of the modalities for the inclusion of those functions of the WEU which will be necessary for the EU to fulfill its new responsibilities in the area of the Petersberg Tasks. In this regard, our aim is to take the necessary decisions by the end of the year 2000. In that event, the WEU as an organisation would have completed its purpose. The different status of Member States with regard to collective defence guarantees will not be affected. (Cologne Presidency Conclusions: Annex III, par. 5)[64]

The member states agreed to create interim institutions, which would become permanent with the IGC in Nice in 2000.

While the military aspects dominated the discussions around a European security institution, the Cologne Council conclusions also mention the introduction of civilian elements of crisis management. It was at the summit more than in the preceding discussions that this issue entered the debate. While Fischer let Scharioth negotiate most of the drafts, with input from Fischer's Green colleague Christoph Pleuger, at the summit, Fischer took up the issue and introduced it to his colleagues. He thereby got support from his Swedish counterpart Anna Lindh. Fischer said that his European counterparts did not take this element of security very seriously and, hence, let it enter into the conclusions as paragraph 56.[65]

While this move did not require Fischer to expend much capital convincing his European colleagues, it was an issue close to his party's

---

[64] The WEU Council of Ministers confirmed this in its meeting in Luxembourg on November 22–23.

[65] Interview # 2 with senior German official in Berlin (November 17, 2006).

ideological core. Pushing for civilian crisis management functions reflects a Green inclination to oppose giving military elements priority over civilian ones as the party has seen the deployment of military force as a last resort. The fact that the SPD's *Frankfurter Kreis* and the Green's *Fundis*, the more pacifist-minded factions of both parties, did not oppose ESDP – though admittedly, they voiced concerns, but no one left the party because of it – can be explained by the inclusion of the civilian aspects. While the *Frankfurter Kreis* and the *Fundis* remained critical of NATO's military character, they had shown in the past that they appreciated the inclusion of political means as components of crisis management.[66] Hence, as Scharioth suggests, out of conviction, and also to calm his party, Fischer introduced the more comprehensive approach to European security cooperation.[67]

Leaving the United States aside   The role and possible influence of the United States during the negotiations was kept to a minimum. During the process of debating and writing the Cologne Council conclusions, the United States was kept informed – though only through bilateral channels and after each proposal had already been discussed.[68] The EU member states refused to have the NATO Secretary-General involved as they wanted to keep the whole process EU-focused. In return, the US government voiced repeatedly that it was not keen on the European endeavor.[69] It was very suspicious of the possibility of a European caucus inside NATO and hence did not want the Europeans to institutionalize this policy domain.[70] Thus, while the US government was kept informed, the United States became increasingly reluctant to give rhetorical support to an autonomous European military capability (Howorth 2003).[71] Nonetheless, despite the worries expressed on the other side of the Atlantic Ocean, the European governments set out to create ESDP. They had no intention of replacing NATO, but wanted to create a robust European security institution autonomous from it.

[66] Interview with Winfried Nachtwei, Security Spokesperson of the Greens, in Berlin (November 24, 2006).

[67] Interview with Joschka Fischer in Princeton (February 21, 2007) and phone interview with Klaus Scharioth (April 12, 2007). Fischer says that the CDU/CSU would never have prioritized the issue.

[68] Interview # 1 with senior German official in Berlin (November 16, 2006).

[69] Interview # 1 with senior German official in Berlin (November 16, 2006) and interview # 3 with former senior British official in London (December 4, 2006).

[70] Interview with Robert Hutchings in Princeton (February 21, 2007).

[71] Interview with former Foreign Minister Fischer in Princeton (February 21, 2007).

A robust institution: ESDP in action   Since its inception in 1999, and its inclusion in the Treaty of Nice and its annexes (signed in February 2001 and in force since February 2003) – which endorses the Cologne language and the legal transfer of existing WEU institutions into the EU framework – ESDP has been declared operational. ESDP has experienced increased resource allocation, new institutional structures and procedures as well as institutional autonomy. All of these elements make it a robust institution (Mérand 2008: 13). For example, governments amended Article 25 of the TEU so that, since the Treaty of Nice, the PSC could take over the responsibilities of the former Political Committee – though with much more decision-making powers and a more frequent meeting schedule.[72] Military expertise was internalized especially through the transfer of most of the WEU to the EU, with WEU experts brought into the EU. A European Security and Defense College was established in 2005. Javier Solana, former NATO Secretary General, was appointed High Representative.[73] Along with military goals for crisis management, a range of civilian instruments such as police forces for post-conflict reconstruction were institutionalized. Concrete military and political commitments followed the institutional groundwork at the capability conference in November 2000. Next to the PSC, EUMS (with over 220 staff members), and EUMC, working groups and cells were created. The staff of all these institutions has increased ever since (Council of Ministers 2009; Vanhoonacker *et al.* 2010). Member states have also increased staff in their permanent representations in Brussels threefold since 1998 (Mérand 2008: 75). The ESDP member states established common command and control, which gives ESDP assets and capacities for independent crisis management and conflict prevention (House of Commons 2000; Smith 2000). The EU's common assets – the Civil-Military Cell and its Operation Centre (OpsCen) – are equipped (in terms of material and human resources) to plan and conduct battalion size missions and operations (Perruche 2006; European Council 2008). ESDP has recourse to NATO resources, especially Supreme Headquarters Allied Powers Europe (SHAPE) – when it wants to conduct high-intensity operations through the "Berlin Plus" agreement.[74] ESDP member states also invested in multinational forces.

---

[72] See Reynolds (2010: 164–7) for a detailed discussion of the PSC's functions.

[73] This triggered the establishment of the "dedicated" CFSP Directorate in the Commission, Directorate A of DG RELEX (Duke 2006: 11; Derks and More 2009).

[74] The Berlin Plus agreement comprises a series of separate accords on the modalities and procedures. In 1996, NATO foreign ministers met in Berlin and decided to make NATO assets and capabilities available to crisis management operations led by the

ESDP created – at least as a planning concept – the European Rapid Reaction Force (1999) and the battle groups (2004).[75]

ESDP has since conducted over 24 operations and missions (while NATO has been engaged in over 15 operations in the same time frame). Between 2001 and 2006, the total number of European troops in crisis management operations increased to more than 80,000 from 65,000 (Dempsey 2008: 3). While European states had contributed to NATO and UN operations before, the increase is mostly due to ESDP. At least six operations have involved relatively large military deployments (see Table 6.2). In five of these cases, ESDP troops have deployed alongside UN or NATO forces. This resulted in instances such as Darfur, where ESDP and NATO insisted on having the same mandate in assisting the African Union with its peace operation in Sudan (Hofmann and Reynolds 2007). Rather than representing an efficient division of labor, such operations are often about asserting institutional presence.

Comparing explanations: party ideologies, realism and rational choice institutionalism

As with the previous two cases of CFSP and Amsterdam, the situation of political parties during the creation of ESDP showed that parties do not nicely align on only one spatial dimension. While I argue that ESDP's creation was the result of ideological congruence across parties in power in major European states, an understanding of ideology as a unidimensional variable should have resulted in characterizing the RPR as a party emphasizing liberty, while Labour and the SPD–Green coalition on the left are associated with equality (Rathbun 2004). Despite different positions on liberty and equality, the RPR, Labour and the SPD–Greens shared fundamental values around Europe, multilateralism in the use of force, and sovereignty. These values provide more traction in analyzing ideological positions than a left–right dichotomy. One wonders, for example, what exactly equality means in the context of European security cooperation: equality between the EU and NATO, or equality among EU members? These different understandings of equality do not translate in the same policy preferences, as we have seen above. In the

WEU. At the time, the EU had not yet developed ESDP, and the WEU was considered both the "European pillar of NATO" and "the defense component of the EU." NATO assets and capabilities (such as NATO planning facilities at SHAPE and the AWACS E-3A radar aircraft) were made available for the WEU to carry out the Petersberg tasks.

[75] NATO established the NATO Response Force (NRF) in 2002. For most member states, the NRF and the battle groups are based on the same pool of national forces and assets (Cornish 2006).

Table 6.2 *Military and civil-military ESDP operations*

Operation	Duration	Troop strength
EUFOR Concordia (Macedonia)*	March 31, 2003 to December 15, 2003	Up to 350
EUFOR Artemis (RD Congo)	June 12, 2003 to September 1, 2003	Up to 1,800
EUFOR Althea (Bosnia-Herzegovina)*	December 4, 2004 to present	Up to 6,000
EUSEC RD Congo (civil-military)	June 8, 2005 to present	Up to 60
Support to AMIS II Sudan/ Darfur (civil-military)	July 18, 2005 to December 31, 2007	Up to 40
EUFOR RD Congo	July 30, 2006 to November 30, 2006	Up to 2,500
EUFOR Tchad/République Centrafricaine	January 28, 2008 to May 18, 2009	Up to 3,700
EU SSR Guinea Bissau (civil-military)	June 2008 to December 30, 2010	Up to 32
EUNAVFOR Atalanta	December 8, 2008 to present	Up to 1,800 (eight frigates, two ocean patrol vessels, maritime patrol and five reconnaissance aircraft, etc.)
EUTM Somalia	April 7, 2010 to present	Up to 141

Source: European Council (www.consilium.europa.eu/showPage. aspx?id=268&lang=EN). * Berlin Plus Operations.

end, an *a priori* definition of a unidimensional policy space distorts preferences toward multilateral European security cooperation.

The divergent domestic policy preferences between parties in 1998–2000 are difficult to account for by conventional IR theories such as the institutionalist's notion of objectively accessible efficient institutional design and cooperation problems, or realist emphasis on soft balancing or security dilemmas. Labour's conception of the UK's role in the world, especially when it comes to the EU and NATO, radically differed from the Conservatives' despite constant international exogenous factors (Gnesotto 1998: 124–5; Whitney 1999: 4; Howorth 2000a; Andréani *et al.* 2001: 12). The same can be said for the French and German governments and their political oppositions.

Realists bring forth two explanations for ESDP. One group of scholars argues that in response to unipolarity, the UK and France have embarked on a strategy of soft balancing vis-à-vis the United States. Here, soft balancing results of structural constellations; states try to counter the dominance of the hegemon. ESDP serves the strategic end by showing the United States that Europe will not accept its unmitigated rule and can instead disagree with US security policy (Posen 2004; Pape 2005; Paul 2005; Walt 2005). In Art's words, the UK and France seek "to enhance their political influence within the transatlantic alliance through soft balancing, but not to challenge America's military hegemony with hard balancing" (Art 2005/6: 199). Posen (2004, 2006) even argues that, because of its reliance on military capabilities, any kind of ESDP can be characterized as a form of hard balancing. In both cases the independent variable stays the same: the distribution of military capabilities explains the creation of ESDP.

Yet the empirical evidence shows that no European government conceived of ESDP as being an institution founded in response to US action or inaction – or power, for that matter. The US power and behavior in the 1990s was a constant; however, European attempts to create a security institution autonomous of NATO varied with regard to their success rate and design. Though Art (2005/06) mentions that Europeans want to increase their influence *within* the Alliance, no European caucus has been formed within NATO, and ESDP is *outside* NATO. Realists often refer to France as the driving factor behind the creation of ESDP. As I have shown, however, this is historically inaccurate, leaving aside the UK's pivotal role in ESDP creation. Moreover, ESDP coincided with a French rapprochement with NATO, and to an extent, US policy, after Chirac came to power.

In their defense, realist theorists are quick to point out that their theories are focused on explaining outcomes rather than intentions: "States and statesmen," writes Posen (2006: 165), "are not necessarily expected to couch their actions in balancing language." Art (2005/06: 180) reinforces this position. However, the problem lies in the fact that any putative progress made by ESDP is quickly co-opted as evidence of balancing behavior and is taken as a vindication of the realist position. Sidelining motives, as realists often do, logically implies that the only possible outcome sufficient to falsify the balancing hypothesis would be a total disintegration of ESDP (Posen 2006: 165). Such a position prompts Howorth (2007: 51) to suggest that "[i]f any action by any state which increases that state's relative power vis-à-vis another one is to be defined as balancing, then ... it essentially strips the term of any conceptual or analytical usefulness."

Another more differentiated explanation argues that, with the US retreat from the European continent, European states were uncertain

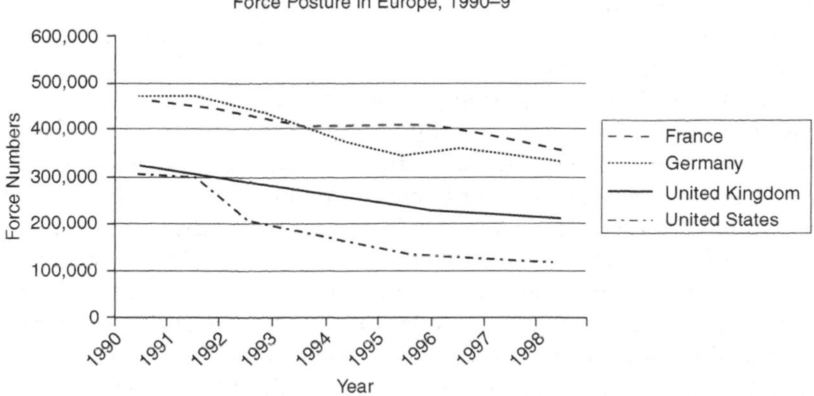

Figure 6.2 Force posture in Europe 1990–9 (France, Germany, UK and United States)
Source: IISS, *The Military Balance*, 1990–1998.

about the stability of their continent, especially concerning a powerful Germany. Hyde-Price (2007: 43) refers to "balanced multipolarity" in Europe. Verdier and Eilstrup-Sangiovanni (2005) speak of the Franco-German rivalry over continental leadership. From this perspective, ESDP is a binding strategy (Jones 2007):

Security cooperation through the European Union has been inversely corre-lated with American power in Europe: the lower the American military pres-ence and commitment to the continent, the greater the incentive for cooperation through the EU to ameliorate a potential security dilemma. It has also been correlated with German power: the greater the power of Germany, the greater the impetus for cooperation. (Jones 2007: 92)

Together with the UK, France has "adopted a binding strategy ... to tie Germany into Europe and increase the likelihood of peace on the continent" (Jones 2007: 11). In this understanding, military presence on the European continent matters. Hence, US power does not matter per se but German power does as it is based in Europe.

Two points have to be made with regard to declining US presence and its implications: first, while the United States decreased its military presence in Europe, so did France, the UK and especially Germany (see Figure 6.2), and, second, the United States far from disengaged from Europe completely but stayed politically and militarily involved, signaling this intention on many occasions. While the decline of the US military presence in Europe might have been worrying to European governments at the very beginning of the end of the Cold War, the

Europeans did not manage to create a strong European security institution during the Maastricht or Amsterdam Treaty negotiations. However, the US force levels declined between 1990 and 1995, and then started to level off. ESDP was only attempted in 1998/9.

More comprehensive also, a definition of security and the new NATO security doctrine called into question the need for overpowering military presence. Aware of the new security environment, governments adjusted their military forces, moving away from territorial defense toward a more rapidly deployable military force (Dyson 2008: 731–4). For this reason, European member states reduced their forces alongside the United States, not exactly the response one would expect of powers balancing against one another or soft balancing against the United States. The United States reduced its forces from 325,000 to 100,000 while the Europeans collectively reduced their forces by more than 500,000 (Wallander 2000: 718). Chirac, for example, streamlined the military from 400,000 to 250,000 (excluding the gendarmerie) from 1996 to 2002 while at the same time increasing the number of forces for global deployment from 12,000 to 60,000 (Irondelle 2003a, 2003b). Also, for the first time, several multinational division-sized units were created, and existing crisis reaction forces were increased from fewer than 5,000 troops to more than 50,000. Zelikow judges the remaining US forces in Europe to be "solid … the forces' capability is high; they are backed by powerful units in the US designed effectively for overseas deployment" (Zelikow 1996: 12). Jones (2007) does not include this change of overall security environment and requirements in his analysis.

Instead of disengaging from Europe and leaving the Europeans to their own devices, the US government had been uneasy about the creation of ESDP and its relationship to NATO (Waltz 2000). While most European governments made an effort to inform the US government about the decisions after they were made, the United States continually reiterated its suspicions about ESDP.[76] When the EU finally took it up to create a European security institution overlapping with NATO, the US government's misgivings over the creation of a European security institution and the fear that NATO would be abandoned became pronounced.[77] The Bush and Clinton administrations "strongly supported the continued existence of NATO as a way to prevent the formation of an independent European force that could potentially challenge US

---

[76] Interview # 1 with senior German official in Berlin (November 16, 2006) and interview # 3 with former senior British official in London (December 4, 2006).

[77] Phone interview with Klaus Scharioth (April 12, 2007).

global supremacy" (Schweller 2001: 181).[78] The American government "demanded that the EU should be obliged, even for an autonomous mission, to turn to NATO's SHAPE ... The Europeans resisted and ultimately persuaded the Americans to accept a provision whereby the EU could, if it wished, resort to SHAPE's expertise" (Andréani *et al.* 2001: 27; see also Talbott 1999). The US government, unenthusiastic to begin with, saw its position in the realm of security contested. This became most evident with Madeleine Albright's 3D speech (no decoupling, no discrimination, no duplication). The EU members were not willing to shape their institution in accordance with NATO and the United States. This unwillingness was not based on soft balancing motivations, as demonstrated above, but originates from congruent ideologically-based national preferences toward a European security institution.

Furthermore, if Jones' (2007) binding argument is correct, we should see the German government early on pushing for ESDP. While Kohl's behavior could be understood as a binding strategy, the Conservative Party blocked such a strategy. The Schröder government was less inclined to follow in Kohl's footsteps. Though the German government certainly was a motor in 1991 and 1996, it did not push for a binding strategy in 1999. Rather, in 1999, Germany was the most agnostic of the three major European governments. Nor did the British or French government in any way mention that Germany needs to be embedded in *another* multilateral institution. They did not decide to balance against Germany in reinforcing the bilateral relationship, nor did Germany try to balance against France and the UK. This result remains surprising in light of a realist view of events. The changes in European security institution building coincide with changes in government.[79]

Two strains of argument in the rational choice institutionalist literature are relevant for ESDP; while both stress the need for further crisis management *capabilities*, surprisingly neither of them mentions the EU–US tensions as a cooperation problem that needed resolution. First, the EU's inability to act in Bosnia, the unsuccessful diplomatic dealings with Kosovo in early 1998, and the US's reluctance to intervene in the European "periphery" frustrated the Europeans, and especially the UK, so much that they decided to create a capability autonomous of NATO. The EU found itself "incapable of dealing with a very present and destabilising security environment ... The crises in

[78] Waltz in 2000 remained unclear whether Europeans are out to balance the United States or whether they appreciate the US power as the only possible leadership in Europe as they cannot agree on a *European* leader (Waltz 2000: 36).
[79] Interview #5 with a senior British official in London (December 5, 2006).

the Balkans … were to create a powerful exogenous stimulus behind ESDP" (Howorth 2007: 55, see also Cameron 1999: 80f.; M.E. Smith 2004: 78). Furthermore, "the EU collectively embraced the entirely logical need to look to its own regional security … This was not strategic calculation; it was historical necessity" (Howorth 2007: 53l; see also Weiss 2011). The EU member states created ESDP because of an existing cooperation problem in crisis management and a debate over distributional gains, which could not be left unattended.

Yet this part of the argument ignores NATO and the reforms that it was undergoing and instead looks at the EU in isolation. At the NATO summit in April 1999, NATO member states – the majority of which are also EU member states – reiterated that NATO was moving toward a crisis management institution, reconfirming this in a change to its institutional mandate. These reforms – in combination with ESDI, NATO's European pillar through which Europeans can conduct operations with recourse to NATO assets and capabilities – should have been enough for Europeans to conduct operations. That is, a reduction of transaction costs a cooperation problem around crisis management could have been effectively achieved in NATO alone.

The second strain of institutionalist argumentation is that Blair and his party initiated ESDP because they feared that NATO was threatened with extinction (Howorth 2000a, 2000b, 2007: 53). "Unless Europe got its security act together, NATO was dead in the water" (Howorth 2007: 53). This argument claims that not one but two cooperation problems would be solved with ESDP. Both cooperation problems are interlinked. The types of new security challenges and new demands for deployable military help on top of existing commitments have put a strain on NATO. Jupille and Snidal (2005: 7) argue that if the suitability of addressing a certain cooperation problem decreases in a status quo institution, institutional change and institutional creation becomes a more likely path that states can pursue. The future of NATO was uncertain as the institution was adapting to the new international environment – to strengthen this adaptation process the European governments created ESDP. Based on Suh's (2007) definition of transaction costs, NATO's equipment, processes, human assets and location specificity should therefore be insufficient for reducing the member states' uncertainty about coping with the new security environment.

However, NATO never stopped using its consultation mechanisms, military planning and command structures, common infrastructure, joint exercises, interoperable weapons systems, and integrated forces

(Wallander 2000). Instead, as the last three chapters have shown, NATO reformed and expanded its mandate and resources (Yost 1998). ESDP had to build those exact processes, equipment and human assets and did not want to rely on NATO input and expertise. The capabilities that were built up with ESDP could just as likely have been created in NATO. After all, the strain that NATO experienced was based on national armed forces of many alliance members. As NATO and ESDP rely to a large degree on the same set of national forces, it remains unclear why a European autonomous institution should be better able to procure more capabilities than NATO and ESDI.

Why, then, did European governments have to get their act together outside of NATO? Why could the WEU not stay as a bridge between both the EU and NATO? As has been laid out in the previous chapters, years before the Kosovo crisis erupted, but during the beginning of the Balkan wars, NATO started to change by adding another mechanism to its institutional structure, that of granting the European allies more flexibility in crisis management operations. NATO persisted after the Cold War; it used its cost advantage to provide the European allies with NATO assets and capabilities in WEU-led operations. Given its institutional design and function, ESDI should have fulfilled the European concerns, were they only interested in costs and efficiencies. ESDI would keep NATO alive while at the same time providing the European allies with NATO assets and capabilities, which could be used for "European" causes. However, the EU NATO allies nonetheless decided to go further, creating a security institution outside of NATO and increasing the likelihood of duplication of institutional structures and specific assets such as equipment, processes and human capacities. The potential for competition between the two institutions increased (Hofmann 2009). Hence, the creation of ESDP remains a puzzle for rational choice institutionalist approaches. ESDP matters in ways that cannot be reduced to its functional role.

Conclusion

As one British MoD official said, "ESDP was not inevitable. European states could have continued having the status quo with NATO as the institution handling European security. NATO had been reinventing itself though it was designed for territorial defense – there was the development of the consciousness of what security means inside NATO."[80]

---

[80] Interview # 8 with a British senior official in London (December 7, 2006).

Uwe Stehr, special advisor for security to the SPD said "ESDP was created based on ideas and not based on an adversary or a threat. It was also not created to save costs as the similarities and overlaps of the national armed forces were already managed by NATO."[81] Both echoed remarks made by many other policy-makers and bureaucrats.

The Balkan experience does not explain the creation of ESDP. The Bosnian crisis started in 1992, and NATO's military intervention in Kosovo, which served as an eye opener for Europeans regarding the military capability gap between themselves and the United States, only happened in the spring of 1999, well after Blair initiated discussions on a European security institution. The material incentive structure (either in terms of distribution of capabilities or in terms of cooperation problems) had been the same for years by 1998. But the Conservative government did not act upon it. As the previous analysis has shown, the Kosovo experience did not inform Blair's thinking independently of his party's wish to be at the heart of Europe. Jones Parry says, "Blair's government, including Blair, were crucial in creating ESDP. Kosovo was not the reason. Nor was the Balkan experience."[82]

In 1998 and 1999, European governments ventured out of the known world and created ESDP. The agreements of the Cologne Summit were "unthinkable a few years ago" (Cameron 1999: 81). They were made possible through ideological congruence of the parties in power in the UK, France and Germany. The major milestone on the way was thereby the Franco-British Summit in Saint Malo which was a result of congruent party ideologies in reference to European security. Yet ideological congruence, at times, left room for disagreements such as ESDP's exact relationship to NATO, or what components of crisis management ESDP should be responsible for. Political leaders therefore resorted to "constructive" ambiguity in the face of disagreement over secondary issues and procedural values.

Over the course of the next years, Labour remained very active in bringing forth new initiatives in the field of ESDP. The presidencies following the German one – Finland and Portugal – were more brokers and note-takers than mediators and initiators in the security policy domain. It was, for example, Richard Hatfield from the British MoD who basically wrote the Helsinki Headline Goal.[83] Even in times of stark disagreement over international foreign and security policy issues, like

---

[81] Interview with Uwe Stehr in Berlin (November 14, 2006).
[82] Interview with Emyr Jones Parry in New York (February 22, 2007).
[83] Interview with Emyr Jones Parry in New York (February 22, 2007).

the participation or critique of the US-led military intervention in Iraq, the Labour government, together with the RPR government, pushed for ESDP initiatives such as the battlegroup concept. As a result, what developed is an institutional overlap between NATO and ESDP in membership, mandate and resources.

7 Conclusion

Ideological orientations and party affiliations structure government preferences in security policy, and ideological congruence across governments in power, therefore, matters in the creation of security institutions. An ideological stance in favor of a European security institution within major European governments, and ideological congruence between major European governments, are sufficient to explain the creation of a security institution. With ideologies guiding the way, institution building is not a "journey to an unknown destination" (Weiler 1993). Instead, governments can have different destinations in mind, which influence the likelihood of international outcomes.

On the whole, the evidence supports these arguments. Each of the case studies analyzed in this book demonstrated a strong correspondence between changes in the degree of ideological congruence dividing partisan decision-makers across states, and the likelihood of the creation of a European security institution outside NATO. The more congruent government ideologies were, the more likely it was that a robust security institution would be created; conversely, the more incongruent these ideologies were, the less likely robust institutionalized security cooperation became. This correspondence between the ideological gap between parties in power and the creation of an autonomous security institution should not be dismissed as either a spurious relationship or the effect of omitted variables. Process-tracing in the case studies strongly supports the argument in favor of the centrality of ideological congruence in the creation of international institutions. In the three attempts examined, governments consistently evaluated the appropriateness of a security institution independent of NATO in terms of party ideologies. In addition, changes in domestic ideology, as through government turnover or *cohabitation*, changed the national policy toward security institutions. Sometimes government policy changed in a matter of weeks, as when the RPR replaced the PS in 1995 and immediately started a rapprochement with NATO. The policy debates in each case study reveal discursive strategies that reflect party ideologies. These

Table 7.1 *Ideological congruence and outcomes*

Case	Ideological congruence	Outcome
Common Foreign and Security Policy (1990–1)	Superficial ideological overlaps	Weak European security institution
Amsterdam Treaty, attempt to merge WEU and EU (1996–7)	Ideological differences	Failure to institutionalize further
European Security and Defense Policy (1998–2000)	Very similar ideological position	Robust European security institution

ideologies went beyond mere rhetoric, as I demonstrated in analyzing government policies. The degree of congruence that emerged from these national government ideologies corresponded to the weak, failed or robust institutional outcomes (see Table 7.1).

No other variable corresponded so closely to institutional creation or failure, including shifts in the distribution of power between the United States and Europe, American responses to proposals for a European security institution autonomous of NATO, as well as functional needs in resolving cooperation problems and the reduction of transaction costs (see Table 7.2). Governments often react differently to the same crises or international changes. One cannot simply look at the nature of the external shock to understand why countries act the way they do. While the balance of power remained relatively constant over the decade examined, European attempts to create a security institution autonomous of NATO varied, including a weak form (1990–1), a failed attempt (1996–7), and a robust institution (1998–2000). First, if a state's position in the international distribution of capabilities is a key factor shaping security policy, as realists argue, we should not observe ideological variation affecting policy at the domestic and international level. Lags in state reactions to changing distributions of power cannot be attributed to the creation of ESDP. The creation of ESDP was not linear. The Amsterdam negotiations show that EU member states did not simply agree more and more over time. Second, if one argues that EU member states eventually realized that they needed to offset US hegemonic tendencies (or "soft balance" the United States), one cannot explain at the same time why these same EU member states also agreed to the transformation of NATO, which confirmed US hegemony. Alongside this argument, we should observe today soft balancing behaviors between ESDP and NATO, but we do not. While tensions

Table 7.2 *Alternative IR explanations*

Case	US position (realism)	Balance of power (realism)	Cooperation problem (rational choice institutionalism)
CFSP	Dislike (of autonomous European security institution)	US > Europe	High
Amsterdam	Dislike to indifference	US > Europe	Medium
ESDP	Dislike	US > Europe	Low

exist between these two institutions, they are far from being accounted for through soft balancing behavior. And third, one could make a plausible counterfactual argument that if the Conservatives had stayed in power after 1997, ESDP would not have been created (at the end of the 1990s).

In terms of institutionalist arguments about functional needs and reduction of transaction costs, NATO was always one step ahead of European initiatives to create an autonomous security institution, making a European alternative unnecessary in functional terms. The US administrations of the 1990s were consecutively in favor of transforming NATO to better suit the new security environment and to develop a European pillar within NATO called ESDI. However, this did not change some European governments' preferences toward a European security institution autonomous from NATO. Instead, institution building was a political project, with little discussion of costs.[1] Building up military capabilities was – though important – secondary to the project. Attempts to reform existing institutions and create new ones did not involve debates over soft balancing or a functional division of labor, but instead involved concerns over the appropriateness of the institutions that were rooted in governing party ideologies. International pressures and constraints had little if any direct causal impact on institutional outcomes, but were instead interpreted according to the ideology of the party in government.

This book also departs from yet another alternative explanation – one that is based on partisan values. Instead of locating ideology on a unidimensional left–right spectrum, I have shown that political parties capture the multidimensionality of politics through interpreting interrelationships between multiple (core) values. Governing parties care

---

[1] Interview with Karsten Voigt in Berlin (October 23, 2007).

about how security cooperation is institutionalized (multilateralism), whether intergovernmentally or supranationally (sovereignty), as well as with whom they cooperate – whether with NATO, the EU, or both (Europe). It is possible that all three core values matter, or that only one or two actually inform policy preferences. Even where parties were built on left–right cleavages, issues such as Europe have emerged that cannot be captured on this single continuum. Though some argue that all important political values can ultimately be captured along a left–right continuum, I have demonstrated that important values around security are often cross-cutting – they did not settle on the left–right dimension – requiring a more complex framework for analyzing ideology. Moreover, based on the cases examined, there is rarely a "national" way of absorbing new values or relating them to one another. Some parties such as the British Conservatives, the French Socialists, and the German Christian Democrats value Europe either not at all or as an-end-in-itself regardless of how they rank other values. In other parties, such as the British Labour Party, the German SPD and Greens, and the French RPR, Europe is valued in light of other values. The RPR sees Europe in light of sovereignty; Labour, the SPD and the Greens, on the other hand, see it in terms of multilateralism-as-an-end-in-itself first and foremost. In the latter cases, when the EU transforms, so do party attitudes toward it. The unidimensional presentation of the policy space based on liberty and equality distorts the more complex reality of parties' issue positions. As Table 7.3 demonstrates, measuring ideological party position in terms of equality and liberty fails to account for institutional outcomes.

Ideologies revisited

I have shown that European security cooperation initiatives are based on democratically legitimized policies pursued by national governments on the EU level. Democracies allow for the alternation of governments and encourage political debate. These debates reflect societies that are pluralist and multidimensional (Miller 1983: 735). Some of these debates are over war and peace. Democratic policy-making has been the focus of much research in relation to questions of war and peace (Doyle 1986; Russett 1993; Fearon 1994; Owen 1994; Brown *et al.* 1995; Bueno de Mesquita *et al.* 1999). However, in explaining international security cooperation patterns, what matters is not only the type of domestic institutions that regulate politics, but also the party in power and its political ideology. Liberalism has many ways of manifesting itself (Hartz 1991; Desch 2007/8; Ikenberry *et al.* 2009). The

Table 7.3 *Partisan values explanation*

Case	Partisan values explanation	Outcome
CFSP	Conservatives: liberty PS: equality CDU/CSU and FDP: liberty	Weak institutionalization
Amsterdam	Conservatives: liberty RPR: liberty CDU/CSU and FDP: liberty	Failed institutionalization
ESDP	Labour: equality RPR: liberty SPD and Greens: equality	Robust institutionalization

values of multilateralism, sovereignty and Europe have been expressed differently across political parties, both within and across states. The various resulting configurations have led to a multitude of party ideologies informing both party and – ultimately – government preferences. Parties shape policy preferences in the field of international security. Party ideologies are central to security policy choices, as they motivate proposals and are the medium through which national leaders and ordinary citizens translate their worldviews into political preferences and choices.

European political party ideologies represent a relatively stable and consistent set of core values. This runs counter to arguments that see ideologies as epiphenomenal. Instead, party ideologies fundamentally shape national preference formation. Mechanisms of democratic accountability encourage parties to stick to their political programs in national and international negotiations. In what turned out to be a crucial decade for the creation of a European security institution, the 1990s, political parties did not reassess their understanding of European security despite major shocks, such as the end of the Cold War, and increased instability at the European periphery and abroad. Instead, parties remained attached to their values of multilateralism-in-the-use-of-force, sovereignty and Europe, keeping their preferences relatively constant. For example, British Conservatives remained opposed to robust European security cooperation throughout the 1990s, despite strong pressures from their European counterparts' transatlantic tensions and the wars on the Bultans that lacked capabilities and assets. In contrast, the Labour Party pushed for a European security institution despite the Conservatives playing on fears of a "European army" that was unpopular domestically.

Thus, political leaders tend to act according to their party's ideology. Their actions reflect a certain faction of their party that recently came to power, or a smaller but dominant faction whose votes are needed to keep parliamentary majority. Even if this structural constellation allows some parliamentary members to disproportionally influence policy-making, as we have seen, the majority of the party has to agree to the policy stance. Looking for common ground, the leader of the party often functions as a manager and interpreter of values. Occasionally, a leader may initiate shifts in party ideology, though she has to reason this in relation to the boundaries of the set of values to which the party subcribes. Blair, for instance, is often cited as a leader who transformed Labour from the socialist left to a center-left, "third way" party. Yet Neil Kinnock had initiated and managed many of these reforms prior to Blair. Moreover, Labour's Europe policy under Blair was premised on shifts in the EU itself. In addition to party leaders, I have shown that factions also matter, especially in the cases of the SPD and the Greens with respect to their stance on multilateralism-in-the-use-of-force.

The oft-claimed demise of ideological differences that organize political preferences may be more anecdotal than substantive (Kirchheimer 1990; Manow *et al.* 2008) – at least in the realm of security policy in Europe. Instead, ideologies continue to provide crucial reference points in the formulation of national policies. Political change in government continues to matter, though not all political change has the same impact and is not equally important to international cooperation. Sometimes, government turnover results in alterations in the nuances of policy, other times it can change an entire policy direction.

ESDP's existence represents a "stickiness of empirical reality" (Abbott 2001: 223), but a reality that does not lead to ideological congruence across time and space. Instead, an institution's existence and purpose are conditional on the ideological congruence across European governments. Although ESDP has existed since 1999, no integration dynamics have overtaken the policy field. ESDP has not been supranationalized but remains under the authority of the Council of Ministers and the European Council. Governing parties, with their own ideological predispositions and compositions, still constitute the decision-making bodies on the EU level. The European Parliament and the Commission only have influence over the ESDP budget for civilian crisis management missions.

Looking beyond the time period covered in this book, all three countries under consideration have experienced changes of both leadership and parties. Nicolas Sarkozy, who heads the RPR's successor

UMP (Union pour un Mouvement Populaire)[2] was elected president in 2007 (until 2012) with a UMP majority in parliament. He has since pursued policies in line with those of Jacques Chirac. Like Chirac did previously, Sarkozy announced in September 2007 that he intended for France to rejoin NATO's integrated command structure, provided that certain conditions were met (*New York Times* 2007; Sciolino 2007). France rejoined NATO in April 2009. The PS, on the other hand, has vehemently criticized this policy step, just as it did a decade earlier. Hubert Védrine has criticized it as "an Occidental temptation."[3] He believes that the commonalities between the United States and Europe are overemphasized and doubts the argument that the reintegration of France into NATO will reinforce France's position in NATO vis-à-vis the United States (Védrine 2007: 37–8).[4]

In the UK, many commentators interpreted Tony Blair's decision to support the United States in its war in Iraq as having chosen the United States over Europe. However, these commentators have ignored the fact that Blair, together with Chirac, initiated a project to create the *battlegroups* in ESDP in February 2003 at the Franco-British summit meeting in Le Touquet. At a November 2003 meeting in London, at the height of the intra-European and transatlantic controversies over Iraq, these proposals were made even more explicit, proposals that would significantly expand ESDP capabilities (Quille 2006). Gordon Brown had continued Blair's line of policy, while the Conservatives under Cameron continue to oppose it. David Cameron, British prime minister since 2010, has often repeated that "Atlanticism is in my DNA and in the DNA of the Conservative Party" (Cameron 2008). Confronted with the reality of ESDP's existence and its more pro-ESDP coalition partner, the Liberal Democrats, the Conservative Party nonetheless wants to ensure that NATO is the primary security institution in Europe. It sees ESDP as subordinate to NATO (Cameron 2008) and has not initiated any EU-wide ESDP actions since coming to power – to the dismay of their coalition partner. Instead, informed by their core value of sovereignty, at the British–French Summit in 2010, both governments focused on the bilateral cooperation between them. Liam Fox, then Secretary of State for Defense, emphasized that the intensified cooperation:

---

[2] The UMP was founded in 2002 as the result of a merger of the RPR and the Christian Democratic wing of the UDF, as well as some smaller parties.
[3] Interview with Hubert Védrine in Paris (May 29, 2008).
[4] Interview with Hubert Védrine in Paris (May 29, 2008).

is not about increasing the defence capabilities of the European Union. I repeat – this is about two sovereign nations, which between them spend 50% of all the defence spending of the NATO members in Europe, and 65% of the research spending. It makes a great deal of sense for us to co-operate, but it is absolutely clear that this is about two sovereign nations that are willing to co-operate when it is in their mutual interest to do so, but keep their ability to act separately when their national interests require it. (Quoted in House of Commons 2010)

Both governments, the Conservatives (with a Liberal Democrat coalition partner) and the UMP cared most about increasing their range of action.

In Germany, from 2005 to 2009, the government has consisted of a *Grosse Koalition* between the CDU/CSU and the SPD. The CDU/CSU tried to tie ESDP more to NATO. By pushing for a consensus on security challenges and means within the transatlantic Alliance (Kamp and Masala 2006). The SPD, however, prefers keeping all multilateral options alive; that is, acting with NATO and the United States – or without them. The CDU/CSU stress synergy while the SPD has been stressing emancipation from NATO as the sole security provider (Kamp and Masala 2006). While both parties were in power, they declared their commitment to Europe but could not specify any particular goals (Koalitionsvertrag 2005). These differences between the ruling parties in the *Grosse Koalition* have prevented the German government from advancing initiatives. With another change in government in 2009, Germany has again a CDU/CSU – FDP coalition in power that is trying to overcome the difficulties that have plagued the EU–NATO relationship ever since ESDP was created. The coalition treaty states as a policy goal the reintroduction of Germany as a leader in the EU (Koalitionsvereinbarung 2009).

As the examination of European security cooperation has demonstrated, some parties' preferences resemble those one would expect to see when studying IR paradigms such as realism or institutionalism (Kowert 2002: 267–8). Preferences that rest on ideological foundations can resemble the sorts of preferences that realism or rational choice institutionalism attribute to states. The behavior of both the British Conservatives and the French Socialists conform to realist predictions in the preceding analysis. However, they do so only in one institutional setting: the Conservatives resemble "realists" in the EU, while the PS does so in NATO. The Conservatives do not want to give up power to a European institution – judging cooperation in the EU in policy fields such as security to be against their view of the national interest and sovereignty. In contrast, the PS followed a very similar logic when arguing against France's full membership in a transformed NATO. The actions of the German Christian Democrats and British Labour resonate with rational choice institutionalist predictions, as they are in favor of both institutions and want to make them work together in a mutually reinforcing way. Picking out these individual stances to make a realist or institutionalist argument is facilitated by the fact that efforts to create a European security institution have never been systematically analyzed in conjunction with NATO and the Alliance's internal developments.

When are ideologies likely to be trumped? As long as the states in question are democracies, this book suggests that it is likely that political party ideologies will play a role in the formulation of policy on the national or international level. We will continue to see disagreements over the appropriate means to handle commonly shared threats, such as terrorism, and economic policy (Hooghe and Marks 1999).[5] However, depending on who holds the political ideology – groups at large or individuals with clientelistic ties to larger groups – we can expect the stability of shared values to vary. In addition, I do not suggest that party ideologies always *dominate* national processes of preference formation or international outcomes, but that they always, albeit to varying degrees, *influence* these processes. It is likely that "the importance of party politics differs across policy fields" (Manow *et al.* 2008: 34) and across democracies. A possible direction for future research would be to inquire into the scope of ideological impact across policy fields and across different democratic regimes. One should thereby bear in mind that when it comes to Europe, not all policy is formulated on the national level.

The transatlantic security relationship revisited

In the 1990s, different institutional possibilities for promoting peace and stability emerged in Europe. During that decade, crisis management policies surpassed defense policies with regard to the actual security activities of states as well as their priority in security policy (SIPRI 2004; UNDPKO 2006; BMVG 2007). Overall, the primary focus on mutual defense during the Cold War has been replaced by a more diverse approach to security with components of collective security and crisis management. In crisis management, states are not obliged to take action against acts of aggression affecting non-allies. In collective security, the belief dominates that states' security is affected

---

[5] Manow *et al.* present evidence that parties across Europe are converging in economic policies, though there is still recognizable variance that matters in terms of policy preferences (Manow *et al.* 2008).

by aggression anywhere (Claude 1962, 1992). The shared logic behind mutual defense, as well as crisis management and collective security, is that they represent attempts "to impose some order on the contingent and unpredictable threats in international politics. They deal, in other words, with the problem of organizing relations among sovereign powers, with a view of preventing war or ... containing its consequences" (Yost 1998: 7).

The 1990s were central given the different possible institutional expressions of European security debated among governments. The three major periods of negotiations over the creation of a European security institution autonomous from NATO have been the focus of this book. Despite predictions to the contrary (Osgood 1962; Mearsheimer 1990; Waltz 1993), NATO "has proven a durable and dynamic actor – a key agent in building security governance in Europe" (Webber *et al.* 2004: 14). So has the EU with its ESDP – on this all theoretical perspectives discussed in this book agree (Jones 2007; Howorth 2010). Between Saint Malo in December 1998 and the following IGC in December 2000 in Nice, a series of practical steps were taken to equip ESDP with the structures and military capabilities to implement a security policy of its own. Anand Menon (2003: 203) said, "no longer can critics (the author included) simply dismiss as mere rhetoric the stated ambitions of Europeans to do more in the military sphere."

NATO's role in the creation of a European security institution has varied according to the parties in power. NATO has depended on the political will and preferences of its member states. Hence, while the French PS was opposed to NATO adaptation to the new security environment at the beginning of the 1990s, other NATO members had to look for alternate ways to transform NATO, which would exclude France from the decision-making process. This slowed down the process of transformation. However, NATO's slow start in the post-Cold War period did not result in the creation of a more robust European security institution because other parties in power, especially the British Conservative Party, were against such a development. Only when British, French and German governments agreed on the relationship between NATO and the EU could a European security institution autonomous from NATO be created.

The Franco-British Saint Malo effort has produced a European institution that overlaps significantly with NATO. As Aggarwal (1998: 1) observes, "International institutions are rarely created in a vacuum. When new institutions are developed, they often must be reconciled with existing ones." This reconciliation is not automatic. A senior specialist for the US Congressional Research Service testified, "The

United States will not depend on individuals in key positions to ensure that ESDP does not split the Alliance. It will want to establish institutions and processes that will lock the European effort into a transatlantic framework" (Sloan 2000: 51). Growing institutional density comes with growing institutional interdependence and vulnerability, which again can result in inefficiencies and the ineffectiveness of institutions. Both NATO and ESDP insist on autonomous control over their strategic and operational planning as well as their resources. While "cleaning up the dishes was politically unacceptable" to most European actors, with the creation of ESDP, the Europeans have assumed "a sharp role"[6] and do not leave military action solely to NATO.

As I have argued throughout the book, the European governments turned NATO into an alliance of choice. These dynamics have weakened NATO's role as Europe's primary security organization, despite US insistence that NATO retains the primary role in European security. Some even speak of the EU as a "global actor" (Howorth 2010) or a "quiet superpower" (Moravcsik 2009, 2010). Clearly the United States would have more influence if NATO were the only security institution in Europe (Nuland 2007; Olson 2007). Speaking of ESDP's increasing autonomy from NATO, the former EU High Representative, Javier Solana, has said, "it won't happen in a way that will destroy NATO. It's true that the United States may lose some leverage as Europe gets stronger, but this is inevitable and by no means an unhealthy thing" (Drozdiak 2000: A01).

The ESDP–NATO overlap has to be understood as an institutional architecture that offers governments many choices with which to conduct their preferred multilateral security policy. Some governments benefit from a range of tools for handling policy issues through forum shopping opportunities (Raustiala and Victor 2004; Alter and Meunier 2009), but the overlap also generates problems and inefficiencies (Hunter 2002; Asmus *et al.* 2003; Peters 2004; *The Economist* 2007). Troop deployments are delayed, communication between both organizations in the field is hindered, and no common strategic guidance exists. All this can put the lives of personnel and the success of operations on the ground in jeopardy (Leaky 2008). NATO and the EU currently have 21 member states in common. But as Jaap de Hoop Scheffer, General Secretary of NATO, observed, "it is astounding how narrow the bandwidth of cooperation between NATO and the Union has remained. There is a remarkable distance between them" (De Hoop Scheffer 2007). The NATO–ESDP overlap has given Turkey (only a

---

[6] Interview with François Heisbourg in Paris (May 27, 2008).

member of NATO) and Cyprus (only an EU member) opportunities to take the inter-institutional relationship hostage to increase their bargaining power (Hofmann 2009). While the governmental change in Cyprus decreased the tensions with Turkey in 2008, thus increasing hopes that the relationship between EU and NATO will improve at least to some degree, the 2010 elections in Turkish Cyprus have brought new issues to the table that stall the rapprochement process (*The Economist* 2011).

The larger point is that the transatlantic relationship cannot be characterized as binary between Europe and the United States. While scholars are quick to identify such binary tensions (Posen 2006; Anderson *et al.* 2008; Ikenberry 2008), this book has shown that European governments neither act as a unity at all times, nor do they understand and interpret Europe as the same entity. Political parties in government, instead, act upon different expressions of Europe and this has repercussions for their valuing and acting within the transatlantic relationship. Depending on their ideological inclinations, different governments perceive the relationship differently. It is not that the EU and the United States disagree over the role and purpose of NATO, it is rather that some political parties within Europe and the United States do – while others do not.

What does this mean for the transatlantic relationship or the "West" at large? The transatlantic relationship has often been called into question – based on its values, identity and institutional expression, as well as action and inaction. But, so far, it has withstood all crises (Risse-Kappen 1995, 1996; Gaddis 1997; Dettke 2009: 9–12; Thies 2009; Tierney 2011). One particularly serious crisis was the disagreement over how to tackle security threats when the war against the regime in Iraq was imminent. The issue pitted the governments of France and Germany (or "old Europe") against the United States, the United Kingdom and "new Europe." While European leaders had pledged their "unlimited solidarity" with the US right after 9/11, disagreements over Iraq were "threatening to render NATO irrelevant at precisely the moment it has been 're-invented' to meet post Cold War challenges" (Black 2003). Philip Gordon and Jeremy Shapiro (2004: 2) observed that "the dispute over Iraq ran so deep that it posed a challenge not only to transatlantic relations, but to the main institutions underpinning world order throughout the post-World War II period." Observers as diverse as Henry Kissinger, Francis Fukuyama, Tony Judt, Charles Kupchan, Robert Kagan and Ivo Daalder all observed deep-seated differences between "Europe" and the United States; Charles Krauthammer even pronounced NATO to be "dead." However, political contestation over the Iraq War was as pronounced *within* the United States, Germany and the UK as it was in the relations between the United States and several European governments. Furthermore, European governments continued to cooperate with the United States on a host of issues, most notably within NATO in Afghanistan. As this book has shown, the security relationship between Europe and the United States is not uniform. One main reason is that Europe is not uniform. Despite the EU, European governments have not harmonized to the extent that their foreign and security policies have become indistinguishable. Instead, different European governments and political politics disagree over policies such as how to relate to the United States (Howorth 2010).

The "West" has never been monolith, but has been marked by bounded competition and political contestation. International disputes and crises between democratic states are in the hands of political parties that have experienced the politics of competing values on the domestic level and that have consistently responded within the normative guidelines of bounded competition (Dixon 1994: 17; Risse-Kappen 1996; Adler and Barnett 1998; Wæver 1998). Disagreements over policy means and substance are not only tolerated but are a necessary component of political life, a demonstration of the plurality of preferences that not only exist but also can be voiced. In such a political space, disagreements happen without fearing for one's survival, security or political standing. One major factor that eases or exacerbates this competition is the degree of ideological congruence within Europe and across the Atlantic. Formalized security institutions can serve as the platform on which this bounded competition is played out (Mérand 2008: 5, 13). Government actors and political parties have to live with the institutional realities that were created at the end of the 1990s. NATO and ESDP are here to stay. But their institutional constraints, the concerns over transaction costs, efficiencies, the distribution of military capabilities, and the future of hegemony, are filtered through party ideological lenses. Political party ideologies make the preferences of governments in key states, and the congruence of them across states, important variables in the study of European security.

References

Abbott, Andrew 2001. *Time Matters: On Theory and Method.* Chicago and London: University of Chicago Press.

Abbott, Kenneth W. and Duncan Snidal 1998. "Why States Act through Formal International Organizations," *Journal of Conflict Resolution* 42, 1: 3–32.

2000. "Hard and Soft Law in International Governance," *International Organization* 54, 3: 421–56.

2004. "Pathways to International Cooperation," in Eyal Benvenisti and Moshe Hirsch (eds.), *The Impact of International Law on International Cooperation: Theoretical Perspectives,* pp. 50–84. New York: Cambridge University Press.

Abramson, Paul, John Aldrich, Andre Blais, Daniel Lee and Renan Levine 2008. "Coalition Considerations and the Vote," in Asher Arian and Michal Shamir (eds.), *The Elections in Israel, 2006,* pp. 45–66. New Brunswick: Transaction.

Acharya, Amitav 2004. "The Role of Regional Organizations: Are Views Changing?" Paper prepared for the Pacific Symposium, National Defense University, Washington, DC, April 22–23. www.ndu.edu/inss/symposia/pacific200.

Adams, James 2001. "A Theory of Spatial Competition with Biased Voters," *British Journal of Political Science* 31: 121–58.

Adams, James, Michael Clark, Lawrence Ezrow and Garrett Glasgow 2004. "Understanding Change and Stability in Party Ideologies: Do Parties Respond to Public Opinion or to Past Election Results?" *British Journal of Political Science* 34, 4: 589–610.

Adler, Emanuel and Michael Barnett (eds.) 1998. *Security Communities.* Cambridge University Press.

Agence Europe 1995. No. 6612 (November 25).

1998a. No. 7330 (October 26/27).

1998b. No. 7336 (November 5).

Aggarwal, Vinod K. (ed.) 1998. *Institutional Designs for a Complex World: Bargaining, Linkages, and Nesting.* Ithaca and London: Cornell University Press.

Aggarwal, Vinod and Edward Fogarty 2005. "The Limits of Interregionalism: The EU and North America," *Journal of European Integration* 27, 3: 327–46.

Albright, Madeleine 1998. "Transcript: Albright Press Conference at NATO HDQS December 8," *USIS Washington File*. www.fas.org/man/nato/news/1998/98120904_tlt.html.

Aldrich, John 1983. "A Downsian Spatial Model with Party Activism," *American Political Science Review* 77: 974–90.

1995. *Why Parties? The Origin and Transformation of Political Parties in America*. University of Chicago Press.

Aldrich, John H., John L. Sullivan and Eugene Borgida 1989. "Foreign Policy and Voting in Presidential Elections: Are Candidates Waltzing before a Blind Audience?" *American Political Science Review* 83, 1: 123–41.

Aldrich, John H., Christopher Gelpi, Peter Feaver, Jason Reifler and Kristin Thompson Sharp 2006. "Foreign Policy and the Electoral Connection," *Annual Review of Political Science* 9: 477–502.

Alesina, Alberto and Howard Rosenthal 1995. *Partisan Politics: Divided Government and the Economy*. Cambridge University Press.

Allen, David 1982. "Political Cooperation and the Euro-Arab Dialogue," in David Allen, Reinhardt Rummel and Wolfgang Wessels (eds.), *European Political Cooperation: Towards a Foreign Policy for Western Europe*, pp. 69–82. London: Butterworth Scientific.

Allen, David and William Wallace 1982. "European Political Cooperation: the Historical and Contemporary Background," in David Allen, Reinhardt Rummel and Wolfgang Wessels (eds.), *European Political Cooperation: Towards a Foreign Policy for Western Europe*, pp. 21–32. London: Butterworth Scientific.

Alter, Karen 1998. "Who are the 'Masters of the Treaty'? European Governments and the European Court of Justice," *International Organization* 52, 1: 121–47.

Alter, Karen and Sophie Meunier 2006. "Nested and Overlapping Regimes in the Transatlantic Banana Trade Dispute," *Journal of European Public Policy* 13, 3: 362–82.

2009. "The Politics of International Regime Complexity," *Perspectives on Politics* 7: 13–24.

Althusser, Louis 1984. *Essays on Ideology*. London: Verso.

Amsterdam Treaty 1997a. *The Treaty of Amsterdam. Amending the Treaty on European Union, the Treaties establishing the European Communities and Certain Related Acts*. www.eurotreaties.com/amsterdamtreaty.pdf.

1997b. *The Treaty of Amsterdam. Amending the Treaty on European Union, the Treaties establishing the European Communities and Certain Related Acts. Final Act and Declarations adopted by the Conference. 2 October 1997*. www.eurotreaties.com/amsterdamfinalact.pdf.

Andersen, Robert and Jocelyn A.J. Evans 2003. "Contemporary Developments in Political Space in France," in Jocelyn A.J. Evans (ed.), *The French Party System*, pp. 171–87. Manchester and New York: Manchester University Press.

Anderson, Jeffrey, G. John Ikenberry and Thomas Risse (eds.) 2008. *The End of the West? Crisis and Change in the Atlantic Order*. Ithaca: Cornell University Press.

Andersson, Jan and Andreas Malm 2006. "Public-Private Partnerships and the Challenge of Critical Infrastructure Protection," in Myriam A. Dunn and Victor Mauer (eds.), *International CIIP Handbook Vol. II*, pp. 139–67. Zurich: ETH Center for Security Studies.

Andréani, Gilles 2000. "Why Institutions Matter," *Survival* 42, 2: 81–95.

Andréani, Gilles, Christoph Bertram and Charles Grant 2001. *Europe's Military Revolution*. London: Center for European Reform.

Art, Robert 2005/6. "Correspondence: Striking the Balance," *International Security* 30, 3: 177–85.

Ash, Timothy Garton 1993. *In Europe's Name: Germany and the Divided Continent*. New York: Random House.

Asmus, Ronald, Rafael L. Bardaji, Christoph Bertram and Carl Bildt 2003. "Declaration on Transatlantic Relations: How to Overcome the Divisions." www.brookings.edu/views/papers/daalder/20030516.htm.

Aspinwall, Mark 2000. "Structuring Europe: Powersharing Institutions and British Preferences on European Integration," *Political Studies* 48: 415–42.

  2002. "Preferring Europe: Ideology and National Preferences on European Integration," *European Union Politics* 3, 1: 81–111.

Atkinson, Rick 1996. "NATO Gives Members Response Flexibility," *Washington Post* (June 4): A14.

Attina, Fulvio and Sarah Repucci 2004. "ESDP and the European Regional Security Partnership," in Martin Holland (ed.), *Common Foreign and Security Policy: The First Ten Years*, 2nd edn, pp. 58–77. London: Continuum.

Axelrod, Robert M. 1970. *Conflict of Interest: A Theory of Divergent Goals with Applications to Politics*. Chicago: Markham.

Baker, David and David Seawright 1998a. "Introduction," in David Baker and David Seawright (eds.), *Britain For and Against Europe: British Politics and the Question of European Integration*, pp. 1–10. Oxford: Clarendon Press.

  1998b. "A 'Rosy' Map of Europe? Labour Parliamentarians and European Integration," in David Baker and David Seawright (eds.), *Britain For and Against Europe: British Politics and the Question of European Integration*, pp. 57–87. Oxford: Clarendon Press.

Baker, David, Andrew Gamble and Peter Ludlow 1994. "The Parliamentary Siege of Maastricht," *Parliamentary Affairs* 47, 1: 37–60.

Balladur, Edouard 1995. *Deux Ans a Matignon*. Paris: Plon.

Barnett, Michael N. and Martha Finnemore 1999. "The Politics, Power, and Pathologies of International Orgnaizations," *International Organization* 53: 699–732.

Barry, Charles 1996. "NATO's Combined Joint Task Forces in Theory and Practice," *Survival* 38, 1: 81–97.

Bartolini, Stefano and Peter Mair (eds.) 1984. *Party Politics in Contemporary Europe*. London: Frank Cass.

Bell, David S. 2000. *Presidential Power in the Fifth Republic France*. New York: Oxford University Press.

  2003. "The French Communist Party: From Revolution to Reform," in Jocelyn A.J. Evans (ed.), *The French Party System*, pp. 29–41. Manchester and New York: Manchester University Press.

Bellamy, Alex J. and Paul Williams 2005. "Who's Keeping the Peace? Regionalization and Contemporary Peace Operations," *International Security* 29, 4: 157–95.

Benoit, Kenneth 2009. "Irish Political Parties and Policy Stances on European Integration," *Irish Political Studies* 24, 4: 447–66.

Benoit, Kenneth and Michael Laver 2012. "The Dimensionality of Political Space: Epistemological and Methodological Considerations," *European Union Politics* 13, 2: 194–218.

Benoit, Kenneth, Thomas Bräuninger and Marc Debus 2009. "Challenges for Estimating Policy Preferences: Announcing an Open Access Archive of Political Documents," *German Politics* 18, 3: 440–53.

Berger, Thomas U. 1996. "Norms, Identity, and National Security in Germany and Japan," in Peter J. Katzenstein (ed.), *The Culture of National Security: Norms and Identity in World Politics*, pp. 317–56. New York: Columbia University Press.

Betz, Hans-Georg 1995. "Alliance 90/Greens: From Fundamental Opposition to Black-Green," in David P. Conradt, Gerald R. Kleinfeld, George K. Romoser and Christian Soe (eds.), *Germany's New Politics: Parties and Issues in the 1990s*, pp. 203–20. Providence and Oxford: Berghahn Books.

Bevins, Anthony 1997. "Tories Face more Bloodletting over Policy on Europe," *The Independent* (November 1): 7.

Beyme, Klaus von 1985. *Political Parties in Western Democracies*. Aldershot: Gower.

Birchfeld, Vicki and Markus M.L. Crepaz 1998. "The Impact of Constitutional Structures and Collective and Competitive Veto Points on Income Inequality in Industrialized Democracies," *European Journal of Political Research* 34, 2: 175–200.

Bitterlich, Joachim 2005. *Europa – Mission impossible?* Düsseldorf: Droste Verlag.

Black, Ian 2003. "Nato Deadlocked as France and Germany Refuse to Back Down," *Guardian* (February 12). www.guardian.co.uk/world/2003/feb/12/iraq.nato.

Black, Ian and Ewen Macaskill 1997. "Cook Confident of Amsterdam Deal," *Guardian* (May 10): 5.

Black, Ian and Nicholas Watt 2000. "Blair Calls for Euro 'Superpower'," *Guardian*. www.guardian.co.uk/EMU/Story/0,2763,378872,00.html.

Blair, Tony 1999. "NATO, Europe, and our Future Security." Speech at NATO 50th Anniversary Conference, Royal United Services Institute London, March 8. www.britainusa.com/sections/articles_show.asp?SarticleType=1&Article_ID=713&i=117.

BMVG 2007. "Bundeswehr im Einsatz." www.einsatz.bundeswehr.de/C1256F1D0022A5C2/Docname/Abgeschlossene_Einsaetze_Home.

Bodenheimer, Suzanne 1967. *Political Union: A Microcosm of European Politics, 1960–1966*. Leyden: A.W. Sijtoff.

Boniface, Pascal 1995. "La France," in Pascal Boniface (ed.), *L'Année Stratégique 1995: Les Equilibres Militaires*, p. 12. Paris: Dunod for the Insitut des Relations Internationales et Stratégiques.

1996. "NATO's Enlargement, France's Dilemmas," in David Haglund (ed.), *Will NATO go East?*, pp. 181–95. Kingston: Queens University Press.

1997. "The NATO Debate in France." Paper presented at Enlargement: The National Debates over Ratification Conference, October 7. www.nato.int/acad/conf/enlarg97/boniface.htm#27.

Boudon, R. 1989. *The Analysis of Ideology*. University of Chicago Press.

Bozo, Frédéric 1991. *La France et l'OTAN. De la guerre froide au nouvel ordre européen*. Paris: Masson.

1999. "De la bataille des euromissiles à la 'guerre' du Kosovo: l'Alliance atlantique face à ses defies (1979–1999)," *Politique étrangère* 3: 587–600.

2005. *Mitterrand, le fin de la guerre froide et l'unification allemande. De Yalta à Maastricht*. Paris: Odile Jacob.

Bradley, Curtis A. and Judith G. Kelley 2008. "The Concept of International Delegation," *Law and Contemporary Problems* 71, 1: 1–36.

Brady, Henry E. and David Collier (eds.) 2004. *Rethinking Social Inquiry: Diverse Tools, Shared Standards*. Lanham: Rowman & Littlefield Publishers, Inc.

Brady, Henry E., David Collier and Jason Seawright 2004. "Refocusing the Discussion of Methodology," in Henry E. Brady and David Collier (eds.), *Rethinking Social Inquiry: Diverse Tools, Shared Standards*, pp. 3–20. Lanham: Rowman & Littlefield Publishers, Inc.

Braunthal, Gerard 1993. "The 1989 Basic Program of the German Social Democratic Party," *Polity* 14, 3: 375–99.

British–Italian Summit Declaration 1999. "Joint Declaration Launching European Defence Capabilities Initiative," July 19. www.britainusa.com/sections/articles_show.asp?SarticleType=1&Article_ID=711&i=117.

Brittan, Samuel 1968. *Left or Right: The Bogus Dilemma*. London: Secker & Warburg.

Brooks, Stephen G. and William C. Wohlforth 2005. "Hard Times for Soft Balancing," *International Security* 30, 1: 72–108.

2008. *World Out of Balance: International Relations Theory and the Challenge of American Primacy*. Princeton University Press.

Brown, Colin 1997a. "Clarke, Kinnock, Jenkins Raise the Euro Banner," *Independent* (November 7): 17.

1997b. "Tory Defector Finds New Labour Very Agreeable," *Independent* (November 25): 10.

Brown, Michael E., Sean M. Lynn-Jones and Steven E. Miller (eds.) 1995. *Debating the Democratic Peace*. Cambridge, MA: MIT Press.

Brown Weiss, E. 1993. "International Environmental Issues and the Emergence of a New World Order," *Georgetown Law Journal* 81, 3: 675–710.

Browne, Eric C., Dennis W. Gleiber and Carolyn S. Mashoba 1984. "Evaluating Conflict of Interest Theory: Western European Cabinet Coalitions, 1945–1980," *British Journal of Political Science* 14: 1–32.

Brzezinski, Zbigniew 1993. "A Bigger – and Safer – Europe," *New York Times* (December 1): A23.

Buchan, David 1993. *Europe: The Strange Superpower*. Dartmouth: Aldershot.

Budge, Ian 1994. "A Spatial Theory of Party Competition: Uncertainty, Ideology and Policy Equilibria," *British Journal of Political Science* 14: 443–67.

Budge, Ian and David Farlie 1983. *Explaining and Predicting Elections: Issue Effects and Party Strategies in Twenty-Three Democracies*. London: Allen & Unwin.

Budge, Ian and Richard I. Hofferbert 1990. "Mandates and Policy Outputs: U.S. Party Platforms and Federal Expenditures," *American Political Science Review* 84: 111–31.

Budge, Ian and Hans Keman 1990. *Parties and Democracy: Coalition Formation and Government Functioning in Twenty States*. New York: Oxford University Press.

Budge, Ian, David Robertson and Derek Hearl (eds.) 1987. *Ideology, Strategy and Party Change: Spatial Analysis of Post-War Election Programmes in 19 Democracies*. Cambridge University Press.

Budge, Ian, Hans-Dieter Klingemann, Andrea Volkens, Judith Bara and Eric Tanenbaum (eds.) 2001. *Mapping Policy Preferences: Estimates for Parties, Electors, and Governments 1945–1998*. Oxford University Press.

Bueno de Mesquita, Bruce 1978. "System Polarization and the Occurrence and Duration of War," *Journal of Conflict Resolution* 22, 2: 241–67.

Bueno de Mesquita, Bruce, James Morrow, Randolph Siverson and Alastair Smith 1999. "An Institutional Explanation of the Democratic Peace," *American Political Science Review* 93, 4: 791–801.

Buhl, Dieter 1999. "Europa muss schneller sein. Der stellvertretende US-Aussenminister Strobe Talbott zu den Problemen der NATO," *Die Zeit* 07/1999. www.zeit.de/1999/07/Europa_muss_schneller_sein.

Bulmer, Simon 1983. "Domestic Politics and European Community Policy-Making," *Journal of Common Market Studies* 21, 4: 349–63.

  2000. "European Policy: Fresh Start or False Dawn?" in David Coates and Peter Lawler (eds.), *New Labour in Power*, pp. 240–53. Manchester University Press.

Bulmer, Simon and Martin Burch 2005. "The Europeanization of UK Government: From Quiet Revolution to Explicit Step-Change?" *Public Administration* 83, 4: 861–90.

Bulmer, Simon and Christian Lequesne (eds.) 2005. *The Member States of the European Union*. Oxford University Press.

Bundesregierung 2000. *Die Bundeswehr – sicher ins 21. Jahrhundert. Eckpfeiler für eine Erneuerung von Grund auf.* www.weltpolitik.net/texte/policy/bundeswehr/2000–06%20Scharping%20Eckpfeiler.pdf.

Burley, Anne-Marie and Walter Mattli 1993. "Europe Before the Court: A Political Theory of Legal Integration," *International Organization* 47, 1: 41–76.

Cameron, David 2008. "Crossroads for NATO – How the Atlantic Alliance Should Work in the 21st Century." Speech given at Chatham House on April 1. www.conservatives.com/tile.do?def=news.story.page&obj_id=143402.

Cameron, Fraser 1999. *The Foreign and Security Policy of the European Union: Past, Present and Future*. Sheffield Academic Press.

Caporaso, James A. 1992. "International Relations Theory and Multilateralism: The Search for Foundations," *International Organization* 46, 3: 599–632.

  1996. "The European Union and Forms of the State: Westphalian, Regulatory or Post-Modern?" *Journal of Common Market Studies* 34, 1: 29–52.

Caporaso, James A., Maria Green Cowles and Thomas Risse (eds.) 2001. *Europeanization and Domestic Change*. Ithaca: Cornell University Press.

Carmines, Edward G. and James A. Stimson 1980. "The Two Faces of Issue Voting," *American Political Science Review* 74, 1: 78–91.

Castles, Francis (ed.) 1982. *The Impact of Parties*. London: Sage.

Castles, Francis and Peter Mair 1984. "Left-Right Political Scales: Some 'Expert' Judgments," *European Journal of Political Research* 12: 73–88.

CDU Party Manifesto 1990. *CDU. Ja zu Deutschland. Ja zur Zukunft. Wahlprogramm der Christlich Demokratischen Union Deutschlands zur gesamtdeutschen Bundestagswahl am 2. Dezember 1990*. Comparative Party manifesto research group, Zentralarchiv für Empirische Sozialforschung an der Universität zu Köln.

CDU/CSU Party Manifesto 1998. *Wahlplattform von CDU and CSU*. Comparative Party manifesto research group, Zentralarchiv für Empirische Sozialforschung an der Universität zu Köln.

Chagnollaud, Dominique and Jean-Louis Quermonne 2000a. *La Ve République. I. Le régime politique*. Paris: Flammarion.

2000b. *La Ve République. II. Le pouvoir exécutif et l'administration*. Paris: Flammarion.

2000c. *La Ve République. III. Le pouvoir legislative et le système de partis*. Paris: Flammarion.

Checkel, Jeffrey T. 1998. "The Constructivist Turn in International Relations Theory," *World Politics* 50: 324–48.

2004. "Social Constructivisms in Global and European Politics: a Review Essay," *Review of International Studies* 30, 2: 229–44.

Cheibub, Jose Antonio and Fernando Limongi 2002. "Democratic Institutions and Regime Survival: Parliamentary and Presidential Democracies Reconsidered," *Annual Review of Political Science* 5: 151–79.

Chevallier, Jean-Jacques, Guy Carcassonne and Olivier Duhamel 2007. *Histoire de la Ve République. 1958–2007*, 12 edn. Paris: Dalloz.

Chiou, Fang-Yi and Lawrence S. Rothenberg 2003. "When Pivotal Politics Meets Partisan Politics," *American Journal of Political Science* 47, 3: 503–22.

Chirac, Jacques 1988. "Discours de Monsieur Jacques Chirac. Vincennes, Dimanche 20 Mars 1988." Comparative Party manifesto research group, Zentralarchiv für Empirische Sozialforschung an der Universität zu Köln.

1999. "Entretien de Monsieur Jacques Chirac," *Armées d'aujourd'hui*, December 1. www.elysee.fr.

2000. "Speech on European Security and Defence by Mr Jacques Chirac, President of the French Republic, to the Presidential Committee of the WEU Assembly at the Elysée Palace, Paris, 30 May 2000." www.assembly-weu.org/en/documents/sessions_ordinaires/rpt/2000/1699.html.

Chittick, William O., Keith R. Billingsley and Rick Travis 1995. "A Three-Dimensional Model of American Foreign Policy Beliefs," *International Studies Quarterly* 39, 3: 313–31.

Chuter, David 1997. "The United Kingdom," in Jolyon Howorth and Anand Menon (eds.), *The European Union and National Defence Policy*, pp. 105–20. London: Routledge.

Cimbalo, Jeffrey L. 2004. "Saving NATO From Europe," *Foreign Affairs* 83, 6: 111–22.

Clare, Joe 2010. "Ideological Fractionalization and the International Conflict Behavior of Parliamentary Democracies," *International Studies Quarterly* 54: 965–87.

Claude, Ines L. Jr. 1962. *Power and International Relations.* New York: Random House.

1992. "Collective Security after the Cold War," in Gary L. Guenter (ed.), *Collective Security in Europe and Asia,* pp. 7–27. Carlisle Barracks: Strategic Studies Institute, U.S. Army War College.

Clift, Ben 2001. "The Jospin Way," *Political Quarterly* 72, 2: 170–9.

2003. "PS Intra-Party Politics and Party System Change," in Jocelyn A.J. Evans (ed.), *The French Party System,* pp. 42–55. Manchester and New York: Manchester University Press.

Coates, David and Peter Lawler (eds.) 2000. *New Labour in Power.* Manchester University Press.

Cogan, Charles G. 2001. *The Third Option: The Emancipation of European Defense, 1989–2000.* Westport and London: Praeger.

Cohen, Roger 1999. "Crisis in the Balkans: The Continent; Europe's Aim: Arms Parity," *New York Times* (June 15): A1.

Cohen, Samy 1989. "La politique étrangère entre l'Elysée and Matignon," *Politique étrangère* 3: 487–503.

Collier, David, James Mahoney and Jason Seawright 2004. "Claiming Too Much: Warnings about Selection Bias," in Henry E. Brady and David Collier (eds.), *Rethinking Social Inquiry: Diverse Tools, Shared Standards,* pp. 85–102. Lanham: Rowman & Littlefield.

Cologne Presidency Conclusions 1999. *Presidency Conclusions. Cologne European Council 3 and 4 June 1999.* Document 150/99 REV 1 EN CAB. http:// ue.eu.int/ueDocs/cms_Data/docs/pressData/en/ec/57886.pdf.

Conover, Pamela Johnston and Stanley Feldman 1981. "The Origins and Meanings of Liberal/Conservative Self-Identifications," *American Journal of Political Science* 25, 4: 617–45.

1984. "How People Organize the Political World: A Schematic Model," *American Journal of Political Science* 28, 1: 95–126.

Conradt, David P. 1995. "The 1994 Campaign and Election: An Overview," in David P. Conradt, Gerald R. Kleinfeld, George K. Romoser and Christian Soe (eds.), *Germany's New Politics: Parties and Issues in the 1990s,* pp. 1–22. Providence and Oxford: Berghahn Books.

Conservative Party Manifesto 1987. *The Next Moves Forward. Foreword by the Rt. Hon. Margaret Thatcher.* Comparative Party manifesto research group, Zentralarchiv für Empirische Sozialforschung an der Universität zu Köln.

1997. *You Can Only Be Sure With The Conservatives.* Comparative Party manifesto research group, Zentralarchiv für Empirische Sozialforschung an der Universität zu Köln.

Cordesman, Anthony H. 2001. *The Lessons and Non-Lessons of the Air and Missile Campaign in Kosovo.* Westport: Praeger.

Cornish, Paul 1996. "European Security: the End of Architecture and the New NATO," *International Affairs* 72, 4: 751–69.

    2006. "EU and NATO: Co-operation or Competition?" *Briefing Paper for the European Parliament, Directorate-General for External Policies of the Union,* October. www.chathamhouse.org.uk/pdf/research/niis/NATO_EU.pdf.

Cornish, Paul and Geoffrey Edwards 2001. "Beyond the EU/NATO Dichotomy: the Beginning of a European Strategic Culture," *International Affairs* 77, 3: 587–603.

Council of Ministers 2009. *"European Security and Defence Policy 1999–2009 ...."* *ESDP Newsletter.* http://consilium.europa.eu/uedocs/cmsupload/ESDP%20newsletter%20-%20Special%20issue%20ESDP@10.pdf.

Cox, Gary W. 1987. *The Efficient Secret: The Cabinet and the Development of Parties in Victorian England.* Cambridge University Press.

Cox, Gary W. and Mathew D. McCubbins 1993. *Legislative Leviathan: Party Government in the House.* Berkeley: University of California Press.

    2005. *Setting the Agenda: Responsible Party Government in the U.S. House of Representatives.* New York: Cambridge University Press.

Dalton, Russell J. 1988. *Citizen Politics in Western Democracies.* Chatham: Chatham House Publishers.

Darnis, Jean-Pierre, Giovanni Gasparini, Christoph Grams, Daniel Keohane, Fabio Liberti, Jean-Pierre Maulny and May-Britt Stumbaum 2007. "Lessons Learned from European Defence Equipment Programmes," *Occasional Paper 69.* www.iss.europa.eu/uploads/media/occ69.pdf.

David, Dominique 1989. *La Politique de Défense de la France. Textes et Documents.* Paris: Foundation pour les Etudes de Défense Nationales.

Davidson, Ian 1992. "French Gaullists Will Try to Block Maastricht Pact," *Financial Times* (February 19).

Debus, Marc 2009. "Analysing Party Politics in Germany with New Approaches for Estimating Policy Preferences of Political Actors," *German Politics* 18, 3: 281–300.

De Hoop Scheffer, Jaap 2007. "NATO and the EU: Time for a New Chapter." Keynote speech by NATO Secretary General Jaap de Hoop Scheffer. www.nato.int/docu/speech/2007/s070129b.html.

Delafon, Gilles and Thomas Sancton 1999. *Dear Jacques, Chers Bill. Au cœur de l'Elysée et de la Maison Blanche 1995–1999.* Paris: Plon.

Delattre, Lucas 1997. "L'Allemagne se fait à Jospin," *Le Monde* (June 14).

Delors, Jacques 1997. "Foreword," in Elfriede Regelsberger, Philippe de Schoutheete de Tervarent and Wolfgang Wessels (eds.), *Foreign Policy of the European Union: From EPC to CFSP and Beyond,* pp. vii–viii. Boulder and London: Lynne Rienner Publishers, Inc.

Dempsey, Judy 2008. "EU Budgets for Defense may Clash with Goals. Deployments are up, but Spending Shrinks," *International Herald Tribune* (May 23): 3.

Derks, Maria and Sylvie More 2009. "The European Union and Internal Challenges for Effectively Supporting Security Sector Reform," The Hague: Netherlands Institute of International Relations "Clingendael." www.clingendael.nl/publications/2009/20090618_cru_ssr_derks_more.pdf.

Desch, Michael C. 2007/8. "America's Liberal Illiberalism: The Ideological Origins of Overreaction in U.S. Foreign Policy," *International Security* 32, 3: 7–43.

Dettke, Dieter 2009. *Germany Says "No." The Iraq War and the Future of German Foreign and Security Policy*. Washington, DC: Woodrow Wilson Center Press.

De Schoutheete de Tervarent, Philippe 1997. "The Creation of the Common Foreign and Security Policy," in Elfriede Regelsberger, Philippe de Schoutheete de Tervarent and Wolfgang Wessels (eds.), *Foreign Policy of the European Union: From EPC to CFSP and Beyond*, pp. 41–63. Boulder and London: Lynne Rienner Publishers, Inc.

De Swaan, Abram 1973. *Coalition Theories and Cabinet Formation*. San Francisco: Jossey-Bass.

De Vries, Catherine E. 2007. "Sleeping Giant: Fact or Fairytale?" *European Union Politics* 8, 3: 363–85.

  2010. "EU Issue Voting: Asset or Liability?" *European Union Politics* 11, 1: 89–117.

De Vries, Catherine E. and Sara B. Hobolt 2012. "When Dimensions Collide: The Electoral Success of Issue Entrepreneurs," *European Union Politics* 13, 2: 246–68.

De Vries, Catherine E. and Gary Marks 2012. "The Struggle over Dimensionality: A Note on Theory and Empirics," *European Union Politics* 13, 2: 185–93.

Dewan, Torun and Arthur Spirling 2011. "Strategic Opposition and Government Cohesion in Westminster Democracies," *American Political Science Review* 105, 2: 337–58.

Diermeier, Daniel and Razvan Vlaicu 2011. "Parties, Coalitions, and the Internal Organization of Legislatures," *American Political Science Review* 105, 2: 359–80.

Diez, Thomas and Antje Wiener 2004. "Introducing the Mosaic of Integration Theory," in Antje Wiener and Thomas Diez (eds.), *European Integration Theory*, pp. 1–21. Oxford University Press.

Dinan, Desmond 1999. *Ever Closer Union: An Introduction to European Integration*. London: Lynne Rienner Publishers.

Dixon, William 1994. "Democracy and the Peaceful Settlement of International Conflict," *American Political Science Review* 88, 1: 14–32.

Dodd, Lawrence C. 1976. *Coalitions in Parliamentary Government*. Princeton University Press.

Döring, Herbert (ed.) 1995. *Parliaments and Majority Rule in Western Europe*. New York: St. Martin's.

Döring, Herbert and Mark Hallerberg (eds.) 2004. *Patterns of Parliamentary Behaviour: Passage of Legislation Across Western Europe*. Aldershot: Ashgate.

Döring-Manteuffel, Anselm 1983. *Die Bundesrepublik Deutschland in der Ära Adenauer. Außenpolitik und innere Entwicklung 1949–1963*. Darmstadt: Wissenschaftliche Buchgesellschaft.

Downs, Anthony 1957. *An Economic Theory of Democracy*. New York: Harper.

Doyle, Michael W. 1986. "Liberalism and World Politics," *American Political Science Review* 80 (December): 1151–70.

1997. *Ways of War and Peace: Realism, Liberalism, and Socialism*. New York: W.W. Norton.

Drezner, Daniel W. (ed.) 2003. *Locating the Proper Authorities: The Interaction of Domestic and International Institutions*. Ann Arbor: University of Michigan Press.

Drozdiak, William 1992. "French-German Brigade to Take a Step Toward European Army," *Washington Post* (May 17): A31.

2000. "U.S. Tepid On European Defense Plan; American Stance Vexes EU Leaders," *Washington Post* (March 7): A01.

Duffield, John S. 1998. "Political Culture and State Behavior: Why Germany Confounds Neorealism," *International Organization* 53, 4: 765–803.

Duke, Simon 1994. *The New European Security Disorder*. London: St Martin's Press.

1996. "The Second Death (or the Second Coming?) of the WEU," *Journal of Common Market Studies* 34, 2: 167–90.

2006. "The Commission and CFSP," *European Institute of Public Administration Working Paper 2006/W/01*. www.eipa.eu/files/repository/product/20070815141210_CFSP_0601e.pdf.

Dumoulin, Andre 1991. "Les forces multinationales," *Defense nationale* 47 (August–September): 67–85.

Duverger, Maurice 1954. *Political Parties: Their Organization and Activities in a Modern State*, trans. B. North and R. North. New York: John Wiley.

Dyson, Tom 2008. "Convergence and Divergence in Post-Cold War British, French, and German Military Reforms: Between International Structure and Executive Autonomy," *Security Studies* 17: 725–74.

Eatwell, Roger 1989a. "The Rise of 'Left-Right' Terminology: The Confusion of Social Science," in Roger Eatwell and Noel O'Sullivan (eds.), *The Nature of the Right: European and American Politics and Political Thought since 1789*, pp. 32–46. London: Pinter Publishers.

1989b. "The Nature of the Right, 1: Is There an 'Essentialist' Philosophical Core?" in Roger Eatwell and Noel O'Sullivan (eds.), *The Nature of the Right: European and American Politics and Political Thought since 1789*, pp. 47–61. London: Printer Publishers.

Economist, The 1991. "A German Idea of Europe" (July 26).

2007. "Berlin Minus. There is no Excuse for the Failure of NATO and the EU to Talk to Each Other" (February 8): 34.

2011. "Sad Island Story. Long Talks have got Little Nearer to Solving Europe's Oldest 'Frozen Conflict'" (March 31). www.economist.com/node/18486379?story_id=18486379&fsrc=rss.

Epstein, David and Sharyn O'Halloran 1996. "Divided Government and the Design for Administrative Procedures: A Formal Model and Empirical Test," *Journal of Politics* 58, 2: 373–97.

Erikson, Robert S., Michael B. MacKuen and James A. Stimson 2002. *The Macro Polity*. New York: Cambridge University Press.

Eurobarometer 32 1989. *Eurobarometer No. 32, December 1989. Public Opinion in the European Community, Vol I: Report*. Brussels: European Commission, Directorate-General Information, Communication and Culture. http://ec.europa.eu/public_opinion/archives/eb/eb32/eb32_en.pdf.

Eurobarometer 35 1991. *Eurobarometer No. 35, June 1991. Public Opinion in the European Community.* Brussels: European Commission, Directorate-General Information, Communication and Culture. http:// ec.europa.eu/public_opinion/archives/eb/eb35/eb35_en.pdf.

Eurobarometer 45 1996. *Standard Eurobarometer No. 45, December 1996.* Brussels: European Commission, Directorate-General Information, Communication and Culture. http://ec.europa.eu/public_opinion/ archives/eb/eb45/eb45_en.htm.

European Commission 1997. *European Dialogue.* Brussels: European Commission.

European Council 2008. "'CFSP Guide' – Compilation of Relevant Texts." 10898/08, PESC 813, RELEX 459. http://register.consilium.europa.eu/ pdf/en/08/st10/st10898.en08.pdf.

European Council Nice Conclusions 2000. www.consilium.europa.eu/ueDocs/ cms_Data/docs/pressData/en/ec/00400-r1.%20ann.en0.htm.

European Voice, November 19, 1999, Vol. 4, no. 42.

Evangelista, Matthew 1999. *Unarmed Forces.* Ithaca: Cornell University Press.

Evans, Geoffrey and Pippa Norris (eds.) 1999. *Critical Elections: British Parties and Voters in Long-Term Perspective.* London: Sage.

Evans, Jocelyn A.J. 2003. "Europe and the French Party System," in Jocelyn A.J. Evans (ed.), *The French Party System,* pp. 155–70. Manchester and New York: Manchester University Press.

Eyal, Jonathan 1993. "A New Europe?" *RUSI Journal* 138, 4: 47–51.

Eysenck, Hans J. 1954. *The Psychology of Politics.* London: Routledge & Kegan Paul.

Fair, John D. and John Hutcheson, Jr. 1987. "British Conservatives in the Twentieth Century: An Emerging Ideological Tradition," *Albion* 19, 4 (Winter): 549–78.

Favier, Pierre and Roland Martin. 1996. *La Decennie Mitterrand,* vol. 3. Paris: Seuil.

FDP Party Manifesto 1990. *Das liberale Deutschland. Programm der FDP zu den Bundestagswahlen am 2. Dezember 1990.* Comparative Party manifesto research group, Zentralarchiv für Empirische Sozialforschung an der Universität zu Köln.

  1998. *Wahlprogramm zur Bundestagswahl 1998 der Freien Demokratischen Partei. "Es ist Ihre Wahl."* Comparative Party manifesto research group, Zentralarchiv für Empirische Sozialforschung an der Universität zu Köln.

Fearon, James D. 1994. "Domestic Political Audiences and the Escalation of International Disputes," *American Political Science Review* 88, 3: 577–92.

Feldman, Stanley and John Zaller 1992. "The Political Culture of Ambivalence: Ideological Responses to the Welfare State," *American Journal of Political Science* 36, 1: 268–307.

Finnemore, Martha and Kathryn Sikkink 2001. "Taking Stock: The Constructivist Research Program in International Relations and Comparative Politics," *Annual Review of Political Science* 4: 391–416.

Fioretos, Orfeo 2011. *Creative Reconstructions: Multilateralism and European Varieties of Capitalism after 1950.* Ithaca: Cornell University Press.

Fiorina, Morris P. 1981. *Retrospective Voting in American Elections*. New Haven: Yale University Press.

Fischer, Joseph 1999a. "Rede des deutschen Aussenministers, Joschka Fischer, am 6. Februar 1999 auf der 'Konferenz für Sicherheitspolitik' in München." www.auswaertiges-amt.de/6_archiv/2/r/R990206a.htm.

  1999b. "Erklärung des deutschen Aussenministers, Joschka Fischer, zur Europäischen Sicherheits- und Verteidigungspolitik auf der WEU-Ministerratstagung am 10. Mai 1999 in Bremen." www.dgap.org/ip9910/fischer100599.htm.

Fitchett, Joseph 1991. "France is Miffed at NATO Plans for Rapid Force," *International Herald Tribune* (June 5).

Flynn, Gregory and Henry Farrell 1999. "Piecing Together the Democratic Peace: the CSCE and the 'Construction' of Security in Post–Cold War Europe," *International Organization* 53, 3: 505–35.

Fordham, Benjamin O. 1998a. "Economic Interests, Party, and Ideology in Early Cold War Era U.S. Foreign Policy," *International Organization* 52, 2: 359–96.

  1998b. "Partisanship, Macroeconomic Policy, and U.S. Uses of Force, 1949–1994," *Journal of Conflict Resolution* 42, 4: 418–39.

Foreign and Commonwealth Office (FCO) 1999. *Annual Departmental Report*. London: The Stationery Office.

Forster, Anthony 1998. "Britain and the Negotiation of the Maastricht Treaty: a Critique of Liberal Intergovernmentalism," *Journal of Common Market Studies* 36, 3: 347–68.

  1999. *Britain and the Maastricht Negotiations*. Houndmills: Macmillan Press Ltd.

Forster, Anthony and William Wallace 2000. "Common Foreign and Security Policy," in Helen and William Wallace (eds.), *Policy-Making in the European Union*, 4th edn, pp. 411–38. Oxford University Press.

Franco-British Summit 1998. *Joint Declaration on European Defence Issued at the British-French Summit*, Saint-Malo, December 3–4. www.fco.gov.uk/servlet/Front?pagename=OpenMarket/Xcelerate/ShowPage&c=Page&cid=1007029391629&aid=1013618395073.

Frankel, Glenn 1990. "NATO Tries to Change With Times; London Summit to Assess Goals," *The Washington Post* (July 5): A1.

Franklin, Mark, Thomas T. Mackie and Henry Valen 1992. *Electoral Change: Responses to Evolving Social and Attitudinal Structures and Western Countries*. Cambridge University Press.

Franklin, Mark N., Michael Marsh and Lauren McLaren 1994. "Uncorking the Bottle: Popular Opposition to European Unification in the Wake of Maastricht," *Journal of Common Market Studies* 32, 4: 455–72.

Franklin, Mark N., Cees van der Eijk and Michael Marsh 1996. "Conclusions: the Electoral Connection and the Democratic Deficit," in Cees van der Eijk and Mark Franklin (eds.), *Choosing Europe? The European Electorate and National Politics in the Face of Union*, pp. 366–88. Ann Arbor: University of Michigan Press.

Friedman, Thomas L. 1989. "Upheaval in the East. Baker, in Berlin, Outlines a Plan to Make NATO a Political Group," *New York Times* (December

13). http://query.nytimes.com/gst/fullpage.html?res=950DE4D9113DF9 30A25751C1A96F948260&sec=&spon=&pagewanted=all.

Gabel, Matthew J. and Christopher J. Anderson 2004. "The Structure of Citizen Attitudes and the European Political Space," in Gary Marks and Marco R. Steenbergen (eds.), *European Integration and Political Conflict*, pp. 13–31. Cambridge University Press.

Gabel, Matthew J. and Simon Hix 2004. "Defining the EU Political Space: an Empirical Study of the European Election Manifestos, 1979–1999," in Gary Marks and Marco R. Steenbergen (eds.), *European Integration and Political Conflict*, pp. 93–119. Cambridge University Press.

Gabel, Matthew and Kenneth Scheve 2007. "Mixed Messages. Party Dissent and Mass Opinion on European Integration," *European Union Politics* 8, 1: 37–59.

Gaddis, John L. 1997. *We Now Know: Rethinking Cold War History*. Oxford University Press.

Gamble, Andrew 1998. "The European Issue in British Politics," in David Baker and David Seawright (eds.), *Britain For and Against Europe: British Politics and the Question of European Integration*, pp. 11–30. Oxford: Clarendon Press.

Geertz, Cliford 1964. "Ideology as a Cultural System," in David E. Apter (ed.), *Ideology and Discontent*, pp. 47–76. London: The Free Press.

Gehring, Thomas and Sebastian Oberthür 2004. "Exploring Regime Interaction: A Framework of Analysis," in Arild Underdal and Oran R. Young (eds.), *Regime Consequences: Methodological Challenges and Research Strategies*, pp. 247–79. Dordrecht, Boston and London: Kluwer Academic Publishers.

Gehring, Thomas and Sebastian Oberthür (eds.) 2006. *Institutional Interaction in Global Environmental Governance: Synergy and Conflict among International and EU Policies*. Cambridge, MA: MIT Press.

Genscher, Hans-Dietrich 1995. *Erinnerungen*. Berlin: Siedler Verlag.

George, Alexander 1979. "Case Studies and Theory Development: the Method of Structure, Focussed Comparisons," in Paul G. Lauren (ed.), *Diplomacy: New Approaches in History, Theory and Policy*, pp. 43–68 New York: Free Press.

George, Alexander L. and Andrew Bennett 2005. *Case Studies and Theory Development in the Social Sciences*. Cambridge, MA: MIT Press.

George, Alexander L. and Timothy J. McKeown 1985. "Case Studies and Theories of Organization Decision-Making," in Robert F. Coulam and Richard A. Smith (eds.), *Advances in Information Processing in Organizations: A Research Annual*, Vol. II, pp. 43–68. Greenwich: JAI Press.

George, Stephen 1998. *An Awkward Partner: Britain and the European Community*, 3rd edn. Oxford University Press.

Gerring, John 1997. "Ideology: A Definitional Analysis," *Political Research Quarterly* 50, 4: 957–94.

Gheciu, Alexandra Ioana 2005. "Security Institutions as Agents of Socialization? NATO and the 'New Europe'," *International Organization* 59, 4: 973–1012.

Giegerich, Bastian 2006. *European Security and Strategic Culture*. Baden-Baden: Nomos.

Giersch, Carsten 1998. *Konfliktregulierung in Jugoslawien 1991–1995. Die Rolle von OSZE, EU, UNO und NATO*. Baden-Baden: Nomos.

Ginsberg, Roy H. 1997. "The EU's CFSP: the Politics of Procedure," in Martin Holland (ed.), *Common Foreign and Security Policy: The Record and Reforms*, pp. 12–33. London and Washington, DC: Pinter.

Glarbo, Kenneth 1999. "Wide-awake Diplomacy: Reconstructing the Common Foreign and Security Policy of the European Union," *Journal of European Public Policy* 6, 4: 634–51.

  2001. "Reconstructing a Common European Foreign Policy," in Thomas Christiansen Knud, Erik Jorgensen and Antje Wiener (eds.), *The Social Construction of Europe*, pp. 140–57. London: Sage.

Glaser, Charles L. 1993. "Why NATO is Still Best: Future Security Arrangements for Europe," *International Security* 18, 1: 5–50.

Gnesotto, Nicole 1996. "Common European Defence and Transatlantic Relations," *Survival* 38, 1: 19–31.

  1998. *La Puissance et l'Europe*. Paris: Presses de Sciences Po.

Goldstein, Judith 1995. "International Law and Domestic Institutions: Reconciling North American 'Unfair' Trade Laws," *International Organization* 50, 4: 541–64.

Goldstein, Judith and Robert O. Keohane 1993. "Ideas and Foreign Policy: An Analytical Framework," in Judith Goldstein and Robert Keohane (eds.), *Ideas and Foreign Policy: Beliefs, Institutions, and Political Change*, pp. 3–30. Ithaca: Cornell University Press.

Gordon, Philip H. 1993. *A Certain Idea of France: French Security Policy and Gaullist Legacy*. Princeton University Press.

  1996. "Recasting the Atlantic Alliance," *Survival* 38, 1: 32–57.

  1997. "Does the WEU have a Role?" *The Washington Quarterly* 20, 1: 125–140.

  1997/8. "Europe's Uncommon Foreign Policy," *International Security* 22, 3: 74–100.

Gordon, Philip H. and Jeremy Shapiro 2004. *Allies at War: America, Europe, and the Crisis over Iraq*. New York: McGraw-Hill.

Gourevitch, Peter 1978. "The Second Image Reversed: the International Sources of Domestic Politics," *International Organization* 32: 881–912.

Gowa, Joanne 1998. "Politics at the Water's Edge: Parties, Voters, and the Use of Force Abroad," *International Organization* 52, 2: 307–24.

Gramsci, Antonio 1971. *Selections from the Prison Notebooks of Antonio Gramsci*. New York: International Publishers Co.

Grant, Robert P. 1996. "France's New Relationship with NATO," *Survival* 38, 1: 58–80.

Gray, John 1997. "He's Behind You, William," *Guardian* (November 14): 21.

Green, David G. 1987. *The New Right: The Counter-Revolution in Political, Social and Economic Thought*. Brighton: Wheatsheaf.

Grieco, Joseph 1993. "Anarchy and the Limits of Cooperation: A Realist Critique of the Newest Liberal Institutionalism," in David A. Baldwin (ed.), *Neorealism and Neoliberalism: The Contemporary Debate*, pp. 116–40. New York: Columbia University Press.

  1995. "Anarchy and the Limits of Cooperation: a Realist Critique of the Newest Liberal Institutionalism," in Charles W. Kegley Jr. (ed.),

Controversies in International Relations Theory. Realism and the Neoliberal Challenge, pp. 151–71. New York: St. Martin's Press.

Grunberg, Gérard and Étienne Schweisguth 1997. "Recompositions idéologiques," in Daniel Boy and Nonna Mayer (eds.), *L'Électeur a ses raisons*, pp. 139–78. Paris: Presses de Sciences Po.

Grünen Party Manifesto 1990. *Das Programm zur 1. Gesamtdeutschen Wahl 1990*. Comparative Party manifesto research group, Zentralarchiv für Empirische Sozialforschung an der Universität zu Köln.

Guilbert, Paul 1997. "Les gaullistes revendiquent le role de première force d'opposition et d'alternance au Parti socialiste," *Le Figaro* (October 7).

Gutner, Tamar and Alexander Thompson 2010. "The Politics of IO Performance: A Framework," *Review of International Organizations* 5: 227–48.

Haas, Ernst 1964. *Beyond the Nation-State: Functionalism and International Organization*. Stanford University Press.

Haas, Mark L. 2003. "Ideology and Alliances: British and French External Balancing Decisions in the 1930s," *Security Studies* 12, 4: 34–79.

  2005. *The Ideological Origins of Great Power Politics, 1789–1989*. Ithaca: Cornell University Press.

Hacker, Jacob 2004. "Privatizing Risk without Privatizing the Welfare State: The Hidden Politics of Social Policy Retrenchment in the United States," *American Political Science Review* 98, 2: 243–60.

Haftel, Yoram Z. and Alexander Thompson 2006. "The Independence of International Organizations: Concepts and Applications," *Journal of Conflict Resolution* 50, 2: 253–75.

Haftendorn, Helga, Robert O. Keohane and Celeste Wallander (eds.) 1999. *Imperfect Unions: Security Institutions over Time and Space*. New York: Oxford University Press.

Hagemann, Sara 2008. "Voting, Statements and Coalition-Building in the Council from 1999 to 2006," in Daniel Naurin and Helen Wallace (eds.), *Unveiling the Council of the European Union: Games Governments Play in Brussels*, pp. 36–63. Basingstoke: Palgrave Macmillan.

Hall, Peter (ed.) 1986. *Governing the Economy*. New York: Oxford University Press.

Hall, Peter (ed.) 1989. *The Political Power of Economic Ideas: Keynesianism across Nations*. Princeton University Press.

Hallerberg, Mark 2003. "Fiscal Rules and Fiscal Policy," in B. Guy Peters and Jon Pierre (eds.), *Handbook of Public Administration*, pp. 393–401. London: Sage.

Hallerberg, Mark and Scott Basinger 1998. "Internationalization and Changes in Tax Policy in OECD Countries: The Importance of Domestic Veto Powers," *Comparative Political Studies* 31, 3: 321–52.

Hanley, David 2003. "Managing the Plural Left: Implications for the Party System," in Jocelyn A.J. Evans (ed.), *The French Party System*, pp. 76–90. Manchester and New York: Manchester University Press.

Hanson, Stephen E. 2010. *Post-Imperial Democracies: Ideology and Party Formation in Third Republic France, Weimar Germany, and Post-Soviet Russia*. New York: Cambridge University Press.

Hartz, Louis 1991. *The Liberal Tradition in America: An Interpretation of American Political Thought Since the Revolution.* San Diego: Harcourt Brace.

Hayward, Jack 1993a. "From Republican Sovereign to Partisan Statesman," in Jack Hayward (ed.), *De Gaulle to Mitterrand: Presidential Power in France,* pp. 1–35. London: Hurst & Company.

1993b. "The President and the Constitution: its Spirit, Articles and Practice," in Jack Hayward (ed.), *De Gaulle to Mitterrand: Presidential Power in France,* pp. 36–75. London: Hurst & Company.

Haywood, Elizabeth 1993. "The European Policy of Francois Mitterrand," *Journal of Common Market Studies* 31, 2: 269–82.

Hellmann, Gunther 1997. "The Sirens of Power and German Foreign Policy: Who is Listening?" *German Politics* 6, 2: 29–57.

Hellström, Johan 2008. "Partisan Responses to Europe: the Role of Ideology for National Political Parties' Positions on European Integration," *Journal of European Public Policy* 15, 2 (March): 189–207.

Helm, Sarah 1997a. "Amsterdam Summit: Europe Fails to Deliver its Own Future," *Independent* (June 18): 16.

1997b. "Labour's Man for EU Seeks New Start," *Independent* (May 6): 6.

Henderson, D. 1998. "The UK Presidency: an Insider's View," *Journal of Common Market Studies* 36, 4: 563–72.

Héritier, Adrienne and Christoph Knill 2001. "Differential Responses to European Policies: a Comparison," in Anne-Cécile Douillet (ed.), *Differential Europe: The European Union Impact on National Policymaking,* pp. 257–94. Lanham and Boulder: Rowman & Littlefield Publishers.

Herrmann, Richard K., Philip E. Tetlock and Penny S. Visser 1999. "Mass Public Decisions to Go to War: A Cognitive-Interactionist Framework," *American Political Science Review* 93, 3: 553–73.

Hilz, Wolfram 2005. *Europas verhindertes Führungstrio: Die Sicherheitspolitik Deutschlands, Frankreichs und Grossbritanniens in den Neunzigern.* Paderborn: Schöningh Ferdinand GmbH.

Hindmoor, Andrew 2004. *New Labour at the Centre: Constructing Political Space.* Oxford University Press.

Hinich, Melvin J. and Michael C. Munger 1992. "A Spatial Theory of Ideology," *Journal of Theoretical Politics* 4, 1: 5–30.

1997. *Analytical Politics.* Cambridge University Press.

Hitchcock, William I. 1998. *France Restored: Cold War Diplomacy and the Quest for Leadership in Europe, 1944–1954.* Chapel Hill and London: University of North Carolina Press.

Hix, Simon 1994. "The Study of the European Community: The Challenge to Comparative Politics," *West European Politics* 17, 1: 1–30.

1996. "IR, CP and the EU: A Rejoinder to Hurrell and Menon," *West European Politics* 19, 4: 802–4.

1999. "Dimensions and Alignments in European Union Politics: Cognitive Constraints and Partisan Responses," *European Journal of Political Research* 35, 1: 69–106.

2005. *The Political System of the European Union,* 2nd edn. London: Palgrave.

Hix, Simon and Christopher Lord 1997. *Political Parties in the European Union.* Basingstoke: Macmillan Press.

Hix, Simon, Abdul Noury and Gerard Roland 2007. *Democratic Politics in the European Parliament*. Cambridge University Press.

Hoffmann, Stanley 1966. "Obstinate or Obsolete? The Fate of the Nation-State and the Case of Western Europe," *Daedalus* 95, 3: 862–915.

2003. "US-European Relations: Past and Future," *International Affairs* 79, 5: 1029–36.

Hofmann, Stephanie 2009. "Overlapping Institutions in the Realm of International Security: The Case of NATO and ESDP," *Perspectives on Politics* 7, 1: 45–52.

Hofmann, Stephanie and Frédéric Mérand 2012. "Regional Institutions *à la Carte*: The Effects of Institutional Elasticity," in TV. Paul (ed.), *International Relations Theory and Regional Transformation*, pp. 133–57. New York: Cambridge University Press.

Hofmann, Stephanie and Christopher Reynolds 2007. "EU-NATO Relations: Time to Thaw the 'Frozen Conflict'," *SWP Comments* (June) 12: 1–9.

Holbrooke, Richard 1998. *To End a War*. New York: Random House.

Holland, Martin (ed.) 1997. *Common Foreign and Security Policy: The Record and Reforms*. London: Pinter.

Holsti, Ole R. 1992. "Public Opinion and Foreign Policy: Challenges of the Almond-Lippmann Consensus," *International Studies Quarterly* 36, 4: 439–66.

1998/9. "A Widening Gap between the Military and Society: Some Evidence 1976–96," *International Security* 23: 5–42.

Holsti, Ole R. and James N. Rosenau 1990. "The Structure of Foreign Policy Attitudes Among American Leaders," *Journal of Politics* 52: 94–125.

Hooghe, Lisbet 2003. "Europe Divided? Elites vs. Public Opinion on European Integration," *European Union Politics* 4, 3: 281–305.

Hooghe, Lisbet and Gary Marks 1999. "The Making of a Polity: the Struggle over European Integration," in Hebert Kitschelt, Peter Lange, Gary Marks and John Stephens (eds.), *Continuity and Change in Contemporary Capitalism*, pp. 70–97. Cambridge University Press.

2006. "Europe's Blues: Theoretical Soul-Searching after the Rejection of the European Constitution," *PS: Political Science and Politics* 34, 2: 247–50.

Hooghe, Lisbet, Gary Marks and Carole J. Wilson 2002. "Does Left/Right Structure Party Positions on European Integration?" *Comparative Political Studies* 35, 8: 965–89.

Hopf, Ted 1998. "The Promise of Constructivism in International Relations Theory," *International Security* 23, 1: 171–200.

2002. *Social Construction of International Politics: Identities and Foreign Policies, Moscow, 1955 and 1999*. Ithaca: Cornell University Press.

House of Commons 2000. "Common European Security and Defence Policy: A Progress Report," *House of Commons Research Paper 00/84*, October 31.

2010. *Franco-British Defense Co-operation*. www.parliament.uk/briefingpapers/commons/lib/research/briefings/snia-05750.pdf.

Howorth, Jolyon 1993. "The President's Special Role in Foreign and Defence Policy," in Jack Hayward (ed.), *De Gaulle to Mitterrand: Presidential Power in France*, pp. 150–89. London: Hurst & Company.

1996. "France and European Security 1944–94: Re-reading the Gaullist 'Consensus'," in Tony Chafer and Brian Jenkins (eds.), *France: From the Cold War to the New World Order*, pp. 17–38. Houndmills and London: Macmillan Press.

2000a. "Britain, France and the European Defence Initiative," *Survival* 42, 2: 33–55.

2000b. "Britain, NATO and CESDP: Fixed Strategy, Changing Tactics," *European Foreign Affairs Review* 5, 3: 1–20.

2003. "ESDP and NATO: Wedlock or Deadlock?" *Cooperation and Conflict* 38, 3: 235–54.

2007. *Security and Defence Policy in the European Union*. London and New York: Palgrave.

2010. "The EU as a Global Actor: Grand Strategy for a Global Grand Bargain?" *Journal of Common Market Studies* 48, 3: 455–74.

Huber, John D. 1989. "Values and Partisanship in Left-Right Orientations: Measuring Ideology," *European Journal of Political Research* 17, 5: 599–621.

Humphreys, Macartan and Michael J. Laver 2010. "Spatial Models, Cognitive Metrics and Majority Rule Equilibria," *British Journal of Political Science* 40: 11–30.

Hunter, Robert E. 2002. *The European Security and Defense Policy: NATO's Companion – or Competitor?* Santa Monica: RAND.

Hurd, Douglas 1991. "No European Defence Identity without NATO," *Financial Times* (April 15): 13.

1994. "Developing the Common Foreign and Security Policy," *International Affairs* 70, 3: 421–8.

Hutchings, Robert L. 1997. *American Diplomacy and the End of the Cold War: An Insider's Account of U.S. Policy in Europe, 1989–1992*. Baltimore: The Johns Hopkins University Press.

Hyde-Price, Adrian 2007. *European Security in the Twenty-First Century: The Challenge of Multipolarity*. London: Routledge.

Ikenberry, G. John 2008. "Explaining Crisis and Change in Transatlantic Relations: An Introduction," in Jeffrey Anderson, G. John Ikenberry and Thomas Risse (eds.), *The End of the West? Crisis and Change in the Atlantic Order*, pp. 1–27. Ithaca: Cornell University Press.

Ikenberry, G. John, Thomas J. Knock, Anne-Marie Slaughter and Tony Smith 2009. *The Crisis of American Foreign Policy: Wilsonianism in the Twenty-First Century*. Princeton University Press.

Inglehart, Ronald 1979. "Political Action: the Impact of Values, Cognitive Level and Social Background," in Samuel Barnes and Max Kaase (eds.), *Political Action*, pp. 343–80. Beverly Hills: Sage.

International Institute for Strategic Studies (IISS) 1990. *The Military Balance, 1990–1991*. London: IISS.

1991. *The Military Balance, 1991–1992*. London: IISS.

1992. *The Military Balance, 1992–1993*. London: IISS.

1993. *The Military Balance, 1993–1994*. London: IISS.

1994. *The Military Balance, 1994–1995*. London: IISS.

1995. *The Military Balance, 1995–1996*. London: IISS.

1996. *The Military Balance, 1996–1997*. London: IISS.

1997. *The Military Balance, 1997–1998*. London: IISS.

Irondelle, Bastien 2003a. "Civil-Military Relations and the End of Conscription in France," *Security Studies* 12, 3: 157–87.

2003b. "Europeanization without the European Union? French Military Reforms 1991–1996," *Journal of European Public Policy* 10, 2: 208–26.

2011. *La réforme des armées en France. Sociologie de la decision.* Paris: Presses de Sciences Po.

Isernia, Pierangelo, Zoltan Juhasz and Hans Rattinger 2002. "Foreign Policy and the Rational Public in Comparative Perspective," *Journal of Conflict Resolution* 46, 2: 201–24.

Isnard, Jacques 1997. "Lionel Jospin expose pour la première fois sa vision de la defense," *Le Monde* (September 5).

Iversen, Torben and John D. Stephens 2007. "Partisan Politics, the Welfare State, and Three Worlds of Human Capital Formation." Paper prepared for the *Research Frontiers in Comparative Politics* Conference, Duke University, April 27–28. www.tcd.ie/iiis/documents/seminar%20papers/ Iversen&Stephens2.pdf.

Jachtenfuchs, Markus and Beate Kohler-Koch 2004. "Governance and Institutional Development," in Thomas Diez and Antje Wiener (eds.), *European Integration Theory*, pp. 97–115. Oxford University Press.

Jäger, Thomas, Kai Oppermann, Alexander Höse and Henrike Viehrig 2009. "The Salience of Foreign Affairs Issues in the German Bundestag," *Parliamentary Affairs* 62, 3: 418–37.

Jarreau, Patrick, Laurent Maudit and Jean Louis Saux 1997. "Entretien avec le president du RPR," *Le Monde* (December 10).

Jennings, M. Kent 1992. "Ideological Thinking among Mass Publics and Political Elites," *Public Opinion Quarterly* 56: 419–41.

Jervis, Robert 1997. *System Effects: Complexity in Political and Social Life.* Princeton University Press.

Joffe, Josef 1994. "German Grand Strategy after the Cold War," in Arnulf Baring (ed.), *Germany's New Position in Europe: Problems and Perspectives*, pp. 79–90. Oxford and Providence: BERG Publishers.

Johansson, Karl M. 1999. "Tracing the Employment Title in the Amsterdam Treaty: Uncovering Transnational Coalitions," *Journal of European Public Policy* 6, 1: 85–101.

2002. "Another Road to Maastricht: The Christian Democrat Coalition and the Quest for European Union," *Journal of Common Market Studies* 40, 3: 871–93.

Jones, Seth G. 2006. "The Rise of European Defense," *Political Science Quarterly* 121, 2: 241–67.

2007. *The Rise of European Security Cooperation.* Cambridge University Press.

Jopp, Mattias 1999. *European Defence Policy: the Debate on the Institutional Aspects.* Berlin: Institut für europäische Politik.

Jørgensen, Knud Erik 1997. "PoCo: the Diplomatic Republic of Europe," in Knut Jorgensen (ed.), *Reflective Approaches to European Governance*, pp. 167–80. Basingstoke: Macmillan.

Juncos, Ana E. and Christopher Reynolds 2007. "The Political and Security Committee: Governing in the Shadow," *European Foreign Affairs Review* 12, 2: 127–47.

Junor, Penny 1993. *The Major Enigma*. London: Michael Joseph.

Jupille, Joseph and Duncan Snidal 2005. "The Choice of International Institutions: Cooperation, Alternatives and Strategies." Paper presented at the annual meeting of the American Political Science Association, Washington, DC, September 1–3.

Jupille, Joseph, James A. Caporaso and Jeffrey T. Checkel 2003. "Integrating Institutions: Rationalism, Constructivism, and the Study of the European Union," *Comparative Political Studies* 36, 1/2: 7–40.

Kaarbo, Juliet 2008. "Coalition Cabinet Decision Making: Institutional and Psychological Factors," *International Studies Review* 10: 57–86.

Kaarbo, Juliet and Ryan K. Beasley 2008. "Taking it to the Extreme: the Effect of Coalition Cabinets on Foreign Policy," *Foreign Policy Analysis* 4, 1: 67–81.

Kam, Christopher 2009. *Party Discipline and Parliamentary Politics*. Cambridge University Press.

Kam, Christopher, William T. Bianco, Itai Sened and Regina Smyth 2010. "Ministerial Selection and Intraparty Organization in the Contemporary British Parliament," *American Political Science Review* 104, 2: 289–306.

Kamp, Karl-Heinz and Carlo Masala 2006. "The New German Foreign and Security Policy: More than a Change in Style," *Konrad Adenauer Stiftung Working Paper/Documentation*. Sankt Augustin: Konrad-Adenauer-Stiftung e.V. www.kas.de/wf/doc/kas_9957–544–1–30.pdf.

Kassim, Hussein 2003. "Meeting the Demands of EU Membership: the Europeanization of National Administrative Systems," in Kevin Featherstone and Claudio Radaelli (eds.), *The Politics of Europeanization*, pp. 83–111. Oxford University Press.

2004. "The United Kingdom and the Future of Europe: Winning the Battle, Losing the War," *Comparative European Politics* 2: 261–81.

2005. "The Europeanization of Member State Institutions," in Simon Bulmer and Christian Lequesne (eds.), *The Member States of the European Union*, pp. 285–316. Oxford University Press.

Katz, Richard S. 1980. *A Theory of Parties and Electoral Systems*. Baltimore: Johns Hopkins.

1997. *Democracy and Elections*. Oxford University Press.

Katz, Richard S. and Peter Mair (eds.) 1994. *How Parties Organize: Change and Adaptation in Party Organizations in Western Democracies*. London: Sage.

Katzenstein, Peter J. 1976. "International Relations and Domestic Structures: Foreign Economic Policies of Advanced Industrial States," *International Organization* 30, 1: 1–45.

1978. *Between Power and Plenty: Foreign Economic Policies of Advanced Industrial States*. Madison: University of Wisconsin Press.

Katzenstein, Peter J. (ed.) 1996. *The Culture of National Security: Norms and Identity in World Politics*. New York: Columbia University Press.

Katzenstein, Peter J. 2005. *A World of Regions: Asia and Europe in the American Imperium*. Ithaca: Cornell University Press.

Keohane, Daniel (ed.) 2008. *Towards a European Defence Market, Chaillot Paper 113*. Paris: EUISS.

Keohane, Robert O. 1984. *After Hegemony: Cooperation and Discord in the World Political Economy*. Princeton University Press.

1989. "Neoliberal Institutionalism: A Perspective on World Politics," in Robert O. Keohane (ed.), *International Institutions and State Power*, pp. 1–20. Boulder: Westview.

1990. "Multilateralism: an Agenda for Research," *International Journal* 45, 4: 731–64.

Keohane, Robert O. and Celeste A. Wallander 1998. "Security in an Era Without Enemies. Expansion will Mark the End of Wars among Europeans. The Alliance Becomes One of Security Management," *Los Angeles Times* (May 6): B7.

Kier, Elizabeth 1995. "Culture and Military Doctrine: France between the Wars," *International Security* 19: 65–93.

Kiewiet, D. Roderick and Mathew D. McCubbins 1991. *The Logic of Delegation: Congressional Parties and the Appropriateness Process*. University of Chicago Press.

King, Gary, Robert O. Keohane and Sidney Verba 1994. *Designing Social Inquiry: Scientific Inference in Qualitative Research*. Princeton University Press.

Kirchheimer, Otto 1990. "The Catch-all Party," in Peter Mair (ed.), *The West European Party System*, pp. 50–60. New York: Oxford University Press.

Kirkpatrick, Jeane 1990. "It's Time Now to Influence Events in Europe," *Washington Post* (June 25): A11.

Kissinger, Henry A. 1965. *The Troubled Partnership: A Reappraisal of the Atlantic Alliance*. New York, Toronto and London: McGraw-Hill for the Council on Foreign Relations.

1990. "Germany, Neutrality and the 'Security System' Trap; Europe doesn't need a United Deutschland Playing Both Sides against the Middle," *Washington Post* (April 15): D7.

Kitschelt, Hebert 1988. "Left-Libertarian Parties: Explaining Competitive Innovation in Comparative Party Systems," *World Politics* 40, 2: 194–234.

1994. *The Transformation of European Social Democracy*. New York: Cambridge University Press.

1995. *The Radical Right in Western Europe*. Ann Arbor: University of Michigan Press.

Kitschelt, Herbert and Staf Hellemans 1999. "The Left-Right Semantics and the New Politics Cleavage," *Comparative Political Studies* 23, 2: 210–38.

Klein, Markus and Jürgen W. Falter 2003. *Der lange Weg der Grünen. Eine Partei zwischen Protest und Regierung*. Munich: Verlag C.H. Beck.

Klingemann, Hans-Dieter, Richard Hofferbert and Ian Budge 1994. *Parties, Policies and Democracy: Theoretical Lenses on Public Policy*. Boulder: Westview.

Klingemann, Hans-Dieter, Andrea Volkens, Judith Bara, Ian Budge and Michael McDonald 2007. *Mapping Policy Preferences II. Estimates for Parties, Electors, and Governments in Eastern Europe, European Union and OECD 1990–2003*. Oxford University Press.

Knapp, Andrew 2003. "From the Gaullist Movement to the President's Party," in Jocelyn A.J. Evans (ed.), *The French Party System*, pp. 121–36. Manchester and New York: Manchester University Press.

Koalitionsvereinbarung 1991. "Koalitionsvereinbarung für die 12. Legislaturperiode des Deutschen Bundestages," *CDU Dokumentation 2/1991*.

  1994. *Das vereinte Deutschland zukunftsfähig machen: Die Koalitionsvereinbarungen von CDU, CSU und FDP für die 13. Legislaturperiode des Deutschen Bundestages*. Bonn: CDU-Bundesgeschäftsstelle, HA Öffentlichkeitsarbeit.

  1998. *Aufbruch und Erneuerung – Deutschlands Weg ins 21. Jahrhundert. Koalitionsvereinbarung zwischen der Sozialdemokratischen Partei Deutschlands und BÜNDNIS 90/DIE GRÜNEN, Bonn, 20. Okotber 1998*. www.gruene-partei.de/cms/themen/dokbin/182/182660.koalitionsvertrag_1998.pdf.

  2009. *Growth, Education, Unity. The Coalition Agreement between the CDU, CSU and FDP*. www.fdp-bundespartei.de/files/363/2009–203_en_Koalitionsvertrag_2009.pdf.

Koalitionsvertrag 2005. *Gemeinsam für Deutschland. Mit Mut und Menschlichkeit. Koalitionsvertrag von CDU, CSU und SPD*. www.cducsu.de/upload/koavertrag0509.pdf.

Koch, Rainer 2003. "USA wollen NATO gegen EU einschwören," *Financial Times Deutschland* (October 17): 11.

Koenig-Archibugi, Mathias 2004. "Explaining Government Preferences for Institutional Change in EU Foreign and Security Policy," *International Organization* 58 (winter): 137–74.

Kohl, Helmut 1989. "La question allemande et la résponsabilité européenne," *Politique étrangère* 4: 755–66.

  1992. "Die Bedeutung der Westeuropäischen Union für die gemeinsame Sicherheitspolitik." Speech in front of the Chiefs of Staff of the WEU members in Bonn. *Bulletin* 11 (January 31): 76–8.

  2005. *Erinnerungen 1982–1990*. Munich: Drömer.

  2007. *Erinnerungen 1990–1994*. Munich: Drömer.

Kohler-Koch, Beate 1999. "The Evolution and Transformation of European Governance," in Beate Kohler-Koch and Rainer Eising (eds.), *The Evolution and Transformation of European Governance*, pp. 14–36. London: Routledge.

Koremenos, Barbara, Charles Lipson and Duncan Snidal 2001. "The Rational Design of International Institutions," *International Organization* 55, 4: 761–99.

Kowert, Paul A. 2002. "Toward a Constructivist Theory of Foreign Policy," in Vendulka Kubalkova (ed.), *Foreign Policy in a Constructed World*, pp. 266–87. Armonk: ME Sharpe.

Krasner, Stephen D. 1972. "Are Bureaucracies Important? (Or Allison Wonderland)," *Foreign Policy* Summer: 459–72.

  1978. *Defending the National Interest: Raw Materials Investments and U.S. Foreign Policy*. Princeton University Press.

  1999. *Sovereignty: Organized Hypocrisy*. Princeton: Princeton University Press.

Krauthammer, Charles 1990/1. "The Unipolar Moment," *Foreign Affairs* 70, 1: 23–33.

Krehbiel, Keith 1991. *Information and Legislative Organization.* Ann Arbor: University of Michigan Press.

1993. "Where's the Party?" *British Journal of Political Science* 23: 235–66.

Kreppel, Amie and Simon Hix 2003. "From 'Grand Coalition' to Left-Right Confrontation," *Comparative Political Studies* 36, 1–2: 75–96.

Kreppel, Amie and George Tsebelis 1999. "Coalition Formation in the European Parliament," *Comparative Political Studies* 32: 933–66.

Labour Party 1995. "The Future of the European Union: Report on Labour's Position in Preparation for the Intergovernmental Conference," Interim Report, Labour Party, September 14, Conference in John Smith House.

Labour Party Manifesto 1987. *Britain Will Win. Introduction by Mr Neil Kinnock, Leader of the Labour Party.* Comparative Party manifesto research group, Zentralarchiv für Empirische Sozialforschung an der Universität zu Köln.

1997. *New Labour Because Britain Deserves Better.* www.psr.keele.ac.uk/area/uk/man/lab97.htm.

Lahav, Gallya 1997. "Ideological and Party Constraints on Immigration Attitudes in Europe," *Journal of Common Market Studies* 35, 3: 377–406.

Lake, David A. and Robert Powell 1999. "International Relations: a Strategic-Choice Approach," in David A. Lake and Robert Powell (eds.), *Strategic Choice and International Relations*, pp. 3–38. Princeton University Press.

Lambert, Sarah 1991. "Washington's Alarm at EC Defence Plan," *Independent* (March 9).

Lambeth, B.S. 2001. *NATO's Air War for Kosovo: A Strategic and Operational Assessment.* Santa Monica: Rand Corporation.

Lamy, Jean-Michel 1997. "OTAN et intégration de l'Est: la leçon de Washington," *Les Echos* (July 9): 56.

Lang, Jack 1997. "Je ne voterai pas le traité d'Amsterdam ..." *Le Monde* (August 19): 1.

Laponce, Jean A. 1981. *Left and Right: The Topography of Political Perceptions.* University of Toronto Press.

Laursen, Finn and Sophie Vanhoonacker (eds.) 1992. *The Intergovernmental Conference on Political Union.* Maastricht: European Institute of Public Administration.

Laver, Michael J. and Kenneth Benoit 2005. "Mapping the Irish Policy Space: Voter and Party Spaces in Preferential Elections," *Economic and Social Review* 36, 2: 83–108.

2006. *Party Policy in Modern Democracies.* London: Routledge.

Laver, Michael J. and Ian Budge (eds.) 1992. *Party Policy and Coalition Government.* London: Macmillan.

Laver, Michael J. and John Garry 2000. "Estimating Policy Positions from Political Texts," *American Journal of Political Science* 44: 619–34.

Laver, Michael J. and W. Ben Hunt 1992. *Policy and Party Competition.* New York: Routledge.

Laver, Michael J. and Norman Schofield 1990. *Multiparty Government: The Politics of Coalition in Europe*. Oxford University Press.

Laver, Michael J. and Kenneth A. Shepsle 1996. *Making and Breaking Governments: Government Formation in Parliamentary Democracies*. New York: Cambridge University Press.

Laver, Michael J., Kenneth Benoit and Nicolas Sauger 2006. "Policy Competition in the 2002 French Legislative and Presidential Elections," *European Journal of Political Research* 45, 4: 667–97.

Leaky, David 2008. "Joint and Separate Priorities for the EU and NATO in 2008," in Security and Defense Agenda (ed.), *Revisiting NATO-ESDP Relations. Part 1*, pp. 17–20. Brussels: SDA Discussion Paper.

Legro, Jeffrey W. 2005. *Rethinking the World: Great Power Strategies and International Order*. Ithaca: Cornell University Press.

Lellouche, Pierre 1991. "OTAN: l'atlantisation," *Le Point* (June 1).

Lemaitre, Philippe 1994. "La réunion des ministres de la défense de l'Alliance atlantique a Séville. La distribution des roles au sein de l'OTAN entre Américains et Européens se fait attendre," *Le Monde* (September 29).

1997. "Les Quinze signent le traité d'Amsterdam," *Le Monde* (October 3).

Lepgold, Joseph 1998. "NATO's Post-Cold War Collective Action Problem," *International Security* 23, 1: 78–106.

Lequesne, Christian 1998. "Une lecture décisionnelle de la politique européenne de François Mitterrand," in Samy Cohen (ed.), *Mitterrand et la sortie de la Guerre froide*, pp. 127–55. Paris: PUF.

Levy, Jack S. 1989. "Domestic Politics and War," in Robert I. Rotberg and Theodore K. Rabb (eds.), *The Origin and Prevention of Major Wars*, pp. 79–101. Cambridge University Press.

Lieber, Keir A. and Gerard Alexander 2005. "Waiting for Balancing: Why the World Is Not Pushing Back," *International Security* 30, 1: 109–39.

Lijphart, Arend 1999. *Patterns of Democracy: Government Forms and Performance in Thirty-Six Countries*. New Haven: Yale University Press.

Linhart, Eric and Susumu Shikano 2009. "Ideological Signals of German Parties in a Multi-dimensional Space: an Estimation of Party Preferences using the CMP Data," *German Politics* 18, 3: 301–22.

Lipset, Seymour M. and Stein Rokkan 1967. "Cleavage Structures, Party Systems, and Voter Alignments: an Introduction," in Seymour M. Lipset and Stein Rokkan (eds.), *Party Systems and Voter Alignments*, pp. 1–64. Glencoe, IL: The Free Press.

Lipset, Seymour M., Paul Lazarfeld, Allen Barton and Juan Linz 1954. "The Psychology of Voting: an Analysis of Political Behavior," in Gardner Lindzey (ed.), *Handbook of Social Psychology*, pp. 1124–75. Cambridge, MA: Addison-Wesley.

Loewenberg, Gerhard and Samuel C. Patterson 1979. *Comparing Legislatures*. Boston: Little Brown.

London Declaration 1990. *Declaration on a transformed North Atlantic Alliance issued by the Heads of State and Government participating in the meeting of the North Atlantic Council ("The London Declaration")*, London, July 6. www. nato.int/docu/basictxt/b900706a.htm.

Lowe, William, Kenneth Benoit, Slava Mikhaylov and Michael Laver 2011. "Scaling Policy Preference From Coded Political Texts," *Legislative Studies Quarterly* 26, 1: 123–55.

Lowi, Theodore J. 1964. "American Business, Case-Studies, and Political Theory," *World Politics* 16, 4: 677–715.

Ludlam, Steve 1998. "The Cauldron: Conservative Parliamentarians and European Integration," in David Baker and David Seawright (eds.), *Britain For and Against Europe: British Politics and the Question of European Integration*, pp. 31–56. Oxford: Clarendon Press.

Ludlow, Peter 1998. "The 1998 UK Presidency: a View From Brussels," *Journal of Common Market Studies* 36, 4: 573–83.

Maastricht Treaty 1992. *The Maastricht Treaty. Maastricht 7 February 1992.* www.eurotreaties.com/maastrichteu.pdf.

Machin, Howard 1993. "The President, the Parties and Parliament," in Jack Hayward (ed.), *De Gaulle to Mitterrand: Presidential Power in France*, pp. 120–49. London: Hurst & Company.

MacIntyre, Andrew 2003. *The Power of Institutions: Political Architecture and Governance*. Ithaca: Cornell University Press.

Mahoney, James 2000. "Path Dependence in Historical Sociology," *Theory and Society* 29, 4: 507–48.

Mair, Peter 2000. "The Limited Impact of Europe on National Party Systems," *West European Politics* 23, 4: 27–51.

Major, John 1993. "Raise Your Eyes, There is a Land Beyond," *The Economist* (September 25).

    1999. *John Major: The Autobiography*. London: HarperCollins.

Manin, Philippe (ed.) 1996. *Le Révision du Traité sur l'Union Européenne Perspectives et Réalités. Rapport du groupe francais d'étude pour la Conférence Intergouvernementale 1996.* Paris: Editions A. Pedone.

Manners, Ian 2002. "Normative Power Europe: a Contradiction in Terms?" *Journal of Common Market Studies* 40, 2: 235–58.

Mannheim, Karl 1936. *Ideology and Utopia*. London: Paul, Trench, Trubner.

Manow, Philip, Armin Schäfer and Hendrik Zorn 2008. "Europe's Party-political Centre of Gravity, 1957–2003," *Journal of European Public Policy* 15, 1: 20–39.

Mansfield, Edward and Eric Reinhardt 2003. "Multilateral Determinants of Regionalism: the Effects of GATT/WTO on the Formation of Preferential Trading Arrangements," *International Organization* 57: 829–62.

Mansfield, Edward and Jack Snyder 1995. "Democratization and the Danger of War," *International Security* 20, 1: 5–38.

Mansfield, Edward D., Helen V. Milner and Jon C. Pevehouse 2008. "Democracy, Veto Players and the Depth of Regional Integration," *The World Economy* 31, 1: 67–96.

March, James G. and Johan P. Olsen 1995. *Democratic Governance*. New York: The Free Press.

Markovits, Andrei S. and Simon Reich 1997. *The German Predicament: Memory and Power in the New Europe*. Ithaca and London: Cornell University Press.

Marks, Gary and Marco R. Steenbergen (eds.) 2004. *European Integration and Political Conflict*. Cambridge University Press.

Marks, Gary and Carole J. Wilson 2000. "The Past in the Present: a Cleavage Theory of Party Response to European Integration," *British Journal of Political Science* 30: 433–59.

Marks, Gary, Lisbet Hooghe and Kermit Blank 1996. "European Integration from the 1980s: State-Centric v. Multi-level Governance," *Journal of Common Market Studies* 34, 3: 341–78.

Marks, Gary, Carole J. Wilson and Leonard Ray 2002. "National Political Parties and European Integration," *American Journal of Political Science* 46, 3: 585–94.

Marsh, Michael 2007. "European Parliament Elections and Losses by Governing Parties," in Wouter Van der Brug and Cees van der Eijk (eds.), *European Elections and Domestic Politics: Lessons from the Past and Scenarios for the Future*, pp. 51–72. University of Notre Dame Press.

Martin, Lisa L. 1992. *Coercive Cooperation: Explaining Multilateral Economic Sanctions*. Princeton University Press.

Martin, Lisa and Beth Simmons 1998. "Theories and Empirical Studies of International Institutions," *International Organization* 52, 4: 729–57.

Marx, Karl and Friedrich Engels 2006 [1848]. *The Communist Manifesto*. New York: Penguin.

Mastanduno, Michael 1997. "Preserving the Unipolar Moment: Realist Theories and U.S. Grand Strategy after the Cold War," *International Security* 21, 4: 49–88.

Mastanduno, Michael, David A. Lake and G. John Ikenberry 1989. "Towards a Realist Theory of State Action," *International Studies Quarterly* 33: 457–74.

Mattila, Mikko 2004. "Contested Decisions: Empirical Analysis of Voting in the European Union Council of Ministers," *European Journal of Political Research* 43, 1: 29–50.

Maull, Hanns 1990/1. "Germany and Japan: The New Civilian Powers," *Foreign Affairs* 69, 5: 91–106.

  2000. "Germany and the Use of Force: Still a 'Civilian Power'?" *Survival* 42, 2: 56–80.

Mayhew, David R. 1991. "Divided Party Control: Does it Make a Difference," *PS: Political Science and Politics* 24, 4: 637 40.

Mazzucelli, Colette 1997. *France and Germany at Maastricht: Politics and Negotiations to Create the European Union*. New York and London: Garland Publishing, Inc.

McDonald, Michael D. and Ian Budge 2005. *Elections, Parties, Democracy: Conferring the Median Mandate*. Oxford University Press.

McElroy, Gail and Kenneth Benoit 2007. "Party Groups and Policy Positions in the European Parliament," *Party Politics* 13, 1: 5–28.

  2010. "Party Policy and Group Affiliation in the European Parliament," *British Journal of Political Science* 40, 2: 377–98.

McGillivray, Fiona and Alistair Smith 2004. "The Impact of Leadership Turnover on Relations Between States," *International Organization* 58: 567–600.

McKeown, Timothy J. 1991. "The Foreign Policy of a Declining Power," *International Organization* 45, 2: 257–79.

Mearsheimer, John J. 1990. "Back to the Future: Instability in Europe after the Cold War," *International Security* 15, 1: 5–56.

Menon, Anand 1996. "The 'Consensus' on Defence Policy and the End of the Cold War: Political Parties and the Limits of Adaptation," in Tony Chafer and Brian Jenkins (eds.), *France: From the Cold War to the New World Order*, pp. 155–68. Houndsmills and London: Macmillan Press.
  2003. "Why ESDP is Misguided and Dangerous for the Alliance," in Jolyon Howorth and John Keeler (eds.), *Defending Europe: The EU, NATO and The Quest for European Autonomy*, pp. 203–18. New York: Palgrave Macmillan.

Menon, Anand and Andrew Hurrell 1996. "Politics like any Other? Comparative Politics, International Relations and the Study of the EU," *West European Politics* 19, 2: 386–402.

Mérand, Frédéric 2008. *European Defence Policy: Beyond the Nation State*. Oxford University Press.

Merkel, Angela 2003. "Schröder Doesn't Speak for All Germans," *Washington Post* (February 20): A 39.

Meyer, Christoph 2005. "Convergence Towards a European Strategic Culture? A Constructivist Framework for Explaining Changing Norms," *European Journal of International Relations* 11, 4: 523–49.

Migdal, Joel S. 1988. *Strong Societies and Weak States: State-Society Relations and State Capabilities in the Third World*. Princeton University Press.

Mikhaylov, Slava, Michael Laver and Kenneth Benoit 2012. "Coder Reliability and Misclassification in the Human Coding of Party Manifestos," *Political Analysis* 20, 1: 78–91.

Miller, Nicolas 1983. "Pluralism and Social Choice," *American Political Science Review* 77, 3: 734–47.

Miller, Warren E. and Donald E. Stokes 1963. "Constituency Influence in Congress," *American Political Science Review* 57: 45–66.

Milward, Alan 1984. *The Reconstruction of Western Europe*. London: Methuen.
  1992. *The European Rescue of the Nation State*. London: Routledge.

Ministère de la Défense 1989. "Livre Blanc sur la Défense Nationale, 1972," in Dominique David (ed.), *La Politique de défense de la France: textes et documents*, pp. 45–63. Paris: Fondation pour les Etudes de Défense Nationale.
  1994. *Livre Blanc sur la Défense*. http://lesrapports.ladocumentationfrancaise.fr/BRP/944048700/0000.pdf.

Mitterrand, Francois 2001. *De l'Allemagne, de la France*. Paris: Odile Jacob.

Moravcsik, Andrew 1993. "Preferences and Power in the European Community: a Liberal Intergovernmentalist Approach," *Journal of Common Market Studies* 31, 4: 473–523.
  1997. "Taking Preferences Seriously: Liberalism and International Relations Theory," *International Organization* 51, 4: 513–53.
  1998. *The Choice for Europe: Social Purpose and State Power from Messina to Maastricht*. Ithaca: Cornell University Press.
  2009. "Europe: the Quiet Superpower," *French Politics* 7, 3/4: 403–22.
  2010. "Europe: Rising Superpower in a Bipolar World," in Alan Alexandroff and Andrew Cooper (eds.), *Rising States, Rising Institutions: Challenges for Global Governance*, pp. 151–74. Washington, DC: Brookings Institution.

Moravcsik, Andrew and Kalypso Nicolaïdis 1999. "Explaining the Treaty of Amsterdam: Interests, Influence, Institutions," *Journal of Common Market Studies* 37, 1: 59–85.

Morrow, James D. 1993. "Arms versus Allies: Trade-Offs in the Search for Security," *International Organization* 47, 2: 207–33.

Mouton, Jean-Denis and Jean Charpentier 1996. "La Politique Etrangère et de Sécurité Commune," in Philippe Manin (ed.), *Le Révision du Traité sur l'Union Européenne Perspectives et Réalités. Rapport du groupe francais d'étude pour la Conférence Intergouvernementale 1996*, pp. 113–22. Paris: Editions A. Pedone.

Mukherjee, Bumba and David Andrew Singer 2008. "Monetary Institutions, Partisanship, and Inflation Targeting," *International Organization* 62 (spring): 323–58.

Müller, Harald and Lars van Dassen 1997. "From Cacophony to Joint Action: Successes and Shortcomings of the European Non-Proliferation Policy," in Martin Holland (ed.), *Common Foreign and Security Policy*, pp. 52–72. London and Washington, DC: Pinter.

Müller, Wolfgang C. and Kaare Strøm 1999. *Policy, Office, or Votes? How Political Parties in Western Europe Make Hard Decisions.* Cambridge University Press.

Müller, Wolfgang C. and Kaare Strøm (eds.) 2000. *Coalition Governments in Western Europe.* Oxford University Press.

Müller, Wolfgang C. and Kaare Strøm 2008. "Coalitions Agreements and Cabinet Governance," in Kaare Strøm, Wolfgang C. Müller, and Torbjoern Bergman (eds.), *Cabinets and Coalition Bargaining: The Democratic Life Cycle in Western Europe*, pp. 159–200. New York: Oxford University Press.

Munck, Gerardo L. 2004. "Tools for Qualitative Research," in Henry E. Brady and David Collier (eds.), *Rethinking Social Inquiry: Diverse Tools, Shared Standards*, pp. 105–22. Lanham and Boulder: Rowman & Littlefield Publishers, Inc.

Murray, Shoon Kathleen and Jonathan A. Cowden 1999. "The Role of 'Enemy Images' and Ideology in Elite Belief Systems," *International Studies Quarterly* 43: 455–81.

Nardulli, B.R., Walter L. Perry, Bruce R. Pirnie, John Gordon IV and John G. McGinn 2002. *Disjointed War: Military Operations in Kosovo, 1999.* Santa Monica: Rand Corporation.

Narizny, Kevin 2003a. "Both Guns and Butter, or Neither: Class Interests in the Political Economy of Rearmament," *American Political Science Review* 97, 2: 203–20.

2003b. "The Political Economy of Alignment: Great Britain's Commitments to Europe, 1905–39," *International Security* 27, 4: 184–219.

2007. *The Political Economy of Grand Strategy.* Ithaca: Cornell University Press.

NATO Press Communique M-1 (94) 3.

NATO Strategic Concept 1999. *The Alliance's Strategic Concept. Approved by the Heads of State and Government participating in the meeting of the North Atlantic Council in Washington D.C. on 23rd and 24th April 1999.* www.nato. int/docu/pr/1999/p99–065e.htm.

Nau, Henry 2002. *At Home Abroad: Identity and Power in American Foreign Policy.* Ithaca: Cornell University Press.

Naurin, Daniel 2007. "Network Capital and Cooperation Patterns in the Working Groups of the Council of the EU," *EUI Working Papers RSCAS* 2007/14.

Naurin, Daniel and Rutger Lindahl 2008. "East-North-South: Coalition-Building in the Council Before and After Enlargement," in Daniel Naurin and Helen Wallace (eds.), *Unveiling the Council of the EU: Games Governments Play in Brussels*, pp. 64–80. Basingstoke: Palgrave.

Newhouse, John 1970. *De Gaulle and the Anglo-Saxons*. New York: Viking Press.

New Strategic Concept 1991. *The Alliance's New Strategic Concept*. www.nato.int/docu/comm/49–95/c911107a.htm.

New York Times 2007. "Excerpts from Interview with Nicolas Sarkozy" (September 23). www.nytimes.com/2007/09/23/world/europe/24excerpts.html?_r=1&ref=europe&oref=slogin.

Noblecourt, Michel 1997. "Il faut faire de l'Europe une véritable république," *Le Monde* (November 17).

Noël, Alain and Jean-Philippe Thérien 2000. "Political Parties and Foreign Aid," *American Political Science Review* 94, 1: 151–62.

2008. *Left and Right in Global Politics*. Cambridge University Press.

Nugent, Neill 1999. *The Government and Politics of the European Union*, 4th edn. Houndmills: Palgrave.

Nuland, Victoria 2007. "Ambassador Nuland Advocates Strengthening NATO's Role." http://nato.usmission.gov/ambassador/2007/Amb_Nuland_Brussels_101607.htm.

Nuttall, Simon J. 1992. *European Political Co-operation*. Oxford: Clarendon Press.

2000. *European Foreign Policy*. New York: Oxford University Press.

Oatley, Thomas 1999. "How Constraining is Capital Mobility? The Partisan Hypothesis in an Open Economy," *American Journal of Political Science* 43, 4: 1003–27.

Ohrgaard, Jakob C. 1997. "Less than Supranational, More than Intergovernmental: European Political Cooperation and the Dynamics of Intergovernmental Integration," *Millenium: Journal of International Studies* 26, 1: 1–29.

Olson, Richard 2007. "From Riga to Bucharest – NATO in Defense of our Common Security and Values." Speech at the Conference on "Europe at the Crossroads: Agenda from Riga to Bucharest," Riga, Latvia. http://nato.usmission.gov/News/Olson_Oct15.htm.

Oppermann, Kai. 2008. "The Blair Government and Europe: the Policy of Containing the Salience of European Integration," *British Politics* 3: 156–82.

Oppermann, Kai and Henrike Viehrig 2009. "The Public Salience of Foreign and Security Policy in Britain, Germany and France," *West European Politics* 32, 5: 925–42.

Osgood, Robert 1962. *NATO: The Entangling Alliance*. University of Chicago Press.

O'Sullivan, Noel 1976. *Conservatism*. New York: St Martin's.

Owen, John M. 1994. "How Liberalism Produces Democratic Peace," *International Security* 19, 2 (fall): 50–86.

2001/2. "Transnational Liberalism and U.S. Primacy," *International Security* 26, 3: 117–52.

Palmer, John 1997a. "Amsterdam Summit: Compromise Deal Removes Obstacles to Treaty," *Guardian* (June 18): 10.

1997b. "Community Converges on the Road to Amsterdam," *Guardian* (April 4): 19.

Palmer, John and Michael White 1997a. "Blair Charms His Way to EU Treaty Deal," *Guardian* (May 24): 1.

1997b. "Blair Wins Double EU Deal," *Guardian* (June 18): 1.

Paolini, J. 1989. "The Gaullist Model Revisited: Long-Range Strategic Vision and Short-Term Political Implementation in French Defence Policy," *French Politics and Society* 7 (autumn): 16–23.

Pape, Robert A. 2005. "Soft Balancing against the United States," *International Security* 30, 1: 7–45.

Pappi, Franz U. and Nicole M. Seher 2009. "Party Election Programs, Signalling Policies and Salience of Specific Policy Domains: the German Parties from 1990 to 2005," *German Politics* 18, 3: 403–25.

Parsons, Craig 2002. "Showing Ideas as Causes: the Origins of the European Union," *International Organization* 56, 1: 47–84.

2003. *A Certain Idea of Europe*. Ithaca: Cornell University Press.

Parsons, Craig and Till Weber 2011. "Cross-Cutting Issues and Party Strategizing in the European Union," *Comparative Political Studies* 44, 4: 383–411.

Parti Socialiste 1980. *Pour la France des années 80*. Paris: Club Socialiste du Livre.

Parti Socialiste Manifesto 1988. *Propositions Pour la France. Texte adopté a la Convention National du Parti Socialiste*. Comparative Party manifesto research group, Zentralarchiv für Empirische Sozialforschung an der Universität zu Köln.

1997. *Changeon D'Avenir. Nos engagements pour la France*. Comparative Party manifesto research group, Zentralarchiv für Empirische Sozialforschung an der Universität zu Köln.

Patterson, Samuel C. 1963. "Legislative Leadership and Political Ideology," *Public Opinion Quarterly* 27, 3: 399–410.

Paul, T.V. 2005. "Soft Balancing in the Age of U.S. Primacy," *International Security* 30, 1: 46–71.

Peele, Gillian 1980. "Commentary. The Changed Character of British Foreign and Security Policy," *International Security* 4, 4 (spring): 185–98.

Pelizzo, Riccardo 2003. "Party Positions or Party Direction? An Analysis of Party Manifesto Data," *West European Politics* 26, 2: 67–89.

Pennings, Paul 2002. "The Dimensionality of the EU Policy Space," *European Union Politics* 3: 59–80.

Perkins, Anne and Larry Elliott 1997. "Hague Locks Horns with CBI on Support for Monetary Union," *Guardian* (November 10): 3.

Perruche, Jean-Paul (Lt. Gen.) 2006. "Progress and Achievements," *Bulletin of the EU Military Staff. Impetus* (autumn/winter): 2–6.

Peters, Ingo 2004. "ESDP as a Transatlantic Issue: Problems of Mutual Ambiguity," *International Studies Review* 6, 3: 381–402.

Peters, J.E., Stuart Johnson, Nora Bensahel, Timothy Liston and Traci Williams 2001. *European Contributions to Operation Allied Force: Implications for Transatlantic Cooperation*. Santa Monica: Rand Corporation.

Peterson, Sue and Christopher Wenk 2001. "Domestic Institutional Change and Foreign Policy: a Comparison of U.S. Intervention in Guatemala and Nicaragua," *Security Studies* 11, 1: 53–76.

Pevehouse, Jon, Timothy Nordstrom and Kevin Warnke 2003. "International Organizations, 1815–2000: New Correlates of War Data Set." www.correlatesofwar.org/.

Pierson, Paul 1996. "The Path to European Integration: a Historical Institutionalist Analysis," *Comparative Political Studies* 29, 2: 123–63.

2000. "Increasing Returns, Path Dependence, and the Study of Politics," *American Political Science Review* 94, 2: 251–67.

2004. *Politics in Time: History, Institutions and Social Analysis*. Princeton University Press.

Pogunkte, Thomas, Nicolas Aylott, Elisabeth Carter, Robert Ladrech and Kurt Richard Luther 2007. *The Europeanization of National Political Parties*. London: Routledge.

Pollack, Mark A. 2005. "Theorizing the European Union: International Organization, Domestic Polity, or Experiment in New Governance?" *Annual Review of Political Science* 8: 357–98.

Posen, Barry R. 2004. "ESDP and the Structure of World Power," *International Spectator* 1: 5–17.

2006. "European Union Security and Defense Policy: Response to Unipolarity?" *Security Studies* 15, 2: 149–86.

Posner, Daniel N. 2005. *Institutions and Ethnic Politics in Africa*. New York: Cambridge University Press.

Pouliot, Vincent 2011. "Multilateralism as an End in Itself," *International Studies Perspectives* 12: 18–26.

Press-Barnathan, Galia 2006. "Managing the Hegemon: NATO under Unipolarity," *Security Studies* 15, 2: 271–309.

Puchala, Donald J. 1975. "Domestic Politics and Regional Harmonization in the European Communities," *World Politics* 27, 4: 496–520.

Putnam, Robert 1988. "Diplomacy and Domestic Politics. The Logic of Two-Level Games," *International Organization* 42, 3: 427–60.

Quille, Gerrard 2006. "The EU Battlegroups," *DGExPo/B/PolDep/Note/2006_145 12 September 2006* (European Parliament Directorate-General For External Policies of the Union, Directorate B, Policy Department). www.europarl.europa.eu/meetdocs/2004_2009/documents/dv/091006eubattlegroups_/091006eubattlegroups_en.pdf.

Quinlan, Michael 2001. *European Defense Cooperation: Asset or Threat to NATO?* Washington, DC: Woodrow Wilson Center Press.

Rabkin, Jeremy A. 2004. *The Case for Sovereignty: Why the World Should Welcome American Independence*. Jackson: AEI Press.

Radaelli, Claudio M. 2000. "Policy Transfer in the European Union," *Governance* 13, 1: 25–43.

Ragin, Charles 1987. *The Comparative Method: Moving beyond Qualitative and Quantitative Strategies*. Berkeley: University of California Press.

2004. "Turning the Tables: How Case-Oriented Research Challenges Variable-Oriented Research," in Henry E. Brady and David Collier (eds.), *Rethinking Social Inquiry: Diverse Tools, Shared Standards,* pp. 123–38. Lanham: Rowman & Littlefield Publishers, Inc.

Rathbun, Brian C. 2004. *Partisan Interventions: European Party Politics and Peace Enforcement in the Balkans.* Ithaca: Cornell University Press.

2007. "Hierarchy and Community at Home and Abroad: Evidence of a Common Structure of Domestic and Foreign Policy Beliefs in American Elites," *Journal of Conflict Resolution* 51, 3: 379–407.

2008. "Does One Right Make a Realist? Conservatism, Neoconservatism, and Isolationism in the Foreign Policy Ideology of American Elites," *Political Science Quarterly* 123, 2: 271–99.

2011a. "Before Hegemony: Generalized Trust and the Creation and Design of International Security Organizations," *International Organization* 65: 243–73.

2011b. "The 'Magnificent Fraud': Trust, International Cooperation, and the Hidden Domestic Politics of American Multilateralism after World War II," *International Studies Quarterly* 55: 1–21.

Raustiala, Kal and David G. Victor 2004. "The Regime Complex for Plant Genetic Resources," *International Organization* 58 (spring): 277–309.

Ray, Leonard 2003. "When Parties Matter: the Conditional Influence of Party Positions on Voter Opinions about European Integration," *Journal of Politics* 65, 4: 978–94.

Regelsberger, Elfriede and Wolfgang Wessels 2005. "The Evolution of the Common Foreign and Security Policy. A Case of an Imperfect Ratchet Fusion," in Amy Verdun and Osvaldo Croci (eds.), *Institutional and Policy-Making Challenges to the EU in Wake of Enlargement,* pp. 91–116. Manchester University Press.

Reichard, Martin 2006. *The EU-NATO Relationship: A Legal and Political Perspective.* Aldershot: Ashgate.

Reiter, Howard L. 2004. "Factional Persistence within Parties in the United States," *Party Politics* 10, 3: 251–71.

Reynolds, Christopher 2010. *Understanding the Emergence of the European Security and Defence Policy.* Baden-Baden: Nomos.

Rhode, David W. 1991. *Parties and Leaders in the Post-reform House.* University of Chicago Press.

Richman, Jesse 2011. "Parties, Pivots, and Policy: the Status Quo Test," *American Political Science Review* 105, 1: 151–65.

Riding, Alan 1991a. "NATO: Still the Defender of Europe," *New York Times* (May 30): A3.

1991b. "Mitterrand Joins Kohl in Proposing a European Army," *New York Times* (October 17): A1.

1992a. "French and Germans Plan an Army Corps Despite NATO Fears," *New York Times* (May 23): 1.

1992b. "Paris and Bonn Seek to End Unease on Joint Force," *New York Times* (December 1): A8.

Risse, Thomas 2001. "A European Identity? Europeanization and the Evolution of Nation-State Identities," in Maria Green Cowles, James A. Caporaso and Thomas Risse (eds.), *Europeanization and Domestic Change*, pp. 198–216. Ithaca: Cornell University Press.

Risse-Kappen, Thomas 1991. "Public Opinion, Domestic Structure, and Foreign Policy in Liberal Democracies," *World Politics* 43, 4: 479–512.

1994. "Ideas do not Float Freely: Transnational Coalitions, Domestic Structures, and the End of the Cold War," *International Organization* 48, 2: 185–214.

1995. *Cooperation Among Democracies: The European Influence on U.S. Foreign Policy*. Princeton University Press.

1996. "Collective Identity in a Democratic Community: the Case of NATO," in Peter J. Katzenstein (ed.), *The Culture of National Security: Norms and Identity in World Politics*, pp. 357–99. New York: Columbia University Press.

Robertson, George 1998. "The Future of European Defence." Speech to the WEU Assembly, Paris, December 1. www.britainusa.com/sections/articles_show.asp?SarticleType=1&Article_ID=714&i=117.

1999a. "The Way Forward on European Defence." Speech at the New Statesman Conference, LSE, September 8. www.britainusa.com/sections/articles_show.asp?SarticleType=1&Article_ID=710&i=117.

1999b. "Military Capabilities for European Security." Speech at the NATO at 50 Conference, March 10. www.britainusa.com/sections/articles_show.asp?SarticleType=1&Article_ID=712&i=117.

Robin, Gabriel 1995. "A Quoi Sert l'OTAN?" *Politique Etrangère* 60, 1: 171–80.

Rosamond, Ben 2000. *Theories of European Integration*. New York: Palgrave.

Rose, Gideon 1998. "Neoclassical Realism and Theories of Foreign Policy," *World Politics* 51, 1: 144–72.

Rotfeld, Adam Daniel and Walter Stützle (eds.) 1991. *Germany and Europe in Transition*. New York: Oxford University Press.

RPR–UDF Party Manifesto 1997. *Un nouvel élan pour la France. Plate-former d'union RPR-UDF*. Comparative Party manifesto research group, Zentralarchiv für Empirische Sozialforschung an der Universität zu Köln.

Ruggie, John G. 1992. "Multilateralism: the Anatomy of an Institution," *International Organization* 46, 3 (summer): 561–98.

1993. "Territoriality and Beyond: Problematizing Modernity in International Relations," *International Organization* 47, 1: 139–74.

Russett, Bruce 1993. *Grasping the Democratic Peace: Principles for a Post-Cold War World*. Princeton University Press.

1996. "Why Democratic Peace?" in Michael E. Brown, Sean M. Lynn-Jones and Steven E. Miller (eds.), *Debating the Democratic Peace*, pp. 82–115. Cambridge, MA: MIT Press.

Rutten, Maartje 2001. "From St-Malo to Nice. European Defence: Core Documents," in *Chaillot Papers* 47. Paris: Institute of Security Studies of the WEU.

Sarotte, Mary Elise 2010. "Perpetuating U.S. Preeminence: the 1990s Deals to 'Bribe the Soviets out' and Move NATO in," *International Security* 35, 1: 110–37.

Sartori, Giovanni 1976. *Parties and Party Systems: A Framework for Analysis*. New York: Cambridge University Press.

1997. *Comparative Constitutional Engineering: An Inquiry into Structures, Incentives and Outcomes*, 2nd edn. New York University Press.

Sauger, Nicolas 2003. "The UDF in the 1990s: the Break-Up of a Party Confederation," in Jocelyn A.J. Evans (ed.), *The French Party System*, pp. 107–20. Manchester and New York: Manchester University Press.

Schake, Kori, Amaya Bloch-Lainé and Charles Grant 1999. "Building a European Defence Capability," *Survival* 41, 1: 20–40.

Schapiro, Leonard 1972. *Totalitarianism*. London: Macmillan.

Scharping, Rudolf 1997. "Ziele und Handlungsprinzipien der deutschen Aussenpolitik an der Schwelle zum 21. Jahrhundert," *Frankfurter Allgemeine Zeitung* (October 16): 14.

1999a. "Erklärung des deutschen Verteidigungsministers, Rudolf Scharping, auf der WEU-Ministerratstagung zur Europäischen Sicherheits- und Verteidigungspolitik am 10. Mai 1999 in Bremen," *Bulletin* (Presse- und Informationsamt der Bundesregierung, Bonn), N. 30, 26.5.1999.

1999b. "One Germany in a Unifying Europe Alongside America," *International Herald Tribune* (November 15).

1999c. "Grundlinien deutscher Sicherheitspolitik. Rede des Bundesministers der Verteidigung, Rudolf Scharping, am 8. September 1999 an der Führungsakademie der Bundeswehr in Hamburg," Bulletin 56/1999: 583–8.

Schattschneider, Elmer E. 1960. *The Semi-Sovereign People*. New York: Holt Rinehart & Winston.

Schäuble, Wolfgang and Karl Lamers 1997. "Reflections on European Policy, Bonn, September 1994," in Trevor C. Salmon and Sir William Nicoll (eds.), *Building European Union: a Documentary History and Analysis*, pp. 255–60. Manchester University Press.

Schell, Peter 1991. *Bündnis im Schatten. Die Westeuropäische Union in den 80er Jahren*. Bonn: Bouvier.

Scheuer, Angelika and Wouter van der Brug 2007. "Locating Support for European Integration," in Wouter van der Brug and Cees van der Eijk (eds.), *European Elections and Domestic Politics: Lessons from the Past and Scenarios for the Future*, pp. 94–115. University of Notre Dame Press.

Schmidt, Peter 1992. "Partner and Rivals: NATO, WEU, EC and the Reorganization of European Security Policy: Taking Stock," in Peter Schmidt (ed.), *In the Midst of Change: On the Development of West European Security and Defence Cooperation*, pp. 187–228. Baden-Baden: Nomos.

Schöllgen, Gregor 2000. "Zehn Jahre als europäische Grossmacht. Eine Bilanz deutscher Aussenpolitik seit der Vereinigung," *Aus Politik und Zeitgeschichte* B 24/00: 6–12.

Schultz, Kenneth A. 2005. "The Politics of Risking Peace: Do Hawks or Doves Deliver the Olive Branch?" *International Organization* 59 (winter): 1–38.

Schumacher, Gijs, Catherine E. de Vries and Barbara Vis forthcoming. "Why Political Parties Change Their Positions: Environmental Incentives and Party Organization," *Journal of Politics*.

Schurmann, Franz 1973. *Ideology and Organization in Communist China*, 2nd edn. Berkeley: University of California Press.

Schweller, Randall L. 1992. "Domestic Structure and Preventive War: are Democracies More Pacific?" *World Politics* 44, 2: 235–69.

  2001. "The Problem of International Order Revisited," *International Security* 26, 1: 161–86.

Sciolino, Elaine 2007. "Sarkozy, a Frenchman in a Hurry, Maps his Path," *New York Times* (September 24). www.nytimes.com/2007/09/23/world/europe/24excerpts.html?_r=1&ref=europe&oref=slogin.

Seliger, Martin 1976. *Ideology and Politics*. London: George Allen & Unwin.

Shanks, Cheryl, Harold K. Jacobson and Jeffrey H. Kaplan 1996. "Inertia and Change in the Constellation of International Governmental Organizations, 1981–1992," *International Organization* 50, 4: 593–628.

Shils, Edward A. 1954. "Authoritarianism: 'Right' and 'Left'," in Richard Christie and Marie Jahoda (eds.), *The Authoritarian Personality*, pp. 24–49. Glencoe, IL: Free Press.

Silverman, Lawrence 1985. "The Ideological Mediation of Party Political Responses to Social Change," *European Journal of Political Research* 19: 393–417.

Silvia, Stephen J. 1995. "The Social Democratic Party of Germany," in David P. Conradt, Gerald R. Kleinfeld, George K. Romoser and Christian Soe (eds.), *Germany's New Politics: Parties and Issues in the 1990s*, pp. 149–70. Providence and Oxford: Berghahn Books.

Simon, Herbert A. 1982. *Models of Bounded Rationality*. Cambridge, MA: MIT Press.

SIPRI 2004. *SIPRI Yearbook 2004. Armaments, Disarmament and International Security*. Oxford University Press.

  2005. Peace Operations Data Set for France, Germany and the UK. http://first.sipri.org/index.php?page=step3&compact=true.

  2008. "Concentration in the Arms Industry: Data on Mergers and Acquisitions." www.sipri.org/contents/milap/milex/aprod/m_and_a_jv.html.

Slapin, Jonathan B. 2008. "Bargaining Power at Europe's Intergovernmental Conferences: Testing Institutional and Intergovernmental Theories," *International Organization* 62 (winter): 131–62.

Sloan, Stanley R. 1995. *Combined Joint Task Forces and New Missions for NATO*. Library of Congress report no. 95–1176 F. Washington, DC: Congressional Research Service.

  2000. "The United States and European Defence," *Chaillot Paper* 39: 1–66.

  2003. *NATO, the European Union, and the Atlantic Community: The Transatlantic Bargain Reconsidered*. Lanham: Rowman & Littlefield Publishers.

Smith, Karen 2000. "The End of Civilian Power EU: a Welcome Demise or Cause for Concern?" *International Spectator* 35, 2: 11–28.

Smith, Michael 2004. "CFSP and ESDP: from Idea to Institution to Policy?" in Martin Holland (ed.), *Common Foreign and Security Policy: The First Ten Years*, 2nd edn, pp. 78–88. London: Continuum.

Smith, Michael E. 1998. "What's Wrong with the CFSP? The Politics of Institutional Reform," in Pierre-Henri Laurent and Marc Maresceau (eds.), *The State of the European Union, Vol. 4, Deepening and Widening*, pp. 149–76. Boulder: Lynne Rienner.

2004. *Europe's Foreign and Security Policy*. New York: Cambridge University Press.

Smith, R. Jeffrey 1991a. "Cheney to Take Up French Proposal For European Force Outside NATO," *Washington Post* (May 27): A27.

1991b. "Cheney, French Differ on European Force; Sides Minimize Dispute on Control of Rapid-Response Unit," *The Washington Post* (28 May): A15.

Snyder, Glenn H. 1997. *Alliance Politics*. Ithaca: Cornell University Press.

Snyder, Jack 1991. *Myths of Empire: Domestic Politics and International Ambition*. Ithaca: Cornell University Press.

Solms, Hermann Otto 1997. "Im Zeitalter der Globalisierung gewinnt Bismarcks Einsicht eine neue Aktualität," *Frankfurter Allgemeine Zeitung* (November 12): 10.

Sontheimer, Kurt 1991. *Die Adenauer-Ära: Grundlegung der Bundesrepublik*. Munich: Deutscher Taschenbuch Verlag.

Soroka, Stuart and Christopher Wlezien 2010. *Degrees of Democracy: Politics, Public Opinion and Policy*. Cambridge University Press.

SPD Party Manifesto 1990. *Regierungsprogramm 1990–1994. Der Neue Weg, ökologisch, sozial, wirtschaftlich stark. Beschlossen vom SPD-Parteitag in Berlin am 28. September 1990*. Comparative Party manifesto research group, Zentralarchiv für Empirische Sozialforschung an der Universität zu Köln.

1998. *Arbeit, Innovation und Gerechtigkeit. SPD-Programm für die Bundestagswahl 1998. Beschlauss des ausserordentlichen Parteitages der SPD am 17. April 1998 in Leipzig*. Comparative Party manifesto research group, Zentralarchiv für Empirische Sozialforschung an der Universität zu Köln.

Spruyt, Hendrik 2005. *Ending Empire: Contested Sovereignty and Territorial Partition*. Ithaca: Cornell University Press.

Starr, Barbara 1997. "Cohen Establishing His Doctrine as Clinton and Congress Look On," *Jane's Defence* (February 5): 19.

Steenbergen, Marco R. and David J. Scott 2004. "Contesting Europe? The Salience of European Integration as a Party Issue," in Gary Marks and Marco R. Steenbergen (eds.), *European Integration and Political Conflict*, pp. 165–92. Cambridge University Press.

Steinmo, Sven and Kathleen Thelen 1992. "Historical Institutionalism in Comparative Politics," in Sven Steinmo, Kathleen Thelen and Frank Longstreth (eds.), *Structuring Politics: Historical Institutionalism in Comparative Analysis*, pp. 1–32. Cambridge University Press.

Stephens, Philip and Robert Mauthner 1990. "Thatcher Calls for Broader NATO Role," *Financial Times* (June 8): 1.

Stinchcombe, Arthur L. 1968. *Constructing Social Theories*. New York: Harcourt, Brace & World.

Stokes, Donald E. 1963. "Spatial Models of Party Competition," *American Political Science Review* 57, 2: 368–77.

Strøm, Kaare 1990. "A Behavioral Theory of Competitive Political Parties," *American Journal of Political Science* 34: 565–98.

Strøm, Kaare, Wolfgang C. Müller and Torbjörn Bergman 2010. *Cabinets and Coalition Bargaining. The Democratic Life Cycle in Western Europe*: Oxford University Press.

Suh, Jae-Jung 2007. *Power, Interest, and Identity in Military Alliances*. New York: Palgrave.

Talbott, Strobe 1999. "The State of the Alliance: An American Perspective." www.nato.int/docu/speech/1999/s991215c.htm.

Taylor, Paul 1991. "The European Community and the State – Assumptions, Theories and Propositions," *Review of International Studies* 17, 2: 109–25.

Tetlock, Philip E. 1984. "Cognitive Style and Political Belief Systems in the British House of Commons," *Journal of Personality and Social Psychology: Personality Processes and Individual Differences* 46: 365–75.

  1985. "Integrative Complexity of American and Soviet Foreign Policy Rhetoric: a Time-Series Analysis," *Journal of Personality and Social Psychology: Interpersonal Relations and Group Processes* 49: 1565–85.

  1986. "Integrative Complexity of Policy Reasoning," in S. Kraus and R. Perloff (eds.), *Mass Media and Political Thought*. Beverly Hills: Sage.

Thatcher, Margaret 1993. *The Downing Street Years*. London: HarperCollins.

Thelen, Kathleen 1999. "Historical Institutionalism in Comparative Politics," *American Review of Political Science* 2: 369–404.

  2003. "How Institutions Evolve: Insights from Comparative Historical Analysis," in James Mahoney and Dietrich Rueschemeyer (eds.), *Comparative Historical Analysis in the Social Sciences*, pp. 208–40. New York: Cambridge University Press.

Thérien, Jean-Philippe and Alain Noël 2000. "Political Parties and Foreign Aid," *American Political Science Review* 94: 151–62.

Thies, Wallace J. 2009. *Why NATO Endures*. Cambridge University Press.

Thompson, John B. 1990. *Ideology and Modern Culture: Critical Social Theory in the Era of Mass Communication*. Cambridge: Polity Press.

Thomson, Robert 2009. "Actor Alignments in the European Union before and after Enlargement," *European Journal of Political Research* 48, 6: 756–81.

Thränhardt, Dietrich 1996. *Geschichte der Bundesrepublik Deutschland. Erweiterte Neuausgabe*. Frankfurt: Suhrkamp.

Thucydides 1951. *The Complete Writings of Thucydides: The Peloponnesian War*. New York: The Modern Library.

Tierney, Dominic 2011. "Multilateralism: America's Insurance Policy Against Loss," *European Journal of International Relations* 17, 4: 655–78.

Tomz, Michael 2007. "Domestic Audience Costs in International Relations: An Experimental Approach," *International Organization* 61 (fall): 821–40.

Tonra, Ben 2001. *Europeanisation of National Foreign Policy: Dutch, Danish and Irish Foreign Policies in CFSP*. London: Ashgate.

Trubowitz, Peter 1998. *Defining the National Interest: Conflict and Change in American Foreign Policy*. University of Chicago Press.

Tsebelis, George 1994. "The Power of the European Parliament as a Conditional Agenda-Setter," *American Political Science Review* 88: 128–42.

  1995. "Decision Making in Political Systems: Veto Players in Presidentialism, Parliamentarism, Multicameralism, and Multipartyism," *British Journal of Political Science* 25: 289–326.

2002. *Veto Players: How Political Institutions Work*. New York: Princeton University Press.

Tsebelis, George and Geoffrey Garrett 2000. "Legislative Politics in the European Union," *European Union Politics* 1: 9–36.

Turner, Henry Ashby Jr. 1987. *The Two Germanies since 1945*. New Haven: Yale University Press.

UNDPKO 2006. "United Nations Military, Police Deployment Reaches All-Time High in October," *Department of Public Information Press Release PKO/152*, November 10. www.un.org/News/Press/docs/2006/pko152.doc.htm.

Usborne, David 1991. "US Warns EC Not to Disrupt Role of NATO," *Independent* (March 6).

US Defense Department 1993. *Report on the Bottom-Up Review*. Washington, DC: United States Department of Defense.

US State Department 1999. *Kosovo Chronology*. www.state.gov/www/regions/eur/fs_kosovo_timeline.html.

Van der Brug, Wouter and Cees van der Eijk (eds.) 2007. *European Elections and Domestic Politics: Lessons from the Past and Scenarios for the Future*. University of Notre Dame Press.

Van der Brug, Wouter, Cees van der Eijk and Mark N. Franklin 2007. "EU Support and Party Choice," in Wouter van der Brug and Cees van der Eijk (eds.), *European Elections and Domestic Politics: Lessons from the Past and Scenarios for the Future*, pp. 168–88. University of Notre Dame Press.

Van der Eijk, Cees and Wouter van der Brug 2007. "Introduction," in Wouter van der Brug and Cees van der Eijk (eds.), *European Elections and Domestic Politics: Lessons from the Past and Scenarios for the Future*, pp. 1–12. University of Notre Dame Press.

Van Ham, Peter 2000. "Europe's Precarious Centre: Franco-German Cooperation and the CFSP," in Simon Duke (ed.), *The Elusive Quest for European Security: From EDC to CFSP*, pp. 65–90. New York and Oxford: St. Martins Press.

Vanhoonacker, Sophie 2001. *The Bush Administration (1989–1993) and the Development of a European Security Identity*. Aldershot: Ashgate.

Vanhoonacker, Sophie, Hylke Dijkstra and Heidi Maurer 2010. "Understanding the Role of Bureaucracy in the European Security and Defence Policy: The State of the Art," *European Integration Online Papers* Special Issue 1, 14. http://eiop.or.at/eiop/index.php/eiop/article/view/2010_004a.

Védrine, Hubert 1997. "Audition du Ministre des Affaires Etrangères, Hubert Védrine, devant la Commission des Affaires Etrangères de l'Assemblée Nationale, Paris, 26. Juin 1997," *Politique Etrangère de la France* (May–June): 219.

2007. *Rapport pour le Président de la République sur la France et la Mondialisation*. www.iris.france.org/docs/pdf/rapport-mondialisation-2007.pdf.

Verdier, Daniel and Mette Eilstrup-Sangiovanni 2005. "European Integration as a Solution to War," *European Journal of International Relations* 11, 1: 99–135.

Vernet, Daniel 1999. "L'europe a son ministre des affaires entrangères," *Le Monde* (October 19).

Vienna Council Conclusions 1998. *Vienna European Council 11 and 12 December 1998. Presidency Conclusions.* http://ue.eu.int/ueDocs/cms_Data/docs/pressData/en/ec/00300-R1.EN8.htm.

Waever, Ole 1998. "Integration as Security: Constructing a Europe at Peace," in Charles Kupchan (ed.), *Atlantic Security,* pp. 45–63. Lillington: Edwards Brothers.

Walker, Martine 1998. "Blair Plans Busy Time at EU Helm. Britain will Exploit its Added Diplomatic Weight," *Guardian* (January 1): 10.

Wall, Stephen 2008. *A Stranger in Europe: Britain and the EU from Thatcher to Blair.* Oxford University Press.

Wallace, William 1991. "British Foreign Policy after the Cold War," *International Affairs* 67: 65–80.

Wallander, Celeste A. 2000. "Institutional Assets and Adaptability: NATO After the Cold War," *International Organization* 54, 4: 705–35.

Walt, Stephen M. 1987. *The Origins of the Alliance.* Ithaca: Cornell University Press.

2005. *Taming American Power: The Global Response to U.S. Primacy.* New York: W.W. Norton & Co.

Waltz, Kenneth N. 1959. *Man, the State, and War.* New York: Columbia University Press.

1979. *Theory of International Politics.* New York: McGraw-Hill Inc.

1993. "The Emerging Structure of International Politics," *International Security* 18, 2: 44–79.

2000. "Structural Realism after the Cold War," *International Security* 25, 1: 5–41.

Ware, Alan 1996. *Political Parties and Party Systems.* Oxford University Press.

Warwick, Paul V. 1992. "Economic Trends and Government Survival in West European Parliamentary Democracies," *American Political Science Review* 86, 4: 875–87.

1995. *Government Survival in Parliamentary Democracies.* Cambridge University Press.

Washington Summit Communiqué 1999. "Washington Summit Communiqué, Issued by the Heads of State and Government participating in the meeting of the North Atlantic Council in Washington, D.C. on 24th April 1999," *NAC-S(99)64.* www.nato.int/docu/pr/1999/p99–064e.htm.

Webber, Mark, Stuart Croft, Jolyon Howorth, Terry Terriff and Elke Krahmann 2004. "The Governance of European Security," *Review of International Studies* 30: 3–26.

Weber, Katja 2000. *Hierarchy Amidst Anarchy: Transaction Costs and Institutional Choice.* Albany: State University of New York Press.

Weeks, Jessica L. 2008. "Autocratic Audience Costs: Regime Type and Signaling Resolve," *International Organization* 62, 1: 35–64.

Weiler, Joseph H.H. 1993. "Journey to an Unknown Destination: a Retrospective and Prospective of the European Court of Justice in the Arena of Political Integration," *Journal of Common Market Studies* 31, 4: 417–46.

Weiss, Moritz 2011. *Transaction Cost and Security Institutions: Unravelling the ESDP.* Houndmills: Palgrave.

Weitsman, Patricia A. 2004. *Dangerous Alliances: Proponents of Peace, Weapons of War*. Stanford University Press.

Weldes, Jutta 1996. "Constructing National Interests," *European Journal of International Relations* 2: 275–318.

Wessels, Wolfgang 1994. "Rationalizing Maastricht: the Search for an Optimal Strategy of the New Europe," *International Affairs* 70, 3: 445–57.

WEU Secretariat General 1991. "Declaration on Western European Union – Maastricht 10 December 1991." www.assembly-weu.org/en/documents/ sessions_ordinaires/key/declaration_maastricht_fromeu_site.php.

White, Michael 1997a. "Back Line on Treaty, Hague Tells Euro Rebels," *Guardian* (November 4): 11.

1997b. "Hague Holds on EU Treaty Vote," *Guardian* (November 13): 12.

White Book 1994. *Weissbuch 1994 zur Sicherheit der Bundesrepublik Deutschland und zur Lage und Zukunft der Bundeswehr*. Bonn: Bundesministerium der Verteidigung.

Whitney, Craig R. 1991. "NATO, Victim of Success, Searches for New Strategy," *New York Times* (October 16): 1.

1997. "Kicking Troubles Down the Road," *New York Times* (June 19): A 14.

1999. "U.S. and NATO Allies Divided Over Defense Needs. Difference Focus on Proposals for an Antimissile System and an All-European Force," *New York Times* (December 3): 4.

Williams, Paul D. 2009. "The African Union's Peace Operations: A Comparative Analysis," *African Security* 2, 2: 97–118.

Williams, Robin M. 1979. "Change and Stability in Values and Value Systems: a Sociological Perspective," in Milton Rokeach (ed.), *Understanding Human Values: Individual and Societal*, pp. 15–46. New York: The Free Press.

Williamson, Oliver 1985. *The Economic Institutions of Capitalism: Firms, Markets, and Relational Contracting*. New York: The Free Press.

Wittkopf, Eugene R. 1981. "The Structure of Foreign Policy Attitudes: An Alternative View," *Social Science Quarterly* 62: 108–23.

1990. *Faces of Internationalism: Public Opinion and American Foreign Policy*. Durham, NC: Duke University Press.

1994. "Faces of Internationalism in a Transitional Environment," *Journal of Conflict Resolution* 38, 3: 376–401.

Wohlforth, William C. 1999. "The Stability of a Unipolar World," *International Security* 24: 5–41.

Woll, Cornelia 2008. *Firm Interests: How Governments Shape Business Lobbying on Global Trade*. Ithaca: Cornell University Press.

Woodward, Stephen. 1997. "NATO's Role in European Defence," *Independent* (September 13): 17.

Woodward, Susan L. 2004. "Transatlantic Harmony or a Stable Kosovo?" in Franz-Lothar Altmann and Eugene Whitlock (eds.), *European and U.S. Policies in the Balkans*, pp. 25–30. Berlin: Stiftung Wissenschaft und Politik.

Wüst, Andreas M. and Hermann Schmitt 2007. "Comparing the View of Parties and Voters in the 1999 Election to the European Parliament," in Wouter van der Brug and Cees van der Eijk (eds.), *European Elections and Domestic Politics: Lessons from the Past and Scenarios for the Future*, pp. 73–93. University of Notre Dame Press.

Yost, David S. 1998. *NATO Transformed: The Alliance's New Roles in International Security*. Washington, DC: United States Institute for Peace Press.

2007. "NATO and International Organizations," *NATO Defense College Forum Paper* No. 3.

Young, Oran R. 1996. "Institutional Linkages in International Society: Polar Perspectives," *Global Governance* 2: 1–24.

2008. "Deriving Insights from the Case of the WTO and the Cartagena Protocol," in Oran R. Young, W. Bradnee Chambers, Joy A. Kim and Claudia ten Have (eds.), *Institutional Interplay: Biosafety and Trade*, pp. 131–58. Tokyo: United Nations University Press.

Zelikow, Philip 1996. "The Masque of Institutions," *Survival* 38, 1: 6–18.

Zimmer, Christina, Gary Schneider and Michael Dobbins 2005. "The Contested Council: Conflict Dimensions of an Intergovernmental EU Institution," *Political Studies* 53, 2: 403–22.

Index